AUGMENTING CUSTOMER RETENTION THROUGH BIG DATA ANALYTICS

AUGMENTING CUSTOMER RETENTION THROUGH BIG DATA ANALYTICS

Reena Malik, PhD
Ambuj Sharma, PhD
Prashant Chaudhary, PhD
Editors

AAP | APPLE ACADEMIC PRESS

First edition published 2025

Apple Academic Press Inc.
1265 Goldenrod Circle, NE,
Palm Bay, FL 32905 USA

760 Laurentian Drive, Unit 19,
Burlington, ON L7N 0A4, CANADA

CRC Press
2385 NW Executive Center Drive,
Suite 320, Boca Raton FL 33431

4 Park Square, Milton Park,
Abingdon, Oxon, OX14 4RN UK

Apple Academic Press exclusively co-publishes with CRC Press, an imprint of Taylor & Francis Group, LLC

Library and Archives Canada Cataloguing in Publication

CIP data on file with Canada Library and Archives

Library of Congress Cataloging-in-Publication Data

CIP data on file with US Library of Congress

ISBN: 978-1-77491-721-3 (hbk)
ISBN: 978-1-77491-722-0 (pbk)
ISBN: 978-1-00353-848-6 (ebk)

About the Editors

Reena Malik, PhD
Assistant Professor, Chitkara Business School, Chitkara University, Punjab, India

Reena Malik, PhD, is currently working as Assistant Professor at Chitkara Business School, Chitkara University, Punjab, India. She is actively involved in research areas such as consumer behavior, brand management, customer satisfaction, etc. She has three books to her credit and has been teaching subjects in her field for the last 10 years. She has published research papers and book chapters with publishers such as Emerald Publishing, IGI Global, CRC/Taylor and Francis, Wiley, and Sage Publications. She holds a PhD in Marketing Management and did her postgraduate work in Commerce and Management.

Ambuj Sharma, PhD
Assistant Professor, Govind Ballabh Pant Social Science Institute, Prayagraj, UP, India

Ambuj Sharma, PhD, is currently working as Assistant Professor at the Govind Ballabh Pant Social Science Institute, Prayagraj, UP, India. His research areas are diversity management, human resources practices, and disability studies He has published many papers in international journals (SCOPUS and WoS indexed) and presented papers at international conferences (Hungary, France, Poland, Slovakia, Italy, Austria, and Czech Republic). He acquired his doctoral degree in Management and Business Administration Sciences from Szent Istvan University, Hungary (with a UGC scholarship). Prior to his PhD, he completed his master's in Business Studies from AMET/Alagappa University, Tamil Nadu, India.

Prashant Chaudhary, PhD
Associate Professor, WPU School of Business at Dr. Vishwanath Karad MIT World Peace University, Pune, India

Prashant Chaudhary, PhD, is currently working as Associate Professor at the WPU School of Business at Dr. Vishwanath Karad MIT World Peace University, Pune, India. He has authored two books, both published by Sage Publications. He has also published many research papers and case studies in internationally reputed journals, indexed in ABDC, Scopus, and Web of Science. He is associated with several book publishers that include John Wiley & Sons, Inc.) and Sage Publications as a content reviewer. He is working as a reviewer with the journals *Marketing and Management of Innovations; Asian Journal of Management Cases;* and *Green and Low-Carbon Economy.* He has been awarded with an Innovative Educator Award, conferred by the Valia Centre of Excellence (Mumbai), in collaboration with The Hindu Business Line, and he holds an honorary Rosalind Membership, awarded by London Journals Press (UK).

Contents

Contributors

Preeti Ahlawat
Department of Business Administration, Chaudhary Devi Lal University, Sirsa, Haryana, India

Rajneesh Ahlawat
Department of Business Administration, Chaudhary Devi Lal University, Sirsa, Haryana, India

Manpreet Arora
HPKVBS, School of Commerce and Management Studies, Central University of Himachal Pradesh, Dharamshala, India

Rekha Attri
Jaipuria Institute of Management, Indore, India

Renu Bala
IBM Department, Jan Nayak Chaudhary Devi Lal Vidyapeeth, Sirsa, India

Jyoti Bansal
JCD Vidyapeeth, Sirsa, Haryana, India

Devesh Bathla
Chitkara Business School, Chitkara University, Punjab, India

Anagha Bhope
Departments of Economics and Finance, Indira School of Business Studies PGDM, Tathawade, Pune, India

Prashant Chaudhary
Dr. Vishwanath Karad MIT World Peace University, Pune, India

Prashant Chauhan
Chitkara Business School, Chitkara University, Punjab, India

Aarti Dangwal
Chitkara Business School, Chitkara University, Punjab, India

Pooja Darda
Jaipuria Institute of Management, Indore, India

Om Jee Gupta
Jaipuria Institute of Management, Lucknow, India

Akanksha Jadhav
Pune Institute of Business Management, Pune, Maharashtra, India

Kiran Shrimant Kakade
School of Business, MIT World Peace University, Pune, India

Shailendra Kumar Kale
Professor, Global Business School and Research Centre, Dr. D. Y. Patil Vidyapeeth, Pune, India

Kamalpreet
University School of Business, Chandigarh University, Punjab, India

Nilesh Kate
Marketing, Pune Institute of Business Management, Pune, Maharashtra, India

Amandeep Kaur
JCD Institute of Business Management, Sirsa, India

Randeep Kaur
JCD Vidyapeeth, Sirsa, Haryana, India

Ashok Kumar
Department of Defence and Strategic Studies, Himachal Pradesh University, Shimla, India

Sumeet Singh Lamba
Chitkara Business School, Chitkara University, Punjab, India

Reena Malik
Chitkara Business School, Chitkara University, Punjab, India

Sulakshana B. Mane
BVCOE, Navi Mumbai, India

Mankaj Mehta
Chitkara Business School, Chitkara University, Punjab, India

Amna Mirza
Department of Political Science, Shyama Prasad Mukherji College for Women, University of Delhi, Delhi, India

Anupal Mongia
Chandigarh University, Chandigarh, India

Ruhi Sarangal
Chitkara Business School, Chitkara University, Punjab, India

Sachin Kumar Sharma
Cluster Innovation Centre, University of Delhi, Delhi, India

Swati Sharma
Chandigarh University, Chandigarh, India

Siddharth Shimpi
School of Retail Management, Symbiosis Skills and Professional University, Pune, India

Pooja Swami
JCD Institute of Business Management, Jan Nayak Chaudhary Devi Lal Vidyapeeth, Sirsa, Haryana, India

Renu Tanwar
Department of Business Administration, Chaudhary Devi Lal University, Sirsa, Haryana, India

Chandraprabha Vaidya
Savitribai Phule Pune University, Pune, Maharashtra, India

Neha Verma
Chitkara Business School, Chitkara University, Punjab, India

Swati A. Vispute
School of Business, MIT World Peace University, Pune, India

Susheel Yadav
Jindal Global Business School, O.P. Jindal Global University, Sonipat, Haryana, India

Acknowledgments

The editors would like to thank and congratulate everyone who has helped make this book a reality. We would like to convey our sincere gratitude to all the chapter authors for their contributions; the book would not have been possible without them. Our sincere gratitude and appreciation also go to the subject matter specialists who worked as reviewers and took the time to examine the chapters and provide them on time, therefore, boosting the book's quality, prominence, and consistent layout.

Preface

Acquiring a new customer can cost the business organizations much more than to retain the ones they already have or are currently serving. Today, it is a proven fact that embedding big data analytics into your operations and processes is helping businesses to increase customer retention and hence loyalty. With this digital capacity building and digital transformation supported by big data analytics, business organizations can act upon the insights they obtain and derive. This essentially gives them an opportunity to meet the needs of their consumer effortlessly by bringing personalization.

With an increased focus on fast-tracking operations and redefining established systems, businesses are increasingly embracing digital transformation and automation. Taking into consideration the present and potential interest of a business customer, predictive analysis proves to be useful for an optimized solution. With this core objective, business organizations are deploying the processes of data analytics in combination with advanced technologies. They are using marketing automation and digital marketing, machine learning (ML), blockchain, generative AI, and robotics, etc. to produce groundbreaking outcomes in terms of effectiveness, overall value to consumers, and sustainable customer loyalty. In order to improve customer experience data is imperative for customer engagement, retention, and growth.

As editors, we feel that this book offers academicians, marketers, human resource managers, advanced students and industrial professionals a valuable viewpoint on the technological knowledge and capability to augment customer retention through the use of big data analytics.

The efforts of all the chapter authors is very much appreciated.

CHAPTER 1

Personalization and Customization of Products and Services in E-Commerce Through Big Data

POOJA SWAMI

JCD Institute of Business Management, Jan Nayak Chaudhary Devi Lal Vidyapeeth, Sirsa, Haryana, India

ABSTRACT

With the increasing digitalization, consumers nowadays are spending more time and money online. Due to the expansion and growth of consumer, online purchase, and usage data e-commerce companies are facing challenges in managing such a high-volume, high-velocity, and high-variety information sets also known as unstructured or "big data" that are too large and complex to be processed by conventional database management tools. Because of this, big data analytics is becoming more popular in the e-commerce industry (BDA). Big data analytics is a means to get the most value out of these large volumes of data, thereby opening up new market prospects and increasing customer retention rates. A paradigm shift has occurred in the e-commerce sector as a result of the enormous expansion of big data. Data for the study were collected through the literature review of recent articles and online publications and various e-commerce websites were also used. The study indicated that e-commerce marketing professionals can adapt marketing efforts to the demands of each consumer by keeping track of user information like browsing requests and preferences. The study also showed that e-commerce companies are using BDA to improve customers' experiences by offering them personalized goods and services. However, it is also suggested in this study about privacy and security issues posed by big data,

Augmenting Customer Retention Through Big Data Analytics.
Reena Malik, Ambuj Sharma, and Prashant Chaudhary (Eds.)

necessitating the adoption of appropriate safeguard measures by e-commerce companies to prevent the misuse and improper handling of their users' data.

1.1 INTRODUCTION

Data have existed for many years. But for the past 40–50 years, these data were generally accessible only after manual compilation either monthly, half-yearly, or annually. With the developments like scanning technologies, data have become the norm. In the 1990s, businesses began to invest significantly in massive customer databases, which resulted in the creation of millions of customer records containing information on their purchase patterns, marketing trends, and other characteristics. With the rise of the Internet, and more recently, social media, data have multiplied enormously, and many organizations now have access to hourly or even real-time data (Verhoef, 2016). This tremendous explosion of data gave rise to a concept known to us all as "big data," which has pushed e-commerce companies to carefully draw value from these data by integrating big data analytics into their technical infrastructure and therefore gaining an advantage over their rivals by providing their customers personalized products, services and user experience. Personalization and customization are like blood for any e-commerce company and vital for its survival and continued success. According to a survey conducted by Fortune Business Insights, the global market for big data analytics is expected to increase from $271.83 billion in 2022 to $655.53 billion in 2029. It is evident that leading industries are emphasizing about using analytical tools to gather information about customers by advancing business intelligence. For instance, Amazon, Inc. introduced its HIPPA-compliant big data analytics services Amazon Health Lake in December 2020 for the healthcare industry, which offers real-time patient data-driven insights (Fortune Business Insights, 2022).

Most sectors in industrialized nations, including Canada, France, Germany, Italy, Japan, Switzerland, the United Kingdom, and the United States of America have entered the big data analytics era thereby motivating experts and scholars to investigate the effects of these analytics and technologies on corporate values and challenges now than ever before (Le and Liaw, 2017). There are not enough studies, though that demonstrate how e-commerce businesses employ big data and analytics to attract new customers and keep their current ones. This study therefore focuses on big data in e-commerce, how analytical tools are used by e-commerce businesses to offer customized products and services to the customers, the difficulties they face, the privacy and security risks big data poses to their customers, and what potential solutions there may be.

1.2 BIG DATA

Massive volumes of data are being gathered, stored, and analyzed by numerous organizations nowadays. Due to its large volume, unprecedented velocity with which it comes, and variety of formats, these data are often referred to as "big data." Big data is the term for the extremely large, diverse information sets that are produced at an accelerating rate and are so complex that they are difficult or impossible to process using conventional techniques (Watson, 2014). The big data can be classified into three categories as given in Table 1.1.

TABLE 1.1 Classification of big data.

Types of Data	Description
Structured data	"Structured data" is a term for data that can be stored, accessed, and processed in a predefined format
Unstructured data	Data that lacks a clear structure and has an unknown form is referred to as "unstructured data"
Semi-structured data	Both structured and unstructured data are included in semi-structured data

Source: Author

There are five different characteristics of big data also known as 5Vs of big data.

- Volume- The term "volume" refers to both the size and the quantity of the data. In today's high-tech world, information is constantly being generated and stored in a wide range of file types, from text documents and Excel spreadsheets to portable document format (PDF) files and multimedia files, such as photographs and videos (Balusamy et al., 2021).
- Velocity: Velocity is a term used to indicate how quickly data are generated and how quickly it flows. In the modern world, data are constantly being transmitted through many channels, including computers, networks, social media, and mobile phones.

- Variety: Variety is a phrase that is used to indicate the many different sources of data as well as the many different sorts of data. It comprises structured, unstructured, and semi-structured data (Ohlhorst, 2012).
- Veracity: The data's accuracy and quality are described by veracity. Due to the fact that the data are obtained from a variety of sources, it is prone to a great number of errors and inconsistencies; as a result, it is essential to review the data to ensure that it is of high quality, credible, and accurate.
- Value: Value is the degree to which data aids in decision-making. The data's value is determined by how likely it is to have a beneficial effect on a company's operations (Techvidvan, n.d.).

1.3 BIG DATA IN E-COMMERCE

E-commerce, short for "electronic commerce," refers to the trading of goods and services electronically. Although buying and selling things online is the traditional focus of e-commerce, it is important to understand that any transaction that is carried out fully electronically is categorized as e-commerce. There are three distinct types of electronic commerce: B2B or Business to Business (Cisco), B2C or Business to Consumer (Amazon), and C2C (eBay), which stands for "consumer-to-consumer. Due to their need to always be one step ahead of the competition, e-commerce companies are among the quickest to use BDA. The majority of the time, online retailers deal with both structured and unstructured forms of data. Clicks, likes, comments, Twitter posts, voices, etc. are examples of unstructured data, while name, gender, age, DOB, address, and interests are examples of structured data. The problem of the BDA environment is dealing with both forms of data to produce useful insights for improving conversions (Akter and Wamba, 2016).

1.3.1 TYPES OF BIG DATA IN E-COMMERCE

1.3.1.1 TRANSACTIONAL OR BUSINESS ACTIVITY DATA

Transactional or business activity data changes over time as a result of the ongoing interaction between the company and its customers. This is structured data and the data come from a wide range of places, such as customer relation management systems (Bakdi and Chakdi, 2021). For different types of big data in e-commerce refer to Figure 1.1.

1.3.1.2 CLICK-STREAM DATA

In the networked world of today, social media and internet marketing, including the usage of click-stream data, play an important role in the continuing promotional strategy of a firm. This role enables management to make accurate tactical and strategic decisions.

1.3.1.3 VIDEO DATA

Videos, unlike text and photos, are unstructured data. It combines audio and visual elements with information. Every other second, videos are recorded and uploaded from many devices on a global scale to cloud sites such as YouTube and Facebook. Companies in the e-commerce sector can analyze massive amounts of unstructured data, including data that is audio or video.

1.3.1.4 VOICE DATA

Voice data, or information gathered from telephone conversations, customer support, or customer service, is a fourth category of information related to the big data group. Data gathered from customers' voices can be used to learn about their shopping habits and find new customers (Gaikwad and Patil, 1826).

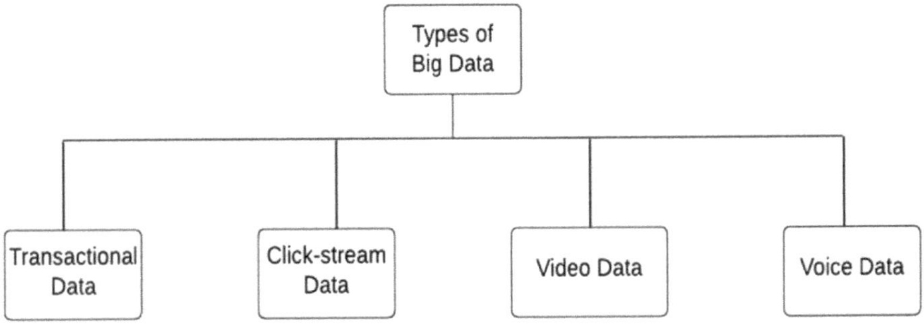

FIGURE 1.1 Types of big data.

Source: Author

1.4 BIG DATA AND CUSTOMER RETENTION

Retaining an existing customer base is less expensive than acquiring a new one. It is essential for e-commerce companies to maintain their current consumer base. Keeping repeat customers helps e-commerce businesses generate more stable revenue. That is why big data has now become a crucial element of a company's success in relationship management with customers because it enables companies to tailor their products and services to consumers and acquire deeper insights into customer behaviors from the huge quantity of data, they have access to. According to research, businesses using big data analytics surpassed their competitors by 5% in productivity and 6% in profitability. 92% of business leaders from 19 different countries were pleased with the results of big data analytics, and they expected big data to have even bigger effects on their organizations, especially on customer relationship management (Cao, 2021).

Retaining existing customers requires massive data to provide better customer experiences in terms of searching for information, recommendation systems, shopping experiences, payment experiences, cancellation and return experiences, and after-sale service experiences. The e-commerce firm gets daily, unlimited access to reams of data. In order to use the payment and shipping options, customers are first required to create an account online by providing details about themselves, such as their name, gender, age, date of birth, area, etc. From the moment a user performs product research online to the moment that the user shares their thoughts on a product or brand via social media, comments, ratings, and returns for a refund, the system collects and stores data such as shopping and browsing histories. By collaborating with SAS institutions, e-commerce companies can simply record and quantify their customers' buying behavior for further study. As a result, businesses proactively modify their products and services to meet the needs of their various customers to boost customer satisfaction, repeat business, and favorable customer perception of the brand (Cao, 2021). As already mentioned, not many studies have looked at how big data affects acquiring and retaining customers. This means that most companies, especially small ones, may not know how to use big data to get new customers or keep the ones they already have. This chapter looks at how big data can be used to keep existing customers coming back. It also looks at how Amazon has used the theory and what the results are.

1.5 PERSONALIZATION AND CUSTOMIZATION

A primary use for big data in the e-commerce sector is the customization or personalization of services and products (Akter and Wamba, 2016). "Even though the general concept of personalization includes customization, we distinguish personalization from customization to come up with simpler and clearer definitions in this study." Customization lets website visitors express their preferences. "My Yahoo" is a good example of customization. If users indicate the zip code for their town and their favorite stock code for tracking, the website could automatically display local news, weather, and stock prices (Nunes and Kambil, 2001; Zo, 2003). The terms "customization" and "personalization" are frequently used interchangeably, but they have important distinctions. Although their ends (improving users' experiences through targeted advertising) are similar, they each take different approaches. Inherently, they are not the same. Personalization is done for the user, whereas customization is done by the user.

1.5.1 CUSTOMIZATION

Customization is performed by the customer. Customers are first asked to identify their preferences, and then they are shown products or services that match those preferences. For instance, Amazon Custom is a store that can be found on Amazon.com. Customers can go there to customize things by adding their own text, images, or logos to them, or they can choose from a range of options that the sellers supply. Text customization allows online shoppers to add their own text to products, with the colors and font options specified by the seller. Some of the other possible applications for this choice are engraving, embroidery, printing, painting, and much more. Image customization allows customers to customize products by uploading their own images. Additionally, the customer also has the option of adding text to the image (sell.amazon, n.d.)

1.5.2 PERSONALIZATION

Personalization is done for the customer. Personalization makes use of datasets, which are statistics about consumers, such as their age, gender, demographics, purchase intent, browsing history, and previous purchases, among other things. This helps to improve the usefulness of advertisements that are presented to the user, which in turn ensures that the offers that are presented to them are relevant (Muhammad, n.d.).Amazon Personalize is a low-code machine learning (ML) service that can generate custom recommendations through an application program interface (API) call for any application running on Amazon Web Services (AWS) infrastructure (Amazon. n.d.). Amazon Personalize's aim is to increase user engagement with personalized product recommendations. Personalize is frequently used by developers to customize marketing promotions, search results, and content recommendations (Lewis, 2019).

1.5.3 PERSONALIZATION: THE SECRET TO CUSTOMER RETENTION

Nowadays, consumers have a growing desire for personalized offerings in the modern era of the digital world. Click data from websites and data from mobile devices are the primary sources of information that can be used to tailor an online shopping experience. By tracking users' clicks and how long they spend doing so online, businesses may better tailor their advertising and promotions to individual consumers. Social media networks, logged-in sites, webpage stays and news, keywords, smartphone click applications, and LBS-based user behavior data are the most common types of user-personalized behavior data (Chen, 2021). The following are examples of how e-commerce sites use the data they collect for personalization purposes:

1.5.3.1 PERSONALIZED PRODUCT RECOMMENDATIONS

Personalizing the product and service recommendations that customers see is one e-commerce personalization strategy that is used by e-commerce companies. For this, cookies can be used to gather data about a customer's location, the products they buy, and their website browsing behavior so that products or services that match their preferences can be recommended to them. The availability of "you might also like" and "recently viewed" features on a website also encourages customers to make additional purchases (Thiagarajan, 2022).

1.5.3.2 LOCATION-SENSITIVE DISPLAY OF PRODUCTS AND CAMPAIGNS

The geographic location and nationality of a customer's purchase can be easily determined by an online store. Companies take advantage of their location to provide more relevant suggestions. Take, as an example, the fact that a major festival is planned for a specific city in the near future. The locals can be given tempting opportunities to shop for festival-related goods and services, such as food and decorations (Thiagarajan, 2022).

1.5.3.3 INFORMATION SEARCH

The quality of an information search is indicative of the quality of the information and the search service as a whole. The credibility of a website's information is measured by how well it is understood by its visitors (Bharati and Chaudhury, 2004). The term "searching service quality" refers to how customers overall perceive the level of responsiveness, suitability, and authenticity of the search results (DeLone and McLean, 2003). A website employing big data analytics software may read and filter a lot of data and offer customers real-time services based on their preferences. For instance, Amazon provides a variety of homepages with a variety of products to practically every visitor. The key is to fully understand their customer by synthesizing information from many sources to understand what they are looking for (Le and Liaw, 2017).

1.5.3.4 INDIVIDUALIZED DYNAMIC PRICING

Individualized dynamic pricing refers to the process of providing goods and services at different prices that change in response to market circumstances (Le and Liaw, 2017). Products and services have prices that fluctuate in real time based on factors including availability, consumption, the market, sales goals, and exchange rates. Discounts and special offers are given to loyal consumers in order to keep them. For example, Amazon continuously modifies its prices on a minute-by-minute basis. Their algorithm sifts through a lot of information, such as market trends, competition pricing, consumer behavior, and more. Their big customer base is the outcome of this (Dearth, 2022).

1.5.3.5 OPTIMIZE CUSTOMER SERVICES

Big data allows e-commerce companies to significantly enhance their customer services. Big data is used by customer service teams to determine common issues with products, track down the origin of a complaint so it may be resolved as soon as possible, and predict which customers are most likely to defect so that preventative measures can be taken. Big data in e-commerce also helps obtain real-time client feedback through live chats, surveys, phone calls, etc. (Le and Liaw, 2017).

The various ways stated above are how e-commerce businesses use big data to offer personalized experiences to their customers, which allows them to retain their current customers and draw in new ones. One of the keys to a customer retention strategy is personalization, which has emerged in this day as a way for businesses to differentiate themselves from one another (Chen, 2021). With the use of real-time data analytics, businesses can provide customers with individualized experiences, including tailored content and offers. In addition, these individualized solutions help companies differentiate between new and repeat customers, which in turn allows for more targeted advertising.

According to Liebowitz (2013), personalization has the potential to increase revenue by at least 10% and improve the yield on marketing efforts by anywhere from five to eight times.

1.5.4 CUSTOMIZATION: AS CUSTOMER IS KING

As previously stated, the customer performs the customization. Young people are becoming an increasingly important consumer target group, and they are not a "one-size-fits-all" group that is satisfied with generic options. Additionally, because of the prevalence of social media and online publishing, fashions and trends are changing more quickly than ever before, thus forcing online retailers to adapt to customers' evolving tastes (Splauding and Perry n.d.). As a result, here comes the big data, which proves to be very useful for customers as it enables them to receive information, products, and services that are especially customized to them (Ghandour, 2015). Now that we know what customization does, let's look at the different ways online stores offer customized products to shoppers.

1.5.4.1 OFFERING PRODUCT BUNDLING FOR COMPLEMENTARY GOODS

One of the simplest methods to provide product customization is through product bundling. It entails the selection of product combinations based on buyer preferences or purchasing patterns. Additionally, it is a great opportunity to cross-sell similar goods while fostering an excellent shopping experience. With the help of product configuration software, online stores group together similar or related items for easier browsing. Better yet, customers mix and match various products in accordance with their specific preferences and view how they will combine before making a purchase (Guldman, 2021).

For instance, if an online seller sells cameras, it makes sense to bundle them with other relevant things like camera cases and lens cleaners in order to enable customers to obtain all they need in one go, and of course, to boost order values.

1.5.4.2 DECORATING THE STANDARD PRODUCTS

When it comes to product customization, e-commerce companies have taken things to a whole new level by letting customers add their own touches to standard items. The company has an advanced product customization platform where customers may upload any number of logos, clip art, or other images to be embroidered or printed on the finished product. Text customization is also available, so customers may add a monogram or special message. In this way, consumers put their own mark on the products they purchase (Guldman, 2021). For example, with Amazon Custom, which is a storefront on Amazon, a customer can customize his passport cover by adding text such as his name, a quote, etc. (Amazon. n.d.).

1.5.4.3 MADE TO ORDER PRODUCTS

Custom-made (or made-to-order) items are one of the most modern forms of product customization. Despite the user interface being comparable to the prior example, production requirements might occasionally be more complicated. This kind of product customization offers customers a great deal of freedom and is one of the most interesting ways to distinguish a brand (Guldman, 2021). Dell Computers is an excellent example of a made-to-order customized product since it employs the MTO production approach and allows customers to order fully customized computers online with options, such as processor, operating system, memory, storage, color and receive them in a few weeks (Jiang et al., 2015).

E-commerce companies that sell everything from dresses to shirts to handbags are seeing the value of letting customers design their own unique products. Big data is used by retailers to provide customers with a customized selection of products; it has been a key factor in Amazon's success. At this point, brands are mass-customizing customization. They are learning how to increase customer retention while utilizing their existing clientele as a source of referrals for new clients. Brands can increase sales on their own websites or win market share on a retailer's website by customizing their products (Splauding and Perry, n.d.).

1.6 SERVICE CUSTOMIZATION

Customizing services is just as significant as customizing products because it improves the way customers see the quality of the service, their satisfaction, their trust, and in the end, their faithfulness to the service provider. Businesses may customize their services for every consumer by maintaining extensive records of their contacts and interactions with those consumers and using this information in the future. One way to provide individualized service is to interact with consumers in ways that are most convenient for them (Coelho and Henseler, 2012). Nowadays, services are highly customized and adapted to customers' needs and it is possible with the help of information gathered about them from both inside and outside the company relationship. By applying the knowledge gained from examining the customer's behavioral patterns, big data analytics helps businesses to cost-effectively adapt service to a only one segment at a time as opposed to bulk customization. A company can automatically customize the user interfaces or the service delivery channels based on the inferred preferences of the consumer (Lehrer et al., 2018). For example, when customers sign up for Netflix, the site allows them to pick a few programs they love before providing them with a range of options based on their choices. Netflix then modifies the user's account depending on the found preferences (Netflix. n.d.).

Personalization and customization frequently go hand in hand. The e-commerce companies that personalize and customize their products and services in accordance with customers' needs, preferences, and likings. Using big data has many advantages, such as increased customer loyalty and the desire to spend more time with the company. This makes it easier for online retailers to retain their customers, which helps them stay one step ahead of the competition and opens up new business opportunities for them. The e-commerce giant Amazon is a great example of this.

1.7 HOW AMAZON IS RULING THE E-COMMERCE MARKET WITH THE USE OF BIG DATA

Amazon.com is a worldwide e-commerce business with headquarters in the United States that specializes in cloud computing, online advertising, digital streaming, and artificial intelligence. As the company's founder and

CEO, Jeff Bezos founded Amazon.com Inc. in 1994 as a bookstore. After a year of business, the company launched online and soon began to provide a variety of products in addition to books, including music media (MP3s, DVDs, and CDs), gadgets, toys, and other home items (Wikipedia. n.d.). With a significant market share in e-commerce, Amazon is the top retailer on the Internet. They heavily rely on the Internet, e-commerce, and information technology in their operations. Along with online shopping, Amazon also provides us with a variety of other services, such as Amazon Pay, Alexa, Amazon Pantry, Amazon Web Services (AWS), and many more. A corporation like Amazon regularly gathers a substantial amount of information. To handle these massive amounts of data, the company employs big data technologies. Amazon uses big data tools to collect information about its customers' viewing habits, search queries, and purchases and uses it to provide personalized and customized products and services to its customers which also helps in the retention of customers (Anshari et al., 2019).

Amazon uses three main types of big data analytics approaches to make the most of its data and provide the best possible service to its consumers at every stage of the buying process, from the first search for a product through its delivery and beyond, if necessary. Predictive analytics, descriptive analytics, and prescriptive analytics all fall under this category. These are discussed below:

1.7.1 PREDICTIVE ANALYTICS

The phrase "predictive analytics" is used to describe the practice of employing data, artificial intelligence methods, and techniques of ML to estimate the likelihood of forthcoming events on the basis of previous information (Finlay, 2014). For instance, Amazon can predict what its consumers will purchase and when by analyzing their purchasing habits. After that, they speculate as to how soon they will be required. The expected products are subsequently sent to a warehouse facility according to the location of the consumers, where they await an order. Amazon predictive analytics takes into account a specific customer's browsing and purchasing history. By doing this, it generates an educated guess that enables it to provide an improved customer experience (Vamanan, 2023).

1.7.2 DESCRIPTIVE ANALYTICS

Descriptive analytics is the process of using data analysis to provide answers to questions like "what is happening?" and "what happened?" in the past through historical analysis (Bakdi and Chadli, 2021). Amazon makes a visual representation of customer data, like past purchases, browsing history, search queries, wish lists, etc., by using descriptive analytics. Amazon can tell from these numbers how likely it is that a buyer will buy a certain product. Additionally, it is helpful for determining what type of price range to establish in order to boost the probability of making a sale (Vaishali, 2020).

1.7.3 PRESCRIPTIVE ANALYTICS

A subset of advanced analytics known as "prescriptive analytics" seeks to answer questions like "what should be done?" and "what can we do to make anything happen?" It is distinguished by techniques such as graph analysis, simulation, intricate real-time evaluation, artificial neural networks, expert systems, analytical tools, and deep learning (Gartner, n.d.).

Amazon has had "anticipatory shipping" copyrighted for a few years now. The goal was to steer products toward certain customers ahead of their actual purchase, all according to a predetermined set of business criteria. Thus, Amazon saves money because of the decreased shipping and fulfilment expenses (Kumar, 2020). Using ML, Amazon aimed to anticipate what a consumer would buy and when they would buy it, and then ship the item to them in advance of their actual purchase. Naturally, if they sent a product that the client had not ordered, the client would not accept the shipment. Customer retention, higher satisfaction, and reduced shipping costs would more than make up for the money lost on the returned items. What we have here is an example of prescriptive analytics (Kumar, 2020).

For example, Amazon uses the vast amounts of structured and unstructured data to create advanced recommendation engines that contribute to over 35% of all sales, automated customer service frameworks to guarantee high levels of customer satisfaction, and dynamic pricing systems that adjust prices against rival sites almost every 15 seconds to maximize profits (Goff et al. 2012). Using big data, Amazon is able to keep tabs on the exact locations of its 1.5 billion items stored in 200 fulfilment centers across the globe, as well as ensure their safety and security. The company then uses predictive analytics for what it calls "anticipatory shipping," in which it anticipates when a customer will buy a product and sends it ahead to a distribution center near the final destination (Zakir et.al., 2015).

There are three main places where Amazon gets its consumer information: The first step is the consumer providing his or her information while making use of the service. Second, it might include information it gathers on the devices, locations, and the like used by its own customers. When everything is said and done, it gathers information from the external environment which involves third parties. E-commerce companies can learn from Amazon's success by looking at how the company uses big data to boost sales. In order to keep consumers, Amazon places a higher value on their satisfaction than on their revenue and statistics, and therefore they use these data to tailor their service to each individual, which is a key to customer retention.

1.8 CHALLENGES FACED BY E-COMMERCE COMPANIES IN HANDLING BIG DATA

Even though it is clear that several e-commerce businesses are gathering enormous volumes of data, only a few are effectively utilizing the knowledge that big data analysis provides. E-commerce businesses' inability to utilize such vast amounts of data is a major issue. Despite the fact that an e-commerce company invests a huge amount of money into learning how to interpret the information that is flowing in from their suppliers and customers, only about 40% of their workforce possesses the necessary skills and expertise to do so (Deshmukh, 2013) Big data is so big that it necessitates big skills to manage and value it. Let us have a look at the challenges of big data.

The marketing departments of e-commerce businesses are struggling to make sense of the flood of information coming in from various sources. Consequently, the first and most significant challenge is sifting through the massive volume of data to locate the relevant details about each individual consumer (Agarwal and Dhar, 2014).

Second, it might be challenging to follow customer behavior, particularly that of dangling customers who are transitioning from brand awareness to conversion. Identifying and establishing the connections between both online and physical stores can be difficult, such as when a buyer first sees or reads about a good or service and when he really decides to buy it (Anshari et al., 2019).

Thirdly, Individual choices can vary in social networks influenced by group emotion. After making a purchase, customers express their views on the service or product on the website. Feedback that is faked in the form of online advertising cannot be accepted (Gaikwad and Patil, 1826). Big data analysis has a negative effect on consumer willingness, which further reduces customers' intentions and encourages inappropriate behavior that eventually results in them rejecting offers to purchase products or services (Guangting and Junxuan, 2014).

The final challenge is to the legitimacy of the data, and it centers on the interest in the data source, which may include Web records, social media, cloud-based content, transactions, and data applications that may require a meaningful power of information to guarantee the data's genuineness and safety. The person in charge of managing all that massive data, for instance, reads every status update and tweet we make (Anshari et al., 2019).

1.9 PRIVACY AND SECURITY ISSUES FACED BY CUSTOMERS BECAUSE OF BIG DATA

As previously said, big data and related analytics are extremely helpful to businesses. They help businesses gain and retain customers. Big data and big data analytics present certain privacy and security-related issues that need to be discussed. A few of these concerns are discussed further down.

Data leaks, brokerage, and discrimination account for the vast majority of privacy issues. When a customer's information is accessed by a third party without their consent, it is considered a data breach and a privacy risk. For instance, Instagram gathers a lot of information about its users and analyses it to learn more about them. However, there is always a chance that the data collector may improperly handle or even misuse the information they have gathered (Wu, 2022).

Organizations gather information from a range of sources, including physical components, software programs, and endpoint devices. It can be difficult to verify the accuracy and reliability of data as it is gathered, as well as the sources from which it came. Wicked users frequently tamper with the data collection device or the data collection software installed on the device, resulting in the entry of malicious data into the centralized data collection system. Malicious individuals may generate fake IDs and enter malicious data into the centralized data collection system using them (Berie et al., n.d.)

Another increasing threat to data security is the unwanted correlation of data and deriving inferences from that data. Trying to find hidden patterns by combining and cross-linking a massive amount of data made by and about people and gathered from various sources raises new risks because big data has the potential to make the privacy and security implications of database relationships much worse (Farkas and Jajodia, 2002). In point of fact, the process of correlating information from various data sources, which is a standard operation with the majority of big data environments, may increase the danger of re-identification and de-anonymization and really, analysts may, either purposefully or unintentionally, draw inferences about the data subject or uncover additional sensitive information that the individual concerned has not consented to disclose (Simo, 2015). Deceptive analysts can use the inferred information and knowledge to draw logical but unjust conclusions, which can have serious negative consequences for the persons whose data is being stored and associated (Parihar and Sc, 2021).

1.10 SAFEGUARD MEASURES

E-commerce businesses have a responsibility to reassure customers that the online information and data they provide will be kept secure and used solely as the customer anticipates it will be. The company owners should carefully consider their security needs and implement appropriate measures.

The confidentiality of big data can be protected by companies through the application of data cryptography (Wu, 2022). The practice of cryptography entails the use of a collection of methods for scrambling or camouflaging data in such a way that it can be accessed only by an individual who is able to restore the data to its initial form. In modern devices, cryptography offers a reliable and cost-effective basis for confirming data integrity and keeping data safe and secure (Ibm, 2021). The strategy involves changing regular text into something that cannot be understood or read. The procedure safeguards information from unauthorized access or modification (Wu, 2022).

Only the relevant information should be collected from customers; do not make them fill out forms with more information than is actually needed. Numerous online retailers have begun amassing massive troves of data for analysis and research purposes. Storing this much information increases the risk that it could be lost or stolen, which could have a negative impact on the company's reputation in the long run (Le and Liaw, 2017).

In addition to taking these precautions, businesses may also take steps to increase the security of their systems to prevent data theft and hacking. When registering or making a purchase on Amazon, for instance, consumers are required to use a strong password generator to create a password containing at least 8 characters, 1 special character, and 2 numbers. Furthermore, reCAPTCHA systems and other additional security methods can be installed to further ensure that users are not automated software or potential hackers.

By using the cloud as a central data repository, many well-known e-commerce firms have alleviated privacy and security worries. The goal of this action is to make use of the established, tried, and true conformity system and security architecture in the cloud. For instance, in order to lessen the chances of breach of security, cloud systems are updated regularly and monitored frequently. However, before relying on the cloud providers' services, businesses must verify that they have sufficient security measures in place (Wu, 2022).

1.11 CONCLUSION

In conclusion, the e-commerce sector is widely recognized as a major user of big data. A sizable portion of this digital universe is devoted to electronic commerce, which stores information about consumers such as their online and offline movements, purchases, and abandoned carts. However, the real value for e-commerce businesses comes from evaluating the data collected from customers. By implementing big data technology correctly, e-commerce businesses can analyze customer buying patterns in light of current market conditions, thereby increasing sales and profits. These businesses then use this information to better target their advertising, develop products that address client complaints, and train their staff to consistently deliver the high-quality service their customers have come to expect.

Nowadays, it is essential for businesses to tailor their offerings to individual customers, from the goods they sell to the promotional materials they distribute. Customers now expect businesses to provide for their unique requirements and get dissatisfied when they are not met. As a result, the significance of personalization and customization has grown in recent years to meet this growing need. The company uses big data, big data analytics, and tailored offerings to further improve the customer experience, which in turn boosts customer acquisition and retention. Similarly, Amazon and other e-commerce giants have realized the value of big data and are employing it to improve customer service and attract and retain more clients. Big data analytics is indeed the key to winning new business and keeping existing customers happy in the modern era of big data, and businesses should take greater advantage of their own data by using big data technology.

It is clear from the present study that e-commerce firms confront a number of obstacles when attempting to use big data. These challenges stem from the fact that big data analytics still has limitations that must be carefully considered when implemented. Additionally, the privacy and security concerns of consumers who generate this data are highlighted, along with the many preventative steps that might be implemented. This chapter uses Amazon as an example to explain how e-commerce businesses make better use of big data to retain customers through the personalization and customization of products and services. This study is incredibly helpful for customers since it explains how even a single click on shopping websites can be used to deliver them exactly what they want. Once customers understand how this science works, they will be able to use it in an informed manner.

KEYWORDS

- **big data**
- **customer**
- **retention**
- **marketing**

REFERENCES

Agarwal, R.; Dhar, V. Big Data, Data Science, and Analytics: The Opportunity and Challenge for IS Research. *Inf. Syst. Res.* **2014,** *25* (3), 443–448.

Akter, S.; Wamba, S. F. Big Data Analytics in E-Commerce: A Systematic Review and Agenda for Future Research. *Electron. Markets* **2016,** *26* (2), 173–194.

Amazon. Amazon Custom, n.d. https://sell.amazon.com/programs/custom

Amazon. What Is Amazon Personalize? n.d. https://docs.aws.amazon.com/personalize/latest/dg/what-is-personalize.html

Anshari, M.; Almunawar, M. N.; Lim, S. A.; Al-Mudimigh, A. Customer Relationship Management and Big Data Enabled: Personalization & Customization of Services. *Appl. Comput. Inf.* **2019,** *15* (2), 94–101.

Bakdi, M.; Chadli, W. Big Data: An Overview. In: *Big Data Analytics: Harnessing Data for New Business Model*; Khelfaoui, M., Kadi, N., Sedkaoui, S., Eds.; Apple Academic Press, 2021. https://www.google.co.in/books/edition/Big_Data_Analytics/3R0lEAAAQBAJ?hl=en&gbpv=0

Betser, J.; Belanger, D. Big Data and Business Analytics. In: *Architecting the Enterprise via Big Data Analytics*; Lebowitz, J., Ed.; CRC Press, 2013. https://books.google.co.in/oks?hl=en&lr=&id=Oq9znTz7FGoC&oi=fnd&pg=PP1&ots=JT2KxILFGm&sig=9ojn4tPAxjPkpghLbyOg0v_2P1A&redir_esc=y#v=onepage&q&f=false

Bharati, P.; Chaudhury, A. An Empirical Investigation of Decision-Making Satisfaction in Web-Based Decision Support Systems. *Decision Support Syst.* **2004,** *37* (2), 187–197.

Cao, P. Big Data in Customer Acquisition and Retention for e-Commerce–Taking Walmart as an Example. In: *2021 3rd International Conference on Economic Management and Cultural Industry (ICEMCI 2021)*; Atlantis Press, 2021; pp 259–262.

Chen, S. Analysis of Customization Strategy for E-Commerce Operation Based on Big Data. *Wireless Commun. Mob. Comput.* **2021,** 2021.

Coelho, P. S.; Henseler, J. Creating Customer Loyalty Through Service Customization. *Eur. J. Market.* **2012,** *46* (3/4), 331–356.

Dearth, B. Dynamic Pricing in Ecommerce: How It Works, 2022. https://www.vaimo.com/dynamic-pricing-in-ecommerce-how-it-works/

DeLone, W. H.; McLean, E. R. The DeLone and McLean Model of Information Systems Success: A Ten-Year Update. *J. Manag. Inf. Syst.* **2003,** *19* (4), 9–30.

Deshmukh, S. Big Data—An Opportunity and Challenge for E-Commerce. *Int. J. Sci. Eng. Res.* **2013,** *4* (12), 79–83.

Farkas, C.; Jajodia, S. The Inference Problem: A Survey. *ACM SIGKDD Explorations Newslett.* **2002,** 4 (2), 6–11.

Fhom, H. S. Big Data: Opportunities and Privacy Challenges, 2015. arXiv preprint arXiv:1502.00823.

Finlay, S. *Predictive Analytics, Data Mining and Big Data: Myths, Misconceptions and Methods*; Palgrave Macmillan, 2014.

Fortune Business Insights. Big Data Analytics Market Size, 2022. https://www.fortunebusinessinsights.com/big-data-analytics-market-106179

Gaikwad, N.; Patil, H. An Overview of Big Data Analytics in E-Commerce. *Int. Res. J. Modernization Eng. Technol. Sci. 2022, 04*, 1826–1831.

Gandomi, A. H.; Abirami R, N.; Balusamy, B.; Kadry, S. *Big Data: Concepts, Technology, and Architecture*; Wiley, 2021.

Gartner. Prescriptive Analytics, n.d. https://www.gartner.com/en/information-technology/glossary/prescriptive-analytics

Ghandour, A. Big Data Driven E-Commerce Architecture. *Int. J. Econ. Commerce Manag.* **2015,** *3* (5), 940–947.

Goff, J.; McInerney, P.; Soni, G. *Need for Speed: Algorithmic Marketing and Customer Data Overload*; McKinsey & Company, McKinsey on Marketing and Sales, 2012.

Guangting, Z.; Junxuan, Z. The Study of Impact of" Big Data" to Purchasing Intention. *Int. J. Bus. Soc. Sci.* **2014,** *5* (10).

Guldman, A. Customization vs. Personalization vs. Configuration, 2021 Sept. https://configureid.com/2021/09/01/what-is-product-customization/

IBM. The Role of Cryptography in Data Security, 2021, June. https://www.ibm.com/docs/en/zos/2.4.0?topic=introduction-role-cryptography-in-data-security

Jiang, P.; Balasubramanian, S. K.; Lambert, Z. V. Responses to Customized Products: The Consumers' Behavioral Intentions. *J. Serv. Market.* **2015,** *29* (4), 314–326.

Kumar, A. Prescriptive Analytics: The Way Forward for Big Data, 2020, Feb. https://herodigital.com/insights/prescriptive-analytics/

Le, T. M.; Liaw, S. Y. Effects of Pros and Cons of Applying Big Data Analytics to Consumers' Responses in an E-Commerce Context. *Sustainability* **2017,** *9* (5), 798.

Lehrer, C.; Wieneke, A.; Vom Brocke, J. A. N.; Jung, R.; Seidel, S. How Big Data Analytics Enables Service Innovation: Materiality, Affordance, and the Individualization of Service. *J. Manag. Inf. Syst.* **2018,** *35* (2), 424–460.

Lewis, S Amazon Personalize, 2019. https://www.techtarget.com/searchaws/definition/Amazon-Personalize
Muhammad, F. Customization vs. Personalization: What Is the Difference? n.d. https://instapage.com/blog/customized-vs-personalized
Netflix. n.d. https://www.netflix.com/in/
Nunes, P. F.; Kambil, A. Personalization? No Thanks. *Harv. Bus. Rev. 2001*, *79* (4), 32–33.
Ohlhorst, F. *Big Data Analytics: Turning Big Data Into Big Money*; Wiley, 2012.
Parihar, M. Big Data Security and Privacy. *Int. J. Eng. Res. Technol.* **2021,** *10* (07), 323–327.
Splauding, E.; Perry, C. Making It Personal: Rules for Success in Product Customization, n.d. https://www.bain.com/contentassets/9e410ebe236d49449c71c44c6b41d8dd/bain_brief_making_it_personal.pdf
Techvidvan. 5 Vs of Big Data, n.d. https://techvidvan.com/tutorials/5-vs-of-big-data/
Thiagarjan, H. 9 E-Commerce Personalization Strategies to Boost Sales, 2022, June. https://www.mailmodo.com/guides/ecommerce-personalization/
Vaishali. 9 Ways Amazon Uses Big Data To Stalk You! [Leaked], 2020 Feb. https://www.datatobiz.com/blog/amazon-uses-big-data-points-to-know/
Vamanan, D. Best Amazon Predictive Analytics Tips You Need to Follow in 2023, 2023, Jan. https://www.sellerapp.com/blog/amazon-predictive-analytics/
Verhoef, P. C.; Kooge, E.; Walk, N. *Creating Value with Big Data Analytics: Making Smarter Marketing Decisions*; Taylor & Francis, 2016.
Watson, H. J. Tutorial: Big Data Analytics: Concepts, Technologies, and Applications. *Commun. Assoc. Inf. Syst.* **2014,** *34* (1), 65.
Wikipedia. Amazon, n.d. https://en.wikipedia.org/wiki/Amazon_(company)
Wu, X. The Use of Big Data in Customer Acquisition and Retention. In: *2022 7th International Conference on Financial Innovation and Economic Development (ICFIED 2022)*; Atlantis Press, 2022; pp 2258–2265.
Zakir, J.; Seymour, T.; Berg, K. Big Data Analytics. *Iss. Inf. Syst.* **2015,** *16* (2).
Zo, H. Personalization vs. Customization: Which Is More Effective in E-Services? *AMCIS 2003 Proc.* 2003, *32*. https://aisel.aisnet.org/amcis2003/32

CHAPTER 2

Unleashing Big Data and Its Role in Retaining Customers

NEHA VERMA[1] and KAMALPREET[2]

[1]*Chitkara Business School, Chitkara University, Punjab, India*

[2]*University School of Business, Chandigarh University, Punjab, India*

ABSTRACT

A customer is the pivot around which a business revolves and a catalyst that makes the business going. Customers are of prime importance to every business concern. Therefore, their retention is of vital concern. There is no exaggeration to say that no company can thrive without keeping its customers intact. Business houses are well aware of the fact that it is relatively easy to retain existing customers than to fetch new ones. Retained customers are perceived as a highly useful entity for businesses as they act as a precursor to the most outstanding mode of marketing, that is, word-of-mouth marketing. Out of the available tools for retaining customers, big data analysis is gaining ground in the current scenario. Big data refers to the sets of data which are usually large enough to unveil the pattern or trend that is capable of revealing the behavior of a human when put to computational analysis. Big data analytics have actually armed today's business leaders to transform themselves in order to cater to their customers in the best possible way. Big data could be used for multiple purposes, such as gaining insights about customer experience, product development, predictive maintenance, fraud and compliance, machine learning, innovation, operational efficiency, etc. The focus of our study is specifically the role of big data in retaining customers.

Augmenting Customer Retention Through Big Data Analytics.
Reena Malik, Ambuj Sharma, and Prashant Chaudhary (Eds.)

2.1 INTRODUCTION

No business can lead in the future if it has not strategized well enough to retain its customers. A customer is the pivot around which a business revolves and a catalyst that makes the business going. Therefore, their retention is of vital concern.

2.2 CUSTOMER RETENTION AND ITS RELEVANCE

Customer retention is the ability of a business house to keep its customers intact for a longer duration through the provision of quality and requisite products to them. In the words of Ascarza et al. (2018), customer retention is the tendency of a customer to remain tied to a company via its continuous transactions with the same. It is worth noticing that the transaction can be monetary or non-monetary. Monetary transactions include buying a product and paying a subscription fee, whereas non-monetary transactions include using emails or any other free services provided by the company. Furthermore, even if the customer ceases to use product A of the company, he shifts to the product B of the company. But in any case, does not part with the company altogether.

Customer retention boosts the profitability of the company (Reichheld and Kenny, 1990; Ascarza et al., 2018). It is believed that nothing is as powerful as customer retention in this highly competitive era Singh (2006). Customer retention can be highlighted as one of the major challenges faced by companies. (Ascarza et al., 2018). Research reveals that the majority of customers feel that companies should put more efforts to retain them (Handley, 2013). Aspinall et al. (2001) held that although companies understand the importance of customer retention, they are yet to understand it better in order to improve it.

Business houses are well aware of the fact that it is relatively easy to retain existing customers than to fetch new ones (Ahmad and Buttle, 2002). Retained customers are perceived as a highly useful entity for businesses. It is believed that it is the loyalty of retained customers only that brings the majority of profits. Every business house needs adequate strategies to retain customers. Retained customers act as a precursor to the most outstanding mode of marketing, that is, word-of-mouth marketing.

2.2.1 CUSTOMER SATISFACTION PAVES THE WAY FOR CUSTOMER RETENTION

Customer satisfaction and customer retention are positively related (Day, 1994; Singh, 2006).

Customer Satisfaction is not only essential for the survival of a business, but the growth and ultimately the profits of the enterprise are highly dependent on it (Bose, 2007; Ali et al., 2021). In order to know whether he is satisfied or not, adequate inputs are required which are possible due to big data.

The main motive of a business is to earn profits and improve shareholder's value. Needless to say this can never be achieved without satisfying and retaining customers. Primarily, a business can compete based on price and quality of products and services they provide. Here latter is a better solution to the problem and it can only be achieved if meaningful inputs related to customer experience are obtained by the business houses (Speiss, 2014). Reducing costs or lowering prices can bring advantages in the short run, but the sustainable growth in the business and its profitability demands much more. There is a need to provide something unique to the customer that retains him with the business. Quality of service is one of the most important factors contributing to customer retention (Venetis and Ghauri, 2004; Alkitbi, 2020).

It is believed that business houses lose most of their customers due to unsatisfactory services given to them. The root of substandard service stems from poor knowledge about the preferences and perceptions of the customer. This gap of not understanding the customer well could be tackled by analyzing the big data.

2.3 WHAT IS BIG DATA?

Under this section, an effort is made to uncover the details of big data giving due consideration to its meaning, evolution, and relevance in the present times. Big data refers to a set of data which are usually large enough to unveil the pattern or trend that is capable of revealing the behavior of a human when put to computational analysis (Santana, 2019). Big data and its analysis have actually armed today's business leaders to transform themselves to cater to their customers in the best possible way. As this era is marked by mushroom growth of digital data, it is no longer a muddle to obtain data from the customers that are needed by the business houses to have insight into their outlook, perspectives, and fancies. Big data is not only all the rage at present, but it is certainly going to have a bright future as well (Tsai, 2015). This is why researchers are not leaving any stone unturned to discover new technologies which can well manage and analyze big data. It can be described as a process that examines and analyzes large amounts of data in order to uncover clandestine patterns, trends, and correlations to make effective decisions which are beneficial to the business (Tiwari et al., 2018). It is by virtue of big data analytics that users can capture, store, and analyze unimaginably huge amounts of data, both from internal and external sources, such as database of a company, radio frequency identification (RFID), records of mobile or phone and even locations or internet to get valuable insights (Zakir et al., 2015).

The starting decade of the 21st century is believed to mark the onset of big data (Davenport and Dyche, 2013). Industry experts are of the opinion that big data may be new for newly emerging startups and online firms but it exists in one or another form for large and well-established business houses. They often associate this newly coined term with the big and updated version of the data they have already been using. The credit for the introduction of the concept of big data can be given to Cox and Ellsworth in October 1997 (Tiwari et al., 2018). Be it government, academia, or professionals; all regard it as indispensable for their success (Jin et al., 2015).

It is believed that analysis of the big data can help in predicting the future and hence in shaping the moves of business houses accordingly. Various models are applied to the big data in order to achieve the desired outcomes. The data-checking process is completely automatic and involves multiple simulations which are being run usually in billions as long as a concrete pattern has emerged to nail a trend that could solve a problem.

Present technologies which are exceedingly data-intensive, improved computation and advanced data resources for data storage have massively contributed to the progress of big data science (Najafabadi et al., 2015). Many companies that are technology-driven, such as Amazon, Google, Microsoft, and Yahoo generate big data big time. Not only these giants but social media favorites, such as YouTube, Facebook, and Twitter are a dominant source of creating myriad sets of big data

Big data could be used for multiple purposes, such as gaining insights about customer experience, product development, predictive maintenance, fraud and compliance, machine learning, innovation, and operational efficiency. The focus of our study is the role of big data in retaining customers.

2.4 FIVE V'S OF BIG DATA EXPLAINING ITS KEY CHARACTERISTICS

Big data is often comprehended by its 5 V's which describe its key characteristics. Although there are other features too, these are the most widely talked about features as shown in Figure 2.1.

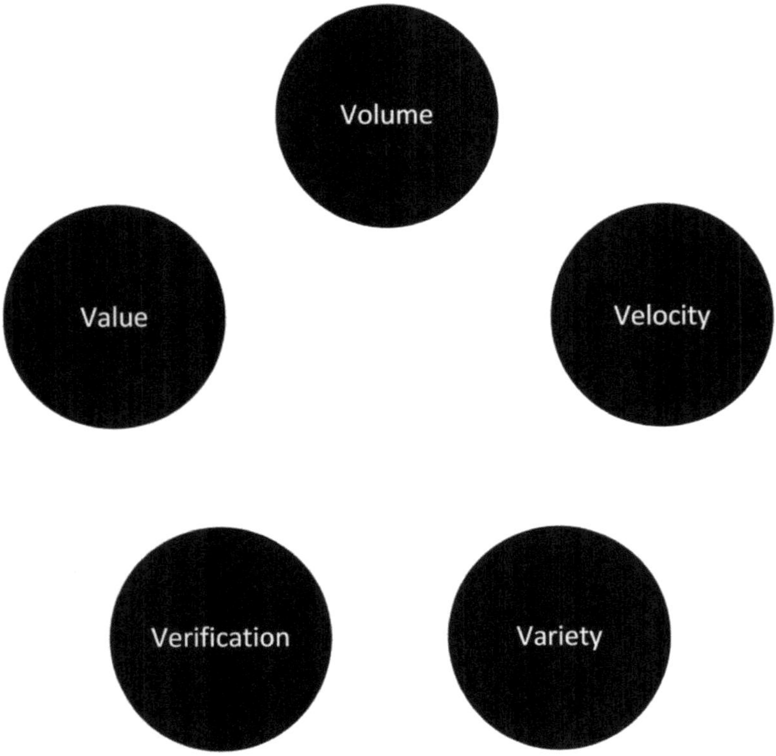

FIGURE 2.1 Principal characteristics of the big data.

These are often referred to as the principal characteristics of the big data. These Five V's bring out the meaning of big data for the users.

2.4.1 VOLUME

The first V of big data connotes the volume of data. It is nothing but the amount or quantity of data. Data can be called big Ddta only when its volume is large enough to be considered so. Customer events that are recorded in a day are generally in multiple billions (Speiss et al., 2014). The larger the volume of the data, the better will be the decisions of the business.

2.4.2 VELOCITY

Second V stands for the velocity or speed at which the data are generated and moved eventually. Speed is very crucial as information not received on time will lose its relevance and hamper the quality of decisions made. Velocity becomes all the more important when real-time data are required to have quick insights into the matter under consideration. A perfect example of such a case could be the healthcare sector where various medical devices are deployed to gather and monitor patients data.

2.4.3 VARIETY

Third V talks about the variety of data obtained. Naturally, there are various sources of data collection. Data can be obtained both from internal and external sources. It is imperative to note that the data obtained could be unstructured, semi-structured, or structured. Structured data are considered to be the best among the three for analysis.

2.4.4 VERIFICATION

Next V relates to the veracity of the data. Data can be incomplete, unreliable, or messy. In that case, the quality of data is compromised and such data lack the power to provide useful insights to make effective decisions. Therefore, the quality of data is as important as the quantity of data to actually derive value from it.

2.4.5 VALUE

The last V is related to the value that can be obtained from the big data. Value can be gauged from the insights the business gets from the big data and what it can do with the insights obtained.

2.5 INDUSTRY-WIDE APPLICATIONS OF BIG DATA

There is no industry today, be it finance, real estate, food, information, retail, management, electronics, auto, pharma, etc. which is not big data-dependent. Big data not only aids in predicting concretely but also helps in gauging the inter-variable relationships. All this leads to making correct decisions. Every business relies on the inputs provided by big data to understand and deliver the best to customers.

Big data has brought a revolution in various industries and is actually aiding them to serve their customers in the best way (Gazis, and Gazi, 2021). Needless to say, no industry can operate efficiently and effectively without having an adequate framework of IT and software. The dependency of businesses on IT and its allied systems needs no introduction at present. Therefore, in order to survive and thrive in the highly competitive era of today, IT adaptability and updation are of paramount importance. Latinovic et al. (2019) emphasized that big data is a boon for the development of industry as it helps to reach correct decisions that have a good impact on production and sales positively. This not only boosts profitability but also has the benefit of cost reduction which is another feather in the cap. The big business houses make it a point that they are cost-efficient operators. Data scientists have proven evidences that storage of big data with the help of Hadoop clusters is far more cost-efficient in comparison to the storage of traditional data. This cost efficiency ultimately reflects on the results of the business in the form of enhanced profitability.

Big data Analytics is highly in demand due to its importance in solving the issues related to national intelligence, fraud detection, cyber security, medical didactics, and marketing, etc. (Najafabadi et al., 2015).

2.6 HOW IS BIG DATA DIFFERENT THAN TRADITIONAL DATA?

The scope of traditional data is narrow, which is primarily obtained at the organization level only, whereas big data encompasses the data at the organization level and beyond, which is outside the organization. Major sources of data in the case of traditional data are CRM data, web transaction data, and ERP transaction data, etc., whereas the popular data sources in the case of big data are social media, videos, images, device data, and log data, etc. As far as data storage is concerned, traditional data are stored in gigabytes or terabytes; however, petabytes, zettabytes, and even exabytes are used in the case of storing big data.

Analysis of big data demands advanced analytical algorithms as data analytics through traditional means becomes futile with large sets of data.

2.6.1 HOW BIG DATA IS ACTUALLY RETAINING CUSTOMERS?

Now that we have discussed what big data is and its importance, we must understand how it helps businesses in retaining customers. The following points will clearly describe the role that big data has in retaining customers as shown in Figure 2.2.

FIGURE 2.2 Role of big data.

2.6.1.1 *PREDICTIVE ANALYSIS*

Big data Analysis helps in predicting the issues that the client might be facing with respect to any product or service. This is a proactive approach to finding solutions to problems before the customer service executive is approached by the client. It makes the customer feel that he is being valued and his concerns are important to the business. It is believed that this would revolutionize customers' relationships.

2.6.1.2 *OPTIMIZING THE PRODUCT OFFER*

Every business is primarily inclined to deliver customized products to its customers in an effort to strengthen their loyalty and hence retain them for a longer period. This requires analyzing the client's transactions to understand their preferences. It is often seen that there is wild mushrooming in existing product versions in an attempt to attract more and more customers. However, this tends to confuse customers. Big data analysis makes business houses understand customer preferences and thus narrow down the options for customers and come up exactly with what the customers need.

2.6.1.3 CASHING IN ON THE REAL-TIME DATA

Big data has made it possible for the business houses to track what customer wants when the customer is looking for products or services. This is to say that big data is the reason why real-time customer engagements are conducted. This gives enough indications and clues as to what to reflect to the customer on a particular medium by analyzing his pattern of research.

2.6.1.4 HELPS TO KEEP POTENTIAL CUSTOMERS

With the help of big data, companies are able to track what customers like and dislike. This helps them to design products that are at par with their needs. This ultimately helps in retaining the customers and making room for potential customers as products are customized as per their whims and fancies.

2.6.1.5 LENDING PERSONAL TOUCH

Big data helps in understanding customers' needs and desires very well and when customized products are reflected to them, they feel that they are being taken care of. This is an excellent way to win customers and keep them for a long period of time.

2.6.1.6 QUICK AND EFFICIENT ANALYSIS

Big data Analytics has made it easier to analyze large-scale and complex calculations by considerably reducing the cycle time involved in the same. It is no exaggeration to say that the analysis that was conducted investing hours and days is now successfully conducted in minutes and sometimes even in seconds.

2.7 CHALLENGES

Although big data has presented businesses with a plethora of opportunities, at the same time, it is also tainted with the challenges that it has posed to data scientists. In order to make big data more useful, its challenges need to be tackled well. Following are the major challenges to be tackled.

2.7.1 LARGE AND COMPLEX DATA SETS

Big data Analytics leads to data sets that are too large and complex to be processed by traditional database and software (Tsai, 2015). This shoots up the cost of computation and can even lead to instability of the algorithms (Fan et al., 2014).

2.7.2 STORAGE AND PROCESSING

It is not easy to store and process the high-velocity data (Marx, 2013). Their rapid storage and processing is a must to come at real-time solutions which are necessary to serve the underlying purpose. In case of a problem in this, the information not obtained timely is of no use.

2.7.3 SORTING THE MEANINGFUL DATA

Out of the large amount of data which comprises different data types, it is a significant muddle to zero in on the data sets which are actually meaningful and have the potential to deliver value. The heterogeneity in data leads to statistical biases which can affect the quality of insights obtained.

2.7.4 HETEROGENEITY

Since big data are obtained from multiple sources which themselves constitute various subpopulations, the issue of heterogeneity of data becomes apparent. This strengthens the need to deploy sophisticated statistical procedures and algorithms as simple methods that work well with small sets of data will lose their suitability in the case of big data.

2.7.5 NOISE ACCUMULATION

While analyzing big data, many parameters are tested. In case any error remains while testing, the decision taken or conclusion drawn will lose its accuracy. This is known as noise accumulation and it usually has a higher probability of existence in the case of big data.

2.7.6 SPURIOUS CORRELATION

Big data are prone to establish erroneous relationship and endangers the quality of discoveries made or inferences drawn from the statistical analysis.

2.7.7 ENDOGENEITY

The statistical data for computation is held valid if it is exogenous. But in the case of big data, this assumption stands violated generally due to large dimensions of data. Such dimensionality of data is responsible for correlating the residual noise with the predictors. This weakens the statistical analysis undertaken on such data.

2.7.8 PRIVACY

One of the biggest issues with big data analytics is that of privacy. Customers are often concerned about getting their personal information public. There is fear of their personal information getting exposed post-analysis. This inhibits them to come forward with their opinions. Therefore, such systems are required which guarantee that the private information of the end users will not be accessible by anyone and everyone (Tsai, 2015).

2.8 CONCLUSION

Big data Analytics can be termed as a creative technology to understand the needs of customers in a better way. Understanding customers is vital to survive and thrive in this highly competitive era. Big data is a non-traditional channel of communication between companies and customers which makes the former familiar with the newly emerging trends which is a key to customer retention in this highly competitive era. And there is no exaggeration to say that big data will become the most sought-after catalyst to perform better in the future.

It is data that has a lot of value for any business house as it is a major input on which many key decisions of a company are based. This data has the power to transform organizations and coax them to innovate harder.

Big data or the blast of information is certainly going to rule the roost as a most resourceful guide to the various business houses in the generations to come. The challenges that come in the way of its fruitful utilization are temporary and lose their relevance in front of the myriad advantages that it potentially offers. It will be a key driver to retain and attain new customers in the future.

KEYWORDS

- **customer retention**
- **big data**
- **big data analytics**

REFERENCES

Ahmad, R.; Buttle, F. Customer Retention Management: A Reflection of Theory and Practice. *Market. Intell. Plan.* **2002,** *20* (3), 149–161.

Ali, B. J.; Saleh, P. F.; Akoi, S.; Abdulrahman, A. A.; Muhamed, A. S.; Noori, H. N.; Anwar, G. *Int. J. Eng. Bus. Manag.* **2021,** *5* (2), 65–77.

Alkitbi, S. S.; Alshurideh, M.; Al Kurdi, B.; Salloum, S. A. Factors Affect Customer Retention: A Systematic Review. In: *International Conference on Advanced Intelligent Systems and Informatics*; Springer: Cham, 2020; pp 656–667.

Ascarza, E.; Neslin, S. A.; Netzer, O.; Anderson, Z.; Fader, P. S.; Gupta, S. et al. In Pursuit of Enhanced Customer Retention Management: Review, Key Issues, and Future Directions. *Customer Needs Solut.* **2018,** *5* (1), 65–81.

Aspinall, E.; Nancarrow, C.; Stone, M. The Meaning and Measurement of Customer Retention. *J. Target. Measure. Anal. Market.* **2001,** *10* (1), 79–87.

Bose, S. K. Customer is the King: A Managerial Perspective in Modern Banking Scenario. *Asia Pac. Bus. Rev.* **2007,** *3* (1), 115–118.

Davenport, T. H.; Dyché, J. Big Data in Big Companies. *Int. Inst. Anal.* **2013,** *3* (1–31).

Day, G. S. The Capabilities of Market-Driven Organizations. *J. Market.* **1994,** *58* (4), 37–52.

Fan, J.; Han, F.; Liu, H. Challenges of Big Data Analysis. *Natl. Sci. Rev.* **2014,** *1* (2), 293–314.

Gazis, A.; Gazi, T. Big Data Applications in Industry Fields. *ITNOW* **2021,** *63* (2), 50–51.

Handley, L. Customer Retention: Brave New World of Consumer Dynamics. *Market. Week Online Edition* **2013,** *21*.

Jin, X.; Wah, B. W.; Cheng, X.; Wang, Y. Significance and Challenges of Big Data Research. *Big Data Res.* **2015,** *2* (2), 59–64.

Latinovic, T.; Preradović, D.; Barz, C. R.; Vadean, A. P.; Todić, M. Big Data as the Basis for the Innovative Development Strategy of the Industry 4.0. In: *IOP Conf. Ser.: Mater. Sci. Eng.* **2019,** *477* (1), 012045.

Marx, V. The Big Challenges of Big Data. *Nature* **2013,** *498* (7453), 255–260.

Najafabadi, M. M.; Villanustre, F.; Khoshgoftaar, T. M.; Seliya, N.; Wald, R.; Muharemagic, E. Deep Learning Applications and Challenges in Big Data Analytics. *J. Big Data* **2015,** *2* (1), 1–21.

Reichheld, F. F.; Kenny, D. W. The Hidden Advantages of Customer Retention. *J. Retail Bank.* **1990,** *12* (4), 19–24.

Santana, J. How Companies Will Use Big Data for Customer Retention, 2019. https://altadigital.com/blog/big-data-customer-retention

Singh, H. The Importance of Customer Satisfaction in Relation to Customer Loyalty and Retention. *Acad. Market. Sci.* **2006,** *60* (193–225), 46.

Spiess, J.; T'Joens, Y.; Dragnea, R.; Spencer, P.; Philippart, L. Using Big Data to Improve Customer Experience and Business Performance. *Bell Labs Techn. J.* **2014,** *18* (4), 3–17.

Tiwari, S.; Wee, H. M.; Daryanto, Y. Big Data Analytics in Supply Chain Management Between 2010 and 2016: Insights to Industries. *Comput. Ind. Eng.* **2018,** *115*, 319–330.-

Tsai, C. W.; Lai, C. F.; Chao, H. C.; Vasilakos, A. V. Big Data Analytics: A Survey. *J. Big Data* **2015,** *2* (1), 1–32.

Venetis, K. A.; Ghauri, P. N. Service Quality and Customer Retention: Building Long-Term Relationships. *Eur. J. Market.* **2004,** *38* (11/12), 1577–1598.

Zakir, J.; Seymour, T.; Berg, K. Big Data Analytics. *Iss. Inf. Syst.* **2015,** *16* (2), 319–330.

CHAPTER 3

The Role of Big Data in Modern Markets for Personalizing and Tailoring Products and Services

SUSHEEL YADAV[1], OM JEE GUPTA[2], POOJA DARDA[3], and PRASHANT CHAUDHARY[4]

[1]*Jindal Global Business School, O.P. Jindal Global University, Sonipat, Haryana, India*

[2]*Jaipuria Institute of Management, Lucknow, India*

[3]*Jaipuria Institute of Management, Indore, India*

[4]*Dr. Vishwanath Karad MIT World Peace University, Pune, India*

ABSTRACT

Personalization enables customers to tailor products and services to their specific needs and preferences, thereby increasing the perceived value of the products and services to the customer. Personalization encourages customer loyalty by enhancing customer experiences. In modern markets, the Internet is one of the most important ways to reach real and potential buyers of goods and services. During these online interactions between businesses and customers, customers generate a lot of data, which businesses can use to give customers more personalized products and services. Sophisticated tools and techniques are used to analyze big data, allowing businesses to better understand, and in some cases, anticipate the needs of their customers. In this chapter, the authors reviewed the role of bigdata for personalization of products and services. Big data analytics is useful not only for personalizing products and services in e-commerce but also in brick-and-mortar stores.

Augmenting Customer Retention Through Big Data Analytics.
Reena Malik, Ambuj Sharma, and Prashant Chaudhary (Eds.)

Businesses study which products are trending online so that the same products can be promoted in physical stores as well. Customers in the modern era are demanding an ever-increasing level of customization in their products and services that big data plays a crucial role in modern markets by enabling companies to personalize and tailor their products and services to meet the specific needs and preferences of individual customers. By analyzing vast amounts of data, companies can gain valuable insights into consumer behavior, demographics, and preferences, which they can use to create more targeted and effective marketing campaigns, as well as to design and develop products and services that better meet the needs of their customers.

3.1 INTRODUCTION

Accurately learning a customer's preference is key to boosting sales and attracting more of those customers who are looking for the kinds of high-quality services that you provide (Wang et al., 2022; Guo et al.,2019). Customer satisfaction and loyalty can be greatly increased through personalization. More and more businesses in the service industry are also realizing that offering personalized services is the best way to boost customer loyalty and cut costs in the face of rising competition in the modern age (Zhou et al., 2022; Grover et al., 2018). Personalization can result in a more favorable brand perception and increased behavioral intent (De Keyzer et al., 2022a, 2022b).

Big data spawns a new wave of customer relationship strategies to support personalized sales, services, and customer support (Anshari et al., 2019). Big data analysis is the analysis of massive data sets that can come from a variety of different sources and formats using sophisticated statistical methods (Yang, 2021). One way companies use big data to personalize their offerings is through customer segmentation. By grouping customers into different segments based on common characteristics, such as demographics, behavior, or purchase history, companies can target their marketing efforts more effectively and tailor their products and services to the specific needs of each segment. For instance, a retailer may segment its customers based on their age, income, and purchase history, and then use this data to create personalized recommendations, promotions, and pricing. In contrast to mass customization, which focuses on fulfilling the needs of clearly delineated market niches, personalization is directed at efficiently and effectively meeting the specific requirements of each individual customer (Tseng et al., 2010; Dong et al., 2011). However, the level of customization is ultimately up to the enterprise, which increases the degree of difficulty. Businesses must meticulously pick the individual characteristics and establish the criteria for personalized evaluation performance (Tan et al., 2017). Predictive modeling is another way businesses utilize big data. Companies can predict future customer behavior, such as which customers are most likely to churn (i.e., stop being customers) or who is most likely to respond to a specific promotional offer, by analyzing individual historical data of the customer. These data can be utilized to enhance customer retention and acquisition efforts, as well as optimize pricing and product offerings.

Big data can also be used to improve product design and development. By analyzing data on customer preferences, needs, and usage patterns, businesses can develop products and services that are more suited to customer requirements. A car manufacturer could, for instance, use data on driving patterns and preferences to design more fuel-efficient and comfortable long-distance vehicles. Big data is a potent tool that businesses can use to enhance their customer understanding and develop more personalized, targeted products and services. It can also be used to improve marketing efforts, increase customer retention and acquisition, and optimize product development and design, ultimately leading to an increase in revenue and market share.

It is also important to note that as the use of big data increases, companies face greater challenges in terms of data privacy and security. Consequently, the majority of companies are implementing security measures and taking actions to protect the data they purchase from their customers, and businesses in the modern era are better equipped, thanks to the growth of internet of things (IoT) and big data analytics, to provide customers with ever-increasing levels of personalization. This chapter focuses on the perspectives of product and service personalization using big data technology. This study is separated into the following sections: Section 3.2 provides a comprehensive literature review. Section 3.3 discusses the various applications of big data to personalize products and services. In Section 3.4, the primary obstacles to the application of big data are examined. Finally, the conclusion is presented in Section 3.5.

3.2 LITERATURE REVIEW

Personalization is tailoring the experience of an individual customer by providing the products and services that suit him according to his needs and wishes. Data about such customers help companies to provide those products and services. A huge amount of data is being generated on a daily basis with the rapid growth of the internet, social media, digitization of the services, and e-commerce. Even COVID-19 pandemic pushed many customers to shop online which they had never opted for before. Online shopping specially for grocery and pharmacy products was boosted during the COVID-19 pandemic (Hallikainen et al., 2022; Statista, 2021). The data which are being generated at such a large scale also created the need to carefully manage the data and generate relevant information from this data for the institutions (Sheng et al., 2020; Zhou and Liu, 2020). Big data is a technology which considers all the three aspects of such data viz., variety, volume, and velocity. Big data utilizes other technologies such as the IoT and Industry 4.0. This aspect is an interdisciplinary element of big data. The application of big data analytics has rapidly spread to the field of management, covering everything from production methods to strategic planning, without ignoring the social impact of these developments.

For this reason, a huge amount of the literature related to big data exists. The authors decided to use both quantitative and qualitative approaches to review the existing big data literature because there is already a substantial body of work on the subject. The authors utilized the Scopus database to complete the literature review. This was done for this study. As a component of a quantitative literature review, the current research makes use of bibliometric analysis to determine the quantity of the big data literature that is currently available. Bibliometric analysis is a well-established scientific methodology in which quantitative methods are used to examine bibliometric data, such as publication and citation information. This methodology was developed in the 1960s and has since gained widespread acceptance (Donthu et al., 2021a; Mukherjee et al., 2021). The strategy is also recognized as a method for conducting scientific research, and it has the potential to be applied in a variety of different areas (Donthu et al., 2021b; Kumar et al., 2021a, b, 2022).

The authors performed a search in the Scopus database using the terms "Big data" OR "Big data," which yielded a total of 215,536 documents. This demonstrates the vast amount of research literature that already exists related to big data. Figure 3.1 also includes a graph that depicts the number of documents along with the year in which they were published. The graph also reveals that after the year 2012, there was a significant rise in the number of papers that were published related to big data research and applications. Figure 3.2 provides a representation of these documents based on the domain in which they were written. This representation demonstrates that research into big data has garnered interest from nearly all of the fields. Given that this is a subject that is associated with technology, it is not surprising that nearly one-third of the documents come from the field of computer science and engineering. In addition, the fields of business, medicine, and the social sciences are all very well represented here because many professionals are attempting to make use of big data to gain insights related to business, health, and social issues. Figure 3.3 shows the top 10 countries in terms of the origin of publications. When it comes to publications about big data research, China is in the lead, followed by the United States and India as shown.

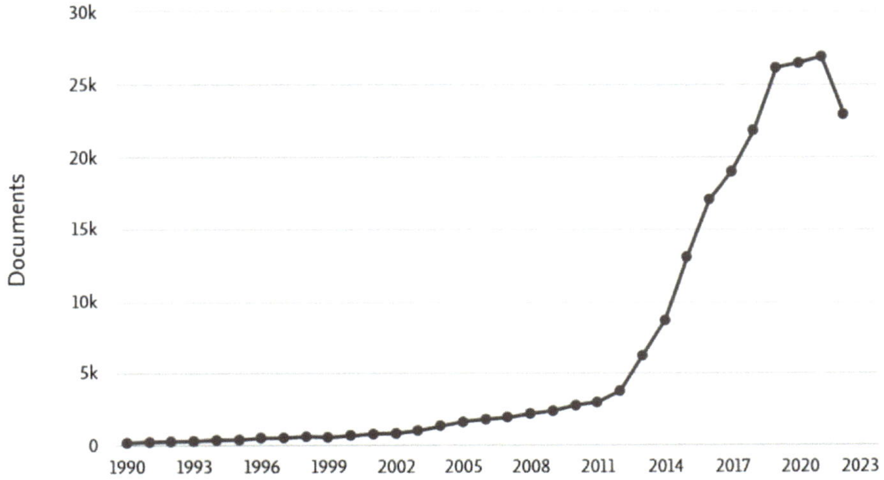

FIGURE 3.1 Documents along with the year of publication.

Source: Author.

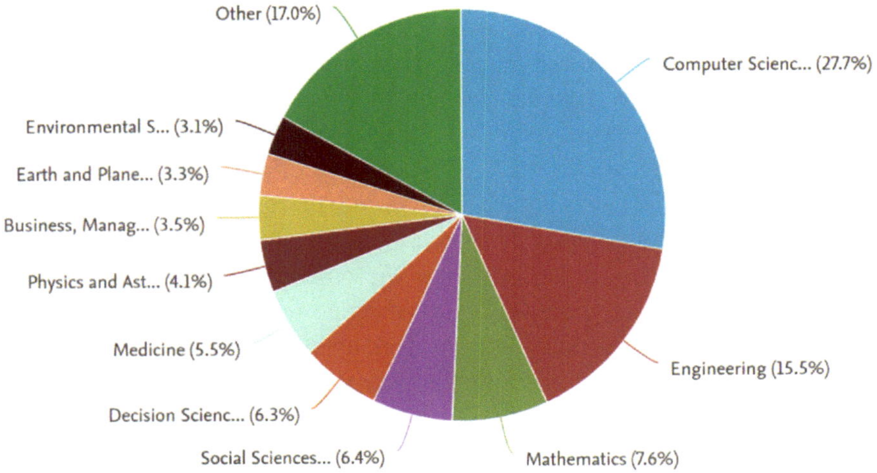

FIGURE 3.2 Domains of the published documents.

Source: Author.

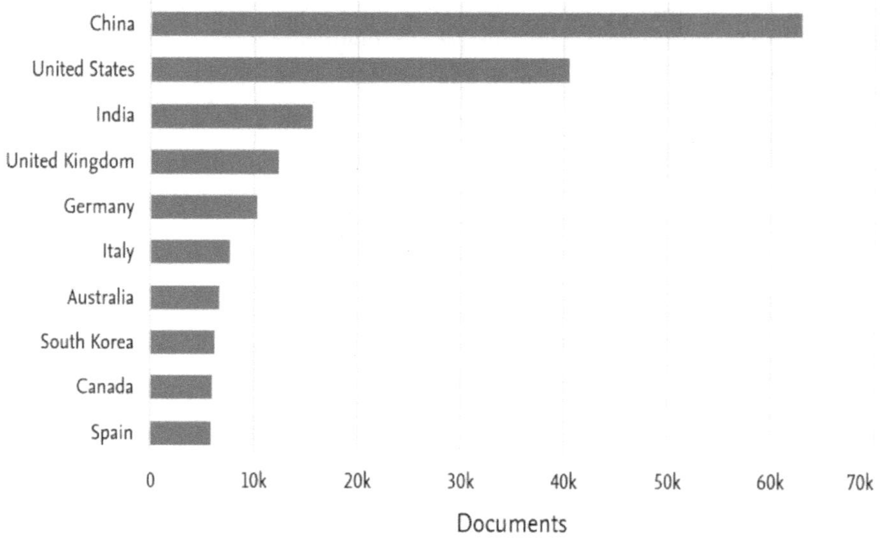

FIGURE 3.3 Number of documents along with the origin of the documents.
Source: Author.

The authors have also carried out a co-occurrence analysis of the author's keywords in order to determine the significant keywords that are applied throughout the body of research. For the purpose of this analysis, the subject matter of the publications was narrowed down to just business and management, and records from the most recent 2000 years were chosen for the analysis. The Scopus database was queried to retrieve a comma-separated value (.csv) file, which was then used to extract the keywords that were associated with each individual article. The VOSviewer® was used to generate the co-occurrence network map that is displayed here. It was required that there be at least 25 occurrences of the keyword, and 43 of the keywords satisfied this requirement. Figure 3.4 presents these keywords in the format of four distinct groups, each of which is represented by a particular color. The proximity of the circles indicates the co-occurrence of the keywords on this map, which in general displays their co-occurrence. The size of the circle indicates how frequently the keyword appears, and the proximity of the circles indicates how frequently they appear together (Van Eck and Waltman, 2010, 2014). Using these newly discovered keywords, the readers will find it much simpler to search the published literature for big data research that pertains to the business and management domain.

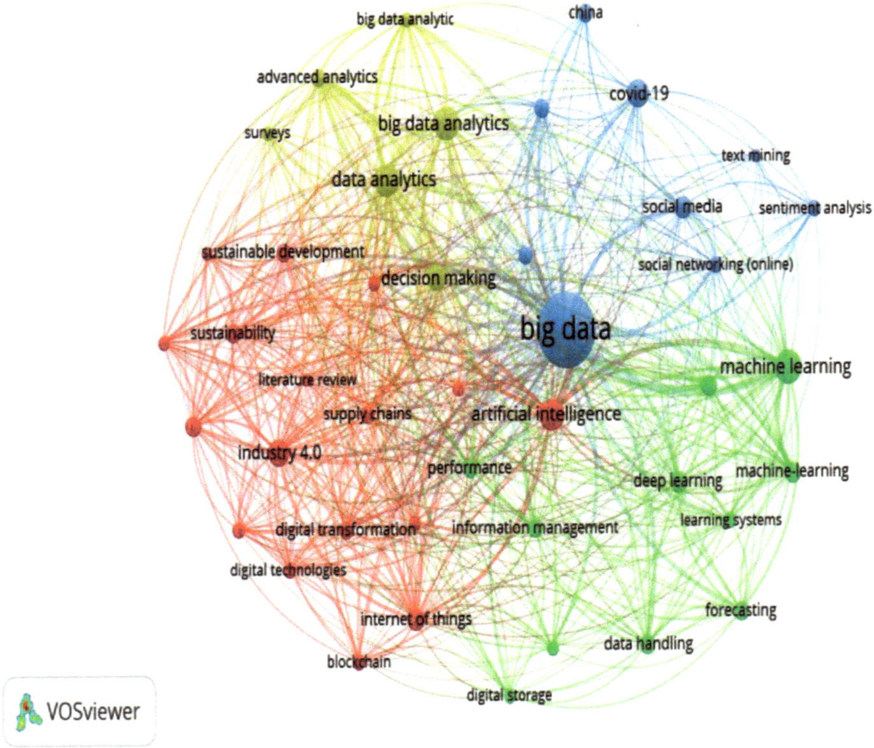

FIGURE 3.4 Co-occurrence analysis of author's keywords.

Source: Author.

The foundation of personalization is the learning of individual tastes. Accurately learning a customer's preferences has many benefits, including higher sales and happier customers. Due to the scarcity of available data, learning individual preferences is an extremely difficult task. Combined modeling of consumer segmentation and preference learning is an efficient and adequate approach to sparsity reduction (Zhu and Liu, 2023). Personality Recommender System (PRS) is to build a personalized model based on each user's traits, interests, and preferences. The system will then show the user resources that were calculated based on the user's preferences (Nunes and Hu, 2012). Zapata et al. (2011) mined LMS metadata, LRM data, and learner characteristics, then applied multiple techniques, including content filtering (CF), CF, and learner primary search. Li et al. (2023) combined deep learning and big data technology to study a personalized recommendation method based on the massive open online course (MOOC) system. They came up with a method that combines the bidirectional encoder representations from the transformers model and the attention mechanism. This includes getting the dataset and cleaning it up first, making a framework for the recommendation model, and using a domain feature difference learning strategy to improve how well the model makes recommendations. Liu (2021) proposed a new approach to solve the challenges of intelligent marketing for agricultural products using big data. Taking into account both functional utility and manufacturing cost, Berry et al. (2013) develop a method for determining suitable product architectures and manufacturing resolutions for achieving personalization. A conceptual framework for a personalized product configuration system built on a flexible open architecture product platform was proposed by Zheng et al. (2017). Strycharz et al. (2019) highlighted the importance of big data in personalization of products and services and referred to as the future of personalization. Big data is rapidly reshaping customer experiences, industries, and organizations by providing more and more personalization (Hentzen et al., 2022; Xu et al., 2020). Big data analysis generates new business strategies aimed at enhancing product and service personalization, boosting brand reputation and customer loyalty, and fortifying customer relationships (Anshari et al., 2019; Del Vecchio et al., 2020; Hallikainen et al., 2022; Del Vecchio et al., 2021).

3.3 PERSONALIZATION OF PRODUCTS AND SERVICES USING BIG DATA

Big data is used to personalize products and services by analyzing consumer behavior, purchasing patterns, and preferences. Big data analytics can be applied to a variety of industries, including retail, healthcare, marketing, and finance, etc. to personalize goods and services. A brief description of the application of big data for personalization of products and services in different industries is given below.

3.3.1 RETAIL AND E-COMMERCE

Information about a shopper's preferences and past purchases can be used to tailor the shopping experience and suggest additional items. A customer's browsing and purchasing history, for instance, can be used to make product recommendations on an online store's website. Retailers can use this information to enhance the shopping experience for their customers and boost sales. Using customer demographics, behavior, and purchase history, retailers can divide their customer base into distinct groups for more targeted marketing. This paves the way for more specific marketing campaigns, individualized product suggestions, and special offers based on shoppers' individual interests and demographics. Through the use of big data analytics, stores can improve their stock management by forecasting future demand based on past sales, customer actions, and even weather conditions. This can help stores keep the products that their customers desire in stock at all times, minimizing product shortages and surpluses. The retail industry can use big data to its advantage by analyzing sales, customer behavior, and the pricing strategies of its competitors in order to develop a pricing strategy that will maximize the profit. For stores to maximize profits while maintaining a competitive edge in the market, this can be very useful information.

When stores use big data, they can learn more about their customers, which in turn enhances the shopping experience and boosts revenue. Retailers can boost customer retention and revenue by catering to individual shoppers' interests and preferences.

3.3.2 HEALTHCARE

Patient data and medical histories can be analyzed using big data to create individualized treatment plans. Because each patient has a unique genetic, lifestyle, and medical history, this can help doctors determine the most effective treatment plan. Patient outcomes and at-risk patients can be predicted and tracked with the help of big data. This can aid doctors in taking preventative measures for their patients' health and halting the progression of potentially dangerous conditions. Clinical decision-making can be aided by utilizing big data by giving healthcare providers access to timely information and guidance. This can aid medical professionals in providing higher quality care by allowing them to make more educated decisions. By analyzing massive datasets for useful patterns and trends, "big data" can aid the medical research process. This can aid the search for novel treatments and the improvement of existing ones.

As a whole, healthcare providers can learn more about their patients, boost their outcomes, and reduce their workload by utilizing big data. Healthcare providers can improve patient health and cut costs by using patient data to make individualized recommendations and focus on specific populations.

3.3.3 MARKETING AND ADVERTISING

Most marketers think their customers expect individualized service, but few think the industry does a good job of providing it (Lindecrantz et al., 2020). In order to meet the needs of their customers, businesses must devote more resources to the study of individual tastes. Targeted marketing campaigns can be developed by analyzing consumer behavior and preferences using big data. This can improve a company's marketing efforts by allowing them to focus their messages on the most receptive customers. By analyzing consumer activity, demographics, and past purchases, big data can tailor ads to each user. Because of this, businesses may see an uptick in conversion rates as ads become more targeted and effective. Through the use of big data analytics, companies can monitor the success of their advertising campaigns and adjust their strategies accordingly. As a result, companies can better gauge the efficacy of their advertising campaigns and make adjustments to boost return on investment.

As a whole, businesses can increase sales, sharpen their marketing focus, and better understand their customers by leveraging big data. Businesses can increase customer loyalty and boost profits by tailoring their recommendations to individual customers and focusing on niche markets.

3.3.4 BANKING AND FINANCE

Financial data and transactions can be analyzed using big data, allowing for more personalized financial services. Financial institutions can use this information to provide clients with individualized banking and investment services. Financial data and transactions can be analyzed with big data to spot patterns and trends that may point to danger. This can aid financial institutions in taking preventative measures against losses by better managing risks. With the help of big data, financial fraud can be uncovered by spotting irregularities and patterns. This can aid financial institutions in safeguarding their clients' money by reducing the likelihood of fraud. Customer credit risk, default probability, and turnover rate can all be predicted with the help of big data. Banks and other financial institutions can use this information to better anticipate and prepare for potential risks. Market trends can be analyzed and high-frequency trading executed with the help of big data. This has the potential to increase profitability and competitiveness for financial institutions.

Banks and other financial institutions can benefit from a better understanding of their customers, enhanced financial product and service effectiveness, and reduced risks thanks to the use of big data. Banks and financial institutions can boost customer loyalty and revenue by tailoring recommendations to individual customers.

3.3.5 TRANSPORTATION AND LOGISTICS

Traffic, weather, and other data can be analyzed with big data to determine the most efficient routes and times for delivery. Because of this, logistics and shipping firms can provide customers with more tailored route and timetable options. Equipment breakdowns can be anticipated and maintenance schedules made more efficient with the help of big data. To keep operations running smoothly, this can help the transportation and logistics sector experience as little downtime as possible. Individual vehicles in a fleet can be tracked and their performance can be monitored using big data. This can aid logistics and transport firms in optimizing their fleet utilization, reducing fuel costs, and maximizing the efficiency of their route planning. By analyzing data on sales, customer behavior, and weather patterns, big data can be used to optimize inventory management by predicting demand and stocking shelves accordingly. This can help logistics and shipping firms keep the goods their customers want in stock and prevent them from running out of stock. By analyzing customer data and preferences with big data, businesses can provide more individualized shipping options. Providing delivery options that are tailored to each individual customer's preferences is one way in which this can help transportation and logistics firms improve their services and attract and retain more clients.

As a whole, transportation and logistics firms can benefit from big data because it provides a more in-depth look at their operations, increases productivity, and decreases overhead. Customers will be more loyal to transportation and logistics firms that offer tailored recommendations and cater to their unique needs.

3.4 CHALLENGES OF PERSONALIZATION OF PRODUCTS AND SERVICES USING BIG DATA

Personalization of products and services using big data requires the collection, storage, and analysis of large amounts of personal information, which raises several challenges. A few of those challenges have been discussed below:

3.4.1 PRIVACY CONCERNS

Organizations typically collect and store extensive individual information, such as demographics, online activities, purchases, and more, when using big data for personalization purposes. With this data, organizations can tailor their offerings to the specific needs of each customer. But there are privacy and security issues associated with data collection and storage. Third-party advertisers and data brokers are two examples of entities that may receive and use customer's identifiable information, which may raise privacy concerns. Personal data can be used for targeted advertising, credit scoring, and other purposes, and this is only made possible by the development of artificial intelligence and machine learning. This may cause people to worry about discrimination and unfair treatment, as well as the possibility of their data being used in ways they did not anticipate or understand. Organizations must be open about their data collection, storage, and use practices and give people a real say over their data if these issues are to be addressed. Typically, the disclosure of information about an organization's internal processes and performance provides a credible signal of brand integrity, which enhances customer appeal and facilitates the personalization of the online customer experience (Lambillotte et al., 2022; Elia et al., 2022Cambier and Poncin, 2020) In addition, businesses must put in place extensive security measures to prevent the loss, misuse, and disclosure of customer data.

3.4.2 QUALITY, ACCURACY, AND INTEGRATION OF DATA

To maximize the success of personalization efforts, it is essential to ensure the high quality and accuracy of the data used for this purpose. However, it can be challenging to construct accurate and complete profiles of individuals from big data sources due to the prevalence of missing, duplicate, or inaccurate data. The success of personalization efforts may suffer as a result of this.

Integrating data helps make sure the right information is being collected, processed, and stored so that products and services can be personalized effectively and efficiently. Integrating data means bringing together information from various locations to form a comprehensive whole. In order to achieve this goal, it may be necessary to clean, transform, and map data from various sources and formats into a common schema. Integrating data from multiple sources is essential for personalization, as it is necessary to collect information from many different areas, such as demographics, behavior, purchase history, browsing history, and feedback. Personalization relies on accurate information that does not infringe on user's privacy, so this requires attention to both data quality and data security.

In order to solve these problems, businesses should have systems in place to guarantee the reliability of the information used in the personalization process. Methods for ensuring high data quality include checking and double-checking collected information, performing regular data cleaning and deduplication, and employing other data quality tools and techniques to spot and fix errors. Successful customization of goods and services relies heavily on data integration as well.

3.4.3 SCALABILITY

Problems with scalability arise when trying to personalize goods and services with large datasets. Processing massive amounts of data in real time is essential for personalization, but this presents a challenge for conventional computing architectures. The system's performance cannot suffer too much as data volume grows; it must be able to handle the increased workload. The use of big data for personalization can lead to several scalability issues, such as those related to data storage, data processing, data analysis, and data governance. Organizations should think about using distributed systems and specialized tools for data storage, processing, analysis, and governance to deal with scalability issues for personalization of products and services using big data. To meet these challenges, businesses must invest heavily in their IT infrastructure.

3.4.4 ALGORITHM BIAS

When using big data for personalized product and service recommendations, algorithm bias can be a serious problem. Improper or inaccurate predictions may result if the data used to train the model does not adequately represent the target audience. Particularly in the context of individualized recommendations for products and services, this can amplify existing biases and lead to a lack of diversity. Bias in personalization can arise from several different places, such as skewed data, flawed algorithms, unreliable feedback loops, etc. Organizations should make sure the data used to train models is diverse and are representative of the population they are meant to serve in order to combat algorithm bias in the personalization of products and services based on big data. Firms should also implement fairness constraints, debiasing techniques, and bias monitoring to lessen the impact of any inherent bias in their algorithms. Organizations can help eliminate bias by continuously monitoring and evaluating the performance of the personalization algorithm. It is important to be aware of the potential biases that can be present in the data and algorithms used in personalization, and to take steps to mitigate them in order to ensure that the personalized recommendations are fair and accurate.

3.5 CONCLUSION

Big data offers a number of opportunities for personalizing and tailoring products and services. Big data analytics provides the ability to analyze vast quantities of data in order to gain customer insights and preferences. This enables businesses to better comprehend their customers and provide them with personalized experiences. However, these opportunities also present obstacles. The complexity of the data presents one of the greatest obstacles to the use of big data for personalization. It is difficult to analyze and extract useful information from big data because it is frequently unstructured and can come from a variety of sources. In addition, companies must be mindful of privacy concerns associated with the collection and use of personal data. The cost of storing and processing massive amounts of data presents a further obstacle. This can be a substantial obstacle for small and medium-sized enterprises. Despite these obstacles, the potential of big data in the future for personalization and tailoring of products and services is extremely promising. Technology advancements, such as artificial intelligence and machine learning, will make it easier to analyze and extract useful information from massive data sets. In addition, as the amount of data generated increases, there will be more opportunities for businesses to use big data to create personalized customer experiences. Big data offers a wealth of opportunities for personalizing and tailoring products and services, but businesses must be aware of the associated challenges and potential privacy concerns.

KEYWORDS

- **personalization**
- **big data**
- **modern markets**
- **customer loyalty**
- **internet of things**
- **unstructured data**

REFERENCES

Anshari, M.; Almunawar, M. N.; Lim, S. A.; Al-Mudimigh, A. Customer Relationship Management and Big Data Enabled: Personalization & Customization of Services. *Appl. Comput. Inf.* **2019,** *15* (2), 94–101.

Berry, C.; Wang, H.; Hu, S. J. Product Architecting for Personalization. *J. Manuf. Syst.* **2013,** *32* (3), 404–411.

Cambier, F.; Poncin, I. Inferring Brand Integrity from Marketing Communications: The Effects of Brand Transparency Signals in a Consumer Empowerment Context. *J. Bus. Res.* **2020,** *109*, 260–270.

De Keyzer, F.; Dens, N.; De Pelsmacker, P. How and When Personalized Advertising Leads to Brand Attitude, Click, and WOM Intention. *J. Advertising 2022a*, *51* (1), 39–56.

De Keyzer, F.; Dens, N.; De Pelsmacker, P. Let's Get Personal: Which Elements Elicit Perceived Personalization in Social Media Advertising? *Electron. Commerce Res. App. 2022b*, *55*, 101183.

Del Vecchio, P.; Mele, G.; Passiante, G.; Vrontis, D.; Fanuli, C. Detecting Customers Knowledge from Social Media Big Data: Toward an Integrated Methodological Framework Based on Netnography and Business Analytics. *J. Knowl. Manag.* **2020,** *24* (4), 799–821.

Del Vecchio, P.; Mele, G.; Siachou, E.; Schito, G. A Structured Literature Review on Big Data for Customer Relationship Management (CRM): Toward a Future Agenda in International Marketing. *Int. Market. Rev.* **2021**.

Dong, M.; Yang, D.; Su, L. Ontology-Based Service Product Configuration System Modeling and Development. *Exp. Syst. App.* **2011,** *38* (9), 11770–11786.

Donthu, N.; Kumar, S.; Mukherjee, D.; Pandey, N.; Lim, W. M. How to Conduct Bibliometric Analysis: An Overview and Guidelines. *J. Bus. Res. 2021a*, *133*, 285–296.

Donthu, N.; Kumar, S.; Pandey, N.; Pandey, N.; Mishra, A. Mapping the Electronic Word-of-Mouth (eWOM) Research: A Systematic Review and Bibliometric Analysis. *J. Bus. Res. 2021b*, *135*, 758–773.

Elia, G.; Raguseo, E.; Solazzo, G.; Pigni, F. Strategic Business Value from Big Data Analytics: An Empirical Analysis of the Mediating Effects of Value Creation Mechanisms. *Inf. Manag.* **2022,** *59* (8), 103701.

Grover, V.; Chiang, R. H.; Liang, T. P.; Zhang, D. Creating Strategic Business Value from Big Data Analytics: A Research Framework. *J. Manag. Inf. Syst.* **2018,** *35* (2), 388–423.

Guo, Y.; Cheng, Z.; Nie, L.; Wang, Y.; Ma, J.; Kankanhalli, M. Attentive Long Short-Term Preference Modeling for Personalized Product Search. *ACM Trans. Inf. Syst. (TOIS)* **2019,** *37* (2), 1–27.

Hallikainen, H.; Luongo, M.; Dhir, A.; Laukkanen, T. Consequences of Personalized Product Recommendations and Price Promotions in Online Grocery Shopping. *J. Retail. Consumer Serv.* **2022,** *69,* 103088.

Hentzen, J. K.; Hoffmann, A.; Dolan, R.; Pala, E. Artificial Intelligence in Customer-Facing Financial Services: A Systematic Literature Review and Agenda for Future Research. *Int. J. Bank Market.* **2022,** *40* (6), 1299–1336.

Kumar, S.; Lim, W. M.; Pandey, N.; Westland, J. C. 20 Years of Electronic Commerce Research. *Electron. Commerce Res. 2021a, 21* (1), 1–40.

Kumar, S.; Lim, W. M.; Sivarajah, U.; Kaur, J. Artificial Intelligence and Blockchain Integration in Business: Trends from a Bibliometric-Content Analysis. *Inf. Syst. Front.* **2022,** 1–26.

Kumar, S.; Pandey, N.; Lim, W. M.; Chatterjee, A. N.; Pandey, N. What Do We Know About Transfer Pricing? Insights from Bibliometric Analysis. *J. Bus. Res.*, 134, 275–287.

Lambillotte, L.; Bart, Y.; Poncin, I. Personalized Online Customer Experience: The Effect of Information Transparency: An Abstract. In: *Academy of Marketing Science Annual Conference*; Springer: Cham, 2022; pp 327–328.

Li, B.; Li, G.; Xu, J.; Li, X.; Liu, X.; Wang, M.; Lv, J. A Personalized Recommendation Framework Based on MOOC System Integrating Deep Learning and Big Data. *Comput. Electr. Eng.* **2023,** *106,* 108571.

Lindecrantz, E.; Gi, M. T. P.; Zerbi, S. Personalizing the Customer Experience: Driving Differentiation in Retail. McKinsey Insights (March). Eriğim Adresi, 2020. https:// www. mckinsey. com/industries/retail/our-insights/personalizing-the-customer experience-driving-differentiation-in-retail

Liu, X. Y. Agricultural Products Intelligent Marketing Technology Innovation in Big Data Era. *Procedia Comput. Sci.* **2021,** 183, 648–654.

Mukherjee, D.; Kumar, S.; Donthu, N.; Pandey, N. Research Published in Management International Review from 2006 to 2020: A Bibliometric Analysis and Future Directions. *Manag. Int. Rev.* **2021,** *61* (5), 599–642.

Nunes, M. A. S.; Hu, R. Personality-Based Recommender Systems: An Overview. In: *Proceedings of the Sixth ACM conference on Recommender Systems*; 2012; pp 5–6.

Sheng, J.; Amankwah-Amoah, J.; Khan, Z.; Wang, X. COVID-19 Pandemic in the New Era of Big Data Analytics: Methodological Innovations and Future Research Directions. *Br. J. Manag.* **2021**. https://doi.org/10.1111/1467–8551.12441.

Statista. E-commerce in the European Union—Statistics and Facts, 2021. htt ps://www. statista.com/topics/3792/e-commerce-in-europe/ (accessed 14 January 2023).

Strycharz, J.; van Noort, G.; Helberger, N.; Smit, E. Contrasting Perspectives–Practitioner's Viewpoint on Personalised Marketing Communication. *Eur. J. Market.* **2019,** *53* (4), 635–660.

Tan, C.; Hu, S. J.; Chung, H.; Barton, K.; Piya, C.; Ramani, K.; Banu, M. Product Personalization Enabled by Assembly Architecture and Cyber Physical Systems. *CIRP Ann.* **2017,** *66* (1), 33–36.

Tseng, M. M.; Jiao, R. J.; Wang, C. Design for Mass Personalization. *CIRP Ann.* **2010,** *59* (1), 175–178.

Van Eck, N. J.; Waltman, L. Software Survey: VOS Viewer, a Computer Program for Bibliometric Mapping. *Scientometrics* **2010,** *84*, 523–538.

Wang, Z.; Chen, J.; Rosas, F. E.; Zhu, T. A Hypergraph-Based Framework for Personalized Recommendations via User Preference and Dynamics Clustering. *Expert Syst. App.* **2022,** 117552.

Xu, Y.; Shieh, C. H.; van Esch, P.; Ling, I. L. AI Customer Service: Task Complexity, Problem-Solving Ability, and Usage Intention. *Aust. Market. J. (AMJ)* **2020,** *28* (4), 189–199.

Yang, X. Business Big Data Analysis Based on Microprocessor System and Mathematical Modeling. *Microprocess. Microsyst.* **2021,** *82*, 103846.

Zapata, A.; Menendez, V. H.; Prieto, M. E.; Romero, C. A Hybrid Recommender Method for Learning Objects. *IJCA Proc. Des. Eval. Digit. Content Educ. (DEDCE)* **2011,** *1*, 1–7.

Zheng, P.; Xu, X.; Yu, S.; Liu, C. Personalized Product Configuration Framework in an Adaptable Open Architecture Product Platform. *J. Manuf. Syst.* **2017,** *43*, 422–435.

Zhou, L. J.; Liu, L. COVID-19 Pandemic in China: Observation and Reflections. *World Leis J.* **2020,** *62*, 315–318.

Zhou, K.; Du, G.; Jiao, R. J. Personalized Service Product Family Design Optimization Considering Crowdsourced Service Operations. *Comput. Ind. Eng.* **2022,** *166*, 107973.

Zhu, T.; Liu, Y. Learning Personalized Preference: A Segmentation Strategy Under Consumer Sparse Data. *Expert Syst. App.* **2023,** *215*, 119333.

CHAPTER 4

Segmentation and Customer Satisfaction: A Study of Insurance Sector

RENU BALA

Jan Nayak Chaudhary Devi Lal Vidyapeeth, IBM Department, Haryana, India

ABSTRACT

Segmentation is the process of dividing the market on different basis, such as age, gender, class, cast, or religion. In the era of 20thcentury, only marketer can survive who can understand and implement the concept of segmentation in their product. A single product cannot satisfy the needs of all consumers. So there is a need to divide the markets of consumers on different grounds. The present study is related to the insurance sector, under which, the advantages of segmentation in the insurance sector, challenges, measures, and the future of such industry based on segmentation, etc. have been discussed. For the study purpose data have been gathered from various private and public sector banks as well as from various insurance companies also. Areas including Haryana and Punjab have been covered. To analyze the data, different statistical tools have been used. The analyzed data revealed that there exist different kinds of insurance companies based on segmentation such as accident and health insurance companies, property and casualty companies, errors and omissions insurance companies, and reinsurance companies, as well as there are a lot of advantages of segmentation for the insurance industry such as it helps to identify the target customers, identify new market opportunities, optimize marketing campaigns and increase customer retention rate, etc. At the end, it has been concluded that segmentation performs an exuberant and vivacious role in the insurance sector and the future of such an industry is going to be very bright and glaring in next few years.

Augmenting Customer Retention Through Big Data Analytics.
Reena Malik, Ambuj Sharma, and Prashant Chaudhary (Eds.)

4.1 INTRODUCTION

Segmentation refers to the process of dividing a market or a group of customers into smaller subgroups based on certain characteristics or attributes, such as demographics, behaviors, or needs (Ryan, 1981). The goal of segmentation is to identify high-yield segments—that is, subgroups of customers that are likely to be the most profitable or that have growth potential—so that a company can tailor its marketing efforts and products to the specific needs and preferences of those segments (Brent, 1999). Now the question arises what is the insurance sector? The insurance sector provides financial protection and risk management services to individuals and organizations (Talonen, 2016). It is an important part of the financial services industry and plays a crucial role in helping individuals and businesses manage the potential financial impact of unexpected events, such as accidents, illnesses, and natural disasters (Fadun, 2013). The insurance sector is made up of a wide range of companies that offer different types of insurance products, including life insurance, health insurance, auto insurance, and property insurance. These companies typically generate revenue by collecting premiums from customers and then using that money to pay out claims to policyholders (Fecher et al., 1993). The insurance sector is heavily regulated by governments around the world to ensure that companies can meet their financial obligations to policyholders and to protect consumers from fraud and other forms of misconduct.

Segmentation plays a crucial role in the insurance sector by helping companies identify and target specific groups of customers that are most likely to purchase their products (Estes et al., 2007). By segmenting the market, insurance companies can better understand the needs and preferences of different groups of customers and tailor their products and marketing efforts accordingly. This can help companies increase their sales and profitability by reaching the most promising segments of the market (Vogel and Winitz, 1989). Segmentation plays a very important role in the insurance sector and there are various bases on which segmentation is done in this sector.

Segmentation in insurance sector is done mainly by:

- ***Demographic Segmentation:*** This includes age, gender, income, education, occupation, and family size (Martin, 2011).
- ***Behavioral Segmentation:*** This includes how customers use a product, how they make purchase decisions, and how they respond to marketing campaigns (Tynan and Drayton, 1987).

- ***Geographic Segmentation:*** This includes the location of customers, climate, and natural hazards (Haley, 1968).
- ***Psychographic Segmentation:*** This includes lifestyle, values, personality, and social class (Beane and Ennis, 1987).

  Through market segmentation, insurance companies can develop targeted marketing campaigns, design customized insurance products, and improve their overall customer service (Dibb, 1999). Additionally, by focusing on specific segments of the market, insurance companies can also reduce their risk by avoiding customers who are less likely to be profitable (Goller et al., 2002).

  Segmentation in the insurance sector refers to the process of dividing the market into smaller groups of customers with similar characteristics (Young et al., 1978). This allows insurance companies to tailor their products and marketing strategies to specific segments, rather than treating all customers the same (Moroko and Uncles, 2009). Some common ways to segment the insurance market include demographic factors, such as age, income, and occupation, as well as behavioral factors, such as risk tolerance and purchasing history (Hellwig et al., 2015). Segmentation can help insurance companies identify new opportunities, reduce marketing costs, and increase customer satisfaction (Cooil et al., 2008).

In the insurance sector, segmentation can be used to identify specific groups of customers that may be more likely to purchase certain types of insurance policies or to tailor insurance products to meet the specific needs of certain segments (Weinstein and Cahill 2014). For example, an insurance company may segment its market based on age, income, or occupation, and then design different insurance products or pricing strategies for each segment (Bock and Uncles 2002). This can help the company to better target its marketing efforts, increase sales, and improve customer satisfaction. Additionally, segmentation can also help insurance companies identify potential risks and develop more effective risk management strategies (Gensch, 1978).

In the future, the use of advanced analytics and technology is likely to play an increasingly important role in the segmentation process within the insurance industry (Rust, 2020). The use of big data, machine learning, and artificial intelligence can help insurers to more accurately identify and understand customer segments, as well as to predict customer behavior and identify new growth opportunities. Additionally, the increasing availability of customer data from a variety of sources, including social media and the Internet of things (IoT) can also provide insurers with more information to use in the segmentation process (Foedermayr, and Diamantopoulos, 2008).

Another trend that could impact the future of segmentation in the insurance industry is the growing focus on personalization (Tsiotsou and Ratten, 2010). As customers become more demanding and technology becomes more advanced, insurers will need to offer more personalized products and services to meet the needs of different customer segments (Shankar et al., 2011). This will require a deeper understanding of individual customer needs and preferences, and the use of advanced analytics and technology to deliver tailored solutions (Constantinides and Stagno, 2011).

Also, with the advent of Insurtech, the customer's digital experience will become more important than ever (Antti, 2013). Segmenting customers based on their digital behavior and preferences will become a crucial aspect of personalizing the customer experience and providing the right products and services (Brand et al., 2017).

Overall, the future of segmentation in the insurance industry is likely to be characterized by the continued use of advanced analytics and technology to more accurately identify customer segments, and an increased focus on personalization and digital experience (Jeong and Heo, 2011).

4.2 REVIEW OF LITERATURE

Almeida et al. (2014) highlighted the advantages of segmentation. For the study purpose, data were gathered from 180 tourists. The analyzed data presented that segmentation provides a lot of opportunities for the growth of different sectors of the economy. Based on the segmentation, entrepreneurs exploit a lot of benefits and earn a very big amount of money. Porrini (2015) described the importance of segmentation for the insurance sector. Data were collected from secondary sources such as newspapers, articles, journals, magazines, and official websites of the organizations. The results of the study presented that segmentation helps organizations to identify what kinds of customer can provide benefits to organizations and what kinds of customers may harm the organizations in monetary terms. Zekaj (2016) showed that how segmentation helps the insurance sector in marketing plans. For the study purpose, data were gathered from the staff of the different insurance organizations. The analysis of the data represented that for the growth of the organizations, there is a big need for marketing strategies and such strategies can be implemented only after the segmentation process. Hence, it can be concluded that segmentation acts as an important tool for the growth of the insurance sector organizations. Padhi and Pattnaik (2017) elaborated on how the employees of the insurance sector organizations use a segmentation approach to manage their work life and personal life. To fulfill the purpose of data collection, data were collected from 156 professionals of insurance sector organizations; out of which 64 were female employees 92 were male. The study indicated that segmentation helps the employees to prioritize their personal and professional work and there in not too much difference in the views of male and female staff members. Pozza et al. (2018) presented a multichannel segmentation approach for identifying the customer segments in the health insurance industry. To analyze the data count regression model and multinomial regression model were used. The analyzed data revealed that multichannel users are very frequent users of call centers and websites as well and they show more heterogeneous profiles in terms of sociodemographics. Krasheninnikova et al. (2019) indicated how segmentation helps the insurance sector to set the prices for their different plans. Data were gathered from the managers of different insurance sector organizations. The outcomes of the data revealed that segmentation firstly categorize the customers based on their incomes and after that helps to set the prizes of different insurance plans on that basis. Bansal and Shukla (2020) showed how insurance organizations use a segmentation approach to identify the different categories of their customers. To analyze, the data cluster techniques were used. The outcomes of the analyzed data described that segmentation helps the organization to identify the customers and to arrange the services for those customers as per their choice. Alt et al. (2021) described the benefits of segmentation specifically for the life insurance sector. Data were collected with the help of a pre-structured questionnaire and a further cross-sectional survey was used. Data were collected from 422 respondents on the basis of convenience sampling. Both online and offline tools were used to fulfill the purpose of data collection. The results of the study presented to provide benefits to the life insurance sector; segmentation can be done on the basis of four grounds, such as young people, mature people, committed people, and cross-channel people. Eckert et al. (2022) presented how the customer satisfaction of the insurance sector's customers depends upon the segmentation strategies. Data were collected with the help of a questionnaire and the responses of the officials revealed that firstly they have to categorize the data of the customer based on different segmentation tools after that they divided up their customers accordingly and then provided the services they need.

4.3 POSITIVE IMPACTS OF SEGMENTATION ON CUSTOMERS OF INSURANCE SECTOR

Segmentation in the insurance sector can have several positive impacts on customers. Some of these include:

4.3.1 TAILORED PRODUCTS AND SERVICES

By segmenting customers based on their needs and demographics, insurance companies can offer more personalized and tailored products and services that better meet the specific needs of each customer segment (Ugwu et al., 2000).

4.3.2 IMPROVED CUSTOMER SATISFACTION

By providing customers with products and services that are tailored to their needs, insurance companies can improve customer satisfaction and loyalty (Adams et al., 2019).

4.3.3 INCREASED EFFICIENCY

Segmentation can help insurance companies to more effectively target and acquire new customers, which can increase the efficiency of their sales and marketing efforts (Leon and Nakayama, 2020).

4.3.4 BETTER PRICING

By segmenting customers, insurance companies can better understand the specific risks and needs of each customer segment, which can help them to more accurately price their products and services (Akhigbe et al., 1993).

4.3.5 BETTER RISK MANAGEMENT

By identifying and understanding the specific risks associated with different customer segments, insurance companies can more effectively manage and mitigate those risks, which can help reduce losses and improve their overall financial stability (Zhou et al., 2022).

4.3.6 *BETTER UNDERWRITING*

Segmentation also helps in underwriting the policies; the underwriters can make better decisions on policy terms and pricing with the help of segmentation (Hsu, 2012).

4.4 NEGATIVE IMPACTS OF SEGMENTATION ON CUSTOMERS OF INSURANCE SECTOR

Segmentation in the insurance sector can also have some negative impacts on customers, including:

4.4.1 *DISCRIMINATION*

If insurance companies use certain characteristics, such as race or ethnicity, as a basis for segmentation, it can lead to discrimination against certain groups of customers (Franke, 2017).

4.4.2 *LIMITED OPTIONS*

By focusing on specific segments, insurance companies may not offer products or services that would be beneficial to customers outside of those segments (Mullins et al., 2021).

4.4.3 *HIGHER PRICES*

Customers in certain segments may be charged higher prices for insurance products and services, which can make them less affordable for some individuals and families (Septina, 2022).

4.4.4 *LACK OF TRANSPARENCY*

Customers may not be aware of how they are being segmented or why they are being charged certain prices, which can lead to mistrust and dissatisfaction (Jorgensen et al., 2020).

4.4.5 COMPLEXITY

Segmentation can make the process of buying insurance more complex and difficult to understand for some customers (Wanke and Barros, 2016).

4.4.6 INACCURATE SEGMENTATION

Sometimes the segmentation process may be inaccurate due to lack of data or wrong assumptions, which can lead to misclassification of customers and result in wrong policies or pricing for the customer (Joof et al., 2022).

4.5 CHALLENGES OF SEGMENTATION

There are several challenges associated with segmentation in the insurance sector, including:

4.5.1 DATA COLLECTION AND ANALYSIS

Accurately segmenting customers requires a significant amount of data, which can be difficult to collect and analyze (Story, 2021).

4.5.2 PRIVACY AND SECURITY

Collecting and storing large amounts of customer data can raise concerns about privacy and security, and insurance companies must ensure that they are complying with relevant laws and regulations (Papadopoulos, and Martin 2011).

4.5.3 CHANGES IN CUSTOMER BEHAVIOR

Customer behavior and needs can change over time, which can make it difficult for insurance companies to maintain accurate segmentation (Hossain and Chen 2019).

4.5.4 DIFFICULTY IN IDENTIFYING SEGMENTS

Identifying the right segments and sub-segments can be difficult and requires expertise in data analysis and market research (Walters, 1997).

4.5.5 COMPLEXITY OF THE INSURANCE PRODUCTS AND SERVICES

Insurance products and services can be complex, making it difficult to understand how different segments may respond to different offerings (Jiang et al., 2020).

4.5.6 LIMITED RESOURCES

Segmentation can be a resource-intensive process, and small and medium-sized insurance companies may not have the resources or expertise to undertake such an effort (Hesamian et al., 2019).

4.5.7 KEEPING UP WITH THE COMPETITION

The insurance industry is highly competitive, and insurance companies must ensure that their segmentation strategies are keeping up with those of their competitors (Despotovic et al., 2015).

4.6 MEASURES TO OVERCOME THE CHALLENGES OF SEGMENTATION

There are several measures that insurance companies can take to overcome the challenges of segmentation, including:

- ***Investing in Data Management andAnalysis:*** To accurately segment customers, insurance companies must invest in data management and analysis tools and resources (Chen et al., 2020).
- ***Ensuring Compliance with Privacy and Security Regulations:*** Insurance companies must ensure that they are complying with all relevant laws and regulations regarding data privacy and security (Prelipcean et al., 2016).
- ***Continuously Monitoring and Updating Customer Segments:*** Insurance companies must continuously monitor and update their segments based on changes in customer behavior and needs (Sharif et al., 2020).
- ***Partnering with Experts:*** Insurance companies can partner with experts in data analysis and market research to help identify and segment customers (Maulik, 2009).

- ***Simplifying the Product and Services:*** Insurance companies can simplify their products and services to make it easier for customers to understand and choose the right coverage (Alkassar et al., 2017).
- ***Investing in Marketing and Communication:*** Insurance companies can invest in marketing and communication campaigns to educate customers about their segmentation strategies and explain how it will benefit them (Irshad et al., 2013).
- ***Adopting a Flexible Approach:*** Insurance companies should adopt a flexible approach and be willing to adapt their segmentation strategy as market conditions change (Xiao et al., 2018).
- ***Leveraging Technology:*** Companies can leverage technology such as artificial intelligence and machine learning to automate the segmentation process and make it more efficient and accurate (Angulakshmi and Lakshmi 2017).

4.7 SIGNIFICANCE OF THE STUDY

The study of segmentation is significant in the insurance sector because it allows insurers to identify specific groups of customers with similar needs and characteristics. This information can then be used to develop targeted products and marketing strategies, which can lead to increased sales and more efficient use of resources (Sofi et al., 2022). By segmenting their customer base, insurers can also better understand and manage the risk associated with different groups, which can help them set more accurate prices and improve their overall financial performance (Kautish et al., 2022). Additionally, Segmentation can also help insurers to identify areas of potential growth and to identify new opportunities for expansion (Singh and Deshmukh 2022). Overall, the study of segmentation can have a positive impact on the insurance sector by improving the effectiveness of products and marketing strategies, enhancing risk management, and driving growth.

4.8 IMPLICATIONS OF THE STUDY

The study of segmentation in the insurance sector can have several implications for both insurance companies and consumers. For insurance companies, segmentation allows them to better understand and target specific groups of consumers, which can lead to more effective marketing and sales efforts (Chang et al., 2022). By segmenting their customer base, insurance companies can also develop more tailored products and pricing strategies that better meet the needs and preferences of different groups of consumers (Singh et al., 2022). For consumers, segmentation can lead to more personalized and relevant insurance options. Consumers may be able to find insurance products that are better suited to their specific needs, rather than having to settle for a one-size-fits-all solution (Yum et al., 2022). Additionally, segmentation can lead to more competitive pricing, as insurance companies may offer different prices to different segments of consumers based on their perceived risk levels. Overall, the study of segmentation in the insurance sector can lead to improved targeting, more tailored products, and more competitive pricing, which can benefit both insurance companies and consumers (Cevolini and Esposito 2022).

KEYWORDS

- **customer**
- **satisfaction**
- **retention**
- **insurance**
- **sector**

REFERENCES

Adams, M.; Upreti, V.; Chen, J. Product-Market Strategy and Underwriting Performance in the United Kingdom's Property–Casualty Insurance Market. *Eur. J. Finance* **2019,** *25* (11), 1012–1031.

Akhigbe, A.; Borde, S. F.; Madura, J. Dividend Policy and Signaling by Insurance Companies. *J. Risk Insurance* **1993,** 413–428.

Alkassar, S.; Woo, W. L.; Dlay, S.; Chambers, J. Sclera Recognition: On the Quality Measure and Segmentation of Degraded Images Captured Under Relaxed Imaging Conditions. *IET Biometrics* **2017,** *6* (4), 266–275.

Almeida, A. M. M.; Correia, A.; Pimpao, A. Segmentation by Benefits Sought: The Case of Rural Tourism in Madeira. *Curr. Iss. Tour.* **2014,** *17* (9), 813–831.

Alt, M. A.; Saplacan, Z.; Benedek, B.; Nagy, B. Z. Digital Touchpoints and Multichannel Segmentation Approach in the Life Insurance Industry. *Int. J. Retail Distrib. Manag.* **2021,** *49* (5), 652–677.

Angulakshmi, M.; Lakshmi Priya, G. G. Automated Brain Tumour Segmentation Techniques—A Review. *Int. J. Imaging Syst. Technol.* **2017,** *27* (1), 66–77.

Antti Pesonen, J. Information and Communications Technology and Market Segmentation in Tourism: A Review. *Tour. Rev. 213, 68* (2), 14–30.

Bansal, A.; Shukla, A. Online Insurance Business Analytics Approach for Customer Segmentation. *Int. J. Adv. Sci. Technol.* **2020,** *29* (10s), 2299–2305.

Beane, T. P.; Ennis, D. M. Market Segmentation: A Review. *Eur. J. Market* **1987,** *21* (5), 20–42.

Bock, T.; Uncles, M. A Taxonomy of Differences Between Consumers for Market Segmentation. *Int. J. Res. Market.* **2002,** *19* (3), 215–224.

Brand, C.; Cluzel, C.; Anable, J. Modeling the Uptake of Plug-in Vehicles in a Heterogeneous Car Market Using a Consumer Segmentation Approach. *Transport. Res. Part A: Policy Practice* **2017,** *97*, 121–136.

Brent, M. R. Speech Segmentation and Word Discovery: A Computational Perspective. *Trends Cogn. Sci.* **1999,** *3* (8), 294–301.

Cevolini, A.; Esposito, E. From Actuarial to Behavioural Valuation: The Impact of Telematics on Motor Insurance. *Valuation Stud.* **2022,** *9* (1), 109–139.

Chang, J. R.; Nalluri, V.; Chen, L. S.; Chen, S. H. Winning Customers' Hearts and Minds Using DFSS in the Insurance Industry. *TQM J.* **2022,** (ahead-of-print).

Chen, J.; Li, Z.; Luo, J.; Xu, C. Learning a Weakly-Supervised Video Actor-Action Segmentation Model with a Wise Selection. In *Proceedings of the IEEE/CVF Conference on Computer Vision and Pattern Recognition*; 2020; pp 9901–9911.

Constantinides, E.; Zinck Stagno, M. C. Potential of the Social Media as Instruments of Higher Education Marketing: A Segmentation Study. *J. Market. High. Educ.* **2011,** *21* (1), 7–24.

Cooil, B.; Aksoy, L.; Keiningham, T. L. Approaches to Customer Segmentation. *J. Relationship Market.* **2008,** *6* (3–4), 9–39.

Dalla Pozza, I.; Brochado, A.; Texier, L.; Najar, D. Multichannel Segmentation in the After-Sales Stage in the Insurance Industry. *Int. J. Bank Market.* **2018,** *36* (6), 1055–1072.

Despotovic, I.; Goossens, B.; Philips, W. MRI Segmentation of the Human Brain: Challenges, Methods, and Applications. *Comput. Math. Methods Med.* **2015,** *2015*.

Dibb, S. Criteria Guiding Segmentation Implementation: Reviewing the Evidence. *J. Strategic Market.* **1999,** *7* (2), 107–129.

Dutta, M. M. Health Insurance Sector in India: An Analysis of Its Performance. *Vilakshan-XIMB J. Manag.* **2020,** *17* (1/2), 97–109.

Eckert, C.; Neunsinger, C.; Osterrieder, K. Managing Customer Satisfaction: Digital Applications for Insurance Companies. *Geneva Papers Risk Insurance—Iss. Practice* **2022,** *47* (3), 569–602.

Estes, K. G.; Evans, J. L.; Alibali, M. W.; Saffran, J. R. Can Infants Map Meaning to Newly Segmented Words? Statistical Segmentation and Word Learning. *Psychol. Sci.* **2007,** *18* (3), 254–260.

Fecher, F.; Kessler, D.; Perelman, S.; Pestieau, P. Productive Performance of the French Insurance Industry. *J. Prod. Anal.* **1993,** *4*, 77–93.

Fadun, O. S. Corporate Governance and Insurance Company Growth: Challenges and Opportunities. *Int. J. Acad. Res. Econ. Manag. Sci.* **2013,** *2* (1), 286–305.

Foedermayr, E. K.; Diamantopoulos, A. Market Segmentation in Practice: Review of Empirical Studies, Methodological Assessment, and Agenda for Future Research. *J. Strategic Market.* **2008,** *16* (3), 223–265.

Franke, U. The Cyber Insurance Market in Sweden. *Comput. Secur.* **2017,** *68*, 130–144.

Goller, S.; Hogg, A.; Kalafatis, S. P. A New Research Agenda for Business Segmentation. *Eur. J. Market.* **2002,** *36* (1/2), 252–271.

Gensch, D. H. Image-Measurement Segmentation. *J. Market. Res.* **1978,** *15* (3), 384–394.

Haley, R. I. Benefit Segmentation: A Decision-Oriented Research Tool. *J. Market.* **1968,** *32* (3), 30–35.

Hellwig, K.; Morhart, F.; Girardin, F.; Hauser, M. Exploring Different Types of Sharing: A Proposed Segmentation of the Market for "Sharing" Businesses. *Psycho. Market.* **2015,** *32* (9), 891–906.

Hesamian, M. H.; Jia, W.; He, X.; Kennedy, P. Deep Learning Techniques for Medical Image Segmentation: Achievements and Challenges. *J. Digit. Imaging* **2019,** *32*, 582–596.

Hossain, M. D.; Chen, D. Segmentation for Object-Based Image Analysis (OBIA): A Review of Algorithms and Challenges from Remote Sensing Perspective. *ISPRS J. Photogrammetry Remote Sens.* **2019,** *150*, 115–134.

Hsu, K. T. The Advertising Effects of Corporate Social Responsibility on Corporate Reputation and Brand Equity: Evidence from the Life Insurance Industry in Taiwan. *J. Bus. Ethics* **2012,** *109*, 189–201.

Irshad, H.; Veillard, A.; Roux, L.; Racoceanu, D. Methods for Nuclei Detection, Segmentation, and Classification in Digital Histopathology: A Review—Current Status and Future Potential. *IEEE Rev. Biomed. Eng.* **2013,** *7*, 97–114.

Jeong, N.; Yoo, Y.; Heo, T. Y. Market Segmentation Strategies for Future Telecommunications services. In *2011 Proceedings of PICMET'11: Technology Management in the Energy Smart World (PICMET)*; IEEE, 2011; pp 1–8.

Jiang, Z.; Ding, C.; Liu, M.; Tao, D. Two-Stage Cascaded U-Net: 1st Place Solution to Brats Challenge 2019 Segmentation Task. In: *Brainlesion: Glioma, Multiple Sclerosis, Stroke and Traumatic Brain Injuries: 5th International Workshop, BrainLes* **2019,** *Held in Conjunction with MICCAI* **2019,** *Shenzhen, China, October 17,* **2019,** *Revised Selected Papers, Part I 5*; Springer International Publishing, 2020; pp 231–241.

Joof, F.; Samour, A.; Tursoy, T.; Ali, M. Climate Change, Insurance Market, Renewable Energy, and Biodiversity: Double-Materiality Concept from BRICS Countries. *Environ. Sci. Pollut. Res.* **2022,** 1–14.

Jorgensen, S. L.; Termansen, M.; Pascual, U. Natural Insurance as Condition for Market Insurance: Climate Change Adaptation in Agriculture. *Ecol. Econ.* **2020,** *169*, 106489.

Kautish, P.; Khare, A.; Sharma, R. Health Insurance Policy Renewal: An Exploration of Reputation, Performance, and Affect to Understand Customer Inertia. *J. Market. Anal.* **2022,** *10* (3), 261–278.

Krasheninnikova, E.; García, J.; Maestre, R.; Fernández, F. Reinforcement Learning for Pricing Strategy Optimization in the Insurance Industry. *Eng. App. Artif. Intell.* **2019,** *80*, 8–19.

Leon, S.; Nakayama, M. Exploring Factors That Influence Positive WOM in the Health Insurance Industry. *Health Market. Quart.* **2020,** *37* (2), 176–192.

Martin, G. The Importance of Marketing Segmentation. *Am. J. Bus. Educ. (AJBE)* **2011,** *4* (6), 15–18.

Maulik, U. Medical Image Segmentation Using Genetic Algorithms. *IEEE Trans. Inf. Technol. Biomed.* **2009,** *13* (2), 166–173.

Moroko, L.; Uncles, M. D. Employer Branding and Market Segmentation. *J. Brand Manag.* **2009,** *17*, 181–196.

Mullins, M.; Holland, C. P.; Cunneen, M. Creating Ethics Guidelines for Artificial Intelligence and Big Data Analytics Customers: The Case of the Consumer European Insurance Market. *Patterns* **2021,** *2* (10), 100362.

Padhi, M.; Pattnaik, S. Role of Integration-Segmentation on Work-Family Interface of Insurance Sector Employees in India. *Int. Jo. Manpower* **2017**.

Porrini, D. Risk Classification Efficiency and the Insurance Market Regulation. *Risks* **2015,** *3* (4), 445–454.

Papadopoulos, N.; Martin Martin, O. International Market Selection and Segmentation: Perspectives and Challenges. *Int. Market. Rev.* **2011,** *28* (2), 132–149.

Prelipcean, A. C.; Gidofalvi, G.; Susilo, Y. O. Measures of Transport Mode Segmentation of Trajectories. *Int. J. Geog. Inf. Sci.* **2016,** *30* (9), 1763–1784.

Rust, R. T. The Future of Marketing. *Int. J. Res. Market.* **2020,** *37* (1), 15–26.

Ryan, P. Segmentation, Duality and the Internal Labour Market. *Dyn. Labour Market Segmentation* **1981,** 3–20.

Septina, F. Leverage, Product Diversification, and Performance of Life Insurance Companies in Indonesia. *JurnalKeuangan Dan Perbankan* **2022,** *26* (2), 301–316.

Shankar, V.; Inman, J. J.; Mantrala, M.; Kelley, E.; Rizley, R. Innovations in Shopper Marketing: Current Insights and Future Research Issues. *J. Retail.* **2011,** *87*, S29–S42.

Sharif, M.; Khan, M. A.; Zahid, F.; Shah, J. H.; Akram, T. Human Action Recognition: A Framework of Statistical Weighted Segmentation and Rank Correlation-Based Selection. *Pattern Anal. App.* **2020,** *23*, 281–294.

Singh, D. P.; Paul, J.; Sharma, P. Segmenting the Bottom of the Pyramid Consumers: Theoretical Approach. *Int. J. Market Res.* **2022,** *64* (3), 397–419.

Singh, R. K.; Deshmukh, A. A. Comparison Between Offline and Online Distribution Practices for the Insurance Industry in India. *Int. J. Asian Bus. Inf. Manag. (IJABIM)* **2022,** *13* (1), 1–19.

Sofi, F.; Dinu, M.; Reboldi, G.; Stracci, F.; Pedretti, R. F.; Valente, S.; Ambrosio, G. Worldwide Differences of Hospitalization for ST-Segment Elevation Myocardial Infarction During COVID-19: A Systematic Review and Meta-Analysis. *Int. J. Cardiol.* **2022,** *347*, 89–96.

Steenkamp, J. B. E.; Ter Hofstede, F. International Market Segmentation: Issues and Perspectives. *Int. J. Res. Market.* **2002,** *19* (3), 185–213.

Story, J. Unique Challenges of Segmentation and Differentiation for Higher Education. *J. Market. High. Educ.* **2021,** 1–20.

Talonen, A. Systematic Literature Review of Research on Mutual Insurance Companies. *J. Co-oper. Organ. Manag.* **2016,** *4* (2), 53–65.

Tsiotsou, R.; Ratten, V. Future Research Directions in Tourism Marketing. *Market. Intell. Plann.* **2010,** *28* (4), 533–544.

Tynan, A. C.; Drayton, J. Market Segmentation. *J. Market. Manag.* **1987,** *2* (3), 301–335.

Ugwu, L. O.; Oyebisi, T. O.; Ilori, M. O.; Adagunodo, E. R. Organisational Impact of Information Technology on the Banking and Insurance Sector in Nigeria. *Technovation* **2000,** *20* (12), 711–721.

Vogel, D.; Winitz, H. World Isolation and Meaning in Segmentation. *J. Psycholinguistic Res.* **1989,** *18*, 473–484.

Walters, P. G. Global Market Segmentation: Methodologies and Challenges. *J. Market. Manag.* **1997,** *13* (1–3), 165–177.

Wanke, P.; Barros, C. P. Efficiency Drivers in Brazilian Insurance: A Two-Stage DEA Meta Frontier-Data Mining Approach. *Econ. Modell.* **2016,** *53*, 8–22.

Weinstein, A.; Cahill, D. J. *Lifestyle Market Segmentation*; Routledge, 2014.

Xiao, X.; Zhou, Y.; Gong, Y. J. Content-Adaptive Superpixel Segmentation. *IEEE Trans. Image Process.* **2018,** *27* (6), 2883–2896.

Young, S.; Ott, L.; Feigin, B. Some Practical Considerations in Market Segmentation. *J. Market. Res.* **1978,** *15* (3), 405–412.

Yum, K.; Yoo, B.; Lee, J. Application of AI-based Customer Segmentation in the Insurance Industry. *Asia Pac. J. Inf. Syst.* **2022,** *32* (3), 496–513.

Zekaj, B. Marketing in Insurance Industry, Marketing Functions in Insurance Industry. *Eur. J. Multidisc. Stud.* **2016,** *1* (5), 33–39.

Zhou, Y. M.; Yang, W.; Ethiraj, S. The Dynamics of Related Diversification: Evidence from the Health Insurance Industry Following the Affordable Care Act. *Strategic Manag. J.* **2022**.

CHAPTER 5

The Underlying Foundation for the E-Commerce Customer Shopping Experience Edge with Big Data Analytics

SIDDHARTH SHIMPI

School of Retail Management, Symbiosis Skills and Professional University, Pune, India

ABSTRACT

E-commerce companies with tightly integrated big data analytics applications rate their customer experience offering at 4.34 on a Likert scale of 1 to 5, whereas others rate their customer shopping experience metrics at 3.62. That is a 20% difference in the customer shopping experience for respondents with tightly integrated big data analytics applications. For many e-commerce companies, improving the shopping experience is just a matter of changing corporate culture and adding desire for customers. However, there is a less discussed area that no amount of culture can replace, that is, big data analytics. Indeed, big data analytics, done right, is the secret element that allows e-commerce companies to create the customer shopping experience edge in a scalable and low-cost way that works not only for a few customers but for millions of customers profitably and sustainably. In this chapter, the author discusses the importance of developing intimate knowledge and understanding of big data analytics for achieving a customer shopping experience edge for e-commerce companies.

5.1 INTRODUCTION

Businesses are utilizing cutting-edge technologies to harness the power of data science in light of the skyrocketing volumes of data. The following

Augmenting Customer Retention Through Big Data Analytics.
Reena Malik, Ambuj Sharma, and Prashant Chaudhary (Eds.)

is a consensus among e-commerce executives: The key to the incredible e-commerce industry's future is big data. Big data enables e-commerce businesses to enhance their performance, products, operational procedures, gain a competitive advantage, and make better decisions. Additionally, it makes it possible to analyze customer behavior and initiates the discovery of relevant insights.

Despite the increasing availability of big data resources, it is easy for e-commerce businesses to become overwhelmed by big data. Businesses already benefit from big data-enabled tools for coupon creation, blog name management, and real-time fraud detection. Despite the fact that big data technology can improve many aspects of a company's operations, such as budgeting and marketing, many executives in the e-commerce industry are still unable to use data science to transform their businesses. Big data has a lot in common with predictive analysis, lead scoring, and targeted personalization.

The term ***'big'*** refers to the technology's volume, velocity, and variety. Companies can access a wide range of data about customer experiences, financial transactions, and the market's competitiveness through volume, velocity, and variety of big data. There are four main ways by which e-commerce companies benefit from big data according to a BARC study (2015): strategic decision-making (69%), enhanced operational process control (54%), deeper comprehension of customers (52%), and cost reductions (47%).

In today's competitive market, businesses must remain adaptable to changes in technology and consumer behavior. The ease of setting up an e-commerce store and the emergence of microbrands have led to reduced customer loyalty. As a result, business owners and e-commerce managers must continuously search for ways to improve the customer experience and retain customers. Despite these challenges, online businesses have an advantage over traditional retailers with physical stores. With the vast amount of information readily available online, e-commerce entrepreneurs have the opportunity to stay ahead of the curve and succeed in this dynamic market.

E-commerce is adaptable and agile; when using third-party logistics providers (3PLs) or running an e-commerce-only operation, these businesses are not restricted to a single location and frequently have to worry about inventory or retail leases. E-commerce businesses do have access to information that brick-and-mortar retailers do not, allowing them to reach a global market. However, it is even more crucial for managers and owners of e-commerce businesses to work within their areas of expertise. Through study and experience, everyone has a circle of competence. The trick is to stay in this circle and use the experience to boost output.

Using big data to the company's advantage will undoubtedly be possible when a circle of competence and an understanding of how the real-world works are combined.

5.2 CONCEPT OF BIG DATA ANALYTICS

In the realm of contemporary business management, the phrase "***big data***" is commonly utilized to describe vast sets of data that can be scrutinized to unveil patterns and trends in human behavior. It is predicted that by the year 2020, the digital universe of information will expand from 4.4 zettabytes to a staggering 44 zettabytes, which is equivalent to 44 trillion gigabytes. This immense growth is due to the production of approximately 1.7 megabytes of novel information every second by individuals.

Many brands believe that big retailers who can afford an inhouse team or data from data brokers can only access big data. BigCommerce and other e-commerce platforms track and provide merchants with access to customer behavior data, which can be used by business owners to make informed decisions. Even though they have a lot of 'power,' less than 0.5% of the data that is available is being used for these purposes.

Big data analytics is the practice of utilizing vast datasets to uncover concealed patterns, market trends, customer preferences, and other valuable information. Through big data analytics, business owners can derive insights that empower them to make informed decisions and extract value from data. In the realm of e-commerce, big data analytics not only enables business owners to gain a deeper understanding of their customers but also predicts market trends and increases revenue. By leveraging big data analytics, e-commerce businesses can unlock significant opportunities for growth and success.

Wikipedia (2016) defines '***big data***' as any collection of datasets that are so large and complex that it is difficult to work with them using standard database management tools. Search, analysis, capture, and storage are among the difficulties. The architecture challenge, the technology challenge, and the talent and organizational challenge are all examples of big data challenges. It would be hard to run an e-commerce business without big data analysis to help make decisions. If you want to personalize shopping experiences and provide better customer service, big data analytics and e-commerce cannot be separated.

5.3 SOURCES OF BIG DATA IN E-COMMERCE

Insights into customer behavior and demand for products or services can be greatly gleaned from transactional data. The buyer's ID and the product's ID, as well as personal information and the amount your customer paid for the purchase using a particular payment method, are typically included in transactional data.

By structuring e-commerce transaction big data, you can gain insight into the following: popularity of a product or service, seasonality in demand, the lifetime value of packaged services, the average check written by customers, the number of sales and funds spent in a particular regional market, the number of orders placed per unit of time, and the value of a particular purchase channel. These are just a few examples.

According to Llewellyn (2019), 87% of online shoppers claim that social media has an impact on their decision to make a purchase, and 30% of social media users typically make purchases directly through social media platforms. The location, hashtags, likes, shares, and records of brand interactions that users place as social data in the form of metadata have the potential to boost the efficiency of e-commerce marketing campaigns. It enables actionable insights into emerging trends and is used for target audience segmentation to provide truly personalized online shopping experiences.

The marketing department of the company might gain from integrating with some data platforms that offer a more in-depth overview of the market. Through these platforms, companies can learn about market pricing policies, the representation of goods and services on various online platforms, largescale shopping trends, and more, making it an excellent method for discovering new profitable opportunities for business expansion. Through their business model, many tech startups offer e-commerce retailers access to platforms with big data.

5.4 DEFINING THE SIGNIFICANCE OF BIG DATA ANALYTICS IN THE CONTEXT OF E-COMMERCE

In recent years, both academic institutions and the e-commerce sector have shown a great deal of interest in big data. This is largely due to the fact that e-commerce businesses that integrate big data analytics into their value chain tend to be 5–6% more productive than their competitors. A recent study conducted in the United States (USA) found that big data analytics contributed to at least 10% of the growth of 56% of businesses (Zhuang et al., 2021). This has led to a significant surge in the adoption of big data analytics, with 91% of Fortune 1000 companies investing in such projects—an 85% increase from the previous year.

Big data analytics can further solidify these impacts by enabling informed decisions based on crucial insights. While emerging internet-based technologies provide e-commerce businesses with transformative benefits such as real-time customer service, dynamic pricing, personalized offers, or improved interaction, big data analytics can further solidify these impacts. In particular, "*big data enables merchants to track the behavior of each user and connect the dots to determine the most effective ways to convert one-time customers into repeat buyers*" applies to e-commerce.

E-commerce companies leverage big data analytics to effectively use data, increase conversion rates, make informed decisions, and provide customers with greater control. By enhancing market transaction cost efficiency, managerial transaction cost efficiency, and time cost efficiency, big data analytics offers significant benefits to online businesses according to e-commerce transaction cost theory. It is a distinctive capability of high-performance business processes that facilitates the identification of loyal and profitable customers, optimal pricing strategies, quality control, and inventory management. Big data analytics is rooted in the resource-based view, but it can also be viewed from a relational ontology of sociomaterialism perspective, where various organizational capabilities are interdependent and mutually supportive in driving firm performance.

Companies like Amazon, Google, and Netflix have all taken advantage of service marketing's perspective on enhancing service innovation models. As a result, big data analytics is the next big thing in innovation—the platform for the growth of employment, increased productivity, and increased consumer surplus.

In the realm of big data analytics, research has honed in on strategy-led analytics, which generates long-term value for businesses. According to LaValle et al. (2011), the use of big data or business analytics for decision-making must be closely intertwined with the organization's strategy. Strategy-driven analytics has garnered significant attention for its ability to facilitate better decision-making. Concurrently, studies have explored competitive advantages and differentiation through the use of real-time data analytics. Biesdorf et al. (2013) similarly underscored the importance of aligning frontline tools, personnel, big data, and process optimization to gain a competitive edge.

The definition of big data analytics as a tool to find new opportunities is centered on the idea of using large volumes of data to identify patterns and trends that would otherwise be difficult to spot. This line of research argues that big data analytics can be used to add value by uncovering new product or service offerings or identifying ways to optimize existing processes. Davenport (2006) emphasized the importance of finding new products and activities that add value through big data analytics. This implies that big data analytics can be used not only to improve operational efficiency but also to drive innovation and business growth. Davenport et al. (2012) similarly highlighted the potential of big data analytics to assess the external environment and spot new opportunities and events. By analyzing data from various sources, businesses can gain insights into market trends, consumer behavior, and emerging technologies that can inform strategic decision-making. However, the significance of behavioral aspects in the definition of big data analytics cannot be ignored. Studies have pointed out that successful big data analytics requires more than just technology and data processing capabilities. Business processes, technology optimization, and an emotional connection to data use are the three components that make up big data analytics according to some researchers. The emotional connection to data use emphasizes the importance of empathy in data analysis, which can help analysts understand the context and significance of the data they are working with. Ferguson (2012) suggested that big data analytics is a multidimensional behavioral analysis that takes into account both internal and external factors. This implies that businesses must consider not only the data they collect but also the people and processes involved in data analysis. In other words, successful big data analytics requires a holistic approach that considers technology, business processes, and human factors.

Big data analytics in e-commerce utilizes statistical, contextual, quantitative, predictive, cognitive models, and other methods (refer to Table 5.1). This approach involves the collection, analysis, utilization, and interpretation of data across multiple functional divisions with the aim of generating business value, creating a competitive edge, and obtaining actionable insights. Overall, big data analytics in e-commerce is a detailed process that encompasses various stages of data processing to derive meaningful insights and achieve strategic advantages in the market.

5.5 SEVERAL TECHNIQUES E-COMMERCE COMPANIES USE TO CREATE A CUSTOMER SHOPPING EXPERIENCE EDGE WITH BIG DATA ANALYTICS

Big data analytics is being used by e-commerce companies in a variety of ways to give customers a better shopping experience. The following are seven ways in which any e-commerce business can benefit from big data:

5.5.1 ENHANCED SHOPPING EXPERIENCE

According to Phucharoen et al. (2021) and Alrumiah and Hadwan (2021), e-commerce businesses can use the vast amount of data they possess to drive predictive analytics, which allows them to forecast how customers will behave in the future. Retail websites can monitor page clicks, the number of products added to shopping carts before making a purchase, and the time it takes for customers to make a purchase after visiting the homepage to gain insights for predictive analytics. Additionally, companies can analyze customer data such as demographics, age, style, size, and socioeconomic status of those who have enrolled in rewards or subscription programs to better understand customer behavior.

Companies can use predictive analytics to come up with new ways to stop customers from abandoning their shopping carts, speed up the purchase process, and take advantage of emerging trends. In a similar vein, e-commerce businesses make use of this data to accurately forecast the requirements for inventory in relation to shifts in the economy or seasonality (Lee, 2017).

5.5.2 SECURER ONLINE PAYMENT METHODS

Customers need to be aware that their payments are safe in order to provide a superior shopping experience (Wang et al., 2018). Big data analysis can detect unusual spending patterns, and customers can be notified in real time when such patterns occur. Companies can establish alerts for a range of fraudulent activities, such as the use of multiple payment methods originating from the same IP address or a sequence of purchases made with the same credit card within a brief timeframe.

Similarly, numerous e-commerce websites now provide multiple payment options on a single, centralized platform. Big data analysis can measure the efficacy of new payment options like 'bill me later' and determine which payment methods work best for which customers. To reduce the likelihood of customers abandoning their shopping carts, some e-commerce websites have made the checkout process simpler. Customers have the option to add an item to a wish list, select the 'bill me later' option, or pay with multiple credit cards on the checkout page (Liu and Arnett, 2000).

5.5.3 ENHANCED PERSONALIZATION

According to Alyass et al. (2015) and Habegger et al. (2014), big data can enable e-commerce businesses to offer personalized shopping experiences and secure payment options, which are highly valued by customers. Research suggests that personalization is a key factor in the purchasing decisions of 86% of consumers, especially among millennials who expect personalized recommendations when shopping online. By utilizing big data analytics, e-commerce businesses can gain a comprehensive understanding of their customers, including their gender, location, and social media presence. This information can be used to segment customers into groups and create targeted marketing campaigns, customized email discounts, and product launches that cater to specific consumer groups.

In fact, numerous retailers capitalize on this tactic by providing loyalty points that customers can use to make subsequent purchases. E-commerce businesses may select a number of dates throughout the year to offer loyalty members additional bonus points on all purchases. This is usually done during a slow time of year and makes customers more engaged, interested, and willing to spend money (Ansari et al., 2019). Loyalty members not only feel like VIPs, but they also provide companies with information that can be used to provide personalized shopping recommendations.

5.5.4 ENHANCED PRICING AND INCREASED SALES

Customers value good deals more than loyalty programs, safe payments, and seamless shopping experiences. In order to increase sales from online purchases, e-commerce businesses are beginning to use big data analytics to determine the most reasonable price for particular customers (Fisher and Raman, 2018; Ghandour, 2015). Customers who have been loyal to a business for a long time may get first dibs on sales, and prices may be higher or lower for customers based on where they live and work.

5.5.5 DYNAMIC CUSTOMER SERVICE

Customer satisfaction is crucial for customer retention, and even businesses with the most competitive prices and products can fail without exceptional customer service. Customers are more likely to remain loyal to a company that provides them with positive experiences, addresses their concerns promptly, and offers personalized solutions to their problems. Customers are more likely to share negative experiences with others than positive ones, which can damage a business's reputation and lead to lost sales. Therefore, it is essential for companies to prioritize customer service and ensure that their customers' needs are met to maintain a loyal customer base. According to Business.com (2022), selling to an existing customer is less expensive than acquiring a new one. In addition, when compared to new customers, loyal customers spend up to 67% more.

Companies that focus on providing the best customer service have a better chance of getting good referrals and can continue to make money from repeat customers. Every e-commerce company should make it a top priority to keep their customers happy and satisfied. Consequently, how does big data enhance customer service? Problems with product delivery, levels of customer satisfaction, and even social media brand perception can all be revealed by big data. In fact, big data analytics is able to pinpoint precisely when changes in customer perception or satisfaction occurred (Mikalef et al., 2021). When businesses have identified areas in which they can improve, it is simpler to implement long-term changes in customer service.

5.5.6 GENERATE INCREASED SALES

E-retailers can tailor their coupons and recommendations based on customer preferences, thanks to big data. This personalized customer experience results in increased traffic and profits (Bughin et al., 2011). E-commerce companies can also use big data about customers to run precise marketing campaigns, provide relevant coupons, and remind customers that they still have something in their cart (McAfee, 2012).

5.5.7 FORECAST TRENDS AND DEMAND

Taking care of a customer's requirements is not just a problem in the present. E-commerce is dependent on having sufficient stock for the future. Companies can use big data to plan marketing campaigns around major events, slow or potentially strong times of the year, and emerging trends (Rathod and Kumar, 2021; Chase, 2013). E-commerce businesses gather extensive datasets that allow them to forecast demand, streamline their operations, plan inventory levels, prepare for peak periods, and analyze data from previous years. They can also use these datasets to address excess inventory by promoting significant discounts through social media during peak shopping hours. This approach can help e-commerce sites efficiently manage their inventory levels while providing customers with attractive deals during high-demand periods.

Big data analytics and machine learning can aid e-commerce sites in optimizing their pricing decisions by enabling them to offer discounts for a limited period of time. With the help of these tools, businesses can determine the most suitable time to offer discounts, the ideal duration for the discount, and the appropriate discounted price. This approach can improve the effectiveness of pricing strategies and increase sales while providing customers with attractive deals.

The e-commerce sector has already been significantly affected by big data, and this trend is likely to continue. By 2040, 95% of all purchases, according to 99 Firms (2022), will be made online. Companies can use big data analytics to improve their copy, improve articles for self-service customer support, and interpret surveys to prepare. In addition, e-commerce companies are able to anticipate seasonal influxes, emerging trends, and customer preferences. Although big data may be the most effective tool for an e-commerce company, only 0.5% of big datasets are utilized.

5.6 DISCUSSION

While big data tends to add value across the entire value chain for businesses, there are a few obstacles that businesses need to overcome before big data benefits flow into their operations. Indeed, there are always obstacles associated with innovative work practices: This is a fact, and big data is no different. Big data has the potential to enhance business performance and add value, but in order for decision-makers to reap the benefits, they must address a variety of business issues (Davenport, 2012; Schroeck et al., 2012; Shah et al., 2012).

Kiron et al. (2014a) identified a significant challenge in the big data environment as it lacks clear guidance on how to align business objectives with the existing organization's capabilities and culture. Barto (2012) emphasized the need for managers to make big data understandable and trustworthy for frontline workers, who may lack the necessary skills or trust in the technology. Barney's (1991) characteristics of rarity, appropriability, nonreproducibility, and nonsubstitutability suggest that innovative capabilities lead to sustained long-term benefits and superior company performance. Kiron et al. (2014b) recommended that managers encourage the adoption of big data by providing incentives, offering training, holding discussions with relevant managers and employees, and demonstrating active leadership. McAfee and Brynjolfsson (2012) argued that to achieve top performance using big data, a specific goal and strategy must be in place.

E-commerce companies' marketing teams are dealing with a lot of data coming in through multiple channels. As a result, the most difficult task is to sort through the vast amount of data to find relevant information about each customer (Agarwal and Dhar, 2014). The vast amount of data available in e-commerce allows marketers to build relationships based on trust and loyalty, giving customers more power than ever before (Gefen, 2000). However, even with access to data from sources such as Facebook, Google, and Twitter, e-commerce companies face challenges in using big data analysis for personalized offers, dynamic pricing, and selecting the appropriate marketing channels to deliver value. The use of sophisticated database management tools is critical for effectively processing big data in marketing as well as in production and operations management. Proponents of big data in e-commerce argue that integrating talent, technology, and information can reduce overall transaction costs (Williamson, 1981).

Access to high-quality big data is crucial for adding value to organizations, while poor-quality data from redundant applications and databases can lead to increased costs for data storage and difficulty in accessing and utilizing data (Beath et al., 2012). Although big data has the potential to increase business value, the presence of redundant, incorrect, or duplicated data can hinder decision-making processes (Nelson et al., 2005; Schroeck et al., 2012). They assert that poor data quality or inadequate data governance is a significant obstacle for big data analytics. It should be noted that even with advanced analytics, the use of incorrect or poor-quality data would be futile (Bose, 2009).

The information revolution has brought about both challenges and opportunities in e-commerce, prompting the emergence of big data analytics as the new frontier of innovation and competition. By utilizing people, processes, and technologies, big data analytics transforms data into insights for effective decision-making and problem-solving, thus adding value to e-commerce businesses. To gain a competitive edge, this comprehensive procedure takes into account data, resources, capabilities, and systems. Big data analytics has already been implemented by major e-commerce companies like Google, Amazon, eBay, ASOS, Netflix, and Facebook, resulting in significant expansion. Through a systematic review and taxonomy development of key aspects, this study provides a useful starting point for applying big data analytics in emerging e-commerce research. The study also presents a method for capturing best practices that shape big data analytics capabilities. If challenges are adequately addressed, the study suggests that a clear definition of big data analytics and its scope, as well as a good understanding of its distinct characteristics and types, will facilitate the widespread use and quick delivery of insights across organizations, thus maximizing business value.

In fact, effective big data analytics is the secret ingredient that enables e-commerce businesses to create a competitive advantage in the customer shopping experience in a low-cost, scalable manner that works not only for a small number of customers but also for millions of customers profitably and sustainably. The author discusses in this chapter how e-commerce businesses can gain an edge in the customer shopping experience by acquiring a thorough understanding of big data analytics. A compiled literature will assist the stakeholders (Table 5.1).

TABLE 5.1 Big Data Analytics in E-Commerce.

Study	Definition	Motive
Davenport (2006)	Quantitative fact-based analysis to support decision-making.	Analytics to get an edge over the competition.
Davenport and Harris (2007)	Utilization of explanatory and predictive models in conjunction with data, statistical, and quantitative analysis to facilitate fact-based management decisions and actions.	Analytics to support the development of distinctive capabilities in a business environment marked by intense competition.
Bose (2009)	A collection of tools used in conjunction to gain insight and direct, optimize, and automate decision-making for the accomplishment of organizational objectives.	Assisting business managers in effectively comprehending the motivations behind the implementation of advanced analytics.
Shanks et al. (2010)	Interpreting data to come up with insights that help make better decisions and make business processes run better.	Value-creating actions that enhance a company's performance and competitive advantage are made possible by analytics-based technology and capabilities.
Manyika et al. (2011)	Improvement in performance, transparency, the discovery of requirements, and the creation of value.	The potential value that big data could bring to businesses and the economy, and how to get that value.
LaValle et al. (2011)	Insights—descriptive, predictive, and prescriptive—to deliver actions that occur at the right time and are closely linked to business strategy and organizational procedures.	Insightful evidence to assist businesses in comprehending the opportunity presented by advanced analytics and information.
Agarwal and Weill (2012)	Enhances data-based evidence based on empathy, emotional connections, and business processes.	Data analytics and process automation and optimization are combined with the incorporation of human emotion.

TABLE 5.1 *(Continued)*

Study	Definition	Motive
Davenport (2012)	Focuses on discovering features, services that add value, and products.	Determining the quality and skill sets that are necessary for handling big data in order to provide high-performance analytics.
Davenport et al. (2012)	Discover and adapt quickly by looking for events, patterns, and opportunities that are always changing.	Revealing the differences between traditional and big data analytics, as well as ways to make use of big data's insights.
Dijcks (2012)	Automates decisions based on analytical models and enables deeper analysis on a wider range of data types, resulting in quicker responses to behavioral shifts.	The significance of business analytics infrastructure in the context of big data.
Ferguson (2012)	The method of multidimensional behavioral analysis is used to identify failure modes ahead of time.	Explains how analytics enables businesses to gain a deeper comprehension of and a means of mitigating a variety of risks, from risky business practices to major undetected risks.
Kiron et al. (2014a)	The process by which applied analytical disciplines use data and business insights to drive fact-based planning, decision-making, action, management, and learning.	Explanations of the real problems that businesses are having when using analytics.

Source: Author.

KEYWORDS

- **E-commerce**
- **big data**
- **shopping experience**

REFERENCES

Agarwal, R.; Dhar, V. Editorial—Big Data, Data Science, and Analytics: The Opportunity and Challenge for IS Research. *Inf. Syst. Res.* **2014,** *25*, 443–448.

Agarwal, R.; Weill, P. The Benefits of Combining Data with Empathy. *MIT Sloan Manag. Rev.* **2012,** *54*, 35.

Alrumiah, S. S.; Hadwan, M. Implementing Big Data Analytics in E-Commerce: Vendor and Customer View. *IEEE Access* **2021,** *9*, 37281–37286.

Alyass, A.; Turcotte, M.; Meyre, D. From Big Data Analysis to Personalized Medicine for All: Challenges and Opportunities. *BMC Med. Genom.* **2015,** *8* (1), 1–12.

Anshari, M.; Almunawar, M. N.; Lim, S. A.; Al-Mudimigh, A. Customer Relationship Management and Big Data Enabled: Personalization & Customization of Services. *Appl. Comput. Inf.* **2019,** *15* (2), 94–101.

Barney, J. Firm Resources and Sustained Competitive Advantage. *J. Manage.* **1991,** *17*, 99–120.

Barton, D.; Court, D. Making Advanced Analytics Work for You. *Harv. Bus. Rev.* **2012,** *90* (10), 78–83.

Beath, C.; Becerra-Fernandez, I.; Ross, J.; Short, J. Finding Value in the Information Explosion. *MIT Sloan Manag. Rev.* **2012,** *53*, 18–20.

Biesdorf, S.; Court, D.; Willmott, P. Big Data: What's Your Plan? *McKinsey Quart.* **2013,** 40–41.

Big Data—Wikipedia. **2016,** April 13. https://en.wikipedia.org/wiki/Big_data (accessed on 16 Jan 2023).

Big Data Use Cases 2015—A BARC Research Study. (n.d.). http://barc-research.com/research/big-data-use-cases-2015/ (accessed on 16 Jan 2023).

Bose, R. Advanced Analytics: Opportunities and Challenges. *Ind. Manag. Data Syst.* **2009,** *109*, 155–172.

Bughin, J.; Livingston, J.; Marwaha, S. Seizing the Potential of 'Big Data'. *McKinsey Quart.* **2011,** *4*, 103–109.

Chase Jr, C. W. Using Big Data to Enhance Demand-Driven Forecasting and Planning. *J. Bus. Forecast.* **2013,** *32* (2), 27.

Davenport, T. H. Competing on Analytics. *Harv. Bus. Rev.* **2006,** *84*, 98–107.

Davenport, T. H. The Human Side of Big Data and High-Performance Analytics. *Int. Inst. Anal.* **2012,** 1–13.

Davenport, T. H.; Harris, J. G. Competing on Analytics: The New Science of Winning. *Language* **2007,** 15 (217p), 24cm.

Davenport, T. H.; Barth, P.; Bean, R. How 'Big Data' is Different. *MIT Sloan Manag. Rev.* **2012,** *54*, 43–46.

Dijcks, J. P. Oracle: Big Data for the Enterprise. Oracle White Paper **2012,** 16.

Ferguson, R. B. Risky Business: How Data Analytics and Behavioral Science Can Help. *MIT Sloan Manag. Rev.* **2012,** 54, 1–5.

Fisher, M.; Raman, A. Using Data and Big Data in Retailing. *Product. Oper. Manag,* **2018,** *27* (9), 1665–1669.

Gefen, D. E-commerce: The Role of Familiarity and Trust. *Omega* **2000,** *28*, 725–737.

Ghandour, A. Big Data Driven E-Commerce Architecture. *Int. J. Econ. Commerce Manag.* **2015,** *3* (5), 940–947.

Habegger, B.; Hasan, O.; Brunie, L.; Bennani, N.; Kosch, H.; Damiani, E. Personalization vs. Privacy in Big Data Analysis. *Int. J. Big Data* **2014,** 25–35.

Kiron, D.; Prentice, P. K.; Ferguson, R. B. The Analytics Mandate. *MIT Sloan Manag. Rev. 2014a*, *55*, 1–25.

Kiron, D.; Prentice, P. K.; Ferguson, R. B. Raising the Bar with Analytics. *MIT Sloan Manag. Rev. 2014b*, *55*, 29–33.

LaValle, S.; Lesser, E.; Shockley, R.; Hopkins, M. S.; Kruschwitz, N. Big Data, Analytics, and the Path from Insights to Value. *MIT Sloan Manag. Rev.* **2011,** *52*, 21–32.

Lee, I. Big Data: Dimensions, Evolution, Impacts, and Challenges. *Bus. Horizons*, 60 (3), 293–303.

Liu, C.; Arnett, K. P. Exploring the Factors Associated with Web Site Success in the Context of Electronic Commerce. *Inf. Manag* **2000,** *38* (1), 23–33.

Llewellyn, G. Social Commerce Trends for 2020 You Need to Look Out for. *Smart Insights.* https://www.smartinsights.com/ecommerce/social-commerce/social-commerce-trends-for-2020-you-need-to-look-out-for/ (accessed on 16 Jan 2023).

Manyika, J.; Chui, M.; Brown, B.; Bughin, J.; Dobbs, R.; Roxburgh, C.; Hung Byers, A. *Big Data: The Next Frontier for Innovation, Competition, and Productivity*; McKinsey Global Institute, 2011.

McAfee, A.; Brynjolfsson, E.; Davenport, T. H.; Patil, D. J.; Barton, D. Big Data: The Management Revolution. *Harv. Bus. Rev.* **2012,** *90* (10), 60–68.

Mikalef, P.; van de Wetering, R.; Krogstie, J. Building Dynamic Capabilities by Leveraging Big Data Analytics: The Role of Organizational Inertia. *Inf. Manag.* **2021,** *58* (6), 103412.

Nelson, R. R.; Todd, P. A.; Wixom, B. H. Antecedents of Information and System Quality: An Empirical Examination Within the Context of Data Warehousing. *J. Manag. Inf. Syst.* **2005,** *21*, 199–235.

Phucharoen, C.; Jarumaneerat, T.; Sangkaew, N. Comparing Shopping Experiences in Department Stores and Street Markets: A Big Data Analysis of Trip Advisor Reviews. *Int. J. Culture Tour. Hosp. Res.* **2021,** *16* (1), 259–275.

Rathod, J.; Kumar, R. Analyzing the Impact of Big Data and Business Analytics in Enhancing Demand-Driven Forecasting in Retailing. *Int. J. Entrepreneurship* **2021,** *25* (2), 1–8.

Schroeck, M.; Shockley, R.; Smart, J.; Romero-Morales, D.; Tufano, P. Analytics: The Real-World Use of Big Data. *IBM Glob. Bus. Serv.* **2012,** *12* (2012), 1–20.

Shah, S.; Horne, A.; Capellá, J.; Good Data Won't Guarantee Good Decisions. *Harv. Bus. Rev.* **2012,** *90*, 23–25.

Shanks, G.; Sharma, R.; Seddon, P.; Reynolds, P. The Impact of Strategy and Maturity on Business Analytics and Firm Performance: A Review and Research Agenda, 7 Nov 2010. https://aisel.aisnet.org/acis2010/51 (accessed on 16 Jan 2023).

Top Big Data Companies—August 2022 | 99firms. 2022. https://99firms.com/big-data-companies (accessed on 16 Jan 2023).

Wang, Y.; Kung, L.; Byrd, T. A. Big Data Analytics: Understanding Its Capabilities and Potential Benefits for Healthcare Organizations. *Technol. Forecast. Soc. Change* **2018,** *126*, 3–13.

What Is Big Data?—business.com. 2022. https://www.business.com/articles/what-is-big-data/ (accessed on 16 Jan 2023).

Williamson, O. E. The Economics of Organization: The Transaction Cost Approach. *Am. J. Sociol.* **1981,** *87*, 548–577.

Zhuang, W.; Wang, M. C.; Nakamoto, I.; Jiang, M. Big Data Analytics in E-Commerce for the U.S. and China Through Literature Reviewing. https://www.degruyter.com/document/doi/10.21078/JSSI-2021–016–29/html (accessed on 16 Jan 2023).

CHAPTER 6

Marketing and Retaining Customers in the World of Brazen Bullshit: Analyzing the Post-Truth Scenario Effect on Strategic Communication

MANPREET ARORA

HPKVBS, School of Commerce and Management Studies, Central University of Himachal Pradesh, Dharamshala, India

ABSTRACT

The biggest challenge of strategic communication, especially in the era of digitalization, is the dark side of media as well as digital platforms, that is, fake news, fake information, fraudulent practices, rumors, propaganda, and distorted information. The blatant lies associated with marketing, especially in post-truth scenarios, are related with fake news, untrue and misleading claims made by the business houses or marketers or the imitators prevalent in the market. This chapter aims at defining the concept of post-truth and its relevance for marketers in order to make counter strategies to deal with bullshit, which can help in turn to devise strategies for customer retention. Fake news and the prevalence of the highest form of distorted information are the negative aspects of big data, which expands at a very great speed and takes the shape of an infodemic and has the capability of putting people into illusions. But on the other hand, it can also act as a strong tool to counter such information. A timely action about any kind of misinformation spread about their brand can only help to curb the more drastic situation of disinformation. In this post-truth era, the antidote will be to direct customers toward official channels, broadcasts, and social media platforms of the company from time

Augmenting Customer Retention Through Big Data Analytics.
Reena Malik, Ambuj Sharma, and Prashant Chaudhary (Eds.)

to time. An extra effort will be required to make customers aware about the reliable sources of communication based on facts. Big data and artificially intelligent solutions can play a decisive role in countering and dealing with the excessive flow of misinformation as well as disinformation.

6.1 INTRODUCTION

Strategic communication is the purposeful communication by the organization in order to fulfill its mission and objectives in the long run. Strategic communication is always based on a certain long-term agenda of the business, where an effort by an organization is made to fulfill its vision, mission, and objectives. In this era of digitalization, where brand reputation, corporate communication, and social media have gained immense importance, it becomes imperative for the organizations to take care of whatever they are communicating to their stakeholders. A single mistake can seriously damage the existence of a brand or a company. A corporate house uses a variety of mediums to strategically communicate with its stakeholders. It can be in the form of a press release, through traditional marketing practices, or even through advertisement campaigns, where the sole purpose is to convey certain messages to the stakeholders, which are well-planned and in consonance with the organizational vision and mission. The biggest challenge of strategic communication, especially in the era of digitalization, is the dark side of media as well as digital platforms, that is, fake news, fake information, fraudulent practices, rumors, propaganda, and distorted information. The biggest example of distorted information is the infodemic during COVID-19, which led to huge economic costs for the companies all over the world and affected the general public at large, in addition to the health crises and concerns that arose during the pandemic. A huge spike/increase was seen during COVID-19 in fake claims and fake news, which were mostly forwarded through social media platforms. Cyber fraud, discrimination, religion, and race-based attacks were common and could be seen in plenty during the pandemic. Not only the societal behavior underwent damage due to an upsurge in fake news and fake posts but the corporates also faced huge risks to sustain their businesses due to infodemics during this time (economic times). This chapter aims at defining the concept of post-truth and its relevance for marketers in order to make counter strategies to deal with bullshit, which in turn leads to customer retention, by exploring the following research questions:

6.2 RESEARCH QUESTIONS

- What is the post-truth scenario?
- How does the post-truth scenario affect a company's decision-making and their response toward the market?
- Why should marketers be cautious enough while making strategies in this digitalized world where post-truth scenarios pose challenges?

6.3 METHODOLOGY

This is a conceptual study, which is literature- and content-based, available on social media platforms, corporate websites, business newspapers, and magazines.

6.4 LITERATURE REVIEW

Rynarzewska (2019) tried to uncover the "morality and dynamics of community of incentivised reviewers" who are basically reviewing products on the online shopping platform, primarily Amazon. The author has used netnography and is of the view that the consumer's morality is suppressed. It is in fact driven by the desire and need to earn benefits by manipulation of reviews. The intention behind this is to boost sales, but there is a presence of bias in such actions. The information or the reviews are manipulated and deceptive. The overconsumption of the product or excessive reviews are done by the consumer in a way intended toward getting free products and benefits of some schemes. The study found that an average consumer who relies on these reviews is influenced and biased. There is also the presence of various unfair business practices on the part of sellers who do so in order to get higher ratings. With the retail sector booming due to high online shopping, it is very easy to fabricate the opinion of the customers. Consumers are, on the other hand, empowered; they have the option to execute purchase decisions from anywhere at any time, 24*7. The onus of making this consumer's online shopping experience positive lies on the sellers and marketers by providing a true and fair view about the product and its usage. But in this age of infodemics, where information is excessive, large, and not free from bias, the challenges are quite high. It has become a very common act on the part of consumers to read the reviews available online before making a purchase decision. Marketing scholars have time and again focused on and highlighted this fact by conducting several studies conducted in this dimension. Positive online reviews have the capability of influencing the buying decisions (Ba et al., 2020; Chen and Barnes, 2007; Zhao et al., 2018; Sparks and Browning, 2011; Dapas et al., 2019; Djafarova and Rushworth, 2017). It is thereby a great motivating factor for the brands to monitor as well as manipulate the product reviews (Li et al., 2020; Sarmad et al., 2016; Weitz et.al., 1986; Chen et al., 1986; Furner et al., 2022). The voluminous data on the internet can be easily filtered for such purposes by the big data analytics, and it can be the darker side of growing technology, which can be misused and misutilized to manipulate the opinion of the public. "Online Review Deception" is a gray area where post-truth dynamics remain at their peak, but we as consumers are unaware of the facts, and our opinions, decisions, and choices remain biased. Online reviews have become an important source of understanding the consumer's behavior, perception, and attitude toward a product in which big data analytics play an important role (Mariani and Borghi, 2020, 2021; Sann et al., 2022; Salehan and Kim, 2016; Ahmed et al., 2021; Ma et al., 2022; Chong et al., 2017). These reviews are also the basis for sale forecasting (Fan et al., 2017; Lau et al., 2018; Zhang et al., 2022; Dellarocas et al., 2007; Ren et al., 2020; Jiménez et al., 2017; Cui et al., 2012; Kulkarni et al., 2012). AI and IoT are providing new dimensions to sale and demand forecasting, supporting the marketer's efforts in this area (Ren et al., 2018; Zohdi et al., 2022; Sohrabpour et al., 2021; Shaikh et al., 2022; Watanabe et al., 2019).

Intentional deceit in any form of act on the part of the seller or brand has a negative impact on brand loyalty (Gillespie et al., 2016; Latif, 2017; Tripathi, 2016; Ketron, 2016; Nuseir, 2018; Rodriguez, 2020). With the newer technologies coming, it is observed that the deliberate manipulation of data, information, and facts is increasing. The desired attitudes and the behavioral implications in favor of a product, seller, or brand could be created by the use of IoT and other supportive technologies in the era of post-truth, where social media platforms and e-commerce channels are playing a decisive role (Shamim et al., 2019; Vedder and Naudts, 2017; Holmlund et al., 2020; Hilbert, 2016; Kunz et al., 2017). Not only brands but also those who indulge in the serious action of creating deliberate false information induce the availability as well as the quality of information to manipulate and falsify information, thereby influencing the consumer's evaluation. Peng et al. (2016) are of the view that online review deceptions are quite prevalent these days. Hiding and deleting the information is another aspect of misrepresentation. On online platforms, hiding and deleting the unfavorable reviews is regarded as the most deceptive and unethical practice. However, locating online review deception is not an easy task. Social media has become a platform for businesses to pursue their long-term strategies in many ways. Arora and Sharma (2022) and Rhodes and Wilson (2018) talk about the firms that have falsely advertised in order to overstate the value of their products. It is an obvious fact that buyers totally rely on the firm's advertisements and promotional activities to learn about the peculiar features or characteristics of the products, which in turn influences their purchase decisions. However, some evidence is available where firms have also resorted to false advertising and engaged in showcasing incorrect or exaggerated product claims. In some countries, many firms were also subjected to legal action and had to pay heavy sums of money in the form of penalties due to their deceptive actions affecting potential consumers. Sawy and Dieter (2022) talk about the use of social media strategies as part of "entrepreneurs' business and marketing strategies". They also talk about the negative consequences of social media for entrepreneurs. According to the authors, entrepreneurs have to engage themselves if they are using social media as a business strategy, and it is a very time-consuming process. One of the negative consequences of using social media is dealing with negative and insulting comments.

6.5 WHAT IS POST-TRUTH SCENARIO?

Post-truth phenomenon is marred by the situation where truth is no longer truth. It takes the form of a fabricated opinion or even a stretched truth for one's own convenience. In the business world, it is more related with fake news, fake messages, and the intentional concealment of facts. The Cambridge Dictionary defines post-truth as "relating to a situation in which people are more likely to accept an argument based on their emotions and beliefs, rather than one based on facts". The objectivity is somewhat missing in the post-truth scenario, and subjectivity overpowers the situation. Deception, lies, fabrication of facts, active concealment, and untrue statements are also associated with the post-truth scenarios. The blatant lies associated with marketing, especially in post-truth scenarios, are related with fake news, untrue and misleading claims made by the business houses or marketers or the imitators prevalent in the market (Arora, 2020).

The distortion, falsification, and misrepresentation of reality can take any form, and particularly, the political scenario across the world is full of this. The ultimate aim is to hit the rational judgment of people in such a way that whatever is preached by the politicians/leaders starts appearing to be rational, coherent, and objective. The inherent purpose of social media platforms is to communicate, connect, and express. When it comes to the dissemination of lies, fake news, distorted facts, distorted viewpoints, propaganda of deception, exaggeration of the truth, cynical realities, outrageous brazen erroneous assertions, and bullshit, anyone could not have guessed that it would become such a large source of misinformation or disinformation. In this scenario, a small bullshit or fake news that goes viral on social media can prove very dangerous for the sustainability of the business. On the other hand, it is very challenging for marketers to retain customers, where the spread of fake news and propaganda is relatively easy for the competitors in order to tarnish the image of the company (refer to Fig. 6.1).

6.6 HOW DOES THE POST-TRUTH SCENARIO AFFECT A COMPANY'S DECISION-MAKING AND RESPONSE TOWARD THE MARKET?

As Ralph Keyes puts it, "in this era of post-truth marketing, the main characteristics of the scenario are dishonesty and deception." The fundamental basis of every marketing activity is knowing your customers. But every customer has his own truth, and every consumer segment is affected by different scenarios. But in the world of multiple realities, the post-truth scenario is the most challenging and difficult to predict as well as handle. Brands target only specific customers sometimes, where AI and big data play an incredible role in understanding their likings and preferences. These likings are generally calculated by AI systems, which are based upon sentiment analysis (Arora and Sharma, 2022). Online shopping platforms are not only platforms to sell and market the products and services for the marketers, but they have also become a platform which communicates about the choices, preferences, likings, consumer behavior, and intentions of the customers. Products in shopping carts and the customer reviews have become the main source of demand predictions as well as production activities. Flash sales of mobiles is one of the biggest examples in front of us. Mi succeeded in India due to this strategy.

Various brands, in order to distort the competition, use deliberate distortion of the truth by using either fake or distorted information, which appeals to the emotions of the public and manipulates the beliefs and emotions of the public or it directly hits the sentiments of the consumer (Arora and Sharma, 2021). This change or, in fact, distortion of the public opinion or any particular segment of the society has a long-lasting effect in terms of a change in consumer attitude toward a brand or product. This can make it a very tough situation for companies to make their decisions in terms of deciding about production and marketing strategies. These strategies should have to be quite strategic in nature, with the capability of influencing the whole market. Communication has become an important aspect in order to sustain in the present scenario, which should have very local and geographical implications, especially in specific market segments of the society. The consumer segments can affect a great deal of communication strategies which target specific customer segments and can prove to be very relevant to them. This era of digitalization has increased the hopes of the customers from the manufacturers to a great extent. The use of the internet has now been perceived by customers as much more than a digital activity. The excessive digitalization has increased the need of anticipatory customer satisfaction as well as hyperpersonalized experiences of the customers and their buying decisions.

Another aspect of this era is that propaganda can be an easy strategy, either to use it in favor or to use it as a vicious tool to manipulate the market or harm the competitor brand; it can be either used for image building or for distorting the image too. Gone are the days when just focusing on mass marketing in order to influence the market was the sole strategy for success, and it was repeated by and large again and again over a period of time by the marketers. The use of different languages and customized messages or products is the new norm of the industry. We can find different advertisements for the same product from country to country or sometimes even from channel to channel. Branding has become more about performance marketing and dealing with the pressures of marketing like handling infodemics, fake news, and propaganda.

The operating models of the businesses have undergone a huge change (Arora and Sharma, 2022), especially where infodemics have come into picture. When the information flow is in abundance on digital platforms, especially social media, a countering strategy must be devised by the companies to save their brand reputation. A single mistake can lead to a disastrous position as well as a dangerous situation, leading the brands to fail miserably.

Many instances of the spread of misinformation and disinformation about brands can be seen worldwide. Misinformation is a wider term and covers all the inaccurate information, whether created deliberately or not. The entire bunch of information is faulty. On the other hand, disinformation is regarded as a "poster child of misinformation" affected by the fake news (Forbes). The intention of defrauding or harming some reputation or distorting the facts is always there. The intention plays a decisive role in the spread of misinformation as well as disinformation. According to the Forbes magazine, marketing has become a success mantra, especially after the pandemic. As per Avi Dan (2021), in his article on "Old Truths and New Marketing Truths after the Pandemic" published in Forbes magazine, "Unquestionably, there was a time when marketing was a cost centre within companies for which the principal accountability was to maximize return on investment. In tough times, when topline results were compromised, it was often one of the first areas to get cut. However, during the pandemic, marketing has been elevated within the C-suite as a driver of digital transformation, a key leader of the customer journey, and the voice of the consumer—all of which are of paramount importance to other functional departments".

The consequences of the fake news or false information on the brands can be drastic, and there is even the possibility of legal consequences of certain actions. The presence of fake news via the internet compels the brands to remain conscious as well as forces them to devise certain strategies for combating the pressures posed by infodemics. Fake news can have an effect on the behavior as well as the intentions of the customers. A great concern that can be seen in almost all the sectors of the society in today's world is that social media plays a drastic role in spreading misinformation, which is associated with false news. The author believes that the dark side of digital marketing is propaganda. There are a plethora of instances available that make us realize that sustaining business for the brands in this digitalized world is not easy. Fake news and offers on the names of brands, fraudulent advertisements and propaganda, fake calls, and schemes often dupe the customers in the name of established brands. Brands have to spend a lot of money and effort to deal with such infodemics of fake news, messages, and emails.

In 2014, Tata Motors cautioned their potential customers as well as the general public about the fraudulent promotional offers and advertisements in the name of the company. In this case, someone was wrongfully extracting or demanding cash in specified banks from the general public who were potential customers of Tata Motors. They were also using the registered trademark of Tata Motors to dupe the public. The fake advertisement was luring the public to fall in the trap of the fake offers to deposit cash in the name of Tata Motors. The company came out in the press and stated that this was purely with the intention of defrauding the general public at large, and they have not authorized any person to require any payment or cash to be made.

In the press statement, the company also stated that these people were asking the prospective buyers to pay a certain amount of money toward the availing price of a lucky draw. Further, an advertisement was also showcased on television by the fraudsters where they were asking to identify the film stars, and by doing so accurately, the people were encouraged to deposit a certain amount of money toward getting registered for that lucky scheme, and then after confirmation, the company would be transferring a vehicle to them. They were also directed to visit the Tata Motors facility to collect the vehicle. This whole scam took place in 2014, and the press release of the incident is available on Tata Motors official website to date (https://www.tatamotors.com).

In another example in 2021, Amazon came forward to the press for clarifying that it is not offering free gifts to all and that a wide circulation of WhatsApp messages was going on. It was a viral message claiming to offer free gifts for all Amazon users as a part of the 30th anniversary celebrations of the company. The link was carrying an incorrect spelling for Amazon, which was not very easy to detect. The link of the offer was carrying the logo of Amazon, which could dupe people very easily. The message was posted across the groups and sent to individuals. The message was so viral that to claim a gift, it should be forwarded to five groups or 20 friends on WhatsApp. And a flood of messages were sent across WhatsApp in order to claim such gifts. In the past, such things happened with some popular brands, like free gifts from Adidas, free tickets from some airlines, foreign trips, etc., which were voluminous data transferred through social media platforms, tarnishing the image of the brands.

Another dimension of the post-truth era is the huge rise in online scams and frauds that have been seen in the past decade, especially through social media. Since the inception of the internet, there has been an upsurge in various kinds of cyber-crimes. It has become quite normal to receive e-mails, phone calls, SMS, WhatsApp, or Telegram messages of some schemes, offers, etc. On any other social media site, we can find plenty of claims providing us with mind-blowing discounts and offers. A wide variety of fraudsters and scammers with the intention of deceiving the general public at large are using these social media platforms to serve their purpose.

If we do not pay attention to these messages and ignore to carefully scrutinize them, we can become victims of fraud and end up losing money as well as personal data. Generally, these fraudsters misappropriate trustworthy brands. Online frauds have become very common due to an increase in e-commerce activities. Most of the online shopping platforms contain sensitive personal information about the customers, like their name, address, phone number, e-mail, etc., and they have got certain features like pay later or electronic gift vouchers or discounts, which remain in that particular website. When a fraudster accesses our account, then this information is also compromised and can be used very easily. The easiest way to dupe an online customer is to create a fake website. They become so similar that, on the very first instance, nobody is able to recognize the difference between the original website and a fake website. They also use trademarks or logos similar to those of these brands. The latest example that highlights social media's effect on brands is of Elon Musk's ownership of Tesla. From the time he has gained ownership of Twitter, he has been posting a lot of posts which are regarded as politically influenced, and a chunk of the population is not liking this approach to using Twitter as a platform to share his beliefs and opinions. It is also shared in the various newspapers that Elon Musk's posts are working as a damaging factor in the electronic vehicle market of Tesla, which is again owned by Elon Musk.

He is also accused of misleading the stakeholders of Tesla by tweeting in 2018 a misleading statement "Funding Secured". It is believed by many that Musk's tweet not only misled the public to invest but he also lied. One of the investors who has filed a petition in the San Francisco Federal Court argues that his tweet cost him trading losses. He claimed a loss of $5000 buying Tesla's stock after Musk sent the tweet. As per Fries, the investor, the tweet saying "Funding secured" means "there had been some vetting, some critical review of those funding sources" (The Guardian). In September 2018, the US Securities and Exchange Commission filed a lawsuit against Musk for fraud and sought to remove him from Tesla (The Economic Times). More recently, on January 17, 2023, as per the Hindustan Times, "Elon Musk shares intriguing post about how Instagram and Twitter can affect people's moods." His tweet is "Instagram makes people depressed & Twitter makes people angry. Which is better?" At the time of writing this piece by the author, the tweet was liked by 654.1 k and was having 148.8 k replies. Disinformation has been regarded as an old story, but it is fueled by new technology.

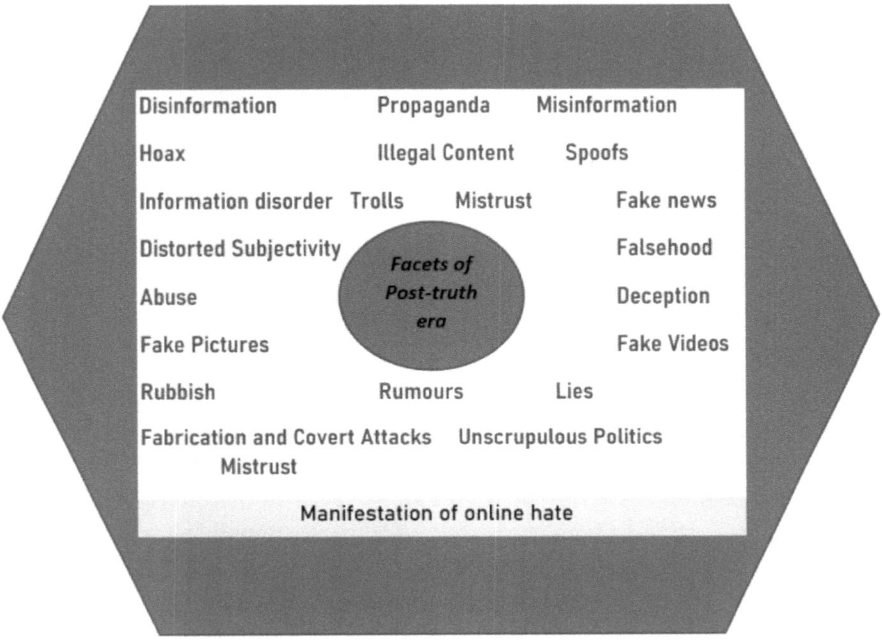

FIGURE 6.1 Facets of the post-truth era.

Source: Author.

A flow of fake messages on WhatsApp, Facebook, Messenger, Telegram, or any other social media platform has become an important feature for companies to deal with in order to deal with the post-truth scenario. One brand's reality is copied, and in a way, it becomes the reality of the customer.

6.7 WHY MARKETERS SHOULD BE CAUTIOUS ENOUGH WHILE MAKING STRATEGIES IN THIS DIGITALIZED WORLD WHERE POST-TRUTH SCENARIO POSES CHALLENGES?

The whole range of products available in the market are consumer-oriented but on the other hand, the customer's orientation toward a product is largely dependent on the consumer's experience. The consumer choices and likings are so wide in their range that new companies are shifting toward artificially intelligent systems, big data solutions, and immersive technologies based on the metaverse in order to predict and forecast accurately. Whatever claims the brands make and are unable to fulfill, especially in the post-truth scenario, can have a serious effect on the image of the brand. The majority of companies have faced relentless criticism in the market because their claims did not match the consumer's experience or the claims were misleading, deceptive, and fabricating the truth. One of the examples recently seen for the Indian product of Unilever, Fair and Lovely, was considered to mislead the public and fell into the category of fabricating the truth.

Critics also regarded that the brand is promoting harmful beauty standards. In this scenario, the brand also faced legal consequences. The situation worsened to the extent that the brand had to change their name from "fair and lovely" to "glow and lovely".

In the past few years, the world has been experiencing a rapid as well as radical change in lifestyle due to the prevalence of the digital revolution in almost every sector. The highest form of data production and usage can be seen in the past few years, which is named big data. A large amount of data generation, which is gigantic in nature, now requires the intervention of data scientists in corporate houses, who are totally responsible for data mining, which helps to extract the relevant information from the huge amount of data. In a world where fake news and propaganda have increased many folds due to social media intervention in advertisement and other related aspects of business strategies, it becomes imperative for the organizations to pay attention to big data solutions in order to deal with the problems which generally arise as a darker side of the digitalized world, i.e., fake news, propaganda, and rumors. Big data solutions will not only help the companies to accurately predict the future, but they will also help you understand the present situation of the organization by extracting the pertinent information for decision-making. Strategic interventions which can be taken by an organization by the use of big data and AI solutions can be many, which have multifaceted orientations for the business.

Undoubtedly, fake news and the prevalence of the highest form of distorted information are the negative aspects of big data, which expands at a very great speed and has the capability of putting people into illusions. But on the other hand, it can also act as a strong tool to counter such information. Fake news and fraudulent information have been perceived as the biggest threat by leaders all around the world. It has been defined as the greatest risk to the brand's reputation and the sustainability of the organization. The unfair practices which are generally prevalent in the markets are supported by the use of these big data darker sides as they are not easy to identify. It is as easy as sharing opinions on social media to disseminate a huge amount of distorted information against the brand by the use of big data. Another complication which arises due to big data is the risk of protection of privacy. Much of the information related with the consumers, which has got privacy issues, can be compromised easily by the intervention of big data and AI. That is why countries like the US have been employing laws to prevent such problems.

Disinformation of any form has been regarded as the biggest global threat in the age of information technology. Not only companies but the communities as well as governments around the world are dealing with disinformation on a regular basis, and the sources are varied like reports, magazines, images, videos, and memes. If, on the one hand, artificial intelligence as well as big data have the power of generating the content, then, on the other hand, they have got the resultant negative aspect in the form of fake news, which can bring any kind of information to a level of infodemic.

The persistent need is to make organizations as well as governments ready to understand the knowledge gaps in this area. A need exists to comprehend the advanced techniques and build algorithms which are required for model building in order to understand the various aspects of misinformation. In fact, it is very difficult to find out the extent of information distortion across the sections of the society as it increases manifold each minute. Only advanced techniques based on big data solutions and Artificial Intelligence can provide solutions to this complicated but important problem prevalent worldwide. Further, as the dimensions of distorted information are many, like whether it is visual content, photo editing, or video manipulation, the tools which may be used to solve multidimensional aspects of misinformation should be based only on advanced technologies. In this era of post-truth where fake news and misinformation are common, big data is both a solution as well as a problem. Therefore, this double-edged sword should be used judiciously.

6.8 SUMMATIVE REMARKS

In this scenario, businesses need to be very proactive about calling for the misinformation. A timely action about any kind of misinformation spread about their brand can only help to curb the more drastic situation of disinformation. In this post-truth era, the antidote will be to direct the customers toward official channels, broadcasts, and social media platforms of the company from time to time. An extra effort will be required to make customers aware of the reliable sources of communication based on facts. Big data and artificially intelligent solutions can play a decisive role in countering and dealing with the excessive flow of misinformation as well as disinformation. Corporate houses have to be very cautious while communicating a true and fair view of the organization. The strategic communication must be directed toward dealing with all the potential harms which could arise from casual communication. It is indispensable for the organizations to provide credible information to the stakeholders so that there is no chance of distortion of any information. However, it is very challenging for the small organizations to counter this phenomenon as it requires infrastructural requirements like speech recognition systems, state-of-the-art computer-aided systems, multimedia analysis programs, etc.

KEYWORDS

- **strategic communication**
- **marketing**
- **post-truth**
- **social media**
- **disinformation**
- **misinformation**
- **digitalization, rumors**

REFERENCES

Ahmed, H. M.; Javed Awan, M.; Khan, N. S.; Yasin, A.; Faisal Shehzad, H. M. Sentiment Analysis of Online Food Reviews Using Big Data Analytics. *Element. Educ. Online* **2021,** *20* (2), 827–836.

Arora, M. Post-Truth and Marketing Communication in Technological Age. In: *Handbook of Research on Innovations in Technology and Marketing for the Connected Consumer*; IGI Global, 2020; pp 94–108.

Arora, M.; Sharma, R. L. Post-Truth (Mis) Communication as Enigmatic Mystification and Misuse of Language. In: *Redefining the Role of Language in a Globalized World*; IGI Global, 2021; pp 43–53.

Arora, M.; Sharma, R. L. Artificial Intelligence and Big Data: Ontological and Communicative Perspectives in Multi-Sectoral Scenarios of Modern Businesses. *Foresight* **2023,** *25* (1), 126–143.

Arora, M.; Sharma, R. L. Integrating Gig Economy and Social Media Platforms as a Business Strategy in the Era of Digitalization. In: *Integrated Business Models in the Digital Age:*

Principles and Practices of Technology Empowered Strategies; Springer International Publishing: Cham, 2022; pp 67–86.

Ba, S.; Jin, Y.; Li, X.; Lu, X. One Size Fits All? The Differential Impact of Online Reviews and Coupons. *Product. Oper. Manag.* **2020,** *29* (10), 2403–2424.

Chen, L.; Jiang, T.; Li, W.; Geng, S.; Hussain, S. Who Should Pay for Online Reviews? Design of an Online User Feedback Mechanism. *Electron. Commerce Res. App.* **2017,** *23*, 38–44.

Chen, Y. H.; Barnes, S. Initial Trust and Online Buyer Behaviour. *Ind. Manag. Data Systems* **2007**.

Chong, A. Y. L.; Ch'ng, E.; Liu, M. J.; Li, B. Predicting Consumer Product Demands via Big Data: The Roles of Online Promotional Marketing and Online Reviews. *Int. J. Product. Res.* **2017,** *55* (17), 5142–5156.

Cui, G.; Lui, H. K.; Guo, X. The Effect of Online Consumer Reviews on New Product Sales. *Int. J. Electron. Commerce* **2012,** *17* (1), 39–58.

Dan Avi. Old Truths and New Marketing Truths After the Pandemic. Retrieved from Old Truths and New Marketing Truths After the Pandemic (forbes.com), 25 Mar 2021.

Dapas, C. C.; Sitorus, T.; Purwanto, E.; Ihalauw, J. J. The effect of Service Quality and Website Quality of Zalora.Com on Purchase Decision as Mediated by Purchase Intention. *Calitatea* **2019,** *20* (169), 87–92.

Dellarocas, C.; Zhang, X.; Awad, N. F. Exploring the Value of Online Product Reviews in Forecasting Sales: The Case of Motion Pictures. *J. Interact. Market.* **2007,** *21* (4), 23–45.

Djafarova, E.; Rushworth, C. Exploring the Credibility of Online Celebrities' Instagram Profiles in Influencing the Purchase Decisions of Young Female Users. *Comput. Hum. Behav.* **2017,** *68*, 1–7.

Fan, Z. P.; Che, Y. J.; Chen, Z. Y. Product Sales Forecasting Using Online Reviews and Historical Sales Data: A Method Combining the Bass Model and Sentiment Analysis. *J. Bus. Res.* **2017,** *74*, 90–100.

Furner, C. P.; Drake, J. R.; Zinko, R.; Kisling, E. Online Review Antecedents of Trust, Purchase, and Recommendation Intention: A Simulation-Based Experiment for Hotels and AirBnBs. *J. Internet Commerce* **2022,** *21* (1), 79–103.

Gillespie, E. A.; Hybnerova, K.; Esmark, C.; Noble, S. M. A Tangled Web: Views of Deception from the Customer's Perspective. *Bus. Ethics: Eur. Rev.* **2016,** *25* (2), 198–216.

Hilbert, M. Big Data for Development: A Review of Promises and Challenges. *Dev. Policy Rev.* **2016,** *34* (1), 135–174.

Holmlund, M.; Van Vaerenbergh, Y.; Ciuchita, R.; Ravald, A.; Sarantopoulos, P.; Ordenes, F. V.; Zaki, M. Customer Experience Management in the Age of Big Data Analytics: A Strategic Framework. *J. Bus. Res.* **2020,** *116*, 356–365.

Jiménez, F.; Sánchez, G.; García, J. M.; Sciavicco, G.; Miralles, L. Multi-Objective Evolutionary Feature Selection for Online Sales Forecasting. *Neurocomputing* **2017,** *234*, 75–92.

Ketron, S. Consumer Cynicism and Perceived Deception in Vanity Sizing: The Moderating Role of Retailer (Dis) honesty. *J. Retail. Consumer Serv.* **2016,** *33*, 33–42.

Kulkarni, G.; Kannan, P. K.; Moe, W. Using Online Search Data to Forecast New Product Sales. *Decision Support Syst.* **2012,** *52* (3), 604–611.

Kunz, W.; Aksoy, L.; Bart, Y.; Heinonen, K.; Kabadayi, S.; Ordenes, F. V. et al. Customer Engagement in a Big Data World. *J. Serv. Market.* **2017.**

Latif, A. A. Volkswagen Brand: The Fall of an Auto Empire. *J. Glob. Bus. Adv.* **2017,** *10* (3), 281–304.

Lau, R. Y. K.; Zhang, W.; Xu, W. Parallel Aspect-Oriented Sentiment Analysis for Sales Forecasting with Big Data. *Product. Oper. Manag.* **2018,** *27* (10), 1775–1794.

Li, K.; Chen, Y.; Zhang, L. Exploring the Influence of Online Reviews and Motivating Factors on Sales: A Meta-Analytic Study and the Moderating Role of Product Category. *J. Retail. Consum. Serv.* **2020,** *55*, 102107.

Ma, G.; Ma, J.; Li, H.; Wang, Y.; Wang, Z.; Zhang, B. Customer Behavior in Purchasing Energy-Saving Products: Big Data Analytics from Online Reviews of E-commerce. *Energy Policy* **2022,** *165*, 112960.

Mariani, M.; Borghi, M. Environmental Discourse in Hotel Online Reviews: A Big Data Analysis. *J. Sustain. Tour.* **2020,** *29* (5), 829–848.

Mariani, M.; Borghi, M. Are Environmental-Related Online Reviews More Helpful? A Big Data Analytics Approach. *Int. J. Contemp. Hosp. Manag.* **2021.**

Nuseir, M. T. Impact of Misleading/False Advertisement to Consumer Behaviour. *Int. J. Econ. Bus. Res.* **2018,** *16* (4), 453–465.

Peng, L.; Cui, G.; Zhuang, M.; Li, C. Consumer Perceptions of Online Review Deceptions: An Empirical Study in China. *J. Consum. Market.* 2016

Ren, S.; Chan, H. L.; Siqin, T. Demand Forecasting in Retail Operations for Fashionable Products: Methods, Practices, and Real Case Study. *Ann. Oper. Res.* **2020,** *291*, 761–777.

Ren, S.; Patrick Hui, C. L.; Jason Choi, T. M. AI-Based Fashion Sales Forecasting Methods in Big Data Era. *Artif. Intell. Fashion Ind. Big Data Era* **2018,** 9–26.

Rhodes, A.; Wilson, C. M. False Advertising. *RAND J. Econ.* **2018,** *49* (2), 348–369.

Rodriguez, M. *Brand Storytelling: Put Customers at the Heart of Your Brand Story*; Kogan Page Publishers, 2020.

Rynarzewska, A. I. It's Not Fake, It's Biased: Insights into Morality of Incentivized Reviewers. *J. Consum. Market.* **2019,** *36* (3), 401–409.

Salehan, M.; Kim, D. J. Predicting the Performance of Online Consumer Reviews: A Sentiment Mining Approach to Big Data Analytics. *Decision Supp. Syst.* **2016,** *81*, 30–40.

Sann, R.; Lai, P. C.; Liaw, S. Y.; Chen, C. T. Predicting Online Complaining Behavior in the Hospitality Industry: Application of Big Data Analytics to Online Reviews. *Sustainability* **2022,** *14* (3), 1800.

Sarmad, M.; Ajmal, M. M.; Shamim, M.; Saleh, M.; Malik, A. Motivation and Compensation as Predictors of Employees' Retention: Evidence From Public Sector Oil and Gas Selling Organizations. *J. Behav. Sci.* **2016,** *26* (2).

Shaikh, A. A.; Lakshmi, K. S.; Tongkachok, K.; Alanya-Beltran, J.; Ramirez-Asis, E.; Perez-Falcon, J. Empirical Analysis in Analysing the Major Factors of Machine Learning in Enhancing the E-Business Through Structural Equation Modelling (SEM) Approach. *Int. J. Syst. Assurance Eng. Manag.* **2022,** *13* (Suppl 1), 681–689.

Shamim, S.; Zeng, J.; Shariq, S. M.; Khan, Z. Role of Big Data Management in Enhancing Big Data Decision-Making Capability and Quality Among Chinese Firms: A Dynamic Capabilities View. *Inf. Manag.* **2019,** *56* (6), 103135.

Sohrabpour, V.; Oghazi, P.; Toorajipour, R.; Nazarpour, A. Export sales forecasting using artificial intelligence. *Technol. Forecast. Soc. Change* **2021,** *163*, 120480.

Sparks, B. A.; Browning, V. The Impact of Online Reviews on Hotel Booking Intentions and Perception of Trust. *Tour. Manag.* **2011,** *32* (6), 1310–1323.

Tripathi, V. The Role of Stealth Marketing Strategy to Manipulate Teenagers. *Asian J. Manag. Res.* **2016,** *7* (2), 189–199.

Vedder Weitz, A.; Naudts, L. Accountability for the Use of Algorithms in a Big Data Environment. *Int. Rev. Law Comput. Technol.* **2017,** *31* (2), 206–224.

Watanabe, I.; Yoshibayashi, T.; Imaoka, T. AI-Based Demand Forecasting for Both Reliable Forecasting and Efficient Operation: Dynamic Ensemble Forecasting. *Fujitsu Sci. Techn. J.* **2019,** *55* (2), 14–22.

Weitz, B. A.; Sujan, H.; Sujan, M. Knowledge, Motivation, and Adaptive Behavior: A Framework for Improving Selling Effectiveness. *J. Market.* **29186,** *50* (4), 174–191.

Zhang, C.; Tian, Y. X.; Fan, Z. P. Forecasting Sales Using Online Review and Search Engine Data: A Method Based on PCA–DSFOA–BPNN. *Int. J. Forecast.* **2022,** *38* (3), 1005–1024.

Zhao, K.; Stylianou, A. C.; Zheng, Y. Sources and Impacts of Social Influence from Online Anonymous User Reviews. *Inf. Manag.*, *55* (1), 16–30.

Zohdi, M.; Rafiee, M.; Kayvanfar, V.; Salamiraad, A. Demand Forecasting Based Machine Learning Algorithms on Customer Information: An Applied Approach. *Int. J. Inf. Technol.* **2022,** *14* (4), 1937–1947.

CHAPTER 7

Big Data as a Tool for Digital Marketers

RUHI SARANGAL[1], PRASHANT CHAUHAN[1], ASHOK KUMAR[2], DEVESH BATHLA[1], AARTI DANGWAL[1], and MANKAJ MEHTA[1]

[1]*Chitkara Business School, Chitkara University, Punjab, India*

[2]*Department of Defence and Strategic Studies, Himachal Pradesh University, Shimla, India*

ABSTRACT

Customers are increasingly performing their activities through digital channels as a result of technical improvements, which also enable marketers to collect enormous amounts of data about consumers, store it, and use it as they see fit. Despite the significance of big data analytics for company marketing, there is little research on this topic. Another is creating future plans that take into account their requirements. In light of this, several tools and techniques have been developed to facilitate the process. These methods include observation, data collection, and analysis, among others. However, the more data you have, the more difficult it will be to manage, and eventually it will exceed human capabilities. This is why we adore big data. Big data enables organizations to comprehend the unmet needs and expectations of customers and achieve long-term commercial success. It is the solution to all of these problems. Truely, this technology is still undergoing development and refinement, but Artificial Intelligence (AI) plays a crucial role in its realization. They have a reciprocal interaction with one another. AI is required to give meaning to big data's information, while big data is required to increase AI's intelligence. Given the four properties of big data—volume, velocity, variety, and veracity—that can lead to more precise data analysis, the use of big data in digital marketing can have a significant influence.

Augmenting Customer Retention Through Big Data Analytics.
Reena Malik, Ambuj Sharma, and Prashant Chaudhary (Eds.)

This chapter's goal is to highlight the value of big data in the context of digital marketing in order to add to the body of literature. In order to achieve this goal, a thorough analysis of the literature that covers big data's definition, elements, sources, function in digital environments, and applications in business is conducted.

7.1 DIGITAL MARKETING

Digital marketing is an incarnation of marketing, which has a broad existence online. Digital marketing provides a platform to promote and advertise a product of their brand or business to gain more visibility and presence, which would lead to sales and revenue generation for the business and value creation and delivery for the customers. The term digital marketing is often used interchangeably with web-based (internet) marketing, online marketing, and internet marketing. Digital marketing can be seen as an umbrella where organizations endeavor online marketing to reach the maximum number of customers. These organizations or firms utilize digital channels available, especially on the internet, such as the Google browser, social media platforms, emails, display advertising, smart phones, and any other websites or digital avenues, to reach, build, and maintain a customer base by targeting relevant prospective customers. Presently, campaigns of digital marketing have appeared more prevalent and efficient as digital platforms are rapidly corroborating with marketing strategies. Digital marketing technologies equip the customers to be updated on the rational information of the companies (Gangeshwer, 2013). Companies update the regular and current pieces of information regarding goods and services. Due to advanced technology adoption by the customers, the company's website, analyzing products with its reviews, and making an online purchase have become affordable and easy for customers. Consumers get the required complete information about the companies owing to these technological platforms (Karp, 2014). Customers can compare the product with all the viable and possible options available on digital platforms. Digital marketing has made it possible for consumers to purchase the products 24/7, and the price is also transparent for them to see anywhere, anytime (Yulihasri, 2011).

7.2 VARIOUS FACETS OF DIGITAL MARKETING

Numerous facets jointly form digital marketing. Electronic devices are used to operate all the facets of digital marketing. The significant digital marketing forms are discussed below:

7.2.1 *ONLINE ADVERTISING*

It is regarded as a subsidiary form of advertising, which is done through the internet, mobile, laptop, and desktop. Over the past decade, technological advancement and internet reach have not only exponentially transformed and shaped the evolution of online advertising and generated several types of digital advertising but also new business models of advertising, market levels, and stakeholders. Internet-based advertising shows ads and content which complement consumer interests. Advertisers, share their services and product information on their websites, where users get to know the required dimensions free of charge.

7.2.2 *EMAIL MARKETING*

Email marketing is the act of reaching out to the customers by sending messages about a business's products and services via email. These emails can be targeted at both the current and the potential customers of the business. To operate this task, core digital marketing is used to send ads, construct consumers' faith, manufacture brand and consumer loyalty, and spread brand awareness. With the use of this facet of digital marketing, companies can recommend their services and products very quickly and at a low cost. The company tries to grab the maximum attention of the customers by bombarding the emails with attractive texts or using various graphics related to the product intended to be sold.

7.2.3 *SOCIAL MEDIA MARKETING (SMM)*

SMM has emerged as a hybrid promotion mix in digital marketing. On this platform, users create, interact, and exchange information, ideas, and photos about the company's products and services. Twitter, Facebook, and LinkedIn are the new components of social media marketing. Through Facebook, LinkedIn, Twitter, or any other social media platform, the company promotes its products and services to its users. On LinkedIn, different professionals make up their profiles and share information. The companies develop their profiles in a strategic and professional manner so as to project the desired image, disseminate, and gather more needful information regarding their products and services.

7.2.4 TEXT MESSAGING

The dissemination of information relating to a product/service by means of a cellphone or a smartphone is termed text messaging. By using these devices, companies move their product and service information in the form of text, audio, pictures, and video. In 2000, marketing via Short Message Service (SMS) emerged rapidly, becoming famous in European countries and a few countries in Asia. This marketing technique is used to confirm orders and send different kinds of alerts. Messages bring substantial and quick outputs for any campaign. Companies are quite confident in this technique about real-time reach and any-time reach, and customers would read messages. Through this technique, the company develops a questionnaire, proposes it, and obtains valuable feedback from customers, which is essential for the development of their products and services in the future as well.

7.2.5 AFFILIATE MARKETING

Affiliate marketing is an exercise where a digital mentor/publisher or website endorses other online retailers and makes a share on each sale or lead that the advertising produces for the same online retailer. This payment is known as Cost per Action. In this marketing, an action is an online sale of goods and services. However, it may have any lead or registration, a download, a phone call, or any other approachable action that meets the desire of the end customer. Affiliate marketing has four primary stakeholders: the merchant, the network, the consumer, and the publisher. If a company chooses to operate an affiliate program, then it needs to pay a referral fee to affiliates for each lead or sale they drive to the company's website. The intention of the company is to find affiliates who can enter the potentially available markets. In the past few years, this technique has grown much and also includes offline sales, provided it can be traced back with a barcode or coupon.

7.2.6 SEARCH ENGINE OPTIMIZATION (SEO)

Search engine optimization is another form of affiliate marketing technique, which is an alternative mode of endorsing the company. With the presence of SEO, the company is being placed among the first shown result pages. The next game-setter is the interface of the website, which enhances the chances of the users clicking on the URL. In SEO, different kinds of searches are included such as news searches, academic searches, image searches, video searches, and industrial-related searches. Pay-per-click is another subsidiary marketing technique of SEO. It is an active and current-trending platform for advertisers and searchers. This technique brings more savings to the company's ads since it works at a low cost and leads to broader engagement with services and products.

7.3 BIG DATA

Technological innovation progressions fundamentally affect advertising methods and practices. Technology aids by providing the opportunities wherein the business has access to gather highly relevant customer data, concentrate on building and developing the customer relationships, increase customer insight, and improve Customer Relationship Management (CRM). The availability of big data has equipped the conventional marketing tools and marketers to function in an evolved and highly strategized manner. For the exorbitant amount of data being produced and converted for each one of the customers and businesses in the world, one cannot let it be and later lose the opportunity of finding out a business opportunity based on that data.

This is a world driven by technology, and the fuel to that technology for business outcomes is data. The data being created every second needs to be kept safe so as to extract the needed information at the given point in time. Big data refers to the data that is hugely large, therefore BIG, Diverse (Variety), and rapidly Evolving (Velocity), making it challenging to manage with existing tools and techniques. It is a large and complex data set which may or may not be structured, and storing, analyzing, and drawing inferences from this integrated data structure may be difficult and complex. The pertained information derivation needs proper extraction and analysis. In the e-business today, there is a tremendous amount of information creation, exchange, and transfer every second; this is where the big data Analytics comes to the marketer's rescue. Online businesses are the prime adopters of the big data Analytics as they are intended to investigate the needs of the customers, their behavior, and customer relationship management including the opportunities and challenges. It is more of a need than a choice for the companies today.

7.4 BIG DATA ANALYTICS

The rate of emergence of technology and the data inflow have increased exponentially. To match the rate of this daily data inflow in the organizations, there is a dire need for an efficient and fast means of data analysis. The raw data lying with the organizations that has not been processed yields no benefit to the institution. The timely availability of the data and information is essential for any organization to compete. It has become challenging for the traditional data management systems and tools to function at the rate of efficiency required in today's scenario, and the infrastructure has become obsolete as well. This calls for the need for new and updated tools and methods that specialize not in data but in big data analytics, along with the required architecture needed for them to function, store, and manage it. The emergence of big data has changed the perspective and implications of everything related to data, from collection to processing to decision derivation.

7.4.1 IMPLICATIONS FOR THE MARKETERS AND DIGITAL MARKETERS

Big data analytics has huge implications for the marketers due to various reasons. The first and foremost is the crucial importance of the data that is being created every moment and stored. That data could be anything and everything, ranging from the name of the customer to the choice of the food he orders online, the medicines that he may be consuming to the car insurance that he has recently purchased, the transactions that he makes every day, and the products that he has searched for recently on the e-commerce websites. Nothing out of this data may be needed anytime any second by the business. It is not just about having the data with you all the time that gives you the edge but the inferences that the company may be able to draw after the analysis to gain the customer insight that helps the company to strengthen its marketing strategy.

It is an accepted fact that the business has only one constant and that is change. The change has just become more insightful, rapid, and unpredictably fast in the era of technological advancement. Technology has eased the process of progressive change but, ironically, made it more challenging as well. The speed and amount of information transfer are tremendously huge and exponential. What has meaning now may become meaningless or obsolete the next day as the reactions on the marketing campaigns are immediate and obvious on the e-business platforms. Therefore, the marketers have huge implications from the big data analysis in the digital marketing era.

7.4.2 SOCIAL MEDIA ANALYTICS

Social media is not just a tool for socializing anymore but has emerged as a tool that needs research on its own for the marketers. The exponential rate and amount of information generation and dissemination have left the marketers wondering how much to dig in the social media analytics. Investing time, effort, and cost in the SMA is a smart choice and the need of the hour for the marketers in the cutting-edge competition. Social media enables businesses to reach a huge audience for brand communication targeted toward their respective interests, but consumers dislike interruptions. This becomes particularly evident when a sales pitch is made to the customer; social media analytics saves the day for the businesses here!

Social media analytics helps businesses with the following dimensions:

- Understanding and identifying the trends related to offerings and brands
- Understand audience conversations
- Attract the customer toward their product and service offerings
- Enabling communication with the customers
- Monitoring the conversations on the digital platforms for their own brand
- Identify key value propositions for a product or service (your own and those of competitors as well)
- Competition monitoring and tracking all digital media conversations online

7.4.3 REAL-TIME CUSTOMER INSIGHTS

Social media analytics are now a part of the core board room discussions, providing input for strategy-making. The competition has become more of a "Digital Race" for the companies, and at the customer's end, it has become a "Transparent Glass". The lead in the competition is not from the one who has data but from the company which analyzes and processes the data in the real-time to draw inferences from it. The needed information at the needed time reflects the consumer insights required.

Real-time big data analysis is giving leverage to all the businesses, whether large or small, out of the huge volume of data more quickly than ever. The companies that are IT-based are on their tips to have real-time consumer insights all the time so as to enable rapid identification of the real-time issues and remediation of the issues for their customers without wasting any time. The real-time Customer Analytics also empowers the business to act instantly to meet the customer needs and, more importantly, to address the issues that are bothering them in real-time. Various tools may be used here to detect, store, and analyze the threats and investigated causes, determining the response to any such occurrences. The impact of real-time big data analytics is not confined to just monitoring and securing the IT infrastructure but goes beyond that. This technology is used to collect the data for all applications that are being used and assess the usability of that function in the cloud. Organizations further use this data to gain insights that may help them decide on the various facets of product development, leading to increased user engagement by focusing on the sought-after features and improvements in the real-time.

7.4.4 PERSONALIZED TARGETING: OPINION MINING AND SENTIMENTAL ANALYSIS

The reason behind it is simple. Understanding the pain points and desires of customers is primary to marketing and sales. With the use of the data gathered from the personal profiles of online shoppers and made actionable through the various online platforms, what used to take years of marketing study now takes days or even hours.

7.4.4.1 PRODUCT RECOMMENDATION

Marketers are able to discern customers' intentions and provide pertinent product recommendations by examining their purchasing behavior. One of the e-commerce corporations that has perfected this art is Amazon. To choose which things to propose, it takes into account past purchasing patterns, search patterns, and interests.

7.4.4.2 TARGETED EMAILS

Marketers may customize email marketing strategies by using big data. They can send the required email to the potential and targeted people at the appropriate times. This enables the marketers to work on a more personalized connection and communication with the users and intrigues the users to press the personalized communications to foster a more intimate connection with clients, which in turn motivates prospects to press the CTA buttons.

7.4.4.3 TARGETED ADVERTISEMENTS

Targeted ads can be made using all the gathered information, including web history. The user believes that he is the only one seeing the advertisement because he is already in the purchase cycle. These ads are highly productive in the advertising campaign.

7.5 ENHANCED PERSONALIZED CUSTOMER CARE AND CUSTOMER RELATIONSHIP MANAGEMENT

The companies often ignore the value of providing extensive customer support via big data analytics to enhance and foster brand loyalty. For the optimum utilization of big data features in customer care, companies need to focus on what is important. The dealing hand should have access to the needed customer information and purchase history of the customers, enabled with the advanced analytics capabilities that are readily used by sales, marketing, etc. The integration of various functions is very important. The representation of the analysis from big data is very crucial as the customer representative has very limited time to act upon the complaints or problems raised by the customers.

7.5.1 BUILD UP LOYALTY

In order to create a relationship with the customers, the business has to transition from nobody to somebody. To bridge the gap from nobody to somebody, one needs to learn about you and you need to learn about them. The customer loyalty works along the same lines. It is essential to have friendly relationships with your customers to inculcate loyalty and association with them. The new customers may mean that your business is growing, but the existing customers make your business keep going. Big data helps to build a very rich and appropriate profile to develop relationships with each of your customers. By offering personalized offerings based on the preferences based on color, size, taste, etc. can help grab attention and also trigger purchases from the customers.

Today, however, large amounts of information (utilizing it, not simply having it) have led to a utilitarian shift from assessed activities to information-driven, prescient decisions. The development of sentiment analysis as a tool for marketing advances a step further. This technology analyzes the emotional undertone of comments made about brands online. Your brand has a tonne of potential as big data and sentiment analysis join forces to create the marketing team of dreams.

7.5.2 MEASURING RESULTS

7.5.2.1 INCREASE IN THE SALES

Big data analysis enables businesses to significantly analyze their targets. They are able to deliver the appropriate offer to them at the appropriate moment by using information such as how frequently they purchase a specific product and their chosen method of payment. Sales have been shown to increase significantly with such accuracy.

7.5.2.2 PRODUCT DEMAND FORECASTING

Both offline and online business owners must make sure that they can meet the demands of their customers at all times. Regrettably, conventional techniques may fall short of what is needed and may not be able to meet those needs. Big data analysis is outstanding in its uses, especially when it comes to prescriptive and predictive analytics to precisely monitor the market and forecast demand. It would help precisely to decide on what needs to be produced, how to produce it, and when and where to distribute it, which can give businesses the needed boost in the era of competition.

7.5.2.3 PREDICTIVE ANALYTICS

Predictive analytics considers what might occur in the market in the future. Based on predictions, predictive analytics provides advice or recommendations. Both analytics work in tandem to reduce the likelihood of stock running out. They also increase production efficiency and reduce losses.

7.5.2.4 PRICE OPTIMIZATION

Knowing how to price the product is a big challenge for the marketers and businesses. The challenge can be addressed to a significant extent with the help of big data analytics. This helps in determining the appropriate price for the products, which may further depend upon many factors, such as:

- Price fluctuations due to seasonal variations (the product might be seasonal)

- Manufacturing cost
- Variable cost
- Competitor's price history

The use of analytics for the price optimization has the power to significantly add to the profits and the revenue of the business.

7.5.2.5 DECISION MAKING

Data science entails principles, processes, and techniques for comprehending phenomena through (automated) data analysis. For the purposes of this article, the ultimate goal of data science is to improve decision-making, which is of paramount importance in business. Analyzing and interpreting the patterns of the data analysis business can improve the decision-making prospects. Identifying the problems and addressing them with a data-backed approach certainly entails an advantage to the business as data enables tracking so as to know whether the solution is actually addressing the problem, improving the situation, or having no change at all.

7.6 CONCLUSIONS

There is always more than one outcome depicted by the data. From identifying the purchase patterns to preferences, every move of the customer can be tracked and analyzed using big data analytics by the marketers. The past data analysis may forecast the future demand and supply in an accurate manner for the firms. The predictive analysis of how the customer may buy or may recommend buying on his social networking circle is a crucial input for the firms. Since the information revolution has transformed the way in which the marketing and businesses operate, their adoption has become more of a necessity for the altered way in which businesses operate. It is beyond doubt that big data is assisting firms in gaining a competitive advantage. These techniques have equipped businesses to gain insights, track patterns, develop or identify correlations, and form associations that would not be possible with conventional and small data. These help businesses and marketers make decisions by using social media data and social media analytics, cost and time reduction strategies, supply chain analytics, web analytics, and so on. Firms that recognize the importance of big data and develop products around it have reaped huge dividends in recent years. Many businesses use analytics in almost every aspect of their operations to reap the benefits of analytics-based decision-making.

KEYWORDS

- **digital marketing**
- **search engine optimization**
- **social media analytics**
- **analytics**
- **big data**
- **opinion mining**
- **sentimental analysis**

REFERENCES

Gangeshwer, D. K. E-Commerce or Internet Marketing: A Business Review from Indian Context. *Int. J. u- e- Serv. Sci. Technol.* **2013,** *6* (6), 187–194. https://doi.org/10.14257/ijunesst.2013.6.6.17

Karp, G. Personal Finance Writer for the Morning Call. *Chickago Tribune* **2014,** *12* (2), 24.

Karp, G. Marketing and Communication and Level (2 edn.) **2014,** *3* (1),128–139.

Eri, Y.; Aminul Islam, M.; Ku Daud, K. A. Factors That Influence Customers' Buying Intention on Shopping Online. *Int. J. Market. Stud. 2011, 3* (1) https://doi.org/10.5539/ijms.v3n1p128

CHAPTER 8

Big Data and Customer Retention with Real-life Examples of Companies

RAJNEESH AHLAWAT, RENU TANWAR, and PREETI AHLAWAT

Department of Business Administration, Chaudhary Devi Lal University, Sirsa, Haryana, India

ABSTRACT

The examination of customer service using big data is a novel method. It seamlessly derives important results from a massive hill of irrelevant information, helping companies increase consumer satisfaction and retention rates. Big data is used in revenue forecasts which identifies customer–buying behavior and trends.The forecast helps to project the market trend and pattern. Utilizing promotions and other actions to raise the likelihood that a client would purchase your products or services again is known as customerretention. Approximately a 25% rise in earnings is produced with just a 5% improvement in client retention. Big data analysis determines the individual's prejudices of prior customers based on all their actions. Big data is an innovative technology. It is not only about technical prowess and artistic flair but also about utilizing technology to facilitate people's fulfillment of their aspirations. By employing big data analytics, firms should be able to effectively explore new trends, connect to buyers in unique and unexpected ways, and, most significantly, use several diversified choices to enhance customer interaction in this hypercompetitive period. This study describes the numerous ways in which big data is meant to improve customer retention. So, this chapter examines how successful big data is for customer retention inbusiness.

Augmenting Customer Retention Through Big Data Analytics.
Reena Malik, Ambuj Sharma, and Prashant Chaudhary (Eds.)

8.1 INTRODUCTION

For any business nowadays, data is the most precious asset! When companies analyze a lot of data and base their decisions on that analysis, they may operate considerably more effectively. So, the modern route to financial success is big data analytics. Big data analytics, which is significantly more objective than conventional methods, will help businesses leverage insights from data to make the most appropriate management decisions. Previously, companies could only communicate with clients one-on-one in person while they were shopping (geeksforgeeks, 2020). On a broad scale, it was also impossible to determine what each particular buyer desired. However, the advent of big data analytics has wholly altered this. Businesses may now interact with every client individually and directly online to understand their needs. Here are some ways businesses may utilize big data analytics to enhance performance over time and become even more prosperous (and successful).

8.2 BUSINESS USAGE OF BIG DATA ANALYTICS TO BOOST CUSTOMER RETENTION

Without clients, a business cannot exist. Therefore, a company must not only draw in consumers but also retain them. Big data analytics can undoubtedly be helpful here. Big data analytics enables a business to identify consumer patterns and promote their products with a focus on those clients. Additionally, the more information a business has about its clientele, the better it will be able to identify consumer trends and behaviors, enabling it to give precisely what its clients need. And doing this is the greatest way to keep customers around longer. After all, satisfied clients are repeated ones. Amazon is a great illustration of a company utilizing big data analytics to increase client retention. Amazon collects as much data on its users as it can including their names, locations, browsing history, billing information, etc. to provide a completely customized experience. This means that Amazon will identify you as soon as you log in! It also provides product recommendations based on your prior purchases to boost the probability that you will make purchases. You are also less likely to stop using Amazon if you do some transactions there!

8.2.1 FIRMS CONSTRUCT ADVERTISING STRATEGIES USING BIG DATA ANALYTICS

How can a business attract new clients? Marketing campaigns, however, just as a successful marketing campaign may bring in new clients for a business;

an unsuccessful one might cause that business to lose even its present clientele. Big data analytics are needed to evaluate the clientele and comprehend what people want for the marketing approach to be successful in getting more consumers. This may be done by staying up to date on the freshest digital movements, studying buyer behavior in the industry, and then using it to create a successful marketing plan. Netflix is one business that uses big data analytics to develop marketing campaigns. Did you ever see how instantly you get listings of films and television series that are tailored specifically for you when you start the Netflix application? This is done by accumulating data from user browsing history and watching interests, after which they serve pertinent advertisements. This means that if you have lately enjoyed mystery films, they will also be suggested to you in the future.

8.3 ALL ABOUT BIG DATA

Extensive, mixed collections of knowledge that are frequently extending are referred to as "big data".The volume of data, the velocity or speed with which it is collected and acquired, and the variety or breadth of the pieces of data addressed are the "three V's" of big data. Big data is typically the outcome ofdata mining and comes in many ways (Troy Segal, 2022).

8.3.1 BIG DATA FEATURES

- Big data is a colossal collection of knowledge produced at an accelerating rate and in pace with the fast numbers.
- Big data (usually quantifiable, conveniently handled, and preserved) can be organized or unorganized.
- Big data analysis results may be used by almost all corporate departments, but managing the complexity and volume it generates can be challenging.
- Survey questions, online orders, digital payment, freely provided information from personal devices and applications, along with publicly available comments on websites and social media sites can all be used to gather big data.
- Software made to manage huge, complicated datasets is frequently used to analyze and store big data and is typically saved in computer databases.

8.3.2 BIG DATA CATEGORIES

Three types of big data exist:

i. **Structured:** Data is said to be structured if it can be saved, retrieved, and processed using a preset format.

ii. **Unstructured data:** Unstructured data are any information that have an arbitrary shape or arrangement. Unstructured data presents other difficulties when processing it to derive value in addition to its substantial volume.

iii. **Semi-structured:** This category of data includes both types of information. The definition of semi-structured data is different from the definition of a table in a relational database management system, even though it appears to be structured. A good illustration of semi-structured data is an extensible markup language (XML) file.

8.3.3 THE APPLICATIONS OF BIG DATA

Data scientists look at how different forms of data, such as census characteristics and shopping habits, are interrelated to each other to discover whether there is any link. Such studies can be done either within the organization or by a third person with expertise in converting huge data into forms that are simple to consume. Businesses usually rely on the opinions of such specialists to translate large data into informative information. Big data is used by several companies, notably Alphabet and Meta (formerly Facebook Company), to target their customers. To profit from advertising, advertisements are shown to social media users and Internet users. Results from data analysis can be applied in almost every department within a business, from marketing and sales to human resources and technology. Big data aims to target audiences, shorten the time and costs needed to gain market adoption, accelerate the release of products to market, and guarantee customer satisfaction.

8.4 REAL-LIFE EXAMPLES OF COMPANIES USING BIG DATA

8.4.1 AMAZON

Amazon is one prominent Internet merchant. They record all data points relating to every individual user to monitor how they spend their money on a certain item. This entire information has been acquired to feed marketing on social media programs, which can subsequently be utilized to enhance customer experiences, propose goods, and develop customer connections. For example, when you add something to your shopping cart/ basket, it proposes other goods you might like or offers regarding things that you may buy together with that item. In this manner, Amazon makes use of big data to enhance customer shopping experiences by facilitating quick purchases.

8.4.2 APPLE

We are all aware of Apple's proficiency with cutting-edge technology. They are doing big data analyticsas a result, such as how many business choices are being influenced by innovation, etc., and employing big data technologies. The information obtained by the firm is used to determine how to approach consumers with fresh offerings and services. Apple may modify future projects to better fit consumer trends by studying large datasets to see how people use applications in practice.

Apple's two main applications for big data are as follows:

- Application architecture.
- The monitoring and improvement of people's lifestyle.

For instance, the Apple w which can collect data in addition to being wearable. Apple watches may analyze what wearers do every day.

As a result, Apple intends to capitalize just on wearable technology's big data potential.

8.4.3 GOOGLE

Based on a range of variables, such as online activity, locations, movements, and a plethora of other aspects, Google examines big data to figure out what we require from it. Google then shows the sorted or positioned index listings that are meant to satisfy the user's needs in terms of relevance and authority aftera complicated estimate method. When a user types a query, Google immediately displays the top-ranked search results that are relevant and authoritative. To better understand customer demands, Google has built several tools, Google Translate, indexed websites, real-time feeds, sorting tools, basic and semantic search, etc.

8.4.4 SPOTIFY

Big data is something that Spotify application genuinely values. They apply a lot of creative computer technology tochange the way we listen to music and like it.

- This firm has a huge amount of customers and is fully data driven.
- They use component details such as when the music was played, where it was played, what device it was played on, and when it was played.
- All of this data gives the music technology industry great insight into how it affects the listeningexperience.
- In short, Spotify application uses big data to digitize user tastes, develop personalized content, and improve marketing strategies including packaging for Spotify application and customized advertisement.

8.4.5 FACEBOOK

Facebook tends to notify us all about upcoming birthdays, and companionship anniversaries, but do you know how Facebook does it?

This work is done by big data that Facebook uses to improve the user experience (UX).

- Facebook made a little remembrance clip from your old images employing big data.
- Data has a crucial function to play in Facebook as they create feedback based on the data they collect.
- Facebook has embraced many big analytics techniques, including face recognition. It is a technique that tells the device how to just point a picture or video at another image to view details in that other image.
- As a result, any time you log in, Facebook assesses every unique piece of data and provides an evenbetter UX.
- Facebook introduced a rainbow filter in 2015, when the US Supreme Court allowed same-sex marriages. This filter lets others know you favor gay marriage.

8.4.6 INSTAGRAM

By collecting and analyzing the generated customer feedback, Instagram ensures that it makes the most ofthe enormous data it collects.

- Every time we scroll through the feed on Instagram, the same kind of stuff appears on our Instagram feed. This Instagram uses a lot of data that collects information about us and gives us recommendations based on it.
- One of the well-established businesses that make excellent use of big data and artificial intelligence (AI) is Instagram.

8.4.7 STARBUCKS

Internationally, Starbucks is recognized as selling the greatest coffee. Managing so much data is not feasible for one customer Therefore, next is the function of large data. When a customer uses a mobile application or orders something, big data gathers all the information about the customer. Recommended items are displayed based on the collected data. The business also use big data to alter menus following consumer tastes. Additionally, they choose sites for new stores, make future menu changes, anddevelop more pertinent promotional campaigns and promotions.

8.4.8 NETFLIX

Netflix have a large number of customers and managing all of the data is tough. As a consequence, big data aids in gathering all customer details and generating cinema recommendations from previous searches. According to Netflix, personalized proposals account for the bulk of a viewer's activity.

Netflix too collects a variety of data to construct an accurate profile of its consumers. As an illustration, Netflix captures the sequences that users have regularly or most often seen to learn about theirpreferences. They also make decisions about whether or not to approve original material using big data and analytics techniques. In a nutshell, Netflix's popularity may be attributed to its ability to collect and interpret data.

8.4.9 MCDONALD'S

The world-famous fast food chain McDonald's has used modern technology in several ways, including ofthe use ofbig data and AI. McDonald's has become a more information-driven company.To enhance customer engagement, they employ big data. To get suggestions on offers and discounts in the future, people who use your smartphone application, or place an order, preserve their information. In addition, it gathers information on sales point traffic, customer interactions, order models, video, and sensor data. They may even learn that consumers are more inclined to go if they observe traffic, which will enable them to plan and increase demand efficiency. They can utilize these insights to create additional menu modifications by continuously monitoring and analyzing the client's behavior.

8.4.10 NEW YORK STOCK EXCHANGE

One terabyte of data is gathered daily by the New York Stock Exchange. There were two points five network connections for each individual globally in 2016, or an estimated 18 point 9 billion connections. By focusing effectively and swiftly on concluding agreements, financial institutions may set themselves apart from their competitors.

8.5 DATA AS A TOOL TO INCREASE CUSTOMER SUCCESS

When we talk about "big data," we are talking about the immense amount of information generated by businesses, governments, organizations, or even individual people. Such precious data consists of machine time, click streams from websites used in web analytics to measure user activity, and client interactions with a firm over the telephone, via mail, or on social networking sites. It is focused on how you use it to generate business value and insight. To make better decisions about product development and design, pricing, and distribution strategies, businesses can use big data analytics to understand their customers by examining data from various sources over time. For your customer success strategy, having more data is better. Big data helps businesses step up their game in many areas, such as increasing customer acquisition and retention rates and marketing strategy effectiveness. The advantages of using big data are as discussed in the following.

8.5.1 FUTURE-LOOKING STATISTICS AND MARKET KNOWLEDGE

Big data helps firms comprehend their customers well. They make decisions regarding which goods to sell, how and when they should promote them, and what pricing is fair for a particular service or product at any given moment.

They make marketing decisions based on historical sales data to support sales-generating campaigns and raise average customer value. Additionally, thanks to open-source and for-profit solutions, their services are now easily accessible on the cloud and internally. Big data analytics can also assist customer success teams in identifying which clients are most likely to leave. These teams can go through the data to find a correlation between individuals who have left and those whose accounts fit certain requirements, such as being inactive on the latest updates for a prolonged period.

8.5.2 MARKETING CAMPAIGNS WITH A PERSONAL TOUCH

Customers prefer to be marketed specifically based on their needs and are no longer interested in generic marketing campaigns. Big data can assist businesses in customizing a message for each customer by examining their online behaviors, such as social media use and web browsing history.

Additionally, it enables targeted marketing campaigns where businesses can send marketing emails or social media posts based on the interests of particular customers. For instance, if a business wants to advertise its new mesh running shoes, it may want to reach out to runners who have recently looked at online posts about footwear. Given that customers receive customized messages based on their interests, this type of messaging is more likely to result in a positive purchasing experience.

8.5.3 MONITORING OF SOCIAL MEDIA

Social media platforms such as Instagram, Twitter, and Facebook may assist you in understanding your clients' demands instantaneously while they are "talking" about you online. Even better, you could see a service or delivery problem before they do, saving the business from losing customers entirely.

8.5.4 OPTIMIZING PAID CAMPAIGNS

Big data can be utilized by businesses to manage paid campaigns. For instance, they can set up alerts in Google Analytics to notify them if a customer has not logged in to their account for 3 months or longer. It enables companies to actively get communicated with clients who are no longer interested in the product or who have stopped using it for a certain amount of time to provide pertinent support and possibly enticethem back to it. All parties benefit when businesses use this kind of proactive outreach to retain morecustomers.

8.5.5 LOYALTY PROGRAM DEVELOPMENT

Customer spending and customer retention can increase with the use of loyalty programs. Big data enables businesses to create better offers that encourage customers to choose them over rivals by assisting them in understanding their customers' purchasing patterns, average order values, and frequency. Customer success includes both acquiring new customers and keeping your current ones satisfied. Big data can help businesses better understand their current and potential customer bases so they can be at the top of customers' minds when it is time to make a purchase decision.

8.6 BIG DATA CASE STUDY

The engaging big data case studies are discussed in the following.

8.6.1 WALMART

Walmart seems to be the world's leading retailer and the greatest enterprise by turnover, with overtwo million workers and 20,000 stores across 28 countries. It started using big data analytics even before the phrase "big data" ever entered the lexicon. Walmart employs data mining to uncover trends that may be utilized to offer item suggestions to the customer based on which goods were bundled. Walmart's customer conversion rate has grown because of the use of sophisticated data mining algorithms. Big data analysis has advanced rapidly to produce best-in-class e-commerce technology to provide an improved consumer experience. The entire aim of Walmart's big data storage is just to improve the browsing customer experiences who visit a retail store.

8.6.2 A CASE STUDY IN BIG DATA: UBER

Uber taxi is the most popular choice among individuals across the world when it comes to transferring people and having deliveries. The user's private information is used carefully track what service elements are the most commonly utilized, to examine consumption patterns, and also to determine where offerings should be prioritized. Uber bases its pricing on market forces, which causes the cost of the services that it provides to fluctuate. As a result, dynamic pricing is one of Uber's key data usages. For example, if you require a taxi in a congested zone yet are late for a scheduled appointment, expect to spend twice the same or more. On New Year's Eve, for instance, the expense on 1 km of transportation may rise from US$200 to 1000. Quick high inflation influences demand rates, however, long-term demand may affect whether or not consumers are kept. Techniques for machine learning are used when there is a huge requirement.

8.6.3 NETFLIX: A BIG DATA CASE STUDY

The most well-liked entertainment business in America focuses on providing customers with online, on-demand streaming video. It has been confirmed that big data enables Netflix to forecast with accuracy the type of content that will peak consumers' interest. Therefore, big data analytics fires its "recommendationengine" developed to accomplish this task. Netflix has just recently begun to promote itself as a content creator instead of as a distribution channel. This strategy has been strongly influenced by data, as should be expected. Data points such as what movie users watch, how often playback is paused, how many stars they give, etc. The company's data framework comprises Hadoop, Hive, and Pig, in contrast to numerous typesof traditional business intelligence. Netflix highlights how easy it can be for enterprises to grasp specifically what its customers want if they discard conventional conceptions and make decisions based on big data.

8.6.4 STUDY OF BIG DATA IN E-COMMERCE

Being a data-intensive firm, eBay faces a substantial technological barrier in using a system that can swiftly evaluate and react to input when it is received (streaming data). There are several quickly growing supporting mechanisms for streaming data analysis. E-Bay use several technologies, including Kafka, Storm, and Apache Spark. It empowers the corporation's data analysts to search for information tags associated with the data (information) and make it accessible to as many individuals as feasible with the necessary level of protection and rights (data governance). The company pioneers the application of big data solutions and actively contributes to the inclusive community by sharing its expertise.

8.7 CUSTOMER RETENTION

The strategies and actions a company does to try to retain its present patrons are considered customer retention. Analytics for customer maintenance give businesses a head start by identifying the activitiesthat customers are most likely to abandon. A data-driven customer preservation strategy, when implemented properly, can result in noteworthy advantages. It has been demonstrated that doing so increases revenue. According to a McKinsey analysis (McKinsey, 2014), firms that use buyer data analytics to inform every company decision saw a 126% increase in profits. Even though big data is a subject that organizations regularly discuss, it does not appear that they are utilizing it to its true ability for repeat purchase statistics. It is intriguing to notice that just 32% of poll respondents whose companies claim to utilize analytics to obtain a competitive edge are happy with this technique. In light of this, there are numerous development opportunities. Machine learning utilized by 38% of companies, is one of the least frequent programs in customer programs. Three critical data science skills—encoding, math, and statistics—are reportedly unavailable to client service representatives or not at all available. According to experts in customer service, their biggest problem is their inability to incorporate customer insights into business operations.

8.7.1 MAKING CONTACT

Big data and predictive analytics will enable professionals to identify customers who are encountering difficulties with such a good or service. As a result, companies may benefit from this essential data and develop good relationship with customers. How? By contacting a client who is having an issue before the user decides to contact us. Customer retention will undoubtedly undergo a revolution thanks to this seemingly telepathic ability to solve problems. Since the customer support representative will be fully aware of the issue before speaking with the customer, this has many advantages for a company. This suggests that before being called, the client will have had some time to consider their options and come up with a solution. Customers would not feel the feared aggravation they all feel at what time they know they will have to squander time phone the buyer support number thanks to this as well. Businesses will be able to tackle problems more proactively than ever before—thanks to big data technology and predictive analytics, which will reassure consumers that they appreciate and care about them and that they are capable of dealing withany challenges that may arise.

8.7.2 CUT PRODUCT FRENZY

There are dozens of distinct cleansers, which all promise beautiful hair, a lot of creams that all pretend to be chemical free, and so on. In a society with so many alternatives and so much product saturation, how may big data be useful? Companies may profit from adopting it to halt the growth of ludicrous products. How? Since businesses will be able to look back and determine what customers truly value, and discover what items were picked as the greatest by customers. Corporations that understand how to set priorities while meeting consumer requirements will see an improvement in retaining customers. Corporations that understand how to set priorities while addressing consumer needs will see an increase in client retention.

Businesses may be able to successfully begin determining client interests by analyzing massive datasets such as capital employed and user actions. As a consequence, businesses will be capable enough to increase the value of their offer. Businesses thrive when organizations commit the time and effort to analyze customer data to make decisions that allow firms to provide the items that consumers desire.

8.7.3 USING UP-TO-DATE DATA

Companies can interact with clientele and comprehend their opinion in a concurrent time thanks to the unstoppable power of big data. Real-time data on the products and topics that customers are most likely topurchase, discuss, and click on online. Big data enables concrete access. Businesses can now create personalized landing pages, advertisements, and mobile apps thanks to the advantages of big data,enabling them to keep in constant communication with their customers. Real-time data will allow customer retention firms to stay in touch with existing clientele, transforming how marketers communicate with their intended audience.

8.7.4 FORECAST THAT MIGHT MATERIALIZE

Customers may get the finest solution by using big data's strong capacity to understand their demands. Consider how a manufacturer could use help desk notes, customer details, behavioral information, and tendencies to choose which item to deliver to a new purchase. Firms can use precise information to connect customers with products, providing them the certainty that they are always being cared for. When it comes to new clients and tailored services, big data will be increasingly advantageous for businesses in the era of innovative innovation and digital transition.

8.7.5 CUSTOMIZATION

Everybody desires to feel significant. Each client desires to be catered to in some way. Because of this, if businesses do not change their offer, customers will make the quick decision to quit and patronize a company that is prepared to go beyond their expectations. Businesses may access specific data, such as social data, gender, or geographic data, with the use of big data. According to this, it might allow marketing specialists to send offers that are tailored to customers' requirements and expectations.

8.7.6 SHORT AND SWEET

Creative technology is all about using technology to assist people in achieving their goals. Ther is more to it than just technical prowess and aesthetic aspirations. With the help of big data analytics, enterprises would be able to recognize the latest advancements, learn about their clients in fresh and unexpectedways, and—most importantly—adopt various strategies to increase customer loyalty in this extremelycompetitive age. Big data and customer retention will converge in the next decades and become crucial business concepts, acting as the difference that might allow corporations to outperform their opponents.

8.7.7 CUSTOMER RETENTION RATE

Keeping the customers as repeat customers is referred to as the definition of customer retention. Theretention rate indicates whether a company's products and services can meet the needs of its present customers. This strategy is essential to the sustainability of organizations and service suppliers with membership business models. Businesses may gauge client retention using the information from the studyof customer success and experience elements. For example, the business might look at a report that showsa reduction in client retention to find out why. This method's superior cost-effectiveness over customer acquisition is one of its most important characteristics. A company's existing customers account for 65% of its revenue, according to SmallBizGenius. Additionally, if a company can increase customer retention by just 5%, it can increase its bottom line by 25–95%.

8.8 CUSTOMER RETENTION STRATEGIES

The following tactics can be used by businesses to improve customer retention:

8.8.1 FOSTER CUSTOMER LOYALTY THROUGH SHARED VALUES

Businesses must strive to share their values with their customers in addition to having easily recognizable ones. Customers' relationships with businesses can improve if they can identify with the company'svalues.

8.8.2 SECOND, REFUNDS, AND RETURNS MUST BE SIMPLE

Errors happen when people buy things, whether they do so online or off. To maintain long-term customer relationships, businesses must make returns and refunds simple. Note that customers seldom use a company's goods or services if they do not accept returns or refunds.

8.8.3 BECOME IRREPLACEABLE IN THE EYES OF YOUR CLIENTS

Companies must make an effort to offer distinctive products. An organization can stand out from its competitors by selling valuable goods that nobody else provides. As a result, customers continue doing business with the company because they are unable to find an alternative. Through exceptional customer service, a company can also stand out from the competition. When clients are aware that they would not find acomparable experience at any other businesses, retaining clients is more accessible.

8.8.4 TAKE THE VALUE PROPOSITION INTO ACCOUNT

Nearly equal weight is given to actual and perceived values. For instance, a product's perceived value is increased by adopting green practices, even though its actual value is unaffected. The value proposition of a business must explain its raison d'être.

8.8.5 TALK TO CUSTOMERS AND REQUEST FEEDBACK

Businesses would not connect with their customers if they do not communicate with them. The organization would not be able to establish a long-lasting relationship as a result. In addition to communication, getting customer feedback is essential for retaining customers. Customer feedback achieves two goals such as it shows customers that the company values their opinions and it gives organizations knowledge of what clients are thinking and experiencing. Businesses may examine their goods or services and make the required improvements using the data acquired from client feedback.

8.8.6 MONITOR AND EXAMINE CHURN METRICS

Software for managing customer relationships can help you learn why and how frequently customers decide not to make purchases from your business because you are unable to solve issues that you do not comprehend.

8.8.7 YOU SHOULD POLISH YOUR USER EXPERIENCE (UX)

In the customer lifecycle, identify and remove any impediments. Make it quick and straightforward for online consumers to locate the products or services they need and finish the checkout process. Invest in improving your customer service skills so that each client receives a prompt response and feels heard. Giving customers self-service options, such as FAQs, is also recommended so they can quickly find answers to simpler questions.

8.8.8 *MAKE YOUR COMMUNICATIONS MORE SPECIFIC*

Create marketing campaigns that are tailored to particular customer segments and interact with them through the platforms they prefer, whether that is social media, email, or live chat.

8.9 FORMULA OF CUSTOMER RETENTION RATE

Your increasing customer retention rate is an easy-to-calculate essential performance metric for your business. The percentage of existing customers that stayed loyal to your brand over a specific time frame is referred to as your customer retention rate. Three factors need to be understood:

- How many customers did you have when you first started (S)?
- The quantity of customers you had at the end (E).
- The total number of new clients you brought on board throughout the same time frame (N).

Apply the following calculation for customer retention now: Divide the result by the starting value (S) after deducting the value of any new clients (N). Once you have a percentage, multiply it by 100.

This is how that formula appears: $[(E - N) \times S] \times 100 = X\%$.

Say, for illustration, that you are interested in learning your customer retention rate for the most recent three months. If you had 1000 consumers at the beginning of the quarter (S), 900 at the end (E), and 200 new customers over the same timeframe, the computation would be as follows (N).

The formula for 70% is $[(900 - 200) \times 1000] \times 100$. That means that during the last three months, you successfully retained 70% of your present clientele. The opposite of that statistic is your customer churn rate, which means that 30% of your current customers have quit doing business with you. As you put tactics to improve customer loyalty into practice, your customer retention rate is a critical sign of theefficacy of your efforts. The goal is to raise your customer retention rate and boost customer lifetime value (CLV), or the projected income you will collect from each client over the term of your partnership.

Example

To better grasp the idea, let us take an example of customer retention.

Let us say Company XYZ has 40,000 clients at the start of a 1-year calculation period. The company had30,000 customers after that period. 2000 new customers were added by Company XYZ during that time.

With the help of the aforementioned formula, we can calculate the rate of customer retention for the company.

Customer retention is equal to (30,000 – 2000)/40,000 multiplied by 100, that is, 70%.

8.10 CUSTOMER RETENTION ANALYTICS

The indicators you monitor to ensure you're doing all possible to retain clients are known as analytics for customer retention. These indicators provide you the ability to evaluate your customers' levels of happiness and whether they are exhibiting brand loyalty. By contrasting empirical data, you may leverage acute insights into customer retention to develop the optimal customer retention plan. If, like most firms, 80% of your revenue comes from just 20% of your current customers, you may use analytics to keep them from leaving. You can predict customer behavior by using machine learning on your customer retention data. Data like demographics and purchase history will be used in customer retention analytics to make inferences and correlations.

8.10.1 FIVE DIFFERENT KINDS OF ANALYTICS ON CUSTOMER RETENTION

Here is a brief overview of five popular types of retention analytics in case you're curious to learn more.

- ***Prescriptive Analytics***

  This improves decision making by assisting in the focus on a specific question, providing options for how to seize an opportunity in the future, or highlighting the effects of each choice. Prescriptive analytics examples for customer retention include following the best action and following the best offer analysis.

- ***Prognostic analytics***

  The most popular approach is this one. To predict what might occur in a specific future situation, predictive analytics uses models. This could be an analysis of the risk of churn and renewal, as well as the next best offers.

- ***Analysis that is descriptive***

  Even though it takes a lot of time and does not always produce the best results, it can help identify trends among a particular customer base. Using this method will give you an understanding of what has previously occurred and patterns and trends that will help you look more closely at the specifics. Some examples of descriptive analytics include the use of statistical measures, clustering, and association rules in market basket analyses.

- ***Analytics for diagnostics***

  This method is frequently employed when attempting to determine the cause of an event. Examples include examining customer usage patterns and churn indicators. Diagnostic analytics include, for instance, analyses of churn factors and customer health scores. It focuses on causal relationships and cycles and mostly looks at previous occurrences.

- ***Analytics of outcomes***

  Outcome analytics also referred to as consumption analytics, provides information on consumer behavior that influences particular outcomes. Consumption patterns and related business outcomes are the main focus of this strategy. Utilize it to better comprehend your clientele and discover how they utilize your services and products.

8.11 CUSTOMER CHURN RATE

The percentage of a company's contractual customers who stop renewing their subscriptions over a predetermined period is measured by the customer churn rate, also known as the customer attrition rate. One crucial business metric for businesses offering certain services (like SaaS businesses) or those using a subscription-based business model is the customer churn rate. The terms "voluntary churn" and "Involuntary churn" refer to the two different ways that customers can leave a company. The percentageof customers who terminate their subscriptions voluntarily (e.g., unhappiness with the company's services). The percentage of consumers that discontinue their subscriptions as a consequence of unavoidable circumstances is known as the involuntary churn rate, and it is the exact opposite (e.g., relocation). Typically, businesses are primarily concerned about voluntary churn that is closely tied to their primary business lines of operation.

8.11.1 METHODS TO REDUCE CHURN USING DATA

8.11.1.1 CREATE A DATA ROADMAP AND FOLLOW IT

Up to 30% of the CEOs in the aforementioned Bain and Co research indicated they had a clear plan for integrating data and analytics into their companies. As per McKinsey's findings, employing an effective system is, perceiving statistics as a strategic driver of development rather than deploying it singularly or only as an aspect of IT—leads to the achievement of the anticipated goal (McKinsey, 2014). The first thing that successful businesses do differently is use the data that they already have. As soon as they comprehend what the data are telling them, they move on to phase two: implementing organizational changes. You now have the data, so make sure to use it and quickly implement any business changes that are required.

Creating a data roadmap and following it religiously is a good strategy. You could take the following actions within the company:

- Automated, repeatable, and scalable corporate key performance indicators (KPIs) are a must.
- Decide on the top three business issues you want to solve and gather important stakeholders.
- Sort the concerns according to whether they are data-related or systemic.

8.11.1.2 CONCENTRATE SOLELY ON LEADS OF HIGH CALIBER

If your customers are similar to your primary target market, they are less likely to leave. If you have access to data on both your current customers and a list of future customers, this is a great opportunity to focus just on individuals who are less likely to go elsewhere. How? By using algorithms to compare the traits and qualities of your current customers to those of your prospective clients. The people who aremost likely to want your product, find it valuable, and stay with you are probably those who share characteristics with your current customers (FTE size, annual spending, job title, type of industry, etc.). Your segmentation is now very important. You can easily identify your next customers thanks to the unique features that each customer segment gives you. For instance, HubSpot's tools offer this type of information in an integrated manner so that you can quickly identify trends and patterns.

8.11.1.3 UTILIZE MACHINE LEARNING STRATEGIES TO CREATE PREDICTION MODELS

Organizations employ a range of analytics, namely advanced analytics that looks at the connections between different variables, to evaluate data. We may utilize predictive analytics to generate future predictions by examining previous data to ascertain what prospective customers might even like or hate. This will help us design successful customer retention methods. Managing and analyzing so manyvariables at once can frequently feel overwhelming. Even if you have a highly qualified data analyst in hand, finding the best predictive model requires a lot of manual labor and time due to the sheer amount of data. Utilize machine learning to quickly and accurately identify the underlying causes of customer churn or brand loyalty to develop the best predictive models of retention. Finding connections between variables that help to optimize crucial outcomes such as retention requires the use of math, statistics, and probability in machine learning. To make predictions, these models are then used with fresh customer data. The algorithms used in machine learning are iterative and continuously improved. They improve as they process more data. Thanks to modern processing power, which can deliver insights more quickly than humans can. For example, analytics may assist you in choosing which upsell or cross-sell goods will be the most pertinent depending on your customers' purchase histories or browsing behavior. Employees with advanced analytics (data science) skills are frequently lacking in companies. The automated integration and analysis of data can be done by third-party providers.

8.11.1.4 YOU CAN ACQUIRE DATA-DRIVEN INSIGHTS VIA TEXT ANALYTICS

If you want smart, information findings, do not miss out on examining the free-text replies to your open-ended survey questions. They might pass you by if you don't! Text analytics software can help you with this. Finding customer pain points is simple with a text analytics tool that employs sentiment analysis. And if you gather a lot of data, make sure to put it to use. Only 15% of senior leaders consistently use customer data to guide business decisions, according to a study (Harvard Business Review). Thematic has created an AI algorithm that automates the analysis of free-text responses to surveys using machine learning and natural language processing. This algorithm has essentially streamlined the method by which firms obtain knowledge through consumer data.

8.11.1.5 FOCUS ON RETAINING THE PROPER CLIENTELE

You may examine how each division responds to your brand and goods by utilizing data analytics to divide the population into different categories. This allows you to study each segment separately and gain insights, after which you can implement new communication and customer care techniques to increase customer loyalty for your most esteemed customers. Analyze information about your customers' demographics, way of life, the products they buy, and how often they buy them, as well as their value andtype of purchase. This will help you identify the customers who generate the most revenue. This will assist you in determining which clients earn the most money. You will know where you intend to focus yourefforts. Some because it costs too much to create money. Sometimes, especially when a business is just getting started, knowing the differences between these types of customers can make or break it. Making important decisions requires having a solid understanding of customer value. You can group customers based on their average lifetime value, historical value, value over the past year, or lifetime value overall. You can then create incredibly targeted product recommendation offers by using the appropriate segmentation. To offer pertinent discounts for various channels (in-store, online, and mobile), segment your customer base. Do not make the same offer to everyone; instead, vary it a little. Monitoring your promotional codes' seasonality and time sensitivity is another smart way to use segmentation. You can check sales data to see if these codes are used more frequently in the mornings, afternoons, or possibly right after a sales communication. You can concentrate on taking the appropriate actions the more you understand how a particular demographic responds.

8.12 CONCLUSION

Businesses can use big data to make informed decisions and better understand their customers' needs.This analysis helps businesses grow quickly by looking at real-time data. It helps businesses to outperform their competition and thrive. Big data technologies assist us in identifying organizational inefficiencies and commercial potential. Big data analytics may help any organization grow and thrive. Big data aids almost every business or industry that seeks to expand with the various technologies it possesses. The company can gain insights to improve customer satisfaction by analyzing large datasets linked to the events of the business. Creative technology is all about using technology to assist people in achieving their objectives. It goes beyond creative aspirations and technical boldness. Big data analytics will enable enterprises to look into innovative trends, hear from customers in surprising and creativeways, and, most significantly, use various diverse strategies to increase customer retention in this era of intense competition. Big data and customer retention will combine in the coming years to form crucial business buzzwords that will enable companies to beat their competitors.

KEYWORDS

- **customer retention**
- **big data**
- **customer satisfaction**
- **churn rate**
- **customer service analysis**

REFERENCES

https://corporatefinanceinstitute.com/resources/valuation/churn-rate/ https://data-flair.training/blogs/big-data-case-studies/

https://dynamics.microsoft.com/en-us/customer-service/what-is-customer-retention/ https://thedatamark.com/importance-of-big-data/

https://vuesol.com/enhance-customer-retention-with-the-help-of-big-data-analytics-services/ https://www.analyticssteps.com/blogs/companies-uses-big-data

https://www.atlantis-press.com/article/125965844.pdf

https://www.clicdata.com/blog/customer-retention-analytics/

https://www.forbes.com/advisor/business/customer-retention-strategies/

https://www.geeksforgeeks.org/how-do-companies-use-big-data-analytics-inrealworld/

https://www.investopedia.com/terms/b/big-data.asp

https://www.linkedin.com/pulse/how-does-big-data-change-game-customer-success-christopher-mesa

https://www.oracle.com/big-data/what-is-big-data/

CHAPTER 9

Impact of Big Data Analytics on Customer Relationship Management

JYOTI BANSAL and RANDEEP KAUR

JCD Vidyapeeth, Sirsa, Haryana, India

ABSTRACT

performs a significant job in business organizations. Therefore, customer plays a major role in the organization's activities and decision-making procedures of the companies. For maintaining better customer relationship management (CRM) big data analytics (BDA) is a key requisite for organizations. In this chapter, we are presenting the procedures to recognize the CRM of various industries, a variety of research of big data analytics (BDA), different statistics pulling out techniques, and big data methodical formation that can be used in CRM. This chapter also describes recent uses of big data in relation to CRM, as well as their drawbacks and potential applications. To acquire, store, and analyze big data, new tools, and techniques are needed. Big data is then utilized to improve decision-making and improve customer management. A literature review and a thematic analysis of recent research will be used to gather the data for this investigation.

9.1 INTRODUCTION

Big data is a general term for datasets that are too massive or complicated to be processed by conventional data dealing with software. Analysis, capture, length, search, sharing, storage, transmission, presentation, and information privacy are the difficulties in data dealing, and they rarely relate to a certain size of dataset; instead they, frequently, only refer to the employ of

Augmenting Customer Retention Through Big Data Analytics.
Reena Malik, Ambuj Sharma, and Prashant Chaudhary (Eds.)

extrapolative analytics or further specific sophisticated ways to extract value from data. It is a general phrase for datasets that are too massive or complicated to be processed by conventional data processing software.

Big data analytics (BDA) has strained exacting interest because of its capability for dynamic decision making. The technology-driven world of today brings a number of unprecedented opportunities and innovative complexities that help people make better decisions and gain a competitive advantage. BDA is the term for the intricate process of extracting information from the vast amounts of organized and unstructured data that help organizations make decisions more effectively, such as hidden patterns, unknown connections, user preferences, and market trends. BDA is described as "the approach of evaluating the massive quantity of data." It is gathered from an extensive variety of sources, including pictures, sensors, videos, social media posts, records of sales transactions, and many more. Although some consider that BDA is a rebellion that will alter the way we make efforts, we believe, and we live, researchers and practitioners have linked BDA with the upcoming frontier for competitiveness, creativity, and productivity. The study of BDA's potential is still in its early stages, and it frequently overlooks the ways in which investments in BDA are translated into competitive success. The literature is essential for learning about the difficulties, benefits, and effects of BDA.

9.1.1 HISTORY AND GROWTH OF BIG DATA ANALYTICS

The purposes of big data have been concerning for many years because before the 1950s anybody even knew of the expression "big data"; companies were using several forms of fundamental analytics consisting of information in a spreadsheet that had to be manually observed to uncover insights and tendencies.

Most business units now understand the considerable value of relating analytics to capture data that flows into their businesses. At the moment, there are fresh benefits that BDA brings to the table; they are rapidity and competence.

9.2 CUSTOMER RELATIONSHIPS MANAGEMENT

The majority of businesses will struggle over the next few years to realize the financial value of BDA techniques for customer relationship management

(CRM) practices. Finding promotion, sales, client service, and e-commerce significant customer operations that could benefit from active, big data customer imminent activities will be the first step toward success. First, major customer processes were determined and then the consumer data from the appropriate sources were organized and incorporated.

- To obtain pertinent customer insights, use BDA.
- Use insights to update customer choice.

  Utilizing the most comprehensive data and analytics to drive customer potential is the first step in being relevant to the customer. Data that are incorrect or irrelevant could cause problems with your consumers. Information acquisition is the first stage in creating value from large data or information.

9.2.1 BIG DATA ANALYSIS RELATED TO CRM

Any marketing department's primary and most important responsibility is CRM, which aims to strengthen customer relationships to boost sales performance. Numerous studies on sales performance have concluded that CRM capabilities play a crucial role in sales performance, but less attention has been paid to this crucial variable in the context of BDA. BDA is additionally the most recent type of data innovation [information technology (IT)], and earlier investigations adroitly presumed that BDA results can impact authoritative execution.

9.3 SCOPE OF BIG DATA ANALYSIS

This study's primary goal is to attempt to provide answers to these aforementioned concerns using data from earlier investigations and information about big data related to CRM from Zerbino et al. (2018). To discover more about the improvement of big data customer analytics (BDCA), to boost the performance of customer connection, this research paper will take a thorough look at preceding research and examine in sequence and organizational elements act attentively and carefully. Furthermore, additionally, this research study identifies and defines associated traits to customer retention that are essential to the use of BDCA and have a significant bearing on CRM and the results of the performance of the company–client relationship management.

9.4 APPLICATION OF BIG DATA ANALYSIS

Customers now receive much more personalized experiences and items for consumption offers that are pertinent to their needs when they connect with websites/applications such as Flipkart and Google. Based on these encounters, customers have comparable demands of other customer-focused businesses including banks, merchants, and news/media. Companies might not be able to match these expectations if they do not have a thorough understanding of their customers. This might have a significant effect on the economy. Companies that should be focused on the customer are falling short when they cannot extract insights from the gold mine of facts. They are enabling their rivals to spot important commercial trends and take benefit of them.

- ***Customer Attainment and Preservation:*** Consumer information always helps immensely in advertising trends, through data-driven activities, to develop customer satisfaction. For gaining customer loyalty and improved customer experience, personalization of Netflix, Amazon, and Spotify is always helpful.
- ***Targeted Customer Advertisements:*** Personalized facts about interface models, order accounts, and seeing manufactured goods page can help enormously to form embattled ad operations for consumers on a better level and at the personage level.
- ***Product Enlargement:*** It can produce insights on expansion decisions, product feasibility, concert dimensions, etc. and express enhancement that completely serves up the consumers.
- ***Pricing Model:*** Pricing models able to be symbolized and used by retailers with the facilitates of a variety of data sources to take advantage of it.
- ***Supply Chain Management and Channel Analytics:*** With Business2Business supplier networks, proactive restocking, course optimizations, stock management, and delivery delay notice, predictive analytical models are helpful.
- ***Hazard Management:*** It assists in identifying new hazards using data trends to create efficient risk management techniques.
- ***Improved Decision Making:*** Enterprises can improve their decision making by using the insights that can be gleaned from the data.

9.5 IMPLEMENTATION OF BIG DATA ANALYTICS IN DIFFERENT SECTORS

9.5.1 RETAILING

The retail industry actively uses BDA. Apply data analytics techniques to understand what your customers are buying and to tailor your products and services to them. Today, Omni channel knowledge and everything. Customers may engage with a brand name on one feed and eventually purchase a product on another while traversing more intermediate channels. Retailers need to track these customers' journeys and leverage marketing and advertising campaigns to improve opportunities to increase sales and reduce costs.

9.5.2 TECHNOLOGICAL

Technology companies are making extensive use of BDA. They study extra regarding how consumers interrelate with her website and apps and collect important information. Based on this, Acquaintance Company's container optimizes sales, customer service, customer satisfaction, and more. This also helps them commence original goods and armed forces as we live in a knowledge-based economy and companies in the technology sector benefit from BDA.

9.5.3 HEALTHCARE INDUSTRY

Healthcare is one more business that can help with BDA tools, procedures, and courses. Healthcare professionals can diagnose a patient's health through a variety of tests and run computers to look for tattletale signs of incongruity, illnesses, and more. It also helps recover enduring care and increase the competence of treatment and medication processes in healthcare. A few diseases can be identified before they develop, so action can be taken to prevent rather than cure.

9.5.4 MANUFACTURING INDUSTRY

Manufacturing is the industrial sector concerned with the development of physical goods. The manufacturing process lifecycle is different for each manufactured goods. Mechanized systems are involved surrounded by industrial facilities and across manufacturing floors. Many technologies are concerned with built-up, such as the Internet of possession (IoP) and robotics, but the backbone of all these is firmly based on BDA. It enables manufacturers to improve yields, speed time to market, improve quality, streamline their supply chains and logistics processes, and prototype products before launching them. We can help manufacturers with all these steps.

9.5.5 ENERGY

Most oil and gas companies in the energy sector are big-time users of BDA. It is used in discovering oil and other natural resources. Vast amounts of big data are used to determine the price of a barrel of oil, how high production is, and whether wells are profitable.

9.6 KEY FACTOR OF CUSTOMER RELATIONSHIP MANAGEMENT

- Offer suggestions based on individual tastes
- Reduce client attrition
- Face-to-face marketing
- customized product offerings
- Mobile wallet for one-to-one marketing
- Manage risk and prevent fraud

9.7 CUSTOMER KNOWLEDGE MANAGEMENT IN MEDIA AND PUBLISHING

- Tailored contented and curriculum.
- Recommendations—advertisements, content, etc.
- Loyalty programed.
- Listeners measurement.

9.8 BACKGROUND

Customer direction is used to organize the firm's shared value and norm frameworks, which may be related to customer BDA culture by Zerbino et al. (2018). Customer orientation is also a type of culture that seeks to improve customer value through gathering, sharing, and using customer information. An organization must make essential improvements to customer orientation to achieve this goal, according to employing customer orientation to create and address customers' expressed and underlying demands could help a managerial benefit from consumer information. To regulate the customers' wants and provide for them, customer orientation relies on knowledge about them.

9.9 CONTRIBUTION OF BIG DATA ANALYTICS

Social media is a factor in the previously unheard-of amount, diversity, and speed of information. Most of this information (wants, needs, and interests) is beyond the organization's boundaries and can be challenging to regularly and properly gather. Associations frequently contain some of this in sequence (sentiment) internally.

It is essential to select the best and most relevant for the bulk of big data CRM initiatives. Integration and management of data will therefore become crucial.

To find the most pertinent insights and choose the best course of action for customers. It is anticipated that the majority of big data CRM initiatives. The majority of information infrastructure and technology can handle one information type or the other, but not both.

The necessity to provide access to several information sources and manage a variety of information types in an incorporated and dependable manner is demonstrated by hybrid use cases. The hybrid use case will require the creation of standard procedure, knowledge, and most excellent practices for content before merging structured data.

To make sure mixture records can be managed and finally evaluated for better consumer insights. CRM leaders will need to collaborate with CIOs.

Customer data can be combined to create some sort of solitary view of the consumer by utilizing various forms of integration and implementing them at various levels of the technology stack, including business processes, applications, data models, and databases, as well as portal/enterprise mashups, portals, and data models. Results from tactical to strategic actions will differ. The case for a strategic strategy must be made by organizations, but the tactical approach is sometimes all that can be done in the short term.

9.10 HOW BIG DATA ANALYTICS WORKS

For business organizations to maintain their big data effectively a large dataset must be gathered, processed, cleaned up, and analyzed as part of BDA.

9.10.1 COLLECTION OF DATA

Every organization has a diverse form of data collection. An organization collects structured and unstructured data from a combination of sources such as cloud storage, many mobile applications, store sensors, and more. Data warehouses will use some of the stored data so that business intelligence apparatus and solutions can rapidly access it. A data house can be used to grasp raw or unstructured data that is too complex or assorted to be stored in a warehouse.

9.10.2 PROCESS DATA

Data processing for businesses is difficult due to the exponential growth of available data. Batch processing is a processing choice that examines big data blocks gradually. When data collection and analysis take more time than expected, batch processing might be helpful. By the stream processing time between data collection and analysis become easy which examines small batches of data at once. The complexity and cost of stream dealing out are generally superior.

9.10.3 CLEAN DATA

To enhance the data eminence and assemble more vigorous results, all the data, regardless of size, have to be scrubbed. Duplicate or preventable data should be detached or accounted for, and each and every information has to be structured correctly. Filthy data can obscure and deceive, leading to erroneous insights.

9.10.4 ANALYZE THE DATA

- It takes much time to convert huge data into a usable form. Highly developed analytics techniques can convert huge data into considerable insights formerly they are ready. Along with these bulky data study techniques are:

- Data removal uses anomalies and data clusters to sort through enormous databases in search of patterns and linkages.

Customer information can be subjected to a variety of analytical techniques and tools. Each will produce a unique kind of customer intelligence. The kind of data collected will define the best consumer decisions that can be made with that data.

A proposal for new skis or boots, for instance, is unlikely to be appropriate in this situation, but a travel discount for the next ski season would be. Selling a variety of retail goods, as well as travel and lodging, is made possible by predicting that a consumer will go skiing in five months.

Four questions can be answered using analytics for customer analysis:

- What is occurring in terms of visibility and descriptive analytics?
- Why is it happening?
- What may be predicted or predicted using predictive analytics?
- How can we (using prescriptive analytics) make it happen?

The foundation of a successful big data CRM endeavor consists of obtaining answers to all four questions. More chances will be provided by predictive and prescriptive analytics to promote and sell to customers as well as proactively stop problems with customer care. For predictive and prescriptive analysis, businesses will need to start with the fundamentals before moving on to more complex layers. Data gathered at levels 1 and 2 frequently offer a stronger basis for advanced analysis with more precise data. The majority of CRM projects put a heavy emphasis on descriptive analytics and are shifting toward more diagnostic types of analytics.

9.11 APPLYING CUSTOMER INSIGHTS

Customer insights derived from big data must be put to use to be efficient and provide corporate value. For instance, a process feedback loop approach which many firms have already started using benefits social network and media research. At this time, societal listening is used to look for fresh or well-established patterns, including complaints about certain products or brands.

Where possible, business rules that can handle complicated events are used to model and automatically make judgments for particular contextual contexts. Marketing automation tools and other workflow automation tools are powered by rule engines. These systems can track and create leads, target user segments with special offers, feed alerts to a customer care center, and modify product suggestions at call centers and websites.

The creation of various context scenarios is perhaps the most challenging phase for businesses to effectively understand and automate decisions, as it involves an intimate grasp of the customer's purchasing experience.

Numerous CRM opportunities are presented by big data. However, the possibility of overwhelming the customer with messages or, worse, of being inconsistent and contradictory comes along with the commercial opportunity. Although it can be challenging to bring various customer activities into harmony, creating a central hub for customer engagement or contact will enable you to priorities customer interactions, have access to consumer insights, and access both organized and unstructured data.

9.12 BIG DATA HELPFUL IN CUSTOMER RELATIONSHIP MANAGEMENT

In most businesses, CRM uses big data. Integrating big data into CRM procedures inside a business is known as big data CRM. Its goals are to improve customer service, anticipate consumer behavior, modify products or services, suggest increasing revenues, and compute the return on savings for various businesses.

9.12.1 BETTER CUSTOMER UNDERSTANDING

If handled correctly, big data can improve and alter relationships between customers and businesses. Your organization can close the gaps between its marketing and sales strategy by analyzing your business operations using big data from the viewpoint of your customers. Additionally, it enables your business to better understand your clientele, including how they see your services or brand. More individualized marketing and communications may result from this, which may boost engagement.

Similar to this, you may segment consumers based on their behaviors by integrating all customer data sources, including social media, the internet, email, and hotlines, using CRM analytics. This will enable you to identify the most lucrative consumers to encourage recurring business by making special offers or giving them preferred treatment. Overall, a better customer experience and level of satisfaction can result from the wise application of big data awareness.

9.12.2 PREDICTIVE MODELING

Customers that are empowered by technology are constantly shifting their preferences. To forecast how clients will be reacting based on their segmented demographics and past behavior in the future, it is essential for businesses to leverage big data and predictive analytics. This will enable you to provide your consumers with recommendations that are appropriate and may increase conversions.

Predictive analytics also has significant advantages for your business. For example, it can reduce the cost, time, and effort involved in predicting business outcomes. To get a thorough picture of your company's future without investing a lot of money, you can incorporate variables akin to the environment, evolving regulations, viable intelligence, and market circumstances into your arithmetical models. Another advantage of predictive analytics is that it can also provide forecasts, that is, headcount planning, competitive analysis, churn analysis, and demand forecasting.

9.12.3 GETTING PERSONAL TOUCH WITH CUSTOMERS

Every time a customer contacts a firm, even with a complaint, they begin a dialogue. An important point of connection that characterizes your brand is this conversation. You have the chance to use personal information to have a meaningful and fruitful interaction with customers when they interact directly with your company.

It is anticipated that brand communications will incorporate a thorough level of client personalization, primarily as a result of social media. However, brand reputation and customer relationships will prosper across all communication channels if organizations make the most of the wealth of offline and online media to incorporate information in the most significant and compelling ways.

9.12.4 BENCHMARKING

By benchmarking, your business can keep tabs on its performance and assess how it stacks up against rivals in the same sector. This analysis also takes into account the rivals' marketing competition techniques for your specific niche. Similarly, using big data, your business may conduct thorough benchmarking over time. Big data benchmarking enables firms to ascertain critical metrics like customer satisfaction, retention, and rate vs. returns per service call.

The use of big data in conjunction with benchmarking can also change descriptive analytics from being retrospective to being prescriptive. Prescriptive analytics assists businesses in processing data in real time to obtain useful insights. Similar to how it can reveal operational areas that are exceeding or falling short of company or industry norms, big data in benchmarking can help businesses. The company may be able to correct its vulnerabilities and retain strategies that are outperforming expectations by using this knowledge of the unique operational locations.

9.12.5 *FINAL THOUGHTS*

The secret to gaining a spirited frame and enhancing company operations is finding and analyzing realistic information from various data sources. Additionally, big data is typically used by businesses for CRM. Its goals include improving client service, modifying manufactured goods and checking offerings to increase revenue, forecasting customer behavior, and calculating the return on investment for different businesses.

The majority of the data connected with CRM is prearranged data, including details about contacts, purchases made by customers, and other items. Furthermore, this situation has changed as a result of the development of big data approaches because businesses may now use amorphous data as a tool to acquire deeper insights. Big data may help firms manage their customer relationships better, overall, because it improves customer comprehension, facilitates benchmarking, enables personalization with customers, and supports predictive modeling.

9.13 PROBLEMS WITH BIG DATA ANALYTICS

- BDA offers more than only broad-reaching advantages:
- Data accessibility: As data volumes rise, the processing and storage of data become more challenging; big data needs to be managed.
- Maintenance of data quality: It takes a lot of time, effort, and resources to maintain data quality.
- Data security: Securing big data systems presents special difficulties due to their complexity. To appropriately address these security issues in large big data ecosystems can be a difficult task.

- Picking the right tools: It can be difficult to choose the best BDA tools among the numerous options in the market. One should be able to choose the optimal tools based on user needs and organizational structure.
- Skills supply-demand gap: Businesses are struggling to fulfill the demand for qualified BDA specialists due to a shortage of experienced professionals.

9.14 LIMITATION

CRM and the use of big data in customer analytics are fairly broad topics. More research and resources are required for the subject. The duration of this study was constrained. The present worldwide pandemic also made it difficult for the researchers to gather data. This increased the difficulty of the study.

The companies that have used BDCA throughout the organization are the topic of this study. As big data is still a relatively new concept for many businesses, the target audiences may be restricted in this area. In large enterprises and IT companies, big data is used for CRM. This study has challenged gathering data from these huge corporations, and it was made even more challenging by the COVID-19 outbreak, which forced some businesses to shut down and forced others to adopt alternate work patterns.

9.15 BIG DATA ANALYTICS' POTENTIAL IN THE FUTURE

In the upcoming years, BDA will engage in recreation a critical role in the business. BDA has already gained popularity, and the majority of large corporations have begun using it to manage their corporations.

- Now is a prime opportunity to observe the phenomenal advancement of cognitive analysis.
- Businesses will use data to its fullest potential to secure financial benefits.
- It is anticipated that the open-source solution will once again be relevant in the market.
- Data security and accuracy will receive increased emphasis from businesses.
- The need for data scientists will grow significantly.

There are currently several job profiles accessible in the field of data analytics. Businesses have begun to strictly shift their focus away from the conventional manner of only looking at degrees.

9.16 CONCLUSION

Businesses must communicate flexibly with their consumers to use CRM. To better understand their customers, engage with them through appropriate marketing strategies, and boost their competitive advantages, businesses must rapidly and efficiently find complicated consumer data from enormous quantities of data using big data. Discussions of big data mining, CRM, and customer value are included in this chapter, along with using information from the automotive maintenance industry.

The empirical findings are based on a variety of earlier literature studies relevant to CRM and big data. To determine the study's findings, surveys were also administered to several organizational business units.

The main challenge might be figuring out how to keep business units supported and developing and influence BDCA within the organization, how to guarantee customer orientation, BDA culture, information quality, and the performance of the customer relationship, increased competition, and how to structure the organization within nature and combine the aid of technology. Other difficulties can include figuring out how organizational leadership improves the organization by incorporating new technological knowledge.

The study offers preliminary evidence that when compared to the number of surveys distributed to various firms, the participants of the business units employing BDCA are fairly few, which is relevant to leadership's lack of technology deployment in the company. However, compared to the modest number of business unit responders, participation has demonstrated the positive in the organization through the application of BDCA, demonstrating the involvement of BDCA in the process and the organization's transformation. The study also contributes by emphasizing the variables that could impact the organization by boosting BDCA to improve presentation.

The organization's explicit informational business unit requirements are met. The BDCA might provide a base upon which to build the advanced customer's competitiveness. The results underscore the importance of the BDCA in ensuring the quality of data-driven information. Corporate decision-makers need simple duties and to accurately comprehend customer information before making hasty decisions. The IT department should be organized simply to ensure that the decision maker receives the customer information that is most important. The incorporation of BDCA tools may enhance the needs of the company in terms of organized format, such as management, integration, and big data technologies, which assist managerial decision makers. The study implies that BDCA might be put into practice.

The study promotes organizational leadership to strengthen the organization with the help of BDCA in organizational business units, with dedication to technology implementation, and with faith in the improvement of BDCA. They may grow their client base, steer clear of big data and recommendation problems, segment the market, choose the best ways to approach customers, calculate the lifetime worth of each customer, and satisfy their demands. Additionally, BDCA has tremendous potential to enhance CRM strategy's performance in terms of customer relationships.

KEYWORDS

- **customer relationship management**
- **big data analytics**
- **decision making**
- **business**

REFERENCES

Anshari, M.; Almunawar, M.; Lim, S.; Al-Mudimigh, A. Customer Relationship Management and Big Data-Enabled: Personalization & Customization of Services. *Appl. Comput. Inf.* **2019,** *15* (2), 94–101.

Bail, C. A. The Cultural Environment: Measuring Culture with Big Data. *Theory Soc. 43* (3–4), 465–482.

Balu, M.-E. V.; Furtuna, F. Principal Component Analysis—Statistical Method of Territorial Profile Factor Analysis. *SSRN Electron. J.* **2006.**

Bell, E.; Bryman, A.; Harley, B. *Business Research Methods*, 4th edn.; Oxford University Press: Oxford, 2015.

Cai, L.; Zhu, Y. The Challenges of Data Quality and Data Quality Assessment in the Big Data Era. *Data Sci. J.* **2015,** *14* (0), 2.

Chang, H. H.; Wong, K. H.; Fang, P. W. The Effects of Customer Relationship Management Relational Information Processes on Customer-Based Performance. *Decision Support Syst.* **2014,** *66*, 146–159.

CMO Survey. CMO Survey Report: Highlights and Insights. *The CMO_Survey—Highlights* **2016**. 10 April 2017.

Dalla Pozza, I.; Goetz, O.; Sahut, J. M. Implementation Effects in the Relationship Between CRM and Its Performance. *J. Bus. Res.* **2018,** 391–403.

Douglas, S. P.; Craig, C. S. On Improving the Conceptual Foundations of International Marketing Research. *J. Int. Market.* **2006,** *14* (1), 1–22.

Dubey, R.; Gunasekaran, A.; Childe, S. J.; Blome, C.; Papadopoulos, T. Big Data and Predictive Analytics and Manufacturing Performance: Integrating Institutional Theory, Resource-Based View and Big Data Culture. *Br. J. Manag.* **2019,** *30* (2), 341–361.

Erevelles, S.; Fukawa, N.; Swayne, L. Big Data Consumer Analytics and the Transformation of Marketing. *J. Bus. Res.* **2016,** *69* (2), pp.897–904.

Falk, R. F.; Miller, N. B. *A Primer for Soft Modeling*; University of Akron Press: Akron, 1992.

Fornell, C.; Larker, D. F. Evaluation Structural Equations Models with Unobservable Variables and Measurement Error. *J. Market. Res.* **1981,** *18*, 39–50.

http://en.wikipedia.org/wiki/Big_data

http://link.springer.com/chapter/10.1007/978-3-319-08254-7_16

http://www.computerweekly.com/news/2240184467/Gartner-Big-data-will-transform-customer-relationship-management-technology

Pandey, P. How Does Marketing Strategy Influence Firm Performance? Implementation of Marketing Strategy for Firm Success. *Int. J. Innov. Econ. Dev.* **2017,** *1* (3), 7–15.

www.finacle/solutions/thought-papers/Documents/CRM-with- big-data.pdf

CHAPTER 10

Influence of Big Data on Customer Relationship Management in Real Estate

NILESH KATE[1], AKANKSHA JADHAV[1], and CHANDRAPRABHA VAIDYA[2]

[1]*Pune Institute of Business Management, Pune, Maharashtra, India*

[2]*Savitribai Phule Pune University, Pune, Maharashtra, India*

ABSTRACT

The concept of big data has been evolving over the years and holds much more importance in today's era than ever. In today's competitive world, it is essential for organizations to use an advanced tools such as big data to get a competitive edge against their rivals. Big data, in many ways, has helped organizations gather and analyze information regarding their customers to improve their experience and lead to better retention rates. This directly affects businesses in a positive manner as it leads to sales and revenue growth. Big data has been influencing the way organizations operate and handle their customers, and the real estate industry is no exception to that. The role and likings of customers are of utmost importance in the real estate industry and therefore, big data becomes an important tool in the effective implementation of CRM. The use of big data helps in understanding the customers in a better way and increases their involvement level. Therefore, it is important to understand how organizations can harness this data and use it to their advantage. This paper aims to understand how big data analytics has influenced customer relationship management (CRM) in the real estate industry by examining its influence on various factors such as customer experience, customization, and services. The paper will also examine how different organizations have used big data in the past and assess its

Augmenting Customer Retention Through Big Data Analytics.
Reena Malik, Ambuj Sharma, and Prashant Chaudhary (Eds.)

effectiveness based on past results. This will further help us to throw light on how big data can be used to improve strategic decisions to increase customer loyalty and thus retention.

10.1 INTRODUCTION

Big data is one of the most important innovations brought to the business world. It is no secret that people have been trying to interpret and use different types of data to give it a meaning that can be used for their own benefit. Businesses have been finding new ways to connect to their customers and understand their requirements. Big data is one big step toward it.

The term big data is often used to define a large amount of data, structured and unstructured, which continues to grow and is analyzed by different organizations to support decision making. In the Business world, big data is basically large-sized data that is mined for information and used for the analysis of consumer behavior in organizations. By using big data to analyze consumer behavior, organizations get a closer understanding of the needs and form their customer base. This data, thus, can be further used to predict future consumer behavior (Winson-Geideman et al., 2017).

The term big data is mainly being used since the 1990s and its scope has been widening ever since. However, it does not confirm whether it had been in existence before that. There have been past attempts in history to capture all existing data by different civilizations. The great attempt of the Roman Empire to analyze the data related to their military strength to use it for optimal distribution is one good example.

Big data has been used for varied purposes by different organizations. Moreover, its use in customer relationship management (CRM) has been proven beneficial for many businesses. Almost all industries have been witnessing to the supremacy of big data and there is no way it can only be considered as an advantage for one and not a necessity.

Currently, we can be considered to be in phase 3.0 of big data, if we have to segment its evolution in years. There has been much buzz around the use and potential of big data in the current times, however, its history traces back a long time. The term "information explosion" was first coined in 1941, which defines a great attempt at quantifying the growth rate in the volume of data. Ever since there have been various small developments in this field. However, it was not until the second half of the 20th century, that the term gained much attention.

The first phase of big data is considered from the 1970s to 2000s when people started to learn about big data through the field of database management. In this phase, the focus was mainly on the storage and extraction of the data. Therefore, this phase is mainly characterized by the use of database management and data warehousing. The current developments in the field of big data are the result of these components only.

The second phase of big data began in the early 2000s. This phase is considered to be very important in the development of big data since the early 2000s also marked the evolution of the Internet and the widening of its access to the local people. As we have all witnessed, with the evolution and increase in the usage of the Internet, there has been an exponential rise in the creation of data. Therefore, an increase in the level and availability of data, mainly in semi-structured and unstructured forms, developed the need to manage it effectively. Consequently, some advanced companies of the current times, such as Amazon, and Yahoo started using these newly created data for analyzing the behavior of their customers. These companies started using data analytics to their advantage to understand, acquire, and retain their customers. However, the range of data increased further with the inception of social media. This created the inevitable demand for new and advanced data technology to put this data into a structured format and extract meaningful information through it.

The third and current phase of big data starts from 2010 onward. This phase is mainly characterized by the presence of huge unstructured data derived from HTTP-based Web traffic. The emphasis of many firms and organizations have been analyzing this data. However, the development in the tech world, especially related to mobile devices, has shown possibilities for retrieving valuable information.

With the significant rise in the number of users of mobile devices and their reach, companies are now able to reach out to a huge number of customers. This further gives them access to different types of data related to their customers and helps them to track their behavior (Lalitha and Hema Latha, 2015). It enables companies to store and analyze different data, to track the movement, health-related information, and the psycho-social and physical behavior of the consumers. This advancement in technology has opened up new possibilities and several opportunities for firms in different fields including the Real Estate industry.

Apart from the advancements in mobile-related technology, there has been a significant level of development with regard to sensor-based devices. This has further added weightage to the generation of huge amounts of data such as wearable technology.

The availability and 3-fold rise in the generation of data has created new opportunities for companies in different sectors to know and understand their customers. Moreover, there is no shortage of data, but with the possibility of opportunities that are brought with it, the companies are now facing steep competition to use it optimally and to their advantage.

The concept of first-mover advantage is proven to be true in many sectors, and real estate is no exception to that. Therefore, many giant firms have been trying to make the most use of big data to understand and manage consumer relations.

10.2 NEED FOR BIG DATA IN THE REAL ESTATE INDUSTRY

Data is the new oil, gold, or whatever is of value to the seekers. There is no doubt that the companies that understand the importance of big data and the potential it holds have been constantly making progress in extracting useful information and developing meaningful resources to harness its power.

Big data is, as the term suggests, huge and infinite, moreover, it is constantly increasing at a significant rate. Therefore, one of the most important things that we can do with big data is harness it to build a better future for everyone. Big data can be used in different industries. For example, in the healthcare industry, we can track people's health using wearable technology and thus, predict and prevent any mishap. This way, we can aim at achieving the goal of good health for all.

With regard to industries that have direct contact with customers, big data has been proven to be of Significant use. Therefore, the real estate industry has a huge scope when with regard to using big data for enhancing the consumer experience.

Because of big data, it has become possible for real estate firms to make more accurate decisions, target the right customer base, mitigate risks, and get insights into their customer base and their needs to improve the overall customer experience as well as the satisfaction level.

There was a time when real estate agents had to put in extra time and effort in even finding the right target audience for their property, who were not only willing but also capable of buying it. However, with the invention of big data analytics, firms can easily track the consumers who need a property or whether or not they would be interested in what businesses are offering. Through big data, one can also predict the kind of property the customer is looking for, and target the ones that are more appropriate for that particular property.

Big data can help real estate firms to get insights into what type of property the customers want, their budget, location, and even the features they are looking for. This data helps not only in the selling stage but also in the development stage. With the help of information provided by big data and its analysis, we can build the properties that are in demand and target the right customers to bring efficiency in selling. The right use of big data can give a competitive advantage to one firm against others, and therefore, its usage has become a necessity rather than a choice.

10.3 OBJECTIVES

- To understand the working models of big data analytics in the real estate industry with respect to the CRM.
- To understand the role that big data analytics plays in the data-driven world.
- To learn the influence of big data on CRM in the real estate industry.
- To suggest strategies to be able to use big data at its full potential to benefit the organization.

10.4 WHO BUYS REAL ESTATE AND HOW BIG DATA CAN HELP?

The real estate industry is one of the most growing industries around the world. With every new step in the development of a country, the need for real estate also grows. Because, with development and growth, rise in the revenue, and gross domestic product (GDP) of a country which in turn increases the employment, investment, and purchasing power of the consumers. When people are looking to invest these extra bucks in their hands, the first thought that comes to their minds is mostly real estate.

There are different reasons why people invest in real estate. However, in recent years it has been observed that real estate is the most preferred source of Investment. This means when people are looking for Investments, they largely prefer to buy a property. It could be in the form of plots, apartments, office spaces, etc. Real estate investments are considered to be one of the most secure forms of investments and therefore people from all classes prefer to invest in them (Du and Zhang, 2014). In this case, the factors such as interest rates and government policies play an important role. If the interest rates are low or the government is providing subsidies to invest in real estate, the buyers will have more incentives to do so.

Apart from that, many people also prefer to invest in real estate for commercial and residential purposes. With regard to commercial purposes, the buyers try to estimate the revenue or profit that can be generated through that particular property. In such cases, big data analysis can prove to be beneficial to provide accurate estimates to the buyers and increase their trust.

With regard to residential investments, the requirements may vary from person to person depending on various demographic, economic, socio-cultural, and geographic factors. This means every customer has different needs and preferences based on which they make their decisions to buy the property. This is where the role of big data and CRM is required the most (Ghavami and Olyaei, 2006). As the customers have different backgrounds and different expectations, the use of big data helps in understanding these customers and matching the right customer with the right property.

Overall, people have the following three main motives to buy properties: Investment, commercial, and residential. Out of these three, currently, Investment has turned out to be a major reason to buy a property, whereas commercial and residential offer more or less the same amount of motive.

There are different ways in which big data can help businesses to understand the buyer segments of all purposes. However, from a strategic point of view, big data can provide help in two main ways: First, by analyzing the sources of knowledge and second, by the influencing factors.

10.5 SOURCES OF KNOWLEDGE

Sources of knowledge are basically the different ways through which the different customer segments receive information about the real estate Industry. It is important to understand which are the most impactful sources, to utilize these sources to bring more customer attention. At the core, there are mainly four sources of information which include print media, digital media, social media, and Networks with 29, 26, 24, and 21% effectiveness, respectively (refer Fig. 10.1).

When we look at the graph, we can observe that print media is the most effective source of knowledge when it comes to the real estate industry. Print media mainly includes advertisements in newspapers, magazines, hoardings, etc. As no one generally wonders about real estate, it has been proven beneficial to engage in this type of promotional method.

The next in line is digital media followed by social media, which are mostly preferred mediums of advertisements in the current times. These are also the methods, that can generate more leads using CRM. Since the advertisements are in digitized form and interactive, it becomes easy to collect the data through these methods and use them for further targeting. Through these mediums, we can understand what type of properties person A and person B are looking for. Based on their previous inquiries we can figure out that maybe person A is looking for a property in a particular location at a certain price range. So, based on this inquiry big data can tell us when such property is available and that property can now be suggested to Person A and similarly, Person B can be suggested a property suitable to his requirements.

This means that through big data, we can provide more personalized suggestions to customers. This filtering of the data and emphasis on customer preferences and requirements in turn can lead to a higher level of consumer satisfaction.

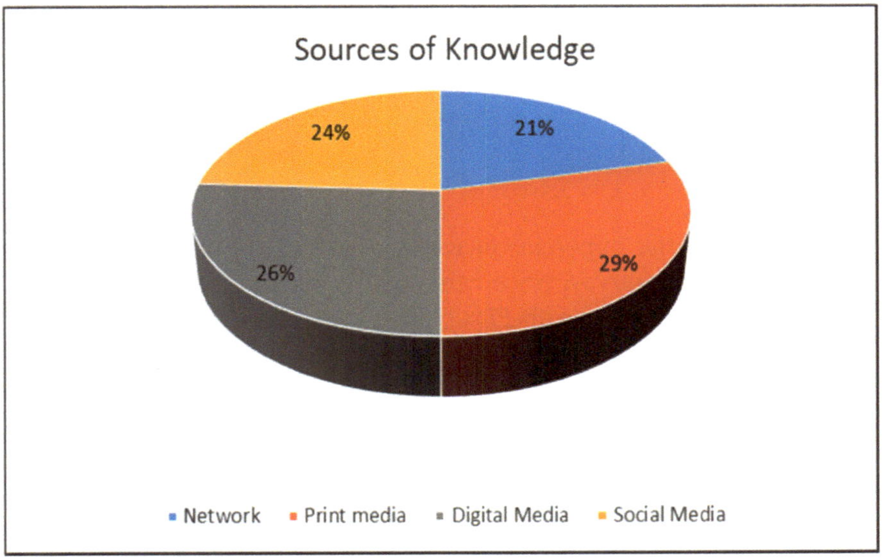

FIGURE 10.1 Sources of knowledge for real estate investment.

Source: Author.

This leaves us with a network as a source of knowledge. The network mostly includes the leads received from families and friends. This is one of the oldest sources to gain information. With regard to family and friends, they already have people's trust, and therefore, it becomes easy to make a deal in real estate. However, sometimes, people may invest solely based on trust without inspecting the property on their own. This can lead to many cases of fraud and dissatisfaction among consumers at a later stage of the purchase.

However, unlike a network of individuals, big data can help you get complete and accurate information about the project and its worth which makes the methods associated with big data more relevant and reliable.

10.6 FACTORS INFLUENCING THE BUYING DECISION IN REAL ESTATE

With regard to the Indian market, real estate industry has its own challenges. India is a family-oriented country, and major decisions such as buying a property will always be influenced by the opinions of the family members. Although this is specific to India, there are many other factors that affect the consumer's decision regarding whether or not to buy a particular property. Thankfully, big data can help us use this information to speed up the decision-making process. How? Let us find out.

10.6.1 PRICE

Price is one of the important factors that affect the buying decisions of customers. In this survey, price came out to be the lead influencer of the property buying decision with 27%. Sometimes, it becomes difficult to make a correct estimate of a property using traditional sources. However, with the arrival of technologies such as big data, it is possible to get insights from the prevalent market conditions, future predictions, and the current state of the property to come up with the most accurate pricing solutions. This helps in building trust at the initial stages of the purchasing process.

10.6.2 LOCATION

Location is another important factor that influences customer buying decisions. According to their needs, people prefer properties in a particular location that suits their needs. It could be any reason—starting from proximity to workplace and markets to price range in that particular area. This could also vary depending on the purpose of buying the property. For example, someone who is buying the property for investment purposes might not be that much concerned about the location as a person looking for residential property.

In this case, big data can help in the selection of the right target audience for a particular property. Based on the data available, we can match the consumer preferences of the location with the given property.

10.6.3 PROPERTY CONDITION

When we are buying a property, sometimes, we may not be fully aware of its condition. For example, an apartment might look good to the eyes, but there may be some damage to the plumbing system. In such cases, we end up paying more for a less-worthy apartment. To avoid such circumstances, we can do an overall estimate of the property which is solely based on its current condition and the market value. Making such estimates has now become possible for businesses.

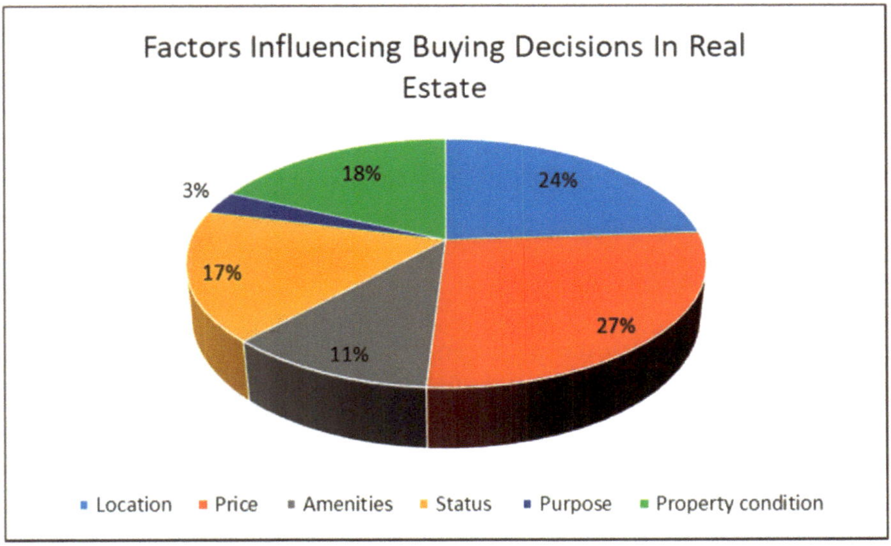

FIGURE 10.2 Factors influencing buying decisions in real estate.

Source: Author.

10.6.4 STATUS

Status plays an important role with regard to the purchase decision of any product in developing countries and the failure of Tata Nano car sales in

India is one of the best examples of it. With regard to India, people can make or break a deal solely based on the value that a particular product offers to their status and real estate is no exception to that. Therefore, it is one of the most influential factors while buying property (refer Fig. 10.2).

This knowledge can particularly help develop a marketing strategy for a particular property. People are more likely to buy a property if we can convince them how much value it adds to their lives and status.

10.6.5 AMENITIES

Another important factor that influences property buying decisions is the amenities offered in that particular project. With changing times, the needs and demands of the people are also changing and therefore, they want different things with their dream home. This includes a swimming pool, gym, club house, sports complex, free Wi-Fi, parking spaces, etc. Therefore, it becomes important to be aware of their preferences before entering the market.

Big data can help us understand all the amenities that should be offered in a particular price range. Big data can gather and analyze data from different sources such as competitors' offers, past deals, etc., and use it to offer a fair number of amenities using it.

10.6.6 PURPOSE

The Purpose for which the customers are buying a particular property also has an impact on the decision regarding buying the property. For Example, If the person is looking for residential property, he will have different requirements than those looking for profit-making or commercial property. This impacts the final decision and therefore it is necessary to know the purpose of purchase before offering a property.

10.7 UNDERSTANDING THE ROLE OF BIG DATA IN CUSTOMER RELATIONSHIP MANAGEMENT IN THE REAL ESTATE INDUSTRY

Big data is considered the next big thing with regard to innovation and technology. It has been useful for various businesses for a number of reasons. Among these, CRM is one of the areas where big data has brought a great amount of efficiency. Because of big data, it has now become possible for big companies to handle massive information and workload without much effort. The real estate industry is gaining success by providing quick solutions to customer problems and a perfect match for their preferences. Be it in decision-making, strategy building, or CRM, big data has influenced many areas in the real estate industry.

10.7.1 RELATIONSHIP BETWEEN BIG DATA AND CUSTOMER RELATIONSHIP MANAGEMENT

CRM has been one of the key elements with regard to ensuring the success of any business. Over the last few years, CRM has been made simple by big data. Since it is now easy to collect and store data, it can be easily used to generate insights from consumer behavior. By emphasizing on customer requirements, businesses can create a better customer experience. This means, due to big data, collecting data has become the easy part, but businesses have to focus on drawing insights from it and using them for their own benefit.

This covers the easy part. Collecting data is easy, but is it enough? No. To tap the complete benefits of big data, we will not only have to generate insights from it but also use them to make the right strategies for the businesses. The insights help us understand consumer behavior. Through big data, we can understand what our customers want, what they buy, and where they buy it. The answers of these questions will help us in developing a strategy for our business. Since we know where the customers are buying from, we can analyze this further to understand why they are buying from that particular place and not others. We can use this information to develop strategies to acquire that particular segment of customers.

However, for the success of any business only acquiring a customer is not enough. We will have to make efforts to retain them and maintain good relations with them (Shrilekha, 2022). Every customer is unique and has different preferences and therefore, we need to use big data to actively reach out to them. This is a key element in CRM. As soon as we accept the uniqueness of each customer, we can make active efforts to build a better relationship with them.

The number of customers you have maintained a good customer relationship with and how quickly you build it will be key to the development of your business. Big data makes it simpler. Through big data, you can find out your target customers, analyze them, and make appropriate decisions to turn them into loyal customers. However, this takes more effort than you think. Here, you not only have to acquire customer but also convince them to buy their next purchase from you. This is where the relationship between CRM and real estate comes into the picture.

10.7.2 RELATIONSHIP BETWEEN CUSTOMER RELATIONSHIP MANAGEMENT AND REAL ESTATE

The proper execution of CRM has proven beneficial for many industries and real estate is no exception to that. Nowadays, CRM acts as a key to building a successful business. CRM helps in understanding the customers in a better way and taking steps to make the process simpler for all the parties involved. This ease of process and trust helps in building better customer relationships.

Most of the time, people see real estate investment as a one-time investment, so why do we need to focus on CRM? It is because maybe not everyone will be interested in buying a second home but they may be interested in buying a different property or someone in their network will be. The importance of CRM does not always surround cracking a deal. The real estate industry needs CRM for different reasons such as enhancing customer relations, lead generation, documentation, process automation, etc.

There have been various innovations in this area to improve CRM in the real estate industry. Over the years, new software has been developed in order to keep the track of the leads and make it easier to convert them. Because of the various applications, companies do not have to maintain records manually.

The availability of such information and software makes it easy to track the actions of our potential and existing customers. This way we can be aware of their needs and requirements at different points in time and provide solutions to their problems.

10.7.3 INTERSECTIONS BETWEEN BIG DATA AND CRM IN THE REAL ESTATE INDUSTRY

There was a time when a lead would live and die with an employee. However, big data and CRM have now enabled the real estate industry to manage the leads in a better way. Since the leads now can be stored in the cloud, they can be maintained for years and used repeatedly to enhance customer relationships.

The application of various serious strategies proves to be beneficial in understanding the customers in a better way and thus, matching their demands at profit. Some applications and software help real estate businesses and agents to get relevant data about a particular property and customers. This way, businesses can easily connect to their target customers. If the past data is available, for example, person XYZ was found looking for property A, at location B, and price C, the other companies having similar property can directly reach out to that certain person rather than reaching out to random people.

Nowadays, businesses do not even have to make a lot of effort, they can just culminate the CRM software with websites and applications to get the relevant information. It does not only help businesses but also various real estate agents as well as investors. This ease in the process of finding and targeting the right customer at the right time is the result of the intersection between big data and CRM in the real estate industry.

10.8 BENEFITS OF USING BIG DATA IN THE REAL ESTATE INDUSTRY

10.8.1 TARGETING THE RIGHT CUSTOMERS

There was a time when real estate agents would target random people using all available and random leads. However, because of the arrival of big data, that is no longer the case. Because of the culmination of big data and CRM in the real estate industry, agents and businesses can now find out the right customers for their products based on the available data. This makes it simple for businesses to target the right set of customers and improve the chances of getting successful leads. With big data, businesses can now better understand the needs and wants of the customers and therefore, it becomes possible to develop the right or customized properties for different customers as per their preferences.

10.8.2 REDUCTION IN THE RISK

Investments in the real estate sector involve huge monetary transactions and therefore the level of risk in this business also becomes high. While investing in a particular property it is important to have accurate information about all the parties involved. Earlier, this used to be a lot more difficult as people could easily manipulate data. However, because of big data, it is now possible to get reliable information about different people from a third party. Big data makes it possible to make a correct estimation of the property by analyzing the condition, location, and other factors related to the property so as to avoid any overpayment from any side. This helps in the mitigation of the financial risk involved in the business.

Apart from that, the investors can also derive information regarding the property itself—including, and not limited to—the designs and construction quality of the property. In this way, the risks other than financial are also minimized regarding the concerned property.

10.8.3 IMPROVES MARKETING STRATEGIES

Big data has certainly opened up new opportunities and new ways to market different products. It enables us to use the available information and draw insights from them (Pawar, 2018). These Insights are collected from various available sources including both public and private channels, and various government and business reports, and nowadays, social media has also become one of the major sources of collecting data. With the availability of enough data, it becomes possible to make the right strategy.

For instance, if there is already a list of potential buyers or people who have shown interest in a particular property in the past, these people can now be considered the target customers for a similar new property.

This way, businesses can now target the right customers who are already potential clients and businesses will not have to start from zero. Also, once we know the potential customers, we can also make appropriate strategies depending on the various characteristics of the potential buyers and what inspires them. This means if there are certain properties, and people living in a particular area have shown interest in the properties, we can use this list to be our leads for a similar property in the future. Earlier, maintaining this list was one difficult task, however, with the arrival of big data, it has now become possible to keep a record of such information.

Apart from that, big data can also help in understanding the needs of the customers at a particular moment. For example, recently people have shown interest in buying a property that has an extra space that can be used for quarantine purposes if needed. Businesses can understand these needs due to big data and offer their customers customized properties as per their needs.

Therefore, by giving us Insights into the needs and wants of the customers, big data proves to be of significant importance in developing marketing strategies for the company (Xie et al., 2016).

10.8.4 MAKE ACCURATE PREDICTIONS

Big data makes it possible to analyze past data to observe recent trends in the sector and predict future results. These predictions are based on past results and therefore help in analyzing future conditions in the market which can help buyer to make purchase decisions regarding a property. They are also helpful in avoiding any kind of risk associated with the property based on market conditions. They help investors as well as home buyers to make a decision. Since home buyers usually want low-risk property they can be referred to these based on the prediction results.

10.8.5 IMPROVEMENT IN CUSTOMER EXPERIENCES

One of the major achievements of big data has been the improvement in the customer experience. A better customer experience always gives you better results, and big data has made it possible. Through the different data collected from various sources, we can get details about our customers. This helps us in understanding their demographic, geographic, and other information which we can use to determine the Preferences of the customers. So, we can use these insights to improve the overall customer experience. This means we can directly offer the customers what they are looking for instead of reaching out to random customers. We can thus target the right customers for a particular property through various mediums that are preferred by them.

10.8.6 ENHANCEMENT IN PROPERTY VALUATIONS

Pricing is one of the important elements that affect decision-making in the real estate industry. Therefore, the success of a property sale can be directly dependent on its valuation. In this scenario, big data can be influential in making the right estimation of the property.

Through big data, businesses can easily make price estimations based on the prices of similar properties in the area, prevailing market conditions, the purpose, and other details. This comparative analysis regarding property can help businesses in determining accurate prices for the given properties (Shimizu, 2017). Using the proper data and information, it becomes possible to make proper offers and target the right audiences. The data can also help the buyers and investors as it can predict the future relative value of the property. So, if someone is buying the property for commercial reasons, the person can estimate the revenue he can earn through the property in the future.

10.8.7 INTELLIGENT CONSTRUCTION

Intelligence construction is one of the critical elements in the real estate industry that is enabled by big data. This means, earlier it would be difficult to gain all the information about a particular project before its construction. However, with big data, people can now understand beforehand the overall cost involved in the project and when and where they can build it. Many companies also make use of 3D models to get an idea of how the whole process will take place and what will be the outcome. Therefore, the businesses can already estimate the efforts and money needed for the investment. This will help them to avoid any unnecessary expenses. Basically, big data has enabled businesses to make more informed decisions with respect to the projects they are working on and know their worth in advance (Director et al., 2022).

10.8.8 PERSONALIZED DATA

Personalization is one of the major benefits derived by the business through big data. Businesses use the insights developed by big data to understand the property and the customers in a better way (Kyung and Lee, 2015). This is how they become more aware of the actual needs of the customers. Some things that were previously ignored by businesses are now given much focus in the customer-driven world. As the customer becomes part of the process, the companies can exactly know what they want and can take efforts to make it a reality. Big data helps businesses in realizing that every customer is unique and has different preferences so, they can accordingly build the properties keeping their target customers in mind (Littlefield, 2015).

10.9 CONCLUSION

The Indian real estate industry has shown significant growth potential. Despite the recent slowdown in the industry, it can be observed to have good potential in the upcoming future. This means the sales, especially of residential properties are expected to rise and with its expansion, the revenue and employment generation will also follow.

Over the years, big data has also played an important role in the development of the sector. Because of big data, it has now become possible to get maximum outcomes with minimum effort.

There have been many changes in the Real Estate process. In recent years, there has been a shift from producer-centric to customer-centric processes with regard to real estate projects. This is mainly due to the realization that customers will buy what they want, so it is important to make what they want instead of trying to sell random properties to random people.

The emphasis on the needs and wants of the customers has been made possible due to the arrival of big data. Since it is now possible to securely collect and restore data, businesses can now use it to draw insights about their customers and reach out to the right ones. This helps in saving time as well as efforts of both businesses and investors. Big data has not only paved the path for customer-centric processes but also infused competition resulting in the best outcomes for customers.

In the data-driven world, there is end number of opportunities for different sectors and real estate is no exception to that. However, with every new technology comes a new risk, there is also an opportunity to rise which can be grabbed by various businesses to become market leaders. With big data, this opportunity comes in the form of the ability to understand their customers in a better way than their customers and being able to meet their needs before anyone else.

As discussed earlier, big data has created a plethora of opportunities for not only businesses but also consumers. On the one hand, businesses have access to data that affects the consumer's buying process; on the other hand, consumers have access to all the available data regarding a particular product from different brands. In the end, whoever is capable of managing that data in better way and utilizing it for their maximum benefit will be able to take control of the market (Kitchens, 2018).

KEYWORDS

- **big data**
- **influence**
- **customer relationship management**
- **real estate**

REFERENCES

Director, H. T. S. et al. *Real Estate Analytics: How Big Data Is Transforming Real Estate, Bright Data.* https://brightdata.com/blog/leadership/how-big-data-is-transforming-real-estate

Du, D., Li, A.; Zhang, L. Survey on the Applications of Big Data in Chinese Real Estate Enterprise. *Procedia Comput. Sci.* **2014,** *30*, 24–33. https://doi.org/10.1016/j.procs.2014.05.377

Edison, J. C. Real Estate Industry in India. *Infrastruct. Dev. Constr. Manag.* **2020,** 66–83. https://doi.org/10.1201/9781003055624-3.

Ghavami, A.; Olyaei, A. The Impact of CRM on Customer Retention. In: *Social Science and Business Administration Programmes*; Lulea University of Technology, 2006.

J, S. Influence of Big Data on Customer Retention Analytics. *J. Asiatic Soc. Mumbai* **2022,** *XCIV* (6).

Kitchens, B. et al. Advanced Customer Analytics: Strategic Value Through Integration of Relationship-Oriented Big Data. *J. Manag. Inf. Syst.* **2018,** *35* (2), 540–574. https://doi.org/10.1080/07421222.2018.1451957.

Kyung, J.-I.; Lee, K.-C. Research on Factors Affecting Intention to Adopt Big Data in the Real Estate Field. *J. Real Estate Anal.* **2015,** *1* (1e), 53–75. https://doi.org/10.30902/jrea.2015.1.1e.53.

Latha, P.; Lalitha, P. Big Data Usage in Customer Relationship Management for Organizations. *Int. J. Eng. Res. Technol.* **2015**.

Littlefield, L. Big Data Can Power Personalized Marketing Campaigns; Right on Interactive, 2015. https://www.rightoninteractive.com/customer-lifecycle-marketing/big-data-personalized-marketing-campaigns.

Pawar, R. Increasing Customer Retention Using Big Data Customer Analytics. *Conference: Seminar—Recent Topics in Business Informatics, Otto-von-Guericke University Magdeburg* [Preprint], 2018.

Shimizu, C. Ways of Real Estate Price Determination from a Big Data Perspective. *Jpn J. Real Estate Sci.* **2017,** *31* (1), 45–51. https://doi.org/10.5736/jares.31.1_45.

Winson-Geideman, K. et al. Gathering Real Estate Data: Real Estate Analysis in the Information Age, 2017; pp 47–51. https://doi.org/10.4324/9781315311135-5.

Xie, K. et al. Value Co-Creation Between Firms and Customers: The Role of Big Data-Based Cooperative Assets. *Inf. Manag.* **2016,** *53* (8), 1034–1048. https://doi.org/10.1016/j.im.2016.06.003.

CHAPTER 11

New Age Communication: Social Media Marketing and Big Data

REKHA ATTRI

Jaipuria Institute of Management, Indore, India

ABSTRACT

Big data has garnered considerable attention from the academic and business communities. Influencer marketing is one of the fastest-growing domains, but finding these influencers in massive datasets is a never-ending difficulty. The increasing popularity of influencer marketing has prompted research scholars to explore their impact on consumer brand knowledge and their attitude toward brands. When preparing for and carrying out their influencer marketing programs, many organizations encounter numerous difficulties. This necessitates the use of up-to-date information, cutting-edge equipment, and automation to address these problems effectively. Studies indicate that the content of the message and congruence of the influencer with the brand significantly influence brand knowledge and brand affection while the credibility of the influencer might not affect brand knowledge or brand affection.

11.1 INTRODUCTION

11.1.1 INFLUENCER MARKETING

Brand managers' attention has shifted toward social media platforms due to changes in how modern consumers consume media (Campbell and Farrell, 2020). Influencer marketing refers to utilizing prominent opinion leaders with considerable popularity on social media to promote favorable consumer

Augmenting Customer Retention Through Big Data Analytics.
Reena Malik, Ambuj Sharma, and Prashant Chaudhary (Eds.)

behaviors and attitudes (Giles and Edwards, 2018; Lou and Yuan, 2019). Influencers are those who are compensated for posting on social media (Campbell and Grimm, 2019). Many corporations have begun paying influencers to promote their products by encouraging individualized consumer involvement through their postings because standard marketing communications methods cannot effectively engage customers naturally (Kowalczyk and Pounders, 2016). Influencer marketing is reportedly nearly 10 times more effective than other digital marketing techniques (Tapinfluence, 2016).

11.1.2 INFLUENCER CATEGORIES

Many brands have employed influencer marketing to connect with their target demographic, increasing sales as a result (Adweek, 2015; ANA, 2018; Wang et al., 2017; Jasrotia et al., 2019). Recent studies on influencer marketing identify their credibility, content, and brand alignment as crucial factors influencing its effectiveness (Campbell and Farrell, 2020; De Veirman et al., 2017; Eisend, 2007; Goldsmith et al., 2000; Kim and Kim, 2021; Lou and Yuan, 2019). Based on authenticity, knowledge, accessibility, and follower count, the Association of National Advertisers has categorized influencers as microinfluencers (50–25,000 followers), midlevel influencers (25,001–100,000 followers), and macroinfluencers (over 100,000 followers). Although these influencers can publish on any social media platform, they prefer posting on Instagram and YouTube (ANA, 2018). In their study, Campbell and Farrell (2020) divided social media influencers into four categories: Nanoinfluencers (0–10K followers; typically have friends and acquaintances as followers; offer highest perceived authenticity and accessibility); microinfluencers (10–100K localized followers but are rated as genuine recommenders); macroinfluencers (100K–1 M followers; are incredibly well-known and have high engagement rates); and megainfluencers (1M+ followers; are social media mavens but unknown beyond the set of their followers) and celebrity-influencers (1 M+ followers; have recognition beyond social media as well).

11.2 BIG DATA IN MARKETING

Big data has garnered considerable attention from the academic and business communities (Cao et al., 2019). Big data consists of extremely large datasets that can be analyzed and interpreted to reveal trends and patterns

(McGuigan, 2019) and has become a catalyst for organizational marketing decision-making while also contributing to the creation of enterprise value (Akhtar et al. 2019). There is a shift from conventional marketing strategies to analytical marketing decision making (Liang and Liu, 2018). Businesses today prioritize marketing analytics, particularly the correct evaluation of marketing performance (Buhalis and Volchek, 2021). Due to the extensive adoption of smart technology, more touchpoints exist between consumers and brands (Gursoy et al., 2019). Data analytics innovations are revolutionizing organizational opportunities for better relationships with their target clients (Senyo et al., 2019). Influencer marketing is one of the fastest-growing domains, but finding these influencers in massive datasets is a never-ending difficulty (Harrigan, et al., 2021). Social media users who interact and express their thoughts on different online social media platforms produce a significant amount of diversity consisting of articles, photographs, or audio clips (Jiménez-Castillo and Sánchez-Fernández, 2019). Researchers in information systems (ISs) have invested much time and money into identifying and validating methods that might process large amounts of social consumer data effectively.

11.3 DATA ANALYTICS IN INFLUENCER MARKETING

Direct interactions between businesses and customers are a result of technological progress, mostly owing to the evolution of social media (Soni et al., 2009; Sudarsanam, 2018; Jasrotia and Koul, 2020). When preparing for and carrying out their influencer marketing programs, many organizations encounter numerous difficulties. This necessitates the use of up-to-date information, cutting-edge equipment, and automation to effectively address these problems (Sharma, 2020). A data-driven framework is required for the identification and selection of influencers who can best promote a company's message or marketing. Mallipeddi et al. (2022) highlighted the cumulative effect of numerous influencers in their empirical investigation and suggested including the multiple exposure effect and forgetting effect in their model. According to 84% of marketing professionals, influencer marketing is very effective and provides the best return on investment (ROI) (Barker, 2020). According to Barker (2020), a data-driven approach as listed in the following can help organizations:

- Identify those products and services that are gaining maximum traction.

- Identify what customers like about the brand.
- Identify achievements in terms of web traffic, brand awareness, conversions, and revenue.
- Identify customer segments that the organization is unable to attract and engage.
- Identify a number of new accounts reached; customer engagement rate; and a number of new followers, comments, and shares.

Thus, data-driven insights can assist in establishing reasonable advertising objectives as well as in locating the appropriate influencers. Platforms for data-driven influencer marketing can help in locating influencers and helping to focus the influencer selection based on factors like region, consumer segment demographics, engagement rate, and the kinds of products the influencer promotes. Before choosing an influencer for their product or service, marketers must carefully consider influencer vetting, which entails assessing the credibility of potential influencers. Big data analytics can help in influencer vetting by the following factors:

- Identifying the impact of influencer messages on the audience.
- Analyzing the quality of the content.
- Evaluating the relevance of audience comments on influencer's posts.
- Calculating the engagement rate of influencer's posts.
- Studying the alignment of the content posted by influencers with the brand's values.
- Identifying the type of content the influencer excels in.

Big data analytics is utilized to find popular subjects, consumer search terms, and the kinds of themes that generate the most comments and engagement (Misra and Singh, 2016). In addition to identifying the ideal influencer for the business, an intelligent, real-time data-driven approach can also recommend which goods will do well with that particular audience by leveraging the significance of conversion rates. Marketers may draw lessons from previous efforts and forecast the performance of the next ones by using data analytics. Data analytics may help in finding the correct influencer, producing effective content, and assessing the effectiveness and return on investment of influencer marketing (Haryacha, 2021). Important factors impacting brand awareness and brand attachment include influencer credibility, message content, and congruence with the brand of the influencer (Quilty, 2022).

11.4 INFLUENCER CREDIBILITY, BRAND KNOWLEDGE AND BRAND AFFECTION

Endorser credibility refers to the magnitude to which a source is viewed as having knowledge about a topic and can be counted upon to present an unbiased viewpoint (Goldsmith et al., 2000; Ohanian, 1990). It has been proposed that the credibility of the source precedes the development of attitudes toward advertisements, which eventually results in the effectiveness of the advertisement (Atkin and Block, 1983; Goldberg and Hartwick, 1990). According to the credibility theory, buyers are influenced by celebrities because they have a higher level of faith in the celebrity than they do in businesses (Erdogan, 1999). In contrast to all other kinds of advertising, a Neilsen study found that 92% of consumers trust recommendations and advice from their reference group of family and friends (ANA, 2018). This is why influencer marketing, rather than focusing on the entire market, targets those people having a large fan following on social media. Through these influencers, businesses can connect with potential customers who find the influencers to be trustworthy and rely on what they have to say about the brand (Adweek, 2015). The degree to which the influencer is regarded as an authority on the issue heavily influences how persuasive they can be (Wang et al., 2017). According to some reports, attractiveness (in terms of familiarity and likeability) and trustworthiness (in terms of perceived honesty and believability) also serve as indicators of a source's veracity (Ohanian, 1990). According to Weinswig (2016), consumers perceive social media influencers as trustworthy and reliable in comparison to supermodels, actors, and athletes. According to the social penetration theory (SPT), influencers' voluntary sharing of experiences and emotions fosters the development of human relationships (Kim and Song, 2016). Through the identification process, the protagonist's feelings and experiences with the brand are transferred vicariously to the audience for the content (Chang, 2013). Customers find visual accounts of influencers' personal lives to be incredibly fascinating, and this attracts their attention, resulting in the growth of brand affection (De Veirman et al., 2017). The expert power of the influencer because of the detailed knowledge in a particular domain, along with the referent power since followers wish to connect with them, provides an explanation of how influencers shape the attitude and purchase intention of customers (Kupfer et al., 2018).

11.5 CONTENT OF MESSAGE, BRAND KNOWLEDGE, AND BRAND AFFECTION

According to reports, the influencer's message's substance determines the level of engagement a post will produce (Lipsman et al., 2012). Additionally, genuineness in the influencer's communication of the brand's various features results in effective influencer marketing (Feng et al., 2020). Contrary to blatantly commercial ads produced by corporations, less invasive ads with a subtly persuasive message from influencers get more consumer attention, engagement, and response (Pereira et al., 2014) and are regarded as being open, sincere, and educational (Kowalczyk and Pounders, 2016). One-sided messaging, in which the influencer only addresses the benefits of the product and ignores its drawbacks, is found to be less trustworthy than two-sided messages, in which the influencer covers both its advantages and problems (Winter and Krämer, 2012). According to studies, people regard influencers as being sincere and honest when they include negative aspects of a product in their messages, improving their credibility (Crowley and Hoyer, 1994; Eisend , 2007). The agencies who hire the influencers use some amount of creative control to make sure the influencer stays on the message even though the influencers are given creative latitude to create and distribute the material (Childers et al., 2019). Influencer posts with a message that is mostly controlled by the brand have been shown to be less effective in terms of waning follower engagement and decreased desire to look for more information (Hwang and Jeong, 2016; Martnez-López et al., 2020).

11.6 INFLUENCER'S CONGRUENCE WITH BRAND, BRAND KNOWLEDGE AND BRAND AFFECTION

Sokolova and Kefi (2019) have observed that effective influencers are typically confined to a specific area of interest and develop expertise in that area as a result of which they are given the chance to endorse the brands in that product category. If the influencer and the brand are a good fit, the followers' trust in the shared material will be increased (Pang et al., 2016; Jung et al., 2016). Customers have indicated a positive attitude toward a brand when they can discern a strong bond between the endorser and the product because it raises the authority of the influencer's opinions, convictions, and experiences (Mathys et al., 2016). The importance of a strong image overlap between the endorser and the brand, which results in favorable attitudinal responses and the influencer's persuasiveness for the brand, has been established by researchers using the "match-up" approach (McCormick, 2016). A good fit between the influencer and the brand boosts the level of cognition as well as attitudinal and conative assessments (Kim and Kim, 2021; Martnez-Lopez et al., 2020).

11.7 CONCLUSION

The establishment of favorable brand affection and purchasing intention is ultimately influenced by brand knowledge. According to Lee and Kim (2020), opinions of the usefulness of a brand are not considerably impacted by judgments of the influencer's legitimacy. According to the "match-up" approach, the congruence of an influencer with a brand has a major positive impact on brand knowledge. A higher congruence with the brand raises the credibility of the influencer's ideas and experiences (Pang et al., 2016; Jung et al, 2016; Mathys et al., 2016; McCormick, 2016).

From a managerial standpoint, it makes sense to recommend that firms should concentrate on the two factors such as when developing influencer marketing because of the content of the message and the influencer's alignment with the brand have a major beneficial impact on brand knowledge and attitude. To capture consumer attention and boost consumer purchase intentions, marketers have been utilizing both earned influencer marketing (which derives from unpaid influencers interested in disseminating information for their own social growth) and paid influencer marketing techniques, such as sponsorships, pre-roll advertising, testimonials, etc. (Sudha and Sheena, 2017). Celebrities and other major influencers with significant social media fan bases typically demand a substantial fee to endorse a product. Some mega, macroinfluencers, and celebrities can be hired for as little as $10,000 to as much as $1 million for each post (Geyser, 2021). Hudders et al. (2021) observed that rather than contacting influencers with a broad following, some of whom may be fake followers, marketers should be on the lookout for those nanoinfluencers who are experts in a particular niche and who, due to their authenticity and relatability, can speak directly to their organic followers, however small in number.

Marketers need to focus more on the message's content and the influencer's alignment with the brand. Since it boosts the message's dependability and believability, which in turn affects attitudes toward the brand and buying intents, it is important to keep an eye on how authentically the message is conveyed.

KEYWORDS

- **influencer marketing**
- **big data**
- **social media**
- **purchase intention**
- **attitude**
- **brand knowledge**
- **brand affection**

REFERENCES

Adweek. 10 Reasons Why Influencer Marketing is the Next Big Thing. https://www.adweek.com/: https://www.adweek.com/performance-marketing/10-reasons-why-influencer-marketing-is-the-next-big-thing/ (accessed on 1 Aug 2021).

Akhtar, P.; Frynas, J.; Mellahi, K.; Ullah, S. Big Data-Savvy Teams' Skills, Big Data-Driven Actions and Business Performance. *Br. J. Manag.* **2019,** *30* (2), 252–271.

ANA. Survey Report: How ANA Members Are Using Influencer Marketing. ANA, 2018. https://www.ana.net/getfile/26389

Atkin, C.; Block, M. Effectiveness of Celebrity Endorsers. *J. Advertis. Res.* **1983,** *23* (1), 57–61.

Barker, S. How to Use Big Data to Boost Your Influencer Marketing Campaign ROI, 3 June 2020. https://blog.crowdfireapp.com/: https://blog.crowdfireapp.com/how-to-use-big-data-to-boost-your-influencer-marketing-campaign-roi-c2b443932720 (accessed on 5 Oct 2022).

Baron, R.; Kenny, D. The Moderator-Mediator Variable Distinction in Social Psychological Research: Conceptual, Strategic and Statistical Considerations. *J. Person. Soc. Psychol.* **1986,** *51* (6), 1173–1182.

Boerman, S.; Van Reijmersdal, E.; Neijens, P. Sponsorship Disclosure: Effects of Duration on Persuation Knowledge and Brand Responses. *J. Commun.* **2912,** *62* (6), 1047–1064.

Buhalis, D.; Volchek, K. Bridging Marketing Theory and Big Data Analytics: The Taxonomy of Marketing Attribution. *Int. J. Inf. Manag.* **2021,** *56*, 102253.

Campbell, C.; Farrell, J. More Than Meets the Eye: The Functional Components Underlying Influencer Marketing. *Bus. Horizons* **2020,** *63* (4), 469–479.

Campbell, C.; Grimm, P. The Challenges Native Advertising Poses: Exploring Potential Federal Trade Commission Responses and Identifying Research Needs. *J. Public Policy Market.* **2019,** *38* (1), 110–123.

Cao, G.; Duan, Y.; El Banna, A. A Dynamic Capability View of Marketing Analytics: Evidence from UK Firms. *Ind. Market. Manag.* **2019,** *76*, 72–83.

Chang, C. Imagery Fluency and Narrative Advertising Effects. *J. Advertis.* **2013,** *42* (1), 54–68.

Childers, C.; Lemon, L.; Hoy, M. # Sponsored# Ad: Agency Perspective on Influencer Marketing Campaigns. *J. Curr. Iss. Res. Advert.* **2019,** *40* (3), 258–274.

Chowdhury, S.; Salam, M. Predicting Attitude Based on Cognitive, Affective and Conative Components: An Online Shopping Perspective. *Stamford J. Bus. Stud.* **2015,** *2* (6), 101–115.

Crowley, A.; Hoyer, W. An Integrative Framework for Understanding Two-Sided Persuasion. *J. Consumer Res.* **1994,** *20* (4), 561–574.

De Veirman, M.; Cauberghe, V.; Hudders, L. Marketing Through Instagram Influencers: The Impact of Number of Followers and Product Divergence on Brand Attitude. *Int. J. Advert.* **2017,** *36* (5), 798–828.

*J. Advert.*Dixit, S.; Maurya , S. Factors Affecting Attitude Towards Private Label Grocery Purchases by Indian Consumers. *LBS J. Manag. Res.* **2021,** *19* (1), 38–51.

Dolega, L.; Rowe, F.; Branagan, E. Going Digital? The Impact of Social Media Marketing on retail website traffic, orders and sales. *J. Retail. Consumer Serv.* **2021,** *102501*, 60.

Eisend , M. Understanding Two-Sided Persuasion: An Empirical Assessment of Theoretical Approaches. *Psychol. Market.* **2007,** *24* (7), 615–640.

Erdogan, B. Celebrity Endorsement: A Literature Review. *J. Market. Manag.* **1999,** *15* (4), 291–314.

Feng, Y.; Chen, H.; Kong, Q. An Expert with Whom I Can Identify: The Role of Narratives in Influencer Marketing. *Int. J. Advert.* **2020,** 1–22.

Fink, M.; Koller, M.; Gartner, J.; Floh, A.; Harms, R. Effective Entrepreneurial Marketing on Facebook—A Longitudinal Study. *J. Bus. Res.* **2019,** *113*, 149–157.

Geyser, W. Influencer Rates: How Much Do Influencers Really Cost in 2021, 28 June 2021. https://influencermarketinghub.com/: https://influencermarketinghub.com/influencer-rates/

Giles, D.; Edwards, L. Instagram and the Rise of the Social Media 'Influencer'. In: *Twenty-First Century Celebrity: Fame in Digital Culture*; Giles, D. C., Ed.; pp 155–173.

Goldberg, M.; Hartwick, J. The Effects of Advertiser Reputation and Extremity of Advertising Claim on Advertising Effectiveness. *J. Consumer Res.* **1990,** *17* (2), 172–179.

Goldsmith, R.; Lafferty, B.; Newell, S. The Impact of Corporate Credibility and Celebrity Credibility on Consumer Reaction to Advertisements and Brands. *J. Advert.* **2000,** *29* (3), 43–54.

Gursoy, D.; Chi, O.; Lu, L.; Nunkoo, R. Consumers Acceptance of Artificially Intelligent (AI) Device Use in Service Delivery. *Int. J. Inf. Manag.* **2019,** *49*, 157–169.

Hair, J.; Black, E.; Babin, B.; Anderson, R. *Multivarite Data Analysis*; Prentice Hall: Upper Saddle River.

Han, H. Consumer Behavior and Environmental Sustainability in Tourism and Hospitality: A review of theories, concepts, and latest research. *J. Sustain. Tour.* **2021,** *29* (7), 1021–1042.

Harrigan, P.; Daly , T.; Coussement, K.; Lee , J.; Soutar, G.; Evers, U. Identifying Influencers on Social Media. *Int. J. Inf. Manag.* **2021,** *56*, 102246.

Haryacha, P. Influencer Marketing in a Data-Driven World, 20 May 2021. https://datafloq.com/: https://datafloq.com/read/influencer-marketing-data-driven-world/ (accessed on 12 Oct 2022).

Hashim, R.; Omar, B.; Al-Samarraie, H. International Tourists Visiting Experiences in Malaysia as Revealed by Travel Bloggers: An Analysis of Travel Blogs Using Tri-component Model of Destination Image. *J. Contemp. Iss. Media Commun. (JCIMC)* **2021,** *1*, 048–074.

Hayes, A. *Methodology in the Social Sciences: Introduction to Mediation, Moderation and Conditional Process Analysis: A Regression-Based Approach*; New York: Guilford Publication.

Hudders, L.; De Jans, S.; De Veirman , M. The Commercialization of Social Media Stars: A Literature Review and Conceptual Framework on the Strategic Use of Social Media Influencers. *Int. J. Advert.* **2021,** *40* (3), 327–375.

Hwang, Y.; Jeong, S. This Is a Sponsored Blog Post, But All Opinions Are My Own: The Effects of Sponsorship Disclosure on Responses to Sponsored Blog Posts. *Comput. Hum Behav.* **2016,** *62*, 528–535.

Jasrotia, S.; Koul, S. Do Young Consumers Buy Country Made Products? Evidence from India. *Int. J. Manag. Enterprise Dev.* **2020,** *19* (4), 378–397.

Jasrotia, S.; Mishra, H.; Koul, S. Brick or click? Channel Choice Disruptions in Travel Industry. *Asia-Pac. J. Manag. Res. Innov.* **2019,** *15* (1–2), 16–26.

Jiménez-Castillo, D.; Sánchez-Fernández, R. The Role of Digital Influencers in Brand Recommendation: Examining Their Impact on Engagement, Expected Value and Purchase Intention. *Int. J. Inf. Manag.* **2019,** *49*, 366–376.

Jung, E.; Walsh-Childers, K.; Kim, S. Factors Influencing the Perceived Credibility of Diet-Nutrition Information Web Sites. *Comput. Hum. Behav.* **2016,** *58*, 37–47.

Katz, D.; Stotland, E. A Preliminary Statement to a Theory of Attitude Structure and Change. In: *Psychology: A Study of a Science: Vol. 3 Formulations of the Person and the Social Context*; Koch, S., Ed; McGraw-Hill: New York, 1959; pp 423–475.

Khan, A. Influencer Marketing Strategies Helped Mamaearth to Earn a Whopping Revenue of Rs 110 crore in FY20, 28 July 2021. https://nextbigbrand.in/: https://nextbigbrand.in/mamaearth-earned-a-whopping-revenue-of-rs-110-crore-in-fy20/ (accessed on 5 August 2021).

Kim, D.; Kim, H. Influencer Advertising on Social Media: The Multiple Inference Model on Influencer-Product Congruence and Sponsorship Disclosure. *J. Bus. Res.* **2021,** *130*, 405–415.

Kim, J.; Song, H. Celebrity's Self-Disclosure on Twitter and Parasocial Relationships: A Mediating Role of Social Presence. *Comput. Hum. Behav.* **2016,** *62*, 570–577.

Kowalczyk, C.; Pounders, K. Transforming Celebrities Through Social Media: The Role of Authenticity and Emotional Attachment. *J. Product Brand Manag.* **2016,** *25* (4), 345–356.

Kupfer, A.; Vor Der Holte, N.; Kubler, R.; Hennig-Thurau, T. The Role of the Partner Brand's Social Media Power in Brand alliances. *J. Market.* **2018,** *82* (3), 25–44.

Lafferty, B.; Goldsmith, R.; Newell, S. The Dual Credibility Model: The Influence of Corporate and Endorser Credibility on Attitudes and Purchase Intentions. *J. Market. Theor. Practice* **2002,** *10* (3), 1–11.

Lee, S.; Kim, E. Influencer Marketing on Instagram: How Sponsorship Disclosure, Influencer Credibility, and Brand Credibility Impact the Effectiveness of Instagram Promotional Post. *J. Glob. Fashion Market.* **2020,** *11* (3), 232–249.

Liang , T.; Liu, Y. Research Landscape of Business Intelligence and Big Data Analytics: A Bibliometrics Study. *Expert Syst. App.* **2018,** *111*, 2–10.

Lim, J.; Ri, S.; Egan, B.; Biocca, F. The Cross-Platform Synergies of Digital Video Advertising: Implications for Cross-Media Campaigns in Television, Internet and Mobile TV. *Comput. Hum. Behav.* **2015,** *48*, 463–472.

Lipsman, A.; Mudd, G.; Rich, M.; Bruich, S. The Power of "Like": How Brands Reach (and Influence) Fans Through Social-Media Marketing. *J. Advert. Res.* **2012,** *52* (1), 40–52.

Lou, C.; Yuan, S. Influencer marketing: How message value and credibility affect consumer trust of branded content on social media. Journal of Interactive Advertising, 19 (1), 58–73.

Macho, S.; Ledermann, T. Estimating, Testing and Comparing Specific Effect in Structural Equation Models: The Phantom Model Approach. *Psychol. Methods* **2011,** *16* (1), 34–43.

Makanyeza, C. Measuring Consumer Attitude Towards Imported Poultry Meat Products in a Developing Market: An Assessment of Reliability, Validity and Dimensionality of the Tri-Component Attitude Model. *Mediterranean J. Soc. Sci.* **2014,** *5* (20), 874.

Mallipeddi, R.; Kumar, S.; Sriskandarajah, C.; Zhu, Y. A Framework for Analyzing Influencer Marketing in Social Networks: Selection and Scheduling of Influencers. *Manag. Sci.* **2022,** *68* (1), 75–104.

Martınez-Lopez, F.; Anaya-Sanchez, R.; Fernandez Giordano, M.; Lopez-Lopez, D. Behind Influencer Marketing: Key Marketing Decisions and Their Effects on Followers' Responses. *J. Market. Manag.* **2020,** *36* (7–8), 579–607.

Martínez-López, F.; Anaya-Sánchez, R.; Fernández Giordano, M.; Lopez-Lopez, D. Behind Influencer Marketing: Key Marketing Decisions and Their Effects on Followers' Responses. *J. Market. Manag.* **2020,** *36* (7–8), 579–607.

Mathys, J.; Burmester, A.; Clement, M. What Drives the Market Popularity of Celebrities? A Longitudinal Analysis of Consumer Interest in Film Stars. *Int. J. Res. Market.* **2016,** *33* (2), 428–448.

McCormick, K. Celebrity Endorsements: Influence of a Product-Endorser Match on Millennials Attitudes and Purchase Intentions. *J. Retail. Consumer Serv.* **2016,** *32*, 39–45.

McGuigan, L. Automating the Audience Commodity: The Unacknowledged Ancestry of Programmatic Advertising. *New Media Soc.* **2019,** *21* (11–12), 2366–2385.

Misra, R.; Singh, D. An Analysis of Factors Affecting Growth of Organic Food: Perception of Consumers in Delhi-NCR (India). *Br. Food J.* **2016,** *118* (9), 2308–2325.

Nasir, N.; Chan, S.; Aprilia, C. The Function of the Attitude of Islamic Banks in Coastal Societies in Mediating the Effect of Emotional Attachment on the Continuance Intention of Islamic Banks. *E3S Web Conf.* **2022,** *339*, 05009.

Ohanian, R. Construction and Validation of a Scale to Measure Celebrity Endorsers' Perceived Expertise, Trustworthiness, and Attractiveness. *J. Advert.* **1990,** *19* (3), 39–52.

Pang, A.; Tan, E.; Qi Lim, R.; Kwan, T.; Lakhanpal, P. Building Effective Relations with Social Media Influencers in Singapore. *Media Asia* **2016,** *43* (1), 56–68.

Pereira, H.; de Fátima Salgueiro, M.; Mateus, I. Say Yes to Facebook and Get Your Customers Involved! Relationships in a World of Social Networks. *Bus. Horizons* **2014,** *57* (6), 695–702.

Podsakoff, P.; Mackenzie, S.; Lee, J.; Podsakoff, N. Common Method Biases in Behavioural Research: A Critical Review of the Literature and Recommended Remedies. *J. Appl. Psychol.* **2003,** *88* (5), 879–903.

Qoruz. Avneet Kaur Official, 2021. https://app.qoruz.com: https://app.qoruz.com/profile/avneetkaur_13

Qoruz. Influencer Marketing Platform for Brands & Agencies, n.d. https://qoruz.com: https://qoruz.com/influencer-marketing-platform-india (accessed on 21 March 2021).

Quilty, F. Using Data Analytics to Drive Influencer Marketing Outcomes, 21 Sept 2022. https://martechseries.com/: https://martechseries.com/mts-insights/guest-authors/using-data-analytics-to-drive-influencer-marketing-outcomes/ (accessed on 5 October 2022)

Rodgers, S. The Effects of Sponsor Relevance on Consumer Reactions to Internet Sponsorships. *J. Advert.* **2003,** *32* (4), 67–76.

Rosenberg, M.; Hovland, C. Cognitive, Affective, and Behavioral Components of Attitudes. In: *Attitude organization and change: an analysis of consistency among attitude components*; Rosenberg, M. J., Ed.; 1960; pp 1–14.

Schouten, A.; Janssen, L.; Verspaget, M. Celebrity vs. Influencer Endorsements in Advertising: The Role of Identification, Credibility, and Product-Endorser Fit. *Int. J. Advert.* **2020,** *39* (2), 258–281.

Sekhar, C.; Krishna, S.; Kayal, G.; Rana, N. Does Brand Credibility Matter? The Case of Organic Food Products. *Br. Food J.* **2022,** *124* (3), 987–1008.

Sengupta, J.; Johar, G. . Effects of Inconsistent Attribute Information on the Predictive Value of Product Attitudes: Toward a Resolution of Opposing Perspectives. *J. Consumer Res.* **2002,** *29* (1), 39–56.

Senyo, P.; Liu, K.; Effah, J. Digital Business Ecosystem: Literature Review and a Framework for Future Research. *Int. J. Inf. Manag.* **2019,** *47*, 52–64.

Sharma, G. How Big Data Can Maximize Your Influencer Marketing Campaign Outcomes, 2020. https://www.smartdatacollective.com/: https://www.smartdatacollective.com/big-data-maximize-influencer-marketing-campaign-outcomes/ (accessed on 25 Oct 2022).

Sokolova, K.; Kefi, H. Instagram and YouTube Bloggers Promote It, Why Should I Buy? How Credibility and Parasocial Interaction Influence Purchase Intentions. *J. Retail. Consumer Serv.* **2019,** *53*, 1–9.

Soni, S.; Sharma, J.; Upadhyaya, M. Communicating Corporate Identity for the Hotel Industry. *J. Market. Commun.* **2009,** *4* (3), 53–58.

Spry, A.; Pappu, R.; Cornwell, T. Celebrity Endorsement, Brand Credibility and Brand Equity. *Eur. J. Market.* **2011,** *45* (6), 882–909.

Srinivasan, L. Indian Cosmetics Go Local, Natural and Organic, 25 Sept 2020. https://www.thehindubusinessline.com/: https://www.thehindubusinessline.com/blink/work/indian-cosmetics-go-local-natural-and-organic/article32690508.ece (accessed on 12 June 2021).

Sudarsanam , S. Social Media Metrics. In: *Social Media Marketing: Breakthroughs in Research and Practice*; 2018; pp 790–808.

Sudha, M.; Sheena, K. Impact of Influencers in Consumer Decision Process: The Fashion Industry. *SCMS J. Indian Manag.* **2017,** *14* (3), 14–30.

Tapinfluence. The Future of Influencer Marketing: 6 Predictions Your Brand or Agency Can Bank on, 2016. https://www.tapinfluence.com: https://www.tapinfluence.com/tp_resource/6-influencermarketing-predictions-brand-agency-can-bank/ (accessed on 23 Feb 2020).

Taylor, C. Is Covid Making Marketing Influencers More Influential? July 2020. www.forbes.com: https://www.forbes.com/sites/charlesrtaylor/2020/07/30/is-covid-making-marketing-influencers-more-influential/#237d789f4200 (accessed on June 2021).

Tewari, S. Consumers Shift to Cleaner Cosmetics, 21 Oct 2020. https://www.livemint.com/: https://www.livemint.com/industry/advertising/cosmetics-startups-latch-on-to-clean-beauty-bandwagon-11603194959112.html (accessed on 12 June 2021).

Thomas, S. Brand Attitude Measurement Using the Tri-Partite Model of Attitude and Evaluating Its Relationship to Customer Satisfaction—A Study of a Hypermarket Brand in UAE. *Int. J. Manag.* **2020,** *11* (10), 548–560.

Tyagi, G. How Mamaearth Used Influencers to Scale Its Income 6.5X to Rs 110 Cr in FY20. https://entrackr.com/: https://entrackr.com/2021/01/how-mamaearth-used-influencers-to-scale-its-income-6–5x-to-rs-110-cr-in-fy20/ (accessed on 24 June 2021).

Wang, S.; Scheinbaum, A. Enhancing Brand Credibility via Celebrity Endorsement: Trustworthiness Trumps Attractiveness and Expertise. *J. Advert. Res.* **2018,** *58* (1), 16–32.
Wang, S.; Kao, G.; Ngamsiriudom, W. Consumers' Attitude of Endorser Credibility, Brand and Intention with Respect to Celebrity Endorsement of the Airline Sector. *J. Air Transp. Manag.* **2017,** *60*, 10–17.
Weinswig, D. Influencers Are the New Brands, 5 Oct 2016. www.forbes.com: https://www.forbes.com/sites/deborahweinswig/2016/10/05/celebritys-are-the-new-brands/#66ad98a37919 (accessed on July 2021).
Winter, S.; Krämer, N. Selecting Science Information in Web 2.0: How Source Cues, Message Sidedness, and Need for Cognition Influence Users' Exposure to Blog Posts. *J. Comput.-Mediated Commun.* **2012,** *18* (1), 80–96.
Zhang, B.; Zhang, Y.; Zhou, P. Consumer Attitude Towards Sustainability of Fast Fashion Products in the UK. *Sustainability* **2021,** *13* (4), 1646.

CHAPTER 12

Innovating Products and Services Using Big Data

ANAGHA BHOPE

Department of Economics and Finance, Indira School of Business Studies PGDM, Tathawade, Pune, India

ABSTRACT

Big data is paving the way for technology and continuously serving to incorporate AI-based modules to bring revolution and innovative vision. Every technology and service that is impacting the human being or gets impacted by society and its behavior can be revolutionized to improve the level of comfort for society and the human being. Big data brings more value and organized execution to the system, which demands innovation. Looking forward to the future and the need of time, it is required to bring all possible technology and services, including retail, traffic management, railway reservation and signaling systems, the fashion world, demand prediction for various sectors, e-commerce, etc., under the umbrella of big data and AI.

12.1 INTRODUCTION

12.1.1 INNOVATING PRODUCTS AND SERVICES USING BIG DATA

Every business focuses on profit and customer satisfaction. Business owners want to understand customer behavior and contemporary trends so that their corresponding businesses can be aligned with customer requirements and to improve customer satisfaction. All kinds of products and services can be categorized and studied to improve customer retention.

Augmenting Customer Retention Through Big Data Analytics.
Reena Malik, Ambuj Sharma, and Prashant Chaudhary (Eds.)

Working with cutting-edge technologies and innovating products and services is a real need to improve the level of customer satisfaction and business revenue by not only retaining existing customers but also by attracting new potential customers.

All profit-making products and services need to be innovated by business owners. The least focused attribute of society, i.e., administration, is also a kind of service, and every individual is a customer for the same. Administrative agencies and the government are the owners of this business. Even though it is said that government does not work on profit, the customer satisfaction index is equally important for the administrators to improve the conditions in the country and the quality of life to compete globally.

The government provides many services to every individual, and there are many problems that need to be addressed innovatively. The traffic management system is a very important service that is provided and controlled by administrative bodies and the government. Every individual who is part of traffic is at the receiving end as a customer of the traffic management system. Everyone expects an improvement in the system of traffic that they are currently experiencing, which is getting worse and worse day by day.

With industrial and economic growth, demand for vehicles and automotives has exponentially increased, but the limitations of roads and infrastructure raise the sensitivity to improve the quality of this system or service so that the rate of accidents, rate of pollution, and commute time can be minimized to the best of their ability, in turn improving the quality of life.

If we see the lifestyle or schedule of anyone, every individual follows a particular trend in his day-to-day activities and travel. Most mornings start with travel toward offices and end in the evening with travel toward home. Unknowingly, every individual has already generated a lot of records over travel trends, travel behaviors, the types of vehicles they are using, and how much time they are spending on commute. Even many administrators have already identified a few areas or zones, like critical zones, where an innovative approach is required to improve the traffic management system on priority.

Big data can be the key for this solution to innovate and control the traffic management system dynamically. Finally, everyone who is traveling can get benefitted and the administrator or government will be getting rewarded for the same in various forms.

In 2015, the number of four-wheelers was anticipated at around 1.3 billion, and by 2040, it is predicted to rise to over 2 billion as developing economies become more prosperous. It calls for the evolutionary system to interact with every vehicle, every individual who is driving the vehicle, and everyone who is part of the traffic. A system which interacts with everyone and technology and organizes the traffic needs time to improve its value. The capacity of the current transportation system may be swiftly exceeded even with increased infrastructure.

Modern information technology, if paired with artificial intelligence (AI) abilities to optimize massive amounts of data in real-time, could make it possible to organize the issue.

Since almost from 1960s, several traffic monitoring devices, such as induction loops, have been around, although more current technologies, like cameras that can follow traffic and read license plates, are newer. Making use of all this data and knowledge is the challenge.

In Bangalore, India, a city known for traffic congestion, the average speed on some routes during peak hours is just ~ 2.5 mph. Siemens Mobility has developed a prototype AI traffic monitoring system. It consists of a "traffic camera-based" component. Vehicles are automatically detected by traffic cameras; the system collects the data and transmits the same to a central control station. Further, an algorithm is executed to determine the volume of traffic on the road. Moreover, the results of the algorithms are used to modify the traffic lights in response to current traffic jams.

Technical institutes throughout the world are working to improve AI's capacity to understand vast amounts of data and information and alter how people move about cities during the day and at night.

In many data research centers, enormous amounts of data are being analyzed. A new study began by The Alan Turing Institute in London in collaboration with researchers from the Toyota Mobility Foundation to investigate how AI can make intelligent traffic and its management systems more responsive and real-time. To help their algorithms learn more and more about the real-time traffic, they are now trying to implement the simulations that scale up in complexity and data and evolve on their own using AI. Although the institute and its teams are still testing the technology, they intend to use it in the real world as soon as possible.

On the other hand, researchers are already collaborating with municipal administrators in Pittsburgh on a comparable strategy that has been in place in the city since 2012. Rapid Flow Tech, a startup, has implemented a traffic control system that was created by academics at Carnegie Mellon University's Robotics Institute. Since the introduction, the business's Surtrac technology has been employed at 50 crossings in Pittsburgh; according to the company, it has decreased intersection wait times by up to 40%. Additionally, it states that automobile emissions have decreased by up to 20% while journey times within the city have decreased by 25%.

Technology not only improves the value of time and shortens travel times but it also helps to lessen CO_2 and GHG emissions, protecting the environment and creating a new way for a better and greener future for Mother Earth.

Every day, technology advances, and people are connecting with one another more and more. With the use of wireless technologies such as cell phones, vehicles are also being connected and brought closer together. They will aid in providing systems with even more data. According to Griffin Schultz of Rapid Flow, networked automobiles will eventually be able to transmit data to surrounding infrastructure regarding their driver behavior, speed, and even potential defects.

Smart roadside technology deployment will do more than just avoiding gridlock. Newer technologies provide a variety of other advantages, according to Mark Nicholson from Vivacity Labs, who oversaw a UK government-funded initiative to install intelligent traffic light signals in Milton Keynes, England. Technology will also contribute to lower costs by reducing the need for human participation in menial chores like monitoring traffic cameras.

In order to prioritize less CO_2-emitting vehicles like bikes, mass transport vehicles like buses, or emergency vehicles like ambulances, for example, automated systems are becoming better at discriminating between vast numbers of road users. This can increase safety. Maintaining traffic can enhance air quality and minimize energy use from stopped vehicles that are left idle. By lowering engine emissions, it can lessen negative environmental effects. It can facilitate parking and give drivers more time to be productive.

The Milton Keynes project's findings are also compelling. Intelligent cameras installed throughout the city that can recognize and categorize all vehicles and other road users have made it possible to gather precise, highly localized data that has helped planners and authorities better understand when and where traffic is most congested, what are the favorite routes of drivers, and where ample parking spaces are available. There are 104 junctions and 812 carriageways in Milton Keynes. Vivacity has installed close to 411 smart traffic cameras to capture data. The sensors can count and categorize road users, assess the amount of time it takes for cars to drive between intersections, and offer real-time images to aid in the creation of future planning.

The data captured from these cameras is further fed into a machine learning model by Vivacity, which blends responses from the traffic to brief changes in the road network with knowledge of regular daily patterns. It improves its prediction ability and reduces the need for human intervention as it develops and adapts over time. It offers both historical and real-time data and forecasts daily traffic patterns.

The creation of a world-class, new, cutting-edge, multifunctional, multi-skilled Road Network Operations Center (RNOC) is at the core of the new capabilities.

The RNOC assembles all the elements of a top-tier smart network operator to manage traffic in a transparent, collaborative, and cutting-edge setting. The workers in each of these areas received extensive training from subject-matter specialists to improve their capabilities, but what really distinguishes Perth's traffic management operation is how seamlessly they all work together.

The Traffic Control Centre, a formidable technological organization that uses cutting-edge information technologies for traffic management, is located even in Moscow. Since the creation of an intelligent transportation system in 2011, there has been an opportunity for ten years to forecast traffic conditions, control traffic flows, and keep track of significant transport infrastructure objects.

While many technological innovations are being made in the field to record human behavior and use it to simplify critical systems like traffic management systems, other innovative research is still going on to raise the safety standard on rods. The creation and implementation of a vehicle-to-infrastructure (V2I) communication system is an important project with the goal of improving road safety levels. V2I is a wireless connection technology that enables cars to exchange information with things like traffic signals and road signs using built-in sensors and detecting equipment. The technology will soon undergo its first Moscow pilot. It is crucial to the development of driverless cars. As the human factor will be minimized, it is anticipated that its introduction in Moscow will boost road safety.

Across the world, numerous startups are also working to help solve the unstructured traffic issue. Software is developed by the Nigerian company Traffic Butter to produce mapping and navigation services. Its in-house-developed mobile application software enables users to create and update traffic maps, communicate with one another via text messaging platforms, and get real-time alerts when traffic and road conditions change.

Surtrac, a firm based in the USA, develops software that integrates data from both previously and recently installed IoT sensors and devices to analyze, optimize, and schedule traffic lights in real-time, changing the signals to reflect changes in traffic or the time of day.

Simplifai Systems, a UK-based startup, develops AI-based traffic management systems to ease congestion in urban areas. With the manipulation of traffic flow and road occupancy, the startup's artificial intelligence enables real-time traffic control techniques and dynamically alters traffic signals throughout a metropolis. By rerouting traffic around important athletic events and managing the flow of traffic close to accidents, the AI also lessens traffic congestion. Cities can use this to decrease the amount of pollution produced by vehicles while simultaneously improving the efficiency of traffic flow.

The Austrian technology company Kapsch TrafficCom established the "Intelligent Corridor" at Nicholson Street in Australia along with the University of Melbourne and the Victorian Department of Transport. Alexandra and Victoria Parades, a 2.5-km length of Nicholson Street, is covered by this corridor. To enhance traffic management, this corridor makes use of sensors, machine learning algorithms, predictive and cloud-based AI models based on big data analysis, and real-time data gathering. It has made a substantial contribution to reducing localized emissions, easing traffic congestion, and enhancing pedestrian, bicycle, and car safety on the road.

AIMES (Australian Integrated Multimodal Ecosystem) is the first, one of its kind, and largest ecosystem for testing cutting-edge linked transport technology at scale. It includes >100 km of road in Melbourne and is supported by the Victorian Department of Transport. It is bordered by Lygon and Hoddle streets and Victoria and Alexandra Parades.

With sensors at every intersection, a number of projects, and a substantial new phase, the Intelligent Corridor ushers in a new era of monitoring and traffic control.

The lifestyle or schedule of every individual, which follows a particular trend in their day-to-day activities and travel, helps technology understand the real-time scenarios and predict the same for the future. Every movement is tracked with AI, and data is collected over time. This data is analyzed and processed to help civic bodies and administrators resolve the critical problems like congestion and unorganized traffic. Big data can be the key for this solution to innovate and control the traffic management system dynamically. Finally, everyone who is traveling can get benefitted and the administrator or government or civic bodies will be getting rewarded for the same in various forms. Collectively, it is helping to create a better organized future.

Big data supports the evolution and transformation of many different enterprises and sectors. One of the foundations of the modern, fast-paced world is the retail industry. Big data in the retail sector aids businesses in anticipating consumer requests, personalizing the shopping experience, and, most significantly, increasing operational effectiveness.

Big data's adoption by a number of retail channels has significantly boosted market competition. Big data analytics is now being looked to by retailers to provide them with a competitive advantage over others.

Companies are quickly embracing it in order to find better ways to connect with clients, comprehend their demands, offer the best available solution, guarantee customer pleasure, etc. Big data utilization in the retail sector is expanding quickly, and with it, so is the need for organizations to identify the best use cases for the technology.

12.2 RETAIL INDUSTRY AND BIG DATA

Some of the retail industry's big data use cases enhance retail sales management's overall effectiveness. It guarantees the following: customer experience personalization; anticipating client needs; operational effectiveness; and customer journey analytics.

12.2.1 CUSTOMER EXPERIENCE PERSONALIZATION

Any company's success is totally determined by how satisfied and well-cared-for its consumers are. A content customer is also a devoted one. Big data offers retailers the chance to improve consumer experiences. Big data Analytics will assist merchants in predicting a client's needs, enabling them to make decisions that are efficient and centered on the needs of the customer and tailoring their marketing strategies accordingly. This consumers' data comes from a variety of sources, including social media, websites, smart mobiles, etc.

This will aid retailers in rising to new heights on the market and, hence, heighten competition. Imagine being able to purchase goods that are precisely tailored to our needs. Modern consumers are obsessed with customization, which is why big data exists.

The ChatBot Revolution study was conducted in the Mall of America in Bloomington, Minnesota. A museum, an indoor theme park, more than 500 stores, 50 restaurants, 14 movie theaters, and the largest shopping center in the Northern States are all located there. It was exceedingly difficult for them to give each individual consumer a tailored experience because they had such a large customer database. What then enabled them to give their clients a better experience? Undoubtedly, big data. To compel their consumers to navigate the enormous mall, IBM gave them a chatbot (a basic text messaging platform) called ELF.

They were able to create a more superior and individualized experience for the clients by using this chatbot to better understand their demands. Delivering a positive shopping experience boosts customer happiness, repeat business, customer loyalty, referrals, sales, and customer engagement according to Accenture.

12.2.2 PREDICTING DEMANDS

Demand forecasting in the Retail Sector is another important factor. Being the first to market a good or service offers numerous benefits and advantages, but it also comes with many obstacles, and big data allows you the flexibility to handle both. Retailers must stay one step ahead of the consumer in this rapidly evolving technical and social media environment if they want to thrive. Retailers will lose customers if they lag behind the market.

Retailers will be able to gain insights into customer behavior through the use of big data analytics, which will help them identify the items and services that are most in demand and those that they should discontinue providing. Also, it would enable them to foresee the future in the retail sector and create new products in accordance with the prevailing market trends. Big data in retail aids merchants in anticipating customer requests in this way. Forecasting weather also helps shops prepare for necessary demand in the retail. The weather is only one aspect of the prediction. It offers a lot more than that. A weather channel forecasts how the weather will affect its audience's feelings.

The partnership between Pantene, Walgreens, and The Weather Channel is an illustration of big data analytics in the retail industry. Data on the air's relative humidity and the time it will be at its peak was gathered by the Weather Channel.

This aided Pantene and Walgreens in marketing their products by connecting them to potential hair issues that women might have as a result of the elevated humidity in the air.

Women were then advised to look for a product at their neighborhood stores to shield themselves from developing any form of hair issues.

This led to a 10% rise in Pantene sales at Walgreens for the months of July and August and a 4% increase in sales overall for the hair category at the pharmacy.

12.2.3 OPERATIONAL EFFICIENCY

The retail company's ability to operate effectively across several channels gives them the freedom to do so. The inventory department's and the production unit's communication must be coordinated at all times.

Big data in retail enables businesses to track in-store demand in real-time and ensure that top-selling products are always available. With ever-quicker product life cycles and increasingly complicated processes, it has helped people comprehend supply chains and product distribution to cut costs. They are now able to handle the enormous demand better to maximize asset management, budget forecasting, performance management, and service quality thanks to big data. A few examples of assets that provide useful data include servers, plant machinery, energy grid infrastructure, and product logs. Every day, there is an exponential increase in the amount of data, making it difficult to gather, prepare, and analyze. Big data analytics can help solve this conundrum.

12.2.4 CUSTOMER JOURNEY ANALYTICS

The cardiac monitoring system, which continuously records your heart's activities, displays a zigzag pattern as a sign that life is there. The path taken by a customer is also the same. Also, it follows a zigzag pattern from study to purchase through several outlets. This is what shows that the market is still active.

The best instrument for managing and analyzing this journey is big data.

Customers now have instant access to information about products at any point of time, thanks to technological improvements and the rise of social media. Nowadays, consumers are king and have more power.

Big data will assist merchants in identifying the most efficient methods to contact customers and persuade them to make a purchase (Fig. 12.1).

Big data is like the heart machine that will let businesses monitor consumer behavior and raise the bar of the customer experience. A customer had to personally inform the store of his requirements before the evolution of big data. Everything, from the things that were out of stock to the products he would need soon, needed to be conveyed to the retailer. Since the evolution of big data Systems, the world has changed. In today's environment, hardly anything goes without being shared on social media networks.

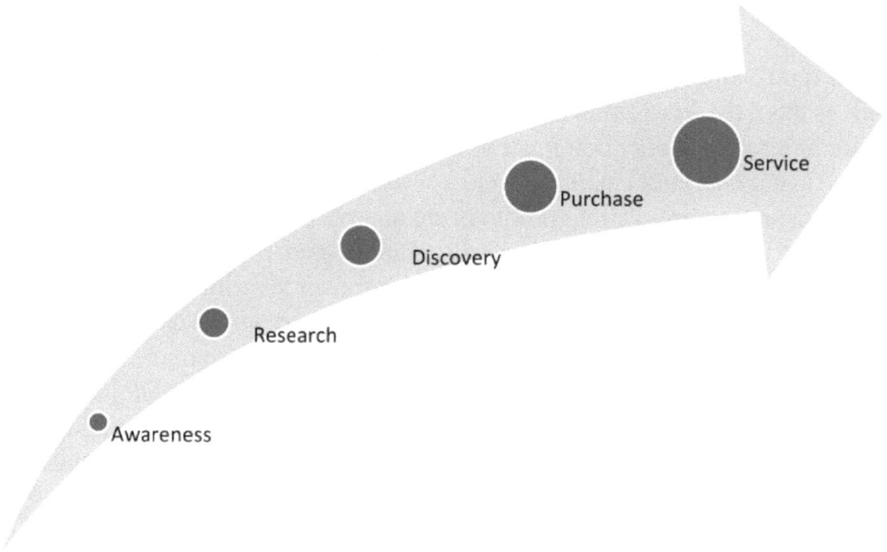

FIGURE 12.1 Customer journey analytics.
Source: Author.

In this quickly developing digital age, big data is everywhere. It is possible to examine the vast majority of online activities. Consumer insights are retailers' most valuable asset and the secret to thriving in the retail industry's future in the continuously changing digital world. If a chance is not seized appropriately and swiftly, a store may fall behind the competition. Yet, big data offers advantages and can help propel the business forward. In the retail industry, big data's contribution has become remarkable. Big data is continuously growing.

Big data analysis may save marketing costs, target the right audience at the right time, foresee future trends, and boost customer happiness. A few common advantages of big data are as follows:

- Know your customer

  Understanding every individual will allow you to deliver the level of individualized attention that clients have grown to expect. The phrase "360 degree perspective" is frequently used and this can be defined as determining the most precise needs of the client. Retailers must make themselves aware of a customer's needs, creating preferences based on using discount, gender, geography, and other details.

Even a small number of these data bits can result in complex marketing tactics.

For instance, fashion retailers frequently spend a lot of money on celebrity brand ambassadors. Yet, by considering the sexes, interests, and social media presence of their customers, fashion firms may locate microinfluencers who are more cost-effective options and capable of promoting their brands on Instagram.

- Optimize pricing

  Determining product prices is the utmost priority for businesses. Big data helps them use trends to set appropriate prices. Companies can predict trends, and retailers can have new goods ready. In such a way, both companies and retailers can plan a dynamic pricing strategy that will work. The 360-degree perspective of the consumer can also be used to inform pricing. This is due to the fact that pricing is heavily influenced by a customer's location and purchasing preferences. Businesses can do beta tests on subsets of their client base to determine which pricing works best. The retailers can find strategies to differentiate themselves from their rivals by knowing what a customer expects to get the most out of emerging trends and understand when and how much to reduce pricing on products that are out of style.

- Backoffice operation ease.

  Imagine having flawless stock levels all-year long and real-time data collection from registered products. Everybody who has worked in retail has felt that dread when their inventory runs out. That manager's whole shift will be spent calming down irate clients. In an ideal world, businesses would completely avoid this circumstance. Big data can assist businesses in managing their supply chains and distribution networks. Product logs can help retailers learn more about the operational performance. Consumers can provide time-to-time feedback on the product's performance, for instance, by registering their views.

- Customer service efficiency

  Big data analysis can help identify the top concerns from recorded calls, which can be used to measure the success of the company and improve quality. Several retail businesses meticulously review in-store video and motion sensor data to improve the customer experience. Intentionally placing items that companies want to sell first in sections of the store where customers commonly gather is not novel. Grocery stores deliberately design their aisles so that customers leave with more food than they intended. Customer comments and reviews might also provide information. By examining these ratings, retailers may inform customers that a particular apparel may fit small or large. To ascertain whether customers are generally speaking favorably or negatively about particular products and businesses, the term "sentiment analysis" can also be employed.

12.3 USING BIG DATA

Knowing how to use big data practically is essential now that everyone is aware of how important it is to keep a competitive advantage in retail. Below are a few stores that are using big data platforms to boost their sales and overall customer satisfaction.

12.3.1 SURVIVING BLACK FRIDAY BOTTLENECKS BY USING BIG DATA

Black Friday, Cyber Monday, and Thanks-Giving-sell are the most exciting and busiest days for retailers. In fact, according to the National Retail Federation, up to 30% of retail annual sales are attributable to sales in November and December.

The Canadian shoe and accessory manufacturer Aldo uses big data analytics to deal with this hectic time of the year. The business integrates systems like payment, billing, and fraud detection through the use of a SOA or service-oriented big data architecture. Aldo can now provide a flawless online shopping experience even on Black Friday, thanks to this integration effort.

12.3.2 OFFICE DEPOT ONLINE AND OFFLINE INTEGRATIONS

In 13+ countries, Office Depot Europe has two brands "Office Depot" and "Viking". By combining its online and physical marketing initiatives, the company is able to maintain its top position. That muchunrelated information is a lot. The company created a big data platform by linking its offline catalog, internet website, customer call centers, and fulfillment processes. Focusing on certain customer segments and utilizing internal funds to increase the productivity of various divisions, Office Depot Europe outcompetes other office supply firms.

12.3.3 GROUPON

An online store called Groupon connects users to deals on trips, events, and other products and services. Each day, Groupon must handle more than one terabyte of raw data in order to satisfy that variety of clients.

Without a big data platform, the dataset would be far too large to store and analyze. Groupon imports, integrates, transforms, and analyzes data in real time using a significant IT framework.

12.3.4 PRICE MINISTER: FLEXIBLE AND AGILE

The French retail company Price Minister (now Rakuten) uses a third-party pricing strategy. They connect their clients with vendors and guarantee the success of every transaction by gathering enormous datasets and tracking buyer and seller behavior.

The Price Ministry combined buyer and seller datasets with a database that houses all 100 million Price Minister products in order to relieve pressure on their IT department. With the aid of this technology, Price Ministers can increase their adaptability and responsiveness. Their buyer and seller information is updated virtually instantly.

12.3.5 MY WORLD SOLUTIONS AG

A shopping network called My World Solutions AG enables its users to earn points and money on their purchases from more than 70,000+ merchants in 47+ different countries. It takes work to manage all of that data.

The company employs a big data platform with a Salesforce connector to consolidate, clean, and transform its customer and merchant data. My World Solutions AG can easily access client information, monitor marketing performance, and, if necessary, correct the path.

12.3.6 FASHION INDUSTRY

French retailer Groupe Zannier (formerly Kidiliz Group) has a brand portfolio that includes every category of children's and adult apparel. Kenzo and Levi's are a few well-known Zannier Group brands.

The Zannier Group must know about the shifting tastes of kids, teenagers, and adults both inside and outside of France if they want to keep their position as a leader in the fashion industry. Data from two important ERPs is combined for this purpose by Zannier Group. The company was able to enable itself to transform retail activity into meaningful customer purchase patterns using this integrated dataset, which can then be used to inform decisions about real-time inventory and sales.

12.3.7 BRINGING DIVERSE BUSINESS UNITS TOGETHER

The main products that Naville markets and sells are press products. The retailer oversees 3,000 periodicals in addition to a chain of candy shops, a tourist guide, a network of comic book stores, and a number of outlet malls.

Naville's SOA, service-oriented big data architecture, enables data flow between all their business units. Naville creates business apps on top of this architecture to help scale and improve connectivity and communication between business units.

Customers today have specific expectations regarding direct sales. They are interested in learning about goods that will interest and appeal to them specifically. Shops must provide their customers with special products and promotions that are catered to their tastes and routines. Catering to individuality is proven to contribute toward an increase in revenue, customer satisfaction, and brand building.

These retailers must simultaneously pay attention to their marketing funding, operations, and pricing optimization. They must create and promote things that are in style. During Black Friday, they need to have enough inventory available. They must suitably price their goods. Retailers may accomplish all of these goals and more by gathering, standardizing, and analyzing big data. The retail sector demonstrates the power of big data today.

12.4 THE INDIAN RAILWAY USES AI AND DATA ANALYTICS TO IMPROVE OPERATIONAL EFFICIENCY

The biggest transporters in India's big data analytics and artificial intelligence are used by the Indian Railway to increase operational effectiveness.

With assets like 121,407+ track km, 34,319+ route km of electrified track, 12,000 locomotives, 74,000 coaches, 7,500 stations, etc., the Indian Railways primarily use artificial intelligence and big data analytics in trains' day-to-day operations, ticket booking, system maintenance, freight operations, etc. With 8.4 billion passengers and 1.2 billion tonnes of freight transported in 2018–2019, India's railway system is enormous and widespread. The Indian Railways are the largest freight and passenger carriers in the world, respectively. Big data and artificial intelligence are being used by India's national railway to explore new possibilities and undoubtedly scale new heights. The official notification states that the Indian Railways analyze data using artificial intelligence and big data analytics before using it in their passenger reservation system (PRS). This can occasionally assist with the rollout of new trains and proactive asset maintenance.

Big data analytics and AI helped the Indian Railway alter the current maintenance system. At the time, they performed periodic maintenance. Predictive asset maintenance will continuously monitor the equipment's conditions and trigger the necessary alarms for immediate maintenance. This lowers not only maintenance costs but also the costs associated with maintaining assets.

With the intention of analyzing the data generated by India's largest transporter, the Indian Railway partnered with the Indian School of Business (ISB), Hyderabad. In addition to data analysis, the Indian Railway assigned ISB the job of creating an introduction to capacity-building programs and a report on the application of AI in the rail transportation industry. The Indian Railway has a sound idea, and they intend to establish an excellence center within the next three months. To create a report on creating a center of excellence and for the capacity-building program, the ISB extends a big helping hand.

The railway has also chosen to appoint a chief technology officer (CTO) in each zonal railway, who will be responsible for keeping track of new developments in analytics and artificial intelligence and efficiently implementing them in each train system. The Indian Railway has already trained over 100 employees in big data analytics and artificial intelligence since they are aware that this will increase their profits.

Long ticket waiting lines were a regular issue, but the Indian Railway has now completed testing an AI program it created. The AI-driven system has allocated open berths in more than 200 trains for the first time, reducing the number of people who must be turned away for lack of a ticket. As a result, there are now shorter waiting lists for certain trains. Railways' internal software division, Center for Railway Information Systems (CRIS), developed this AI module, which is titled Ideal Train Profile. It was supplied with information about how many people bought tickets on these trains, which origin–destination pairs were popular and which were not at what time of the year, which seats were vacant for how long of a trip, etc. The AI has been fed a combination of "training data" spanning three years.

Railways have flagged in internal policy discussions that it is not practical to increase the number of trains in every sector on a continuous basis based on demand. However, if a passenger does not get a confirmed train ticket, she will turn away from the Indian Railway and go somewhere else. Thus, the solution is to take a look at its own inventory of berths and apportion them intelligently.

The traveler is currently given a wait-listed ticket and instructed to wait until four hours prior to departure when the final seat chart is prepared to find out if she made to the list. This is due to the fact that a substantial number of berths are set aside for different quotas and different origin–destination combinations of the train's routes. Not everything is used. Hence, the true image only becomes apparent throughout the chart-making process. There are 1,800 different ticket combinations with origin and destination if a long-distance train has 60 halts. There are normally roughly 45 ticket permutations for 10 halts and so forth. According to officials, there are around one billion different ticket combinations available on Indian Railways. During internal policy discussions, The Railway has brought up the concern that it is not logistically possible to continue increasing the number of trains in every sector depending on demand. Nonetheless, a traveler will choose alternative transportation options, such as long-haul flights and short-haul buses, if she does not obtain a confirmed train ticket from Indian Railways. So, the correct distribution of its own inventory of berths is the solution.

The traveler has been handed a wait-listed ticket and has been told to wait until the final seat map is prepared four hours before departure to learn if she made to the list. This is because a sizeable portion of berths are reserved for various quotas and origin–destination combinations of the train's routes. Not all of it is used. Hence, the true image is only revealed when the chart is being created. If a long-distance train has 60 stops, there are 1,800 potential ticket combinations with origin and destination. For 10 halts, there are typically 45 ticket combinations and so on. In Indian Railways, there are around one billion potential ticket combinations available according to officials. Since most people travel between Delhi and Lucknow by rail, the problem is most obvious in publications that are published overnight, such as the Lucknow Mail. The other long-distance trains with numerous stops are similarly impacted by this issue. The AI in the Ideal Train Profile instructs the Passenger Reservation System on how and for which sectors to distribute confirmed tickets. The AI makes data-driven decisions about remote sites, fully automates quota distribution, and presents the best quota for different ticket combinations based on historical demand.

Indian Railway is of such huge proportions that adjectives like "gigantic" and "enormous" do not seem to justify it. Indian Railway (IR), the fourth-largest freight carrier in the world with a route length of 95,981 km, transported 8.4 billion passengers and 1.2 billion tonnes of freight in 2018–2019. From the perspective of operational analytics, this also means a humongous amount of data. Nevertheless, Railway is now unable to utilize this data to produce precise, pertinent, and useful business insights.

Datasets can be analyzed and inferences can be drawn about them using big data analysis algorithms, enabling firms to make better business decisions. Big data analytics is a type of advanced analytics that entails sophisticated applications powered by high-performance analytics systems that include aspects like regression models, predictive algorithms, and data analysis.

Big data analytics has a wide range of prospects for IR to investigate. A few of them are customer experience, train scheduling, timetabling, inventory management, and IRCTC. To generate commercial benefits in the aforementioned sectors, it is quite possible to use this vast amount of data already available from the various systems. Real-time Train Information System (RTIS), the national train enquiry system (NTES), and the control office application (COA) are a few examples of IR IT systems that generate meaningful information.

Data analytics is very essential when it comes to asset management. An asset inventory, suitable staffing and training, preventative maintenance, and a sufficient budget level are all included in asset management. An organization must determine its demands and costs in addition to creating long-term financial plans in order to satisfy these criteria. Planning for asset management is what it is called. It entails creating a strategy to cut expenses while boosting the effectiveness and dependability of the assets.

Several gigabytes of asset data are kept by Indian Railways. The data can be evaluated into useful information to increase asset usage and availability via connected IoT sensors, historical data, and analytics. By implementing better maintenance procedures, certain efforts have been undertaken to increase asset availability as of late.

These initiatives lack a cohesive strategy and have been produced in departmental silos. There is a chance for everyone to step up and enhance asset usage in general across India.

12.5 EXISTING TECHNOLOGIES FOR COLLECTING DATA AND MONITORING CONDITIONS IN IR

12.5.1 SIGNALING SYSTEM

Data loggers are used to monitor the health of equipment such as axle counters, track circuits, point machines, and other gears and to send SMS notifications for different problem alarms. Also, out of 7.5K stations, more than 5.5K have Wi-Fi capabilities. Although the capabilities are present, they are not fully used. To reduce the need for maintenance, it is necessary to take a more effective approach to gathering all types of asset data through advanced sensors and contemporary big data tools.

12.5.2 ROLLING STOCK

For the automatic discovery of faults, defects, and deficiencies in freight wagons, Indian Railway plans to transform its "freight examination yards" into technologically advanced "Smart Yards." The automatic defect detection equipment is required to provide prior information about spare parts, like hot axles, wheel flats, wheel profiles and diameter, load imbalance, loose and hanging components, etc., even before the rake arrives at the repair yard. It will then employ this data for proactive staffing and objective fault evaluation, shortening turnaround times while increasing safety and productivity. Phase 1 of the conversion to Smart Yards has found 40 yards initially. Data integration is difficult because distinct subsystems are offered by various suppliers.

12.5.3 TRACK

The OMS Car, TRC Run, and other field inspections are part of the current method for keeping tabs on the condition of the track. The goal of Indian Railways is to introduce an integrated track monitoring system, which will include the following:

- A method for recording track parameters
- Rear window video recording of the track
- Track component recording and image processing analysis for the state of the track components
- Additional sensors/transducers

Despite the fact that numerous systems have been implemented for condition monitoring and data collection for various assets, these systems' analytics capabilities are very constrained. Additionally, each of these data-gathering systems has its own acronym and operates in a technical silo, making it challenging to integrate data in order to gather useful information.

Indian Railways should get this humongous data and capture it in a national intelligence model, one that can serve this data-driven railway in a cohesive, safe, and cost-effective manner.

Big data is like a reservoir of information, and if anyone wants to add more value to the data and transform the value proposition to alleviate the pains of consumers and optimize the monetary benefits, this reservoir of big data should be processed and converted into knowledge to make the most of it. This process should be driven intellectually and relentlessly.

12.6 CONCLUSIONS

Having enormous amount of data does not always help. It is required to organize and get it structured to add more value to it and support the technology or services to meet the needs of the future. Data should be rigorously analyzed and monitored to understand the trends and patterns in user and consumer behaviors, which in turn are to be studied and revolutionized to create a better tomorrow for everyone. Various sectors have already entered this race to add more value propositions into their respective deliverables to their users and consumers. The application of big data and AI to every single possible technology and service is really going to set the momentum for an affordable future with a revolutionary vision.

KEYWORDS

- **demand prediction**
- **forecast**
- **consumer behavior**
- **sales**
- **services**
- **networks**
- **cycle time**
- **strategy**

REFERENCES

The Australian traffic management system driving the super highways of tomorrow | Johnson Controls

"World's smartest traffic management system" launches in Australia (newatlas.com)

https://www.intertraffic.com/news/traffic-management/three-smart-cities-in-traffic-management-perth-mexico-city-moscow/

https://www.talend.com/resources/smart-retailing/

https://www.ibm.com/downloads/cas/VXOJQW1L

https://www.proptiger.com/guide/post/what-india-can-learn-from-the-world-for-managing-traffic-better Sneha Sharon Mammen, 17/07/2017

https://slashdot.org/software/traffic-management/

https://www.startus-insights.com/innovators-guide/4-top-traffic-management-startups-impacting-smart-cities/

https://www.startus-insights.com/innovators-guide/smart-traffic-management-startups/

Role of Data Science and Data Analytics in Indian Railways (onleitechnologies.com)

https://www.unimelb.edu.au/newsroom/news/2022/march/worlds-smartest-traffic-management-system-launches-in melbourne#:~:text=AIMES%20(Australian%20 Integrated%20Multimodal%20EcoSystem,scale%20in%20complex%20urban%20 environments.

https://www.googleadservices.com/pagead/aclk?sa=L&ai=DChcSEwiY0KPqovH8AhWt2UwCHZEFDZkYABAAGgJ0bQ&ae=2&ohost=www.google.com&cid=CAESbeD2buOvpAOjWKYuLklHSWrgp5iizj5y1kiN7ry189oiu5keq_IUO6G1sUSKPricoXzquYIRKZFc2Mu-jSkgEagKHVDM7ZHW7RjQEdkxHysgnKQSUk9xMR8wei0MCKktFlCW8Uksqgsihgn4ACg&sig=AOD64_2-_5dfuTgHBC1X837BpR85jEBXA&q&adurl&ved=2ahUKEwimw5rqovH8AhXQ7HMBHf15BTsQ0Qx6BAgJEAE

https://www.google.com/l?sa=t&rct=j&q=&esrc=s&source=web&cd=&cad=rja&uact=8&ved=2ahUKEwimw5rqovH8AhXQ7HMBHf15BTsQFnoECBwQAQ&url=https%3A%2F%2Fnewatlas.com%2Fautomotive%2Fworld-smartest-traffic-management-system-kapsch%2F&usg=AOvVaw2epQXgOUK0pDaikMwgXyjX

CHAPTER 13

Revamping Internal Customer Experience (ICX) with AI

KIRAN SHRIMANT KAKADE[1], SHAILENDRA KUMAR KALE[2], SWATI A. VISPUTE[1], and SULAKSHANA B. MANE[3]

[1]*School of Business, MIT World Peace University, Pune, India*

[2]*Global Business School and Research Centre, Dr. D. Y. Patil Vidyapeeth, Pune, India*

[3]*BVCOE, Navi Mumbai, India*

ABSTRACT

The patterns of life we all took for granted have been disrupted by rapidly changing business environments, technological advancements, and climate change. Tech is at the forefront of disruption, which is a prospect for progress. The Industrial Revolution 4.0 transformed the transactional aspects of businesses. The Industrial Revolution 5.0 was considered the next upsurge of new technologies, bringing the promise of increased productivity and efficiencies. Technological growth has also highly impacted the HR function, transforming HR from transactions to a transformational approach with a much higher impact on businesses and employees than ever before. It is now more about the customer experience. The idea of Internal Customer Experience (ICX) has drawn significant attention from researchers. Previous literature shows that ICX has the prospect of improving employee experience, motivation, outcome, and behavior. This research examines how new technologies can enable HR to deliver the Internal Customer Experience.

Augmenting Customer Retention Through Big Data Analytics.
Reena Malik, Ambuj Sharma, and Prashant Chaudhary (Eds.)

13.1 INTRODUCTION

We are experiencing a revolution that is ongoing, pervasive, and data-exploding. The phrase "the outcome" has been replaced by "the experience." Enterprises are leveraging advances in technology to take advantage of this revolution. Latest technologies, such as AI, ML, and big data, can improve HR strategies by implementing developed automated techniques for human resource management. The latest technologies can make this advancement a reality. This research seeks to discover the need for generating a new technology to address HR-related issues for the new generation in an efficient way. The design system is an intelligent HR solution for the Internal Customer Experience Management System (ICEMS) and employee retention, primarily based on an HR intelligence module. The main goal of this program is to strengthen linkages between the internal customer and planning features. We investigate organized machine learning approaches using a cutting-edge methodology. This approach is a crucial part of a comprehensive framework for advanced solutions. The DOIT model was created in order to solve new technology-related problems (Faqihi and Miah, 2023). The rapidly developing technology that is currently dominating this revolution is AI. AI technologies can understand, learn, and then act based on that big data. A technological strategy that uses AI can solve the problem of organizing such data by transforming it into wisdom that can be used for organizational decision-making (Faqihi and Miah, 2023). AI systems recognize patterns and construct logical connections that would otherwise have been a mammoth, effort-intensive, and time-consuming task for any human being. Digital assistants, chatbots, and machine learning are examples of AI. HR may also use AI to effectively and efficiently provide the next-generation customer experience. To benefit their firms, decision-makers must start testing all aspects of AI. HR has started testing AI to transform the internal customer experience, following businesses' discovery of the ability of AI to generate extraordinary customer experiences. It is crucial to weigh the benefits and drawbacks of implementing such systems. Management at the highest level should make sure that new technologies operate in a manner that lessens the possibility of eternalizing discrimination. AI can be seen as a driving force in the Internal Customer Experience (ICX) system (Faqihi and Miah, 2023).

With an agile workforce, the task of Human Resources is all the more important as administrations require them to connect to the experience offered to their internal customers. The increase in popularity of delivering feedback willingly has also made organizations do some stringent thinking into analyzing whether employees enjoy their jobs, believe themselves contributing and feel valued, believe they are a member of a group, and are connected to attaining the mission of the organization. What experience are internal customers getting in the organization? What are the ways to improve these experiences? How will internal customers perform well? This instructs Human Resources to change from "process support" to an "experience architect" by concentrating on internal customer experience.

13.2 LITERATURE REVIEW

AI is evolving to assist human resources by having the capacity to act, analyze, solve, and envision difficult problems. According to a PwC survey, 67% of firms feel that using AI will make it easier for people to interact with computers and connect human and digital intelligence in the most beneficial manner. According to the Deloitte report, 38% of businesses already use AI in their workplace. 33% of internal customers expect AI will soon augment their jobs. AI-based big data analytics tools help organizations handle enormous amounts of information in a better manner, as well as identify trends and gather data that would be challenging to ascertain using conventional techniques. In Human Resource experience (EX), AI can improve the accuracy of Internal Customer assessments and customize the career plan as per individual customer requirements (Faqihi and Miah, 2023). In order to replicate dialogs during the interventions in the Acquisition-to-Retire employee lifecycle, HR is using AI. Virtual assistants or chatbots developed utilizing sophisticated business algorithms are used to provide this experience. The survey conducted by 350 HR leaders finds that chatbots are the future of employee service. Additionally, according to ServiceNow, chatbot adoption in the workplace could reach adoption rates of up to 75%, with staff members using chatbots to find answers to frequently asked HR questions and access HR solutions at any time. Most people think workers would be fine working with an AI manager if it meant having more freedom and flexibility to work from home (71%) and having a more evenly distributed task (64%). There has been a 746% rise in 5 years, and investment in new technologies has surged. According to research firm IDC, the artificial intelligence demand grew to $47 billion in 2020, changing all business procedures in practically every industry. According to an IBM survey of HR executives, 49% of respondents and 46% of respondents, respectively, anticipate that AI will revolutionize payroll and benefit management. Real-time analytics must be used by HR to monitor employee complaints, and sentiment analysis must be used to address those complaints. AI functions in three different ways, says PwC. For instance, Assisted Intelligence increases the effectiveness of individuals and organizations; Augmented Intelligence enables individuals and organizations to achieve their potential. Machines with autonomous intelligence take action based on their learning (Davenport, 2015). The typical HR strategy to analyze big data is Machine Learning-based algorithms. Machine Learning performs an automated data pattern recognition process, an essential element of machine learning. The goal of new technologies is not only to understand employee experience but also to build an environment around them to enhance employee experience (EX) (Ali Faqihi, 2023). Employee experience includes *the digital environment*, *digital workspace*, and *individual traits* (Sharmila Rani Moganadas, 2022).

13.3 INTERNAL CUSTOMER

An internal customer is someone within an organization who receives goods or services from another member of the organization. For example, a department within a company may provide IT support services to other departments within the same company, making those other departments internal customers of the IT departments within the same company. Providing good customer service to internal customers is important because it helps to maintain good working relationships within the organization and ensures that every customer has the support to complete their jobs effectively. Internal customers are typically employees within an organization who depend on the work or services of another employee within the same organization to perform their own jobs effectively. This can include tasks such as providing technical support, processing payroll, managing inventory, or any other service that supports the work of other employees within the organization. The effectiveness and productivity of the organization as a whole may be directly impacted by the level of service offered to internal consumers. When an organization places emphasis on treating internal customers well and providing them with quality service, it can have several positive effects on the organization as a whole and helps in establishing a positive workplace environment, boosts general productivity, enhances prioritization strategies, simplifies internal communication, and has a favorable impact on outside customers.

13.4 MODERN TECHNOLOGY

Technology can play a crucial role in helping employees perform their tasks more efficiently and effectively, improving collaboration between team members, and providing a secure environment for sensitive data and communications. It can help employees be more productive, collaborative, and secure, which can ultimately benefit the organization as a whole. Technology can be a powerful tool for creating a positive experience for employees, helping them feel supported, empowered, and engaged in their work. It is true that technology has rapidly advanced in recent years, and there is a wide range of new and emerging technologies available to organizations and individuals alike. However, it is also true that many establishments struggle to effectively implement these technologies in their operations.

In this digital era, businesses seek a competitive advantage and gain profitability by offering a smooth customer experience (CX) (Malik et al., 2020; Zel and Kongar, 2020; Pillai et al., 2020). It has benefits and drawbacks. Working from home is one of its advantages. Flexible work timings, the greatest professional representation in remote locations (geographically dispersed), and traveling and crossing boundaries to share knowledge can save costs that are now accessible with the help of virtual groups. The drawbacks could be communication issues, technological glitches, less team engagement, etc. (Dulebohna and Hoch, 2017). Virtual teams facilitate communication via virtual tools (Gibson and Cohen, 2003a). The study says that virtual groups take longer time to perform the job given to them (Marlow, 2017). A study by Gustafson (2012) has shown that virtual and physical work complement one another and cannot be separated. They do not serve as stand-ins for one another.

13.5 TECHNOLOGY AND INTERNAL CUSTOMER EXPERIENCE

There has been global growth of interest in employee experience management in recent years, and such a novel strategy represents a paradigm shift in HR strategy. Employee experience management stresses the importance of crafting a positive and enthralling workplace that fosters satisfaction among members, happiness, and productivity. This approach recognizes that employees are more than simply machine parts; they are people with distinctive demands and preferences so that creating a positive work experience can lead to better performance, greater loyalty, and a stronger organizational culture. Overall, the shift toward employee experience management represents an important evolution in human resource management, one that recognizes the critical role that employees play in an organization's success and that prioritizes their well-being and satisfaction as key factors in achieving that success. Taking into account the research done thus far, it is clear that the term "employee experience (EX)" is heavily predisposed by the phrase "experience economy" and then "customer/user experience (CX/UX)" strategies and techniques with their application in the fields of "information technologies" and "marketing/sales." According to Morgan (2017), the total of all contacts between an employee and an organization is referred to as employee experience, which is the interaction of the company's physical, technological, and cultural settings as experienced by its employees.

Digital transformation has been an ongoing process for many companies, and AI is increasingly playing a more significant role in this evolution. New technologies such as ML, AI, computer vision, and robotics are being adopted by companies across various industries to improve their operations, enhance their customer experience, and increase their competitiveness. AI has the potential to transform businesses by enabling them to computerize their work, use big datasets to obtain new insights, and enhance decision-making. For instance, AI-powered chatbots can help companies provide better customer service by identifying customer data patterns that will assist businesses in tailoring their marketing and sales strategies (Joerres, 2016).

The chatbot is used to predict customer expectations, human emotions, and solve issues (Smith, 2019; Batat, 2022). The AI-powered chatbots are equipped with computerized HR practices, allowing users to avail assistance from everywhere. This gives them a seamless user experience (Meister, 2017). Several kinds of AI-based chatbots are employed to improve the working environment for employees (EEX), such as (1) HR chatbot—provides HR assistance and helps in various HR matters and (2) Career Development Chatbot—supports talent management (Zel and Kongar, 2020). Chatbots are employed to deliver employee services with the primary goal of enhancing employee experience (EEX) in five areas: (a) HR self-service: like applying for leave or Key Performance Indicator data, (b) Data insights: related to information on performance and other HR-related tasks, (c) Problem-solving: related to concerns raised and resolved for the employees, (d) Emotional support: concerns can be raised by the employees related to their emotional issues, and (e) Talent coach: advice on the career.

13.6 TYPES OF AI FOR HR PRACTICES

In the current digital world, chatbots can exchange text or chat messages with people by using automated systems (Ashfaq et al., 2020). Organizations use AI-based chatbots for a variety of HR tasks, including talent acquisition, employee engagement, employee help, and communication, as a result of the development of artificial intelligence (AI) technology (Gkinko and Elbanna, 2022a).

13.6.1 TALENT ACQUISITION

AI-powered chatbots can help automate the initial stages of the recruitment process by screening resumes, answering candidate questions, and scheduling interviews. This can save recruiters a lot of time and effort and make the hiring process more efficient.

13.6.2 EMPLOYEE ENGAGEMENT

AI-powered chatbots can help keep employees engaged by sending out regular updates, notifications, and reminders. They can also conduct surveys to gather feedback from employees and provide personalized recommendations for training and development opportunities.

13.6.3 EMPLOYEE HELP

AI-powered chatbots can be used as a first point of contact for employees who need help with HR-related questions. They can answer common queries related to benefits, leave policies, and payroll and escalate more complex issues to HR staff if needed. AI has the potential to help employees in many ways, including the following:

Streamlining tasks: Automating time-consuming and repetitive processes with AI can free up staff time for more strategic and innovative work.

Personalized learning and development: AI-powered training tools can personalize learning content to an employee's needs and learning style, helping them acquire new skills and knowledge more efficiently.

Improved decision-making: AI can investigate tremendous data and provide insights that can help employees make better-informed decisions.

Enhanced communication: AI-powered chatbots and virtual assistants can assist employees with their inquiries and provide real-time feedback.

Health and wellness: AI can monitor employee health and wellness by analyzing data such as heart rate, sleep patterns, and stress levels. This data can help employees make informed decisions about their health and well-being.

Improved work-life balance: AI can help employees manage their workload more efficiently, reducing stress and improving their overall work-life balance.

13.6.4 EMPLOYEE COMMUNICATION

Chatbots can be used to facilitate communication between employees and HR staff. They can provide updates on company policies, upcoming events, and other important information, and they can also collect feedback from employees on various HR initiatives. A better EEX depends on effective employee interaction with numerous internal and external actors. To deliver a more useful employee experience, efficient communication and relationships with diverse actors are essential (EEX). Organizations may ensure quicker and more effective communication with their staff thanks to technology-driven communication tools. With video conferencing, mobile apps, intranet social networks, instant messaging and chat programs, and mobile apps, for instance, technology can help improve communication (Swanson et al., 2020; Terblanche, 2020; Winarto, 2018).

13.6.5 WORKPLACE SAFETY

Wearable technology is used by employers in the organizations to: (a) track productivity; (b) spot safety concerns or hazards and take appropriate action; (c) deliver augmented training to enhance job management; and (d) promote health and wellness (Kalantari, 2017; Melian-Gonzalez et al., 2021).

Artificial Intelligence (AI) has a significant role in employee safety. Here are some examples of how AI can be used to improve employee safety:

Predictive analytics: AI can analyze data from various sources, such as sensor data, employee behavior patterns, and weather conditions, to identify potential safety hazards and predict the likelihood of accidents or incidents. This information can be used to take proactive measures to prevent accidents before they occur.

Monitoring and detection: AI can monitor employees' behavior and environmental conditions to detect safety hazards and potential incidents. For example, AI can monitor video feeds to identify unsafe behavior, such as an employee not wearing safety equipment, and alert supervisors to take corrective action.

Hazard recognition: AI can recognize potential hazards in real-time, such as an object in the workspace that could cause an accident or a hazardous chemical leak, and alert employees and supervisors to take appropriate action.

Training and education: AI is sometimes employed to deliver personalized safety training to employees, including simulations and virtual reality scenarios, to help them identify potential safety hazards and respond to emergencies.

13.7 BENEFITS OF AI-DRIVEN HR

Although employees believe that AI-driven HR technology helps them make choices more quickly and execute their jobs more effectively, many find it difficult to continuously utilize this AI technology at work and feel anxiety related to technology adoption. It enables businesses to cut back on employee assistance and engagement costs (Johannsen et al., 2021). In addition, it makes use of 24/7 individualized employee support, which gives workers more access and convenience. Chatbots (Majumder et al., 2021) streamline the HR process and make it easier to find information and conduct searches. Chatbots provide proactive HR outreach and facilitate regular computerized commentary (Malik and Budhwar, 2022; McGloin, 2022).

AI and technology have a significant impact. Because of technology, instead of being concentrated in the middle, jobs are more focused at either the inferior or high-skill level of the skills continuum, a phenomenon known as the "hollowing out of work" (Gratton and Scott, 2016; Lee et al., 2014).

Thus, AI-driven HR helps in improving efficiency, enhancing objectivity, better hiring outcomes, improved employee experience, and cost savings.

13.8 ACCEPTANCE OF AI IN INTERNAL CUSTOMER EXPERIENCE (ICX)

The implementation of virtual teams and other technology-based solutions at the executive level can indeed face numerous barriers that can slow down or prevent adoption altogether.

Factors like employee beliefs, budget, type of machine, relationship between user and data evaluator, job type of employee, designation, and familiarity with technology affect the reception of the same in an organization (Choi et al., 2017; Kwee-Meier et al., 2016; Schall et al., 2018; Spagnolli et al., 2014).

The fear of losing their jobs as a result of technology potentially replacing human labor is the root cause of employees' negative opinions regarding AI (Winick, 2018; Laumer et al., 2019).

One major barrier to acceptance of AI is a lack of understanding or familiarity with the technology itself. Executives may not be as familiar with the latest technology trends or may not have the technical skills needed to effectively use and implement these solutions. This can make it difficult for them to evaluate the benefits of virtual teams and other technology-based solutions and may cause them to be hesitant to invest in these tools.

Another barrier is resistance to change. Executives and other decision-makers may be comfortable with the current ways of working and may be resistant to introducing new tools or processes that could disrupt existing workflows or require significant changes in the organization's structure.

Additionally, there may be concerns around security and data privacy, which can make executives hesitant to adopt virtual teams or other technology solutions that involve remote access to sensitive information.

Finally, there may be a lack of resources, including financial resources and IT support, to effectively implement and manage virtual teams and other technology-based solutions.

To overcome these barriers, it is important for organizations to provide executives with the education and training needed to effectively evaluate and implement technology solutions. It may also be necessary to provide additional resources, including IT support and funding, to facilitate the adoption of virtual teams and other technology-based solutions. Additionally, organizations should be transparent about the benefits of these solutions, including improved productivity and efficiency, and should work to address concerns around security and data privacy. By taking a strategic approach to technology implementation, organizations can help ensure that virtual teams and other technology-based solutions are adopted at the executive level and used to their full potential.

13.9 RELATED THEORIES

There are studies done in numerous fields that use some of these theories to talk about the adoption of chatbots. The researchers' study has mostly been centered on theories like the technology adoption model (TAM), and using adoption theories, advanced technology adoption in human resource management is investigated.

13.10 RELATED FINDINGS

13.10.1 AI IN TALENT ACQUISITION

Talent acquisition function has been undergoing a transformation with AI from being a mere applicant management function to more of a strategic function driving an organization's branding initiative with a superior candidate experience. By defining the applicant characteristics (credentials, knowledge, skills, and demographics), AI can facilitate choices with reference to advertisement, analysis, communication, and interview of candidates based on the verbal–nonverbal language, interviews, feedback, and negotiation processes.

13.10.2 AI IN ONBOARDING

The delay between a candidate accepting an offer and joining the company has long troubled organizations. With the help of AI, businesses may actively facilitate informative dialogs with prospective hires and reduce the percentage of "no-shows" at the time of joining. Artificial intelligence can automatically designate the proposed employee to join courses based on the preplanned dialogs, assign a suitable mentor, and deliver news feeds in advance. In this way, organizations can guarantee that employees are ready to contribute from day one.

13.10.3 AI IN EMPLOYEE LIFE CYCLE MANAGEMENT

Regular HR transactions, such as onboarding, employee self-service HRMS, transfers, approvals and probations, and inquiries, can be transformed into more meaningful discussions with AI charting employees' growth, productivity, and involvement toward the business. Organizations receive critical feedback from AI interventions created for these employee life cycle events, which can be related to attrition and talent management. Artificial Intelligence is able to analyze the two-way input and offer insights to workers who are maturing into future leaders.

13.10.4 AI IN PERFORMANCE MANAGEMENT

With agile management and a constant feedback system that encourages frequent dialog and course adjustments, organizations are changing how they assess the performance of their staff. Qualitative metrics based on personality traits, brand association, engagement levels, leadership quality, capacity to handle pressure levels, group spirit, coaching and mentoring ability, and concern for co-workers are growing in popularity for evaluating employees, peers, and managers.

13.10.5 AI IN LEARNING AND DEVELOPMENT

Learning and development are now constant practices since the usefulness of acquired abilities is eroding at an exponential rate. How individuals learn and develop is also drastically changing as a result of the usage of video and mobility in educational technologies. Proactively identifying and training personnel who can upgrade their current abilities or those who can be reskilled is becoming more important as firms implement continuous and healthy learning and development methods. A customized Employee Learning and Development plan can be created using AI's evaluation of qualitative and quantitative trends. By doing this, you may increase productivity while maintaining employee loyalty.

13.11 CONCLUSIONS

Future organizations must make significant investments in corporate connectivity, cooperation, and consolidation using technology. Organizations will deliver the new generation customer experience, which is a competitive advantage in luring and keeping talent, by synchronizing data, analysis, and intelligence. By enabling businesses to build inclusive workplace environments, foster open and collaborative work environments, enhance current services, and promote leadership development, leveraging AI will be crucial in delivering this experience. AI chatbots will initially digitize HR procedures, resulting in a seamless, conversational, tailored, and responsive customer experience in real-time. Chatbots provide an excellent level of customer experience for workers, including individualized learning and development and real-time HR inquiry responses. By accelerating responses to often-asked HR inquiries, simplifying the talent management process, and upgrading the online learning customer experience, chatbots are perfectly suited for HR directors to improve talent acquisition and onboarding procedures (Botha et al., 2011).

13.12 WAY AHEAD

While technology has the potential to greatly enhance and streamline operations, its successful implementation requires careful planning, investment, and expertise. It is essential for organizations to carefully evaluate their needs and capabilities and to work closely with technology specialists to ensure that they can fully realize the benefits of emerging technologies.

In addition to automating work culture, organizations should concentrate on how technology can improve the working environment for employees. Because today is the era of digitally driven organizations, it is imperative for HR managers to embrace technologies like AI chatbots. Without it, businesses would struggle to strategically establish a competitive edge and cater to the demands of a diverse workforce (Malik et al., 2020; McGloin, 2022).

KEYWORDS

- **artificial intelligence (AI)**
- **big data**
- **customer experience**
- **HR**
- **digital**

REFERENCES

Ashfaq, Yun, J.; Yu, S.; Loureiro, S. M. C. I, Chatbot: Modeling the Determinants of Users' Satisfaction and Continuance Intention of AI-Powered Service Agents. *Telemat. Inf.* **2020,** *54*, 101473.

Batat, W. The Employee Experience (EMX) Framework for Well-Being: An Agenda for the Future. **2022,** *44* (5), 993–1013.

Botha, A.; Bussin, M.; de Swardt, L. An Employer Brand Predictive Model for Talent Attraction and Retention. *SA J. Hum. Resour. Manag.* **2011,** *9* (1), 1–12.

Choi, B.; Hwang, S.; Lee, S.; What Drives Construction Workers' Acceptance of Wearable Technologies in the Workplace? Indoor Localization and Wearable Health Devices for Occupational Safety and Health. *Autom. Construct.* **2017,** *84*, 31–41.

Davenport, T. H.; Kirby, J.; Beyond Automation: Strategies for Remaining Gainfully Employed in an Era of Very Smart Machines. *Harv. Bus. Rev.* **2015,** *93* (6), 58–65.

Dulebohna, J.; Hoch, J. Virtual Teams in Organizations. *Hum. Resour. Manag. Rev.* **2017,** *27* (4), 569–574.

EY. How EY's AI Journey Created a Major Business Impact. *EY India* **2019,** 1–2. https://www.ey.com/en_in/alliances/how-ey-s-ai-journey-created-a-major-business-impact.

Faqihi, A.; Miah, S. J. Artificial Intelligence-Driven Talent Management System: Exploring the Risks and Options for Constructing a Theoretical Foundation, Special Issue Risk of Artificial Intelligence and International Business. *J. Risk Financial Manag.* **2023,** *16* (1), 31. https://doi.org/10.3390/jrfm16010031

Gibson, C.; Cohen, S. *Virtual Teams That Work Creating Conditions for Virtual Team Effectiveness*; Wiley: New York, 2003.

Gkinko, L.; Elbanna, A. The Appropriation of Conversational AI in the Workplace: A Taxonomy of AI Chatbot Users. *Int. J. Inf. Manag,* **2022a,** 102568.

Gratton, L.; Scott, A.; *The 100-Year Life: Living and Working in the Age of Longevity*; Bloomsbury: London, 2016.

Gustafson, P. Managing Business Travel: Developments and Dilemmas in Corporate Travel Management. *Tourism Management* **2012,** *33* (2), 276–284.

IBM. *5900-A1H IBM Watson Candidate Assistant*; IBM Corporation: Armonk, NY, 2020; pp 1–2.

Joerres, J.; Globalization, Robots, and the Future of Work: An Interview with Jeffrey Joerres. *Harv. Bus. Rev.* **2016,** *94* (10), 74–79.

Johannsen, F.; Schaller, D.; Klus, M. F. Value Propositions of Chatbots to Support Innovation Management Processes. *Inf. Syst. E-Bus. Manag.* **2021,** *19* (1), 205–246.

Kalantari, M.; Consumers' Adoption of Wearable Technologies: Literature Review, Synthesis, and Future Research Agenda. *Int. J. Technol. Mark.* **2017,** *12*, 274–307.

Kwee-Meier, S. T.; Bützler, J. E.; Schlick, C.; Development and Validation of a Technology Acceptance Model for Safety-Enhancing, Wearable Locating Systems. *Behav. Inf. Technol.* **2016,** *35*, 394–409.

Laumer, S.; Maier, C.; Gubler, F. T. Chatbot Acceptance in Healthcare: Explaining User Adoption of Conversational Agents for Disease Diagnosis. Twenty-Seventh European Conference on Information Systems (ECIS2019), Stockholm-Uppsala, Sweden, 2019; pp 0–18.

Lee, J.; Zo, H.; Lee, H. Smart Learning Adoption in Employees and HRD Managers. *Br. J. Educ. Technol.* **2014,** *45* (6), 1082–1096.

Majumder, S.; Mondal, A. Are Chatbots Really Useful for Human Resource Management? *Int. J. Speech Technol.* **2021,** *24* (4), 969–997.

Malik, A.; Budhwar, P. Employee Experience——The Missing Link for Engaging Employees: Insights from an MNE's AI-Based HR Ecosystem. *Hum. Resour. Manag.* **2022,** 1–19.

Malik, A.; Budhwar, P.; Patel, C.; Srikanth, N. R. May the Bots Be with You! Delivering HR Cost-Effectiveness and Individualised Employee Experiences in an MNE. *Int. J. Hum. Resour. Manag.* **2020,** *33* (6), 1–31.

Malik, N.; Tripathi, S. N.; Kar, A. K.; Gupta, S. Impact of Artificial Intelligence on Employees Working in Industry 4.0 Led Organizations. *Int. J. Manpower* **2022,** *43* (2), 334–354.

Marlow, S.; Lacerenza, C.; Salas, E. Communication in Virtual Teams: A Conceptual Framework and Research Agenda. *Hum. Resour. Manag. Rev.* **2017,** *27* (4), 575–589.

McGloin, C. HR Chatbots: 5 Inspiring Tips for Improving Employee Experience with Bots. Servisbot.Com, 2022. https://servisbot.com/hr-employee-chatbots/

Meister, J. The Future of Work: How Artificial Intelligence Will Transform the Employee Experience. *Forbes*, 2017.

Melian-Gonzalez, S.; Gutierrez-Tano, D.; Bulchand-Gidumal, J. Predicting the Intentions to Use Chatbots for Travel and Tourism. *Curr. Iss. Tour.* **2021,** *24*, 192–210.

Morgan, J. *The Employee Experience Advantage: How to Win the War for Talent by Giving Employees the Workspaces They Want, the Tools They Need, and a Culture They Can Celebrate*; John Wiley: Hoboken, 2017.

Pillai, R.; Sivathanu, B. Adoption of AI-Based Chatbots for Hospitality and Tourism. *Int. J. Contemp. Hosp. Manag.* **2020,** *32* (10), 3199–3226.

Schall, M. C.; Sesek, R. F.; Cavuoto, L. A.; Barriers to the Adoption of Wearable Sensors in the Workplace: A Survey of Occupational Safety and Health Professionals. *Hum. Factors* **2018,** *60*, 351–362.

Sharmila Rani Moganadas, G. G. Digital Employee Experience Constructs and Measurement Framework: A Review and Synthesis. *Int. J. Technol.* **2022,** 999–1012.

Smith, C. An Employee's Best Friend? How AI Can Boost Employee Engagement and Performance. *Strat. HR Rev.* **2019,** *18* (1), 17–20.

Spagnolli, A.; Guardigli, E.; Orso, V.; Varotto, A.; Gamberini, L.; Measuring User Acceptance of Wearable Symbiotic Devices: Validation Study Across Application Scenarios. *Int. Workshop Symbiotic Interaction* **2014,** 87–98.

Swanson, E. B. Available to Meet: Advances in Professional Communications. *Inf. Technol. People* **2020,** *33* (6), 1543–1553.

Terblanche, N. H. D. Factors that Influence Users' Adoption of Being Coached by an Artificial Intelligence Coach. *Phil. Coach.: Int. J.* **2020,** *5* (1), 61–70.

Winarto, W. Electronic Human Resources Management (e-HRM) Adoption Studies: Past and Future Research. *DeReMa (Development Research of Management): Jurnal Manajemen* **2018,** *13* (1), 100.

Winick, E Every Study We Could Find on What Automation Will Do to Jobs, in One Chart. *MIT Technol. Rev.* **2018**. https://www.technologyreview.com/s/610005/every-study-we-could-find-on-what-automation-will-do-to-jobs-in-one-chart/

Zel, S.; Kongar, E. Transforming Digital Employee Experience with Artificial Intelligence. *2020 IEEE/ITU International Conference on Artificial Intelligence for Good, AI4G* **2020,** *2020*, 176–179.

CHAPTER 14

Big Data: The Covert Artillery Backing Customer Loyalty Programs

ANUPAL MONGIA and SWATI SHARMA

Chandigarh University, Chandigarh, Punjab, India

ABSTRACT

Numerous sectors, including healthcare, finance, retail, and telecommunications, now depend heavily on big data. Organizations can spot patterns, trends, and linkages that would be impossible to spot using more conventional techniques by analyzing vast amounts of data. This could result in fresh perspectives and better decision-making, which would boost effectiveness and performance. Big data also presents obstacles, such as ensuring data quality, safeguarding privacy and security, and acquiring new knowledge and skills. Despite these difficulties, big data can help firms gain huge benefits and completely transform their particular sectors. Big data is a component that is gaining importance across a range of businesses and has the ability to significantly affect and enhance performance. Making data-driven decisions, gaining new insights, and completely changing industries are all possible thanks to big data. Despite its potential, big data presents a number of difficulties, including the need to ensure data quality, safeguard users' privacy and security, and acquire new knowledge and skills. Businesses that successfully use big data and overcome these obstacles can reap enormous rewards and succeed in their objectives. Big data's significance in the modern world cannot be overemphasized, and it is essential for enterprises to comprehend both the advantages and difficulties of using it. Big data refers to the massive volume of organized and unstructured data that a firm must continually deal with. The quantity of data is not important, though. What companies do with

Augmenting Customer Retention Through Big Data Analytics.
Reena Malik, Ambuj Sharma, and Prashant Chaudhary (Eds.)

the data is what really matters. Big data analysis may yield information that aids in making more informed judgments in general as well as strategic business decisions. A company can use big data to retain consumers by making use of the amount of customer information it contains. No matter the size of the business, utilizing the data that has been collected effectively can lead to superior customer service throughout the entire organization. Big data enables rapid customer response and mass personalization of service. It seeks to improve the capacity of customer service teams to amaze and facilitate real-time personalization. Big data assists in quickly locating innovative and lucrative product offerings. Smaller businesses may find big data intimidating.

14.1 INTRODUCTION

Many sectors, including banking, healthcare, retail, and telecommunications, now depend heavily on big data. Organizations can get important insights and information through the analysis of vast volumes of data that would not be achievable using more conventional techniques. These insights may result in more effective decision-making and more efficiency, which would improve the organization's performance (McAfee et al., 2012).

However, the use of big data also presents several challenges. Ensuring data quality is a critical issue as big data is often generated from various sources and may not always be accurate, complete, or relevant. Privacy and security are also important considerations as big data often contains sensitive information that must be protected from unauthorized access and misuse (Gandomi et al., 2015). Additionally, while the technology and techniques involved are continually expanding, using big data involves the development of new skills and experiences.

Despite these obstacles, businesses that successfully use big data may reap significant rewards and completely change their sectors. Big data utilization has already contributed to the development of tailored treatments in the field of healthcare as well as new financial services and products in the financial services sector. In summary, big data is an essential component of the modern world, and its significance cannot be overemphasized (Gandomi et al., 2015). To fully exploit the potential of big data and achieve their objectives, organizations must comprehend both the advantages and difficulties connected with its utilization. They must also make an investment in resolving the difficulties (Chen et al., 2012). The capacity of big data to provide businesses with a competitive edge is one of its main advantages. Organizations may get insights about their customers, rivals, and the market by analyzing vast volumes of data, enabling them to make wise decisions and remain ahead of the competition (Fan et al., 2015).

Enhancing operational efficiency is one of big data's other key advantages. For instance, firms may find inefficiencies and streamline their procedures by evaluating data from the supply chain, which lowers costs and boosts productivity.

Organizations need to be mindful of the ethical issues surrounding the use of big data in addition to its advantages (Chen et al., 2012). For example, there are concerns about the collection and use of personal data and the potential for discrimination based on data-driven decisions. It is important for organizations to ensure that they are using big data in a responsible and ethical manner and to implement privacy and security measures to protect sensitive information.

Organizations must have the proper infrastructure in place in order to properly utilize the potential of big data. This entails having a reliable system for managing data as well as the capacity to store, handle, and analyze vast volumes of data. To properly analyze and interpret the data, organizations must also have the appropriate technology and tools, such as data visualization and machine learning tools.

In conclusion, big data has several advantages for businesses, such as better decision-making, fresh insights, and enhanced productivity. Organizations must invest in the required infrastructure and technologies, however, in order to fully utilize their potential. They must also be cognizant of the difficulties and ethical issues related to its usage (McAfee et al., 2012). Organizations may accomplish their objectives and maintain their competitiveness in the fast-paced, data-driven world of today by doing this.

One of the most significant characteristics of big data is its ability to identify patterns and trends that would be challenging to identify using traditional methods. Organizations may better understand their customers, rivals, and the market by analyzing vast volumes of data, and they can then utilize this information to guide their actions. Big data may be utilized, for instance, in the retail sector to assess client purchasing patterns and preferences, resulting in the production of targeted marketing campaigns and new goods and services. Big data's capacity to assist with real-time decision-making is a key feature. Organizations can adapt swiftly to shifting market circumstances and consumer requirements because they have the capacity to handle and analyze massive volumes of data in real-time, helping them to stay competitive and agile. Big data may also help customers have a better overall experience (Fan et al., 2015). Organizations may build individualized experiences that cater to their particular requirements and increase customer satisfaction by analyzing consumer data to acquire insights into their behavior, preferences, and pain spots. Big data may also assist in innovation and the creation of new goods and services. Ultimately, big data has the potential to help enterprises save a lot of money. Organizations may eliminate waste and enhance operations by analyzing data and finding inefficiencies, which lowers costs and boosts profitability. In conclusion, big data has the ability to completely change how businesses function and how they make choices. Organizations may gather insightful information, enhance consumer experiences, foster innovation, and generate cost savings by utilizing its power. Organizations must, however, make the financial investment in the infrastructure and personnel needed to fully harness the potential of big data and meet the related obstacles.

Big data has a wide range of uses and is not just used in a few industries or sectors. By analyzing vast volumes of data from electronic health records, clinical trials, and other sources, big data may be utilized in the healthcare industry, for instance, to enhance patient outcomes.

14.2 CHARACTERISTICS OF BIG DATA

Big data stands out for its abundance, rapidity, diversity, and authenticity. These characteristics have a significant influence on how firms collect, store, and analyze data, and they are crucial for determining the value that can be derived from big data for enterprises.

Volume is the term used to represent the massive amounts of data that enterprises create and keep, which can be measured in petabytes or even exabytes. The volume of data has dramatically expanded in recent years as a result of the growing use of digital technologies and linked gadgets. As a result of this expansion, businesses are finding it harder and more difficult to manage, store, and analyze data using traditional methods. Velocity is a unit of measurement for the rate at which data is generated and the rate at which it must be processed in order to be valuable. Due to the increasing usage of real-time technology and the velocity of data, businesses must process and analyze data in real-time in order to keep up with shifting market circumstances and consumer expectations.

Structured, semistructured, and unstructured data are only a few of the several types of data that are created and are referred to as "variety." Structured data is data that has been predetermined in its organization, such as names, dates, and numbers. Semistructured data, which has some structure but is not as well-organized as structured data, includes emails and social media postings.

The pace at which information is generated and must be processed in order to be useful is known as its velocity. Real-time technologies are being used more often, which has increased the velocity of data. As a result, businesses must process and analyze data in real-time to keep up with changing market circumstances and client demands.

Variety is the term used to describe the various sorts of data produced, such as structured, semistructured, and unstructured data. Data that is organized in a present way, such as numbers, dates, and people, is referred to as structured data. Semistructured data, like emails or social media posts, is data that has some structure but is not as well-organized as structured data.

14.3 BENEFITS OF BIG DATA

Big data has a wide range of advantages; however, some of the more important advantages include the following:

- Better Consumer Insights: Organizations can better understand customer behavior and preferences by analyzing vast amounts of customer data. This includes data on demographics, spending patterns, product preferences, and much more. The marketing strategies and product selections can then be adjusted to better suit the needs of particular consumer groupings. Organizations can also learn about client preferences and opinions by analyzing social media data and customer feedback, which enables them to continuously improve their goods and services. Customers are more satisfied and loyal as a result.
- Enhanced Productivity and Efficiency: Big data analytics can assist businesses in identifying areas for process simplification and operational improvement. For instance, by optimizing their supply chain and lowering costs and delivery times, firms can benefit from the analysis of logistics data. Organizations can also find bottlenecks and inefficiencies by evaluating data from manufacturing processes, which enables them to make changes that speed up production and

save costs. Organizations can gain a competitive edge by utilizing big data through improved productivity and efficiency.

- Superior Decision-Making: Organizations that have access to a lot of data are better able to make decisions based on current knowledge. This results in more accurate decisions, quicker decision-making processes, and more efficient decision-making procedures. Organizations might, for instance, employ big data analytics to find trends and patterns in financial data, enabling them to make wise investment and risk management decisions. Organizations can utilize big data to study consumer behavior and market trends, which enables them to make data-driven decisions about product development and marketing strategies.
- Enhancing Risk Management: Organizations can more efficiently detect and minimize possible hazards by examining data from a number of sources. In order to reduce the risk of financial losses, businesses might, for instance, uncover fraudulent activity by analyzing financial data. Big data can also be used by businesses to recognize and control operational hazards like equipment breakdowns and supply chain interruptions. Organizations may lessen the effect of potential hazards and maintain business continuity by proactively managing risk using big data.
- Improved Fraud Detection and Prevention: By examining patterns and trends in data from diverse sources, big data analytics may be utilized to detect and prevent fraud. Data from social media and banking transactions are all included. Organizations can discover potential fraudulent actions and take measures to stop them by evaluating this data. By displaying a dedication to safeguarding the data and assets of their clients, this aids firms in lowering the danger of financial losses and enhancing customer trust.
- Better Predictive Maintenance: Organizations can forecast when equipment is likely to fail by evaluating data from sensors and machines. This makes it possible for businesses to plan maintenance in advance, cutting downtime and increasing overall effectiveness. Organizations might, for instance, utilize big data to examine equipment data to forecast when a machine is likely to fail. By scheduling maintenance during a planned downtime, they can lessen the impact on operations and boost efficiency. Big data analytics can help firms use predictive maintenance to lower costs and increase equipment reliability.

- Improved Patient Outcomes and Lower Healthcare Costs: Organizations can enhance patient outcomes and lower healthcare costs by evaluating vast amounts of healthcare data. In order to improve patient outcomes and lower the risk of complications, healthcare organizations can, for instance, design individualized treatment plans with the aid of patient data analysis. Organizations can also utilize big data to examine population health data, which enables them to spot and handle public health problems before they spread widely. Healthcare businesses may enhance patient outcomes, cut expenses, and deliver better care to their patients by utilizing big data.
- Enhanced Marketing and Advertising: Organizations can better target their marketing and advertising efforts by evaluating client data, increasing the efficiency of their operations while cutting expenses. For instance, businesses can utilize big data to evaluate client information and identify the best channels and times to deliver marketing messages. Organizations can therefore adjust their marketing initiatives to fit the particular demands of each client segment by examining data on customer purchase patterns, product preferences, and channel preferences. Organizations can also employ big data to evaluate social media data, giving them the ability to recognize and react in real-time to client sentiment. As a result, businesses are able to improve their overall marketing performance and forge closer ties with their clients.
- Better supply chain management: Businesses can pinpoint areas for improvement and streamline operations by evaluating data from the whole supply chain. Organizations can utilize big data, for instance, to analyze information on inventory levels, shipping prices, and delivery times, enabling them to make wise decisions about inventory management and delivery procedures. Big data analysis from suppliers can also be used by businesses to identify and manage supplier risk, lowering the chance of supply chain interruptions. Organizations may enhance operations and cut costs by utilizing big data in their supply chain management efforts.
- Better Resource Management: The usage of resources like electricity, water, and labor can be optimized with the help of big data analytics. Organizations can, for instance, evaluate energy usage data using big data to find potential for cost- and energy-saving energy efficiency. Organizations can also utilize big data to examine data on water use,

which enables them to squander less and use resources more effectively. Organizations can lower expenses and enhance their overall sustainability efforts by leveraging big data to manage resources.

14.4 CHALLENGES OF BIG DATA

- Data Collection and Management: Gathering and managing the enormous volumes of data that are generated is one of the main problems with big data. This entails gathering information from both internal and external sources, including social media and sensors, in addition to internal sources like transactional systems. Organizations must have a strong data management infrastructure in place, including data storage and retrieval systems, data processing and analysis tools, and data security and privacy safeguards, in order to handle this data successfully. Organizations must have well-defined data management policies and procedures in place as well as a thorough grasp of the data they are gathering and managing in order to guarantee that data is managed properly.
- Data Quality: Another major problem with big data is ensuring the quality of the data being collected and analyzed. This entails making sure that data is accurate, full, and consistent, as well as taking care of problems like data bias and data privacy. To overcome these obstacles and make sure the data they use is of the highest quality, businesses must put in place reliable data quality processes and systems, including data validation and data cleaning techniques. The sources of data bias and data privacy issues must also be thoroughly understood by businesses in order for them to put appropriate solutions in place.
- Data Integration: Another significant problem with big data is integrating data from many sources. This entails combining external data sources, like social media and sensors, with internal data sources like transactional systems and internal databases. Organizations must use efficient data integration procedures, such as data mapping, data warehousing, and data interchange standards, to guarantee that data is accurately and effectively integrated in order to meet these difficulties. Organizations must also have a thorough grasp of the data sources and the connections between them, as well as the tools

and processes for data integration that are most suited to satisfy their requirements.

- Data Privacy and Security: A fundamental difficulty of big data is ensuring the security and privacy of the data that is being collected and analyzed. This includes guarding against data breaches, cyberattacks, and other security risks in order to secure sensitive consumer and business data. Organizations must also address issues with data privacy, such as making sure that consumer personal information is not misused or disclosed without permission. Organizations must establish strong data security and privacy measures, such as data encryption, firewalls, and access control systems, as well as privacy policies and processes to ensure that customer data is secured, in order to overcome these difficulties. Organizations must also have a thorough awareness of data privacy and security laws and make sure that their data management procedures adhere to their regulations.
- Data Analytics and Interpretation: Another major problem with big data is analyzing and interpreting the massive volumes of data that are generated. Organizations must be equipped with the appropriate procedures, tools, and a thorough understanding of data analytics and data visualization techniques in order to accomplish this. To guarantee that the data is being properly examined and interpreted, firms must also have the appropriate expertise in place, including data scientists and business analysts. Organizations must invest in the appropriate data analytics procedures and tools, as well as make sure that their data analytics teams have the necessary knowledge and skills to efficiently analyze and interpret the data.
- Data Governance: Another major difficulty with big data is effective data governance. To guarantee that data is being gathered, managed, and used in an ethical and responsible manner, clear policies and processes must be in place. To guarantee that data is precise, secure, and guarded against misuse, enterprises must also have efficient data management systems in place, including data quality control and data security. Organizations must adopt efficient data governance procedures and systems, such as data quality control, data security, and data privacy rules, to overcome these obstacles and guarantee that the data being utilized is of high quality and secure from potential threats. To guarantee that data is utilized in accordance with legal and ethical requirements, they must also have clear policies

and procedures for data management, including data retention, data deletion, and data sharing.

- Data Skilled Labor Shortage: Another issue in big data is the scarcity of skilled workers who can manage and analyze enormous amounts of data. This comprises experts in data management, data analytics, and data visualization, as well as data scientists, data analysts, and other specialists. Organizations must invest in employee training and development programs to meet this challenge, as well as competitive pay and benefits to attract and keep the finest personnel. In order to ensure that their data management and analysis teams are representatives of the diverse populations they serve, they must actively recruit and retain diverse talent as well as collaborate with educational institutions to support the development of the next generation of data professionals.
- Technical Restrictions: Big data also faces technical restrictions, such as the inability to instantly store, process, and analyze enormous amounts of data. Along with having the technical know-how to manage and use these systems, this necessitates that enterprises have reliable and scalable data management and analytic platforms in place. Organizations need to make investments in cutting-edge infrastructure and technology to meet these challenges, including systems for data storage and retrieval, data processing and analysis, and data visualization and reporting. This will give them the technical capacity to efficiently manage and analyze their big data.
- Data Interoperability: Another difficulty with big data is ensuring that various data systems and technologies can cooperate efficiently. To ensure that data is accurately and effectively integrated, companies must have in place defined data exchange standards and protocols as well as efficient data integration processes. Organizations must invest in data interoperability technologies and standards, including APIs and data exchange protocols, to overcome this difficulty and make sure that their data systems can interact and cooperate successfully.
- Cost: This necessitates the establishment of clear data interchange standards and protocols inside businesses as well as efficient data integration processes to guarantee accurate and effective data integration. To address this issue, businesses must invest in data interoperability technologies and standards, such as APIs and data exchange protocols, in order to make sure that their data systems can properly communicate with one another.

14.5 BIG DATA TECHNOLOGIES

Large and complex data sets that are beyond the capacity of conventional data management systems must be stored, processed, and analyzed using a combination of tools and techniques referred to as "big data technologies." Because of the expansion of the Internet and the growing volume of data produced by numerous sources, including social media, online transactions, and machine-generated data, these technologies have grown in significance over the past several years.

Hadoop is an open-source platform for storing and handling large amounts of data. By breaking up the data into smaller bits and distributing it across numerous servers, it is made to manage massive volumes of data. In addition to a processing framework called MapReduce that can process the data in parallel across multiple nodes, Hadoop also offers a distributed file system called HDFS that can store and manage enormous volumes of data.

Large data sets may be processed quickly and effectively with Spark, an open-source big data processing engine. It is intended to be a general-purpose cluster computing system for machine learning, real-time data streaming, and batch processing. Spark is interoperable with Hadoop and other big data technologies, and it offers high-level APIs in various programing languages, including Scala, Python, and Java.

NoSQL databases are nonrelational databases made specifically to manage large amounts of data. They differ from conventional relational databases in that they can accept unstructured data and do not have a set schema. MongoDB, Cassandra, and CouchDB are a few examples of NoSQL databases that are frequently used to handle massive volumes of data in real-time.

Data Lakes: An organization may store all of its structured and unstructured data in a data lake, which is a centralized repository that can accommodate any volume of data. Data lakes offer a single point of access for analytics and data processing while handling enormous amounts of data from diverse sources. They are frequently used in conjunction with big data tools like Spark and Hadoop. A model for distributing computer resources across the Internet is called "cloud computing." It enables businesses to store and handle huge amounts of data on the cloud, eliminating the need for expensive hardware and simplifying scaling up and down as necessary. Amazon Web Services (AWS), Microsoft Azure, and Google Cloud Platform (GCP) are popular big data cloud providers.

These are some of the most common big data technologies in use right now. The best ones to use will depend on the particular demands and requirements of the company. There are other additional tools and technologies out there, each with unique strengths and drawbacks.

14.6 THE IMPLICATIONS OF BIG DATA FOR CUSTOMER LOYALTY

The prospect of nearly automated customer experience programs makes big data analytics alluring. The idea is that you can track and analyze client behavior as well as what they think about their experience with your company's product or service if you just tune the most recent analytics software to your customer interactions and to social media sites. It is not that easy. Many of the interactions that customers have with a firm include human communication between customers and employees. Yes, algorithms can immediately recommend fixes following a negative interaction or strengthen the brand of the organization following a positive one. Additionally, some episodes will do better when distributed only digitally, such as with straightforward online purchases. The underlying procedures and guidelines that determine the quality of the customer experience, whether it be digital or physical, can only be fixed or improved by people. Only people are able to understand the subtleties of a customer's worries and respond to them sympathetically. Big data analytics is without a doubt the newest major advancment in customer experience and advocacy.

The combination of these technologies gives businesses strong new capabilities to deepen interpersonal communication and increase consumer loyalty. Companies may now continuously monitor almost all client impressions at any moment, as opposed to the past when they could only evaluate limited samples of customers at one point in time. Over the next few years, it is expected that the gap between loyalty leaders and laggards will expand in many sectors as early analytics adopters gain proficiency with the tools. Consider big data as the most recent advancement in a long line of tools and methods for executing loyalty-based tactics, which began in the 1980s with customer retention initiatives by forerunner airlines like American Airlines and credit card firms like American Express. The Loyalty Effect, published by Bain & Company in the 1990s, discussed the significance of loyalty. By the early 2000s, Bain had developed a critical loyalty metric called the Net Promoter Score and expanded the focus beyond customer retention to include other benefits of loyalty in its work for clients. These benefits include a stronger focus on customer lifetime value in strategy and execution, as well as smarter acquisition and retention tactics and client segmentation. By the early 2010s, we had worked with businesses to develop and codify a management system that continuously incorporates consumer feedback to enhance the experience. The cutting edge of customer-centered tools and methods has expanded continuously.

The cornerstone for improving the customer experience is observational analytics. For instance, a lot of mobile telecom operators watch the patterns of missed calls using analytics, and software-as-a-service providers track the performance of their applications and the utilization of particular features as fundamental markers of the user experience. This instrumentation can capture expressed sentiment in human interactions as well as fine-grained usage patterns.

The use of predictive analytics extends far beyond the use of recommendation algorithms by companies like Netflix. Big data analytics, for instance, can forecast the possibility that a client will become a detractor when they have a string of bad experiences (including lengthy wait times, defective goods, or service interruptions); the customer may limit purchases, cease visiting a website, or even defect to a rival. Without having to personally survey clients, a business can also successfully analyze the sentiment of contact center calls to generate predictions.

14.7 BIG DATA MAY THEREFORE SUPPORT AND BROADEN SOME OF THE CORE TENETS OF GAINING CUSTOMER ADVOCACY

Get the experience's fundamentals right. Leading online wine retailer Wine.com has made investments in recommendation algorithms and an easy-to-use digital platform for selection and shipment, but it also encourages customers to speak with sommeliers. Customers' loyalty and lifetime value to the company have improved as a result of these experts' assistance in learning about and exploring a wider range.

More information without action causes an organization to regress. Only if you integrate the data into customer feedback loops that directly improve the relevant experience, it will be valuable. Consider software programs that request millions of crash reports from users but never follow up with them or make the program better. Even though the software industry is awash in experience data, no changes are being made as a result.

The most successful businesses scale up their capacity to cater to, customize, and improve the experience for their customers using big data analytics. In all instances where human judgment and empathy are crucial, such as when evaluating tradeoffs and interacting with customers, they continue to rely on human innovation.

14.8 BIG DATA TECHNIQUES THAT CAN AID YOUR COMPANY IN RETAINING CUSTOMERS

Improved big data analytics aid in boosting client loyalty. You will be able to move quickly on the insights you obtain, giving you the chance to easily satisfy customer requests. Here are a few big data techniques your company may employ to increase customer loyalty, gain insights from customer happiness, and become more competitive.

- ***Adaptability*** – Be flexible in how you handle delivery. Customer needs are constantly evolving as a result of technology. Your analysts need to be flexible and able to stay up. Your company will be better able to adapt to shifting demands and priorities if you have big data agility.
- ***Superior quality to quantity*** – Make sure that the most important information is fed into your analytical solutions. Pick the information that is most pertinent to the current scenario from all the data you collect. Place more emphasis on data quality than data quantity.
- ***Eliminate blind spots*** – Ensure you document everything. If there are blind spots, the image of the customer's experience and behavior will be distorted overall since you will not have captured everything that affects the customer's experience and behavior.
- What do your customers need or want? Never presume anything. You should accept your customers for who they are, not what you think they are doing. Allow data to provide insight while being impartial.
- Consider the activity on your network as a gold mine. The knowledge you glean from the traffic is the real treasure. You can use it to enhance delivery and eventually boost revenue.

14.9 CONCLUSIONS

Big data is a fast-expanding and constantly changing sector that is changing how businesses function and make decisions. Big data is becoming an essential tool for businesses and organizations all over the world due to the growing amount of data being produced daily. Big data has several advantages, including better decision-making, better customer service, enhanced production and efficiency, and the creation of new goods and services. Despite the many advantages, big data also poses a number of difficulties that businesses must overcome in order to fully realize their potential. The integration of new technology, data privacy and security, and the requirement for qualified people are some of these problems. Organizations must make investments in cutting-edge technology, put best practices into place, and invest in staff training to meet these difficulties. Big data has a bright future ahead of it as technology advances, and we may anticipate even more cutting-edge uses in the years to come. The chapter has given a thorough review of the main traits, advantages, difficulties, and outcomes and conclusions of big data. Big data will continue to play a crucial role in determining the future of businesses and sectors throughout the world with the correct strategy and investment. It is also crucial to remember that the use of big data also presents social and ethical issues. Organizations must take steps to safeguard data privacy and security as they gather and handle enormous volumes of sensitive and personal data. In order to avoid prejudice and detrimental effects on society, big data algorithms and analytics must be transparent, impartial, and fair. Big data must be used responsibly if it is to succeed and flourish in the future; thus, businesses must take these issues into account when they design and put into practice their big data strategy.

KEYWORDS

- **big data**
- **customer loyalty**
- **artillery**

REFERENCES

Aggarwal, C. C. Big data: A Survey. *Mob. Netw. App.* **2015,** *20* (2), 169–183.

Agrawal, D.; Srikant, R. Fast Algorithms for Mining Association Rules in Large Databases. In: *Proceedings of the 20th International Conference on Data Engineering (ICDE'04)*; 2014; pp 778–785.

Bote-Lorenzo, M. L.; De la Fuente-Valentín, A.; Pérez-Euodia, A. Big Data Processing with Apache Spark. *J. Big Data* **2017,** *4* (1), 2.

Chen, H.; Chiang, R. H. L.; Storey, V. C. Business Intelligence and Analytics: From Big Data to Big Impact. *MIS Quart.* **2012,** *36* (4), 1165–1188.

Chiu, D.; Nguyen, N.; Li, J. Big Data: A Review of Technologies, Challenges, and Future Prospects. *J. Ambient Intell. Human. Comput.* **2016,** *7* (1), 1–12.

Cukier, K.; Mayer-Schönberger, V. *Big Data: A Revolution That Will Transform How We Live, Work, and Think*; John Murray Publishers Ltd, 2013.

Dhar, V.; Stein, E. Big data: A review of the literature. Journal of Business Research, 69 (1), 3–10.

Efthimios's, E. N. Big Data: An Overview of Issues and Research Challenges. *Big Data Res.* **2015,** *2* (2), 60–65.

Fan, W.; Han, J.; Yao, Y. Y. Challenges and Opportunities of Big Data Research. In: *Proceedings of the 2015 ACM SIGMOD International Conference on Management of Data*; 2015; pp 1057–1058.

Gandomi, A.; Haider, M. Beyond the Hype: Big Data Concepts, Methods, and Analytics. *Int. J. Inf. Manag.* **2015,** *35* (2), 137–144.

Jain, A. K.; Murty, M. N.; Flynn, P. J. Data Clustering: A Review. *ACM Computing Surveys (CSUR)* **1999,** *31* (3), 264–323.

Jordan, M. I. Machine Learning: Trends, Perspectives, and Prospects. *Science* **2015,** *349* (6245), 255–260.

Kelleher, C. D.; Mac Namee, B.; D'Arcy, A. *Data Science: An Introduction*; John Wiley & Sons, 2015.

Khatri, N. Big Data and IoT Security. *Computer* **2015,** *48* (3), 27–31.

Kim, D.; Lee, H. Big Data Analytics in Marketing. *Int. J. Inf. Manag.* **2015,** *35* (2), 132–136.

Kim, D.; Lee, H. Big Data Analytics for Business Intelligence and Decision Support. *J. Organ. Comput. Electron. Commerce* **2016,** *26* (4), 291–308.

Kumar, V.; Lin, J.; Yu, P. S. Big Data and Its Technical Challenges. *Proc. VLDB Endowment* **2015,** *8* (12), 1802–1803.

Li, J.; Li, Z.; Li, M.; Tian, J. Big Data: A Survey. *Mob. Netw. App.* **2015,** *20* (2), 171–209.

Liu, B. *Web Data Mining: Exploring Hyperlinks, Contents, and Usage Data*; Springer, 2015.

McAfee, A.; Brynjolfsson, E. Big Data: The Management Revolution. *Harv. Bus. Rev.* **2012,** *90* (10), 28–38.

Shmuel, G.; Patel, N. R.; Bruce, P. C. *Data Mining for Business Intelligence: Concepts, Techniques, and Applications in Microsoft Office Excel with Limner*; John Wiley & Sons, 2015.

Shmueli, G.; Patel, N. R.; Bruce, P. C. *Data Mining for Business Intelligence: Concepts, Techniques, and Applications in Microsoft Office Excel with XLMiner*; John Wiley & Sons, 2010.

Tao, X.; Santamaria Kannan, R. Big Data Privacy: A Review of Current Developments and Future Prospects. Information Systems Frontiers, 19 (2), 397–413.

Wei, W. Big Data and Cloud Computing: A Review. *Int. J. Web Grid Serv.* **2015,** *11* (3), 277–290.

White, T. *Hadoop: The Definitive Guide*; O'Reilly Media, Inc, 2012.

Witten, I. H.; Frank, E.; Hall, M. A.; Pal, C. J. *Data Mining: Practical Machine Learning Tools and Techniques*, 3rd edn.; Morgan Kaufmann Publishers, 2016.

Zaharia, M.; Chowdhury, M.; Franklin, M. J.; Shenker, S.; Stoica, I. Spark: Cluster Computing with Working Sets. In: *Proceedings of the 2010 ACM SIGMOD International Conference on Management of Data*; 2010; pp 1023–1035.

Zaslavsky, A.; Keogh, E.; Lin, J. Data Management and Analysis in the Cloud: Opportunities and Challenges. In: *Proceedings of the 2015 ACM SIGMOD International Conference on Management of Data*; 2015; pp 961–966.

https://www.bain.com/insights/what-big-data-means-for-customer-loyalty/

CHAPTER 15

Role of Big Data Analytics in Enhancing Customer Experience

RANDEEP KAUR and JYOTI BANSAL

JCD Vidhyapeeth, Sirsa, Haryana, India

ABSTRACT

Information technology is rapidly booming in tandem with the international business revolution. As a result of these technological developments, customer experience (CX) has become a viable source of competitive difference. Each firm must make sure that their customers have a good experience. All techniques and technology are being used by businesses to improve CX. The best method for gaining customer insights for managing the CX is big data analytics (BDA). In recent years, the emergence of BDA has been noticed, which is now playing a crucial role in CX. Therefore, there is a need for a conceptual framework that would give a broad overview of BDA's potential applications for CXM and would direct management practice because there is little research in this area. The major objective of this chapter is to make a conceptual and strategic framework for CX obtained from BDA that would help managers make smart and concurrent decisions. For this study, secondary data has been used. The paper provides a conceptual framework of BD and BDA, the evolution of BD, the main characteristics and various types of BD, data sources, and the opportunities and challenges of BDA. In the last section, the conclusion, followed by future research opportunities, is presented.

15.1 INTRODUCTION

With the increasing revolution of information in every industry or business, big data analytics (BDA) is now more capable of improving customer

Augmenting Customer Retention Through Big Data Analytics.
Reena Malik, Ambuj Sharma, and Prashant Chaudhary (Eds.)

experience (CX). Big data helps managers to make discreet decisions based on data as compared to only forecasting. Business organizations are collecting huge data as compared what is actually required (McAfee et al., 2012). Researchers, practitioners, and academicians are now showing an increased interest in BDA. The emergence and spread of digital devices, like the Internet, tablets, and smartphones, are persistently producing massive amounts of data. It helps to make smart decisions based upon good intuitions. Renowned corporate houses are using big data for better and fair managerial practices. The researchers have undertaken abundant studies in a variety of fields, including supply chain big data, social media data, electronic data, and transactional data. Nevertheless, to meet the challenges, computing, storage, and analysis have improved. In the present times, it has become very economical and easy to store large datasets. Along with traditional business data, data obtained from social media sites has become very important for organizations as these data help them in enhancing CX of customers visiting these social sites and advertising and convincing them to buy their products.

E-commerce or social sites such as Instagram, First Cry, Ajio, Reliance mart, etc., have shown the ability to gather business intelligence, which is crucial for developing competitive strategies. However, the decision-makers' grasp of the possibilities of BDA has not been meticulously reviewed yet in any research study. To fulfill this need, this study discusses how it is used in a variety of decision-making processes. This chapter will bridge this gap by providing a detailed conceptual framework for the decision-makers. Big data is being extensively used in the commercial, healthcare, e-commerce, and institutions of higher learning in the 21st century. This research study is beneficial for managers to take timely and accurate decision with the help of big data and would help to make better predictions and decisions.

15.2 LITERATURE REVIEW

In literature review, researchers has to study the research work done by various researchers. This study will present an outcome of various researches that support the decision makers to decide based on facts that are concluded after studying different platforms of BDA. In our study, we employed various search engines, like Google, Google Chrome, etc. We also used some online platforms like Online Journals, ResearchGate, E-books of Conferences, Scopus, Google Scholar, etc., were used to select relevant research papers. Some keywords were used to find research papers like big data, BDA, etc., to get in-depth knowledge of big data.

15.3 DEVELOPMENT OF INFORMATION SYSTEMS IN BIG DATA

In recent years, the information systems and the web have become the primary facilitators of international business. With the advancement in technology and with the usage of advanced information systems software, this system is used for technical applications, like Android software in smartphones, that has made the world a global village. The revolution in computer science engineering and Information Technology resulted in an information revolution across the world (Chan et al. (2012). The Internet has played a very significant role in the evolution of big data. The enlargement of the Internet and e-commerce firms, like Yahoo, Google Chrome, Paytm, Nyka, Instagram, Amazon, etc., has increased the significance of web-based business, which has resulted in the development of big data. The development of different computer storage devices, the Internet, and high-speed communications devices are all also included in this.

15.3.1 MEANING OF BIG DATA

Several authors have defined big data in several ways. Some researchers described big data as the ocean of information, while others described it as a phenomenon of cultural, technological, and academics. It is described by Kitchin (2014) as structured and unstructured data. Massive data refers to datasets that are difficult to process by traditional data processing techniques; that's why new data technologies are invented. Big data are those large datasets and analysis methods which are used during applications. These methods are very complex, when used in cutting-edge methods for storing, management, interpretation, and presentation. In a nutshell, it can be described as datasets with terabytes and petabytes of data that were produced in a few hours. It refers to the enormous amount of data, both organized and unorganized. It is not important that how much data is there, but what matters is what businesses do with the data. Big data analysis can provide a better understanding to the decision-makers, which helps them to take better strategic, tactical, and business decisions.

Big data is mostly used to solve the problem of analysis of huge data with advanced technology in any specific area of application. In the initial years, big data was welcomed by the Internet and e-commerce. There are many applications that help in decision-making that facilitate the use of data. A variety of methods and technologies are used to make decisions for improved data analyses in business organizations. Businesses like Voot apps, Hotstar, Max Players, etc., have created algorithms to determine the association between consumer searches and past purchases to forecast the things customers would like to buy. On the basis of previous experiences, consumers are informed of their searches. This gives clients the chance to purchase some of the things that are suggested, thereby increasing sales. Their maximum new sales are due to this method (Artun and Levin, 2015). To identify which consumers are most likely to be retained, telecom corporations sift through enormous amounts of data. This facilitates the business organizations to create better policies for their client retention.

15.3.2 CHARACTERISTICS OF BIG DATA

Big data includes a huge amount of data which otherwise is not possible by the traditional methods to process. Many researchers have contributed in this area and they said that two things are more important, e.g., truthfulness and value. In the present era, many multinational and e-commerce websites are using this for the development of their business to save time and money. The main characteristics of big data are as follow:

15.3.2.1 VOLUME

In a little span of time, social media sites gathered data in terabytes or pantabytes for corporates, which indicates the huge size of the big data volume. Data volume has been doubling with a very fast speed (Davenport, 2014). The rate of growth for mobile devices is unprecedented. According to John Chambers of Cisco, it is predicted that approximately 40 billion wireless devices will be used to connect the Internet in the coming years. The role of big data involves its contribution to data analysis, which results in more efficient operations, greater relationships with customers, and other understandable and measurable commercial advantages.

15.3.2.2 VELOCITY

In social media as well as traditional enterprise systems, data is accumulating at previously unheard-of rates. Sales managers leave a huge quantity of data in their supply chain. Social media allows for considerably faster data generation—the rate at which businesses acquire, retain, and handle data, such as the quantity of social media postings or search queries that are posted in a day, hour, or other period of time.

15.3.2.3 VARIETY

A large amount of information is stored, some of which are required to be organized and analyzed. In addition to conventional sources, new kinds of large datasets include those from social networks as well as mobile devices. Examples include audio as well as video recordings, photographs, GPS data, medical records, instrument measurements, graphics, web documents, bonus cards, and online search activity. Processing and categorizing data is more difficult when it includes unstructured data, including voice and social media. Enterprise systems like SAP ERP, social media sites, and all the online platforms are some of the sources of big data.

15.3.2.4 VERACITY

Veracity means to comprehend the actual percentage of data and also to know the accuracy of data. Veracity in big data shows accuracy and trustworthiness. The standard of the data that will be studied to check the accuracy is referred as veracity. It helps the user to understand the market to make a wise decision to retain customers.

15.3.2.5 VALUE

Eventually, it is the need of the firms to understand what kind of models firms can create to enhance financial results and extract "value" from big data. The development and growth of every industry depend on how firms extract value from massive amounts of heterogeneous data to make their business profitable. When large amounts of data are concerned, a renowned data analytics company uses different data extraction softwares, like SAP ERP and Oracle ERP, to extract and analyze data collected from different formats.

15.3.2.6 VARIABILITY

Variability means data which is changing continuously. Mostly organizations are required to understand the context of programs and decode their meaning. The data volumes can also exhibit regular peaks that are very erratic. It is difficult to handle huge data loads regularly, mainly true unstructured data.

15.3.2.7 COMPLEXITY

Data that is collected from different social media platforms is required to be analyzed. But these big data are so complex in nature that their analysis, transformation, and interpretation are very difficult and also this data comes from multiple sources. However, without linking and associating hierarchies and huge data, daily data is not easy to manage.

The aforementioned seven big data features have allowed BDA to play a significant part in the advancement of organizations in terms of fulfilling client needs, comprehending market conditions, and growing of revenues. Organizations must be aware of their consumers' perspectives in the context of CX. That has been made feasible by BDA by using a collection of sophisticated algorithms to turn unstructured data into data that is important (Said et al., 2015).

15.4 CUSTOMER EXPERIENCE (CX)

When used in business, the term "CX" means the several points of contact that a client has with a business, all of which combine to create the client's perception of that business as a whole. Researchers defined CX as an organization's direct or indirect interaction with its current or prospective consumers that results in an overall impression in the eyes of those customers. To improve the CX, BDA is a very important instrument for management decision-making. Even while BDA is crucial for providing excellent CX for corporates, there are no specific tactics that businesses may always use to succeed. The researchers explained that big data discovery initiatives may turn up previously undiscovered information and produce insights that will be useful for management customer acquisition decision-making. The capacity of humans to retain and process data was constrained before the development of computers. Big data was utilized as the basis for choices made by experts. Earlier, BDA techniques like regression, factor analysis, etc., were used for statistical analysis. Techniques like real-time data mining from sensor data are involved for the analysis. Big data is a multidisciplinary field that draws on data from data from different subjects like mathematics, computer science, statistics, and many other fields. It requires a methodical approach for gathering and analyzing business data, development of a descriptive analytics model to explain the phenomenon, a predictive analytics model to predict future outcomes based on variable inputs, and the development of an optimization or simulation model using alternative inputs. Correlation, regression, F-test, T-test, ANOVA, and other mathematical skills are employed while formulating equations.

15.5 BIG DATA ANALYTICS (BDA)

Big data has emerged as an important tool to enhance management decision-making. As per a renowned researcher, big data discovery initiative can produce findings that were not previously known, leading to insights that are beneficial for management decision-making. People's capacity for data processing and storing was constrained before the development of computers. In the past, decision-making was done by professionals. The roots of BDA can be found in earlier approaches to analyze information that made use of quantitative methodology like Anova, multivariate statistical, etc. It employs rapid datasets and inertial sensors analysis to acquire real-time insights (Chen et al., 2012). Math, statistics, computer science, and data science are all used in this multidisciplinary discipline. It requires a rigorous approach to acquiring and analyzing corporate data, creating a statistical model (descriptive analytics), and creating a model (predictive analytics) that forecasts future results based on changing inputs, and constructing a model (optimization or simulation) that optimizes or simulates outcomes based on changing inputs (prescriptive analytics). It uses many statistical tools to create equations to solve big data problems.

15.5.1 TYPES OF ANALYTICS

In this competitive era, researchers are not concerned only with descriptive analytics that refers to what is happened or why it is happened. But it helps to know the answers to questions related to the data that may happen in the future, also known as predictive analytics, and what steps should be taken to determine the best outcomes, also known as prescriptive analytics, is the key topic of concern. Business analytics is divided into three categories: descriptive, predictive, and prescriptive analytics.

When managers have a thorough knowledge of the anticipated results, they may make decisions and prepare for contingencies. Managers can take decisions and make plan for alternatives when they expect good results. The method that can be applied to analyze data depends significantly on the sources of that data.

15.5.1.1 TEXT ANALYTICS

Customer behavior can be predicted through many factors like search systems, search engines, etc., on particular platform and this is known as text analytics. When a customer visits their website again, the stored data can be analyzed to predict what they would prefer to buy; this function is used by various e-commerce platforms like Ajio, Nyka, First Cry, Hotstar, etc., to suggest goods or trips, increasing the likelihood that they would make a purchase.

15.5.1.2 AUDIO AND VIDEO ANALYTICS

A technology called audio analytics processes audio in a matter of seconds, mostly for safety purposes in any organization. It can track a variety of environmental sounds. Videos from many different sectors and industries are processed and analyzed using video analytics. This aids in the extraction of events and helps to make strategic and managerial decisions.

15.5.1.3 WEB ANALYTICS

Many companies employ data mining methods to extract intelligence from massive data, including click streams, site searches, order histories, and other online activities. For businesses like Ajio, Nyka, First Cry, Hotstar, etc., this intelligence is successfully used to make decisions about how to promote products. Based on previous purchases that were similar to the anticipated current purchase, a correlation between the two is found. Using digital channels like Gmail, Instagram, or flashing messages on Amazon. com, this correlation is utilized to identify new buyers and market various things to them.

15.5.1.4 NETWORK ANALYTICS

Network analytics gives information on the network-connected devices and their interactions with one another. This data aids in the creation of network policies and the ability to take meaningful actions that enhances company performance and cut costs for communications on Amazon.com.

15.6 VARIOUS TYPES OF DATA

In the present scenario, big data is used in every sphere of life. Data can be divide into different categories. Broadly, different sources of data can be used, which can be categorized into three categories—structured data, unstructured data, and semi-structured data. These can be defined in details as follow:

15.6.1 STRUCTURED DATA

Structure data can be stored in the database in a tabular form as rows and columns. They have relational keys and can easily be mapped into pre-designed fields. Today, those data are mostly processed in the development and simplest way to manage information, for example, relational data. The information system of batch processing and expanded enterprise softwares like supply chain management (SCM) and supply chain control (SCC) are used as structured data sources. Additionally, this data is organized in tabular structured forms. Tools used by conventional databases help to extract, transform, and load data into different data warehouses.

15.6.2 UNSTRUCTURED DATA

This data is referred to those information that are not organized using a predetermined data model or schema and which are not stored in a conventional relational database system, also known as an RDBMS. The main sources of unstructured data are e-commerce sites, social media, emails, attachments, videos, photos, and sound file. This represents more than 90% of the major datasets in terms of volume and velocity.

15.6.3 SEMI-STRUCTURED DATA

This type of data form contains both types of data, that is, structured and unstructured data and it comes from a wide range of sources. Several information systems have been used to exchange information with stakeholders quickly, effectively, and accurately. Businesses can communicate via email, employ RFID technology for quicker processing in logistics, or track goods using sensor devices. There are several tags that contain structured user information, an IP address, and a date and time stamp. Moreover, unstructured text forms for error messages, SQL statements, and event logs exist.

15.7 BIG DATA VS. TRADITIONAL DATA

In the past, corporate data was kept in an unambiguous relational database management system. Over the past few decades, a number of large businesses have used ERP systems to increase operational effectiveness and control expenses (Bharathi and Mandal, 2015). Large amounts of transactional data are continuously collected by these ERP systems or customized application solutions. For the short- and medium-term applications, these assist operational and tactical choices. Data volume and velocity are dependent on business volume. Various levels of management have employed information systems as a decision support system. Within this network of proximate stakeholders, the extent of data gathering was constrained. There higher volumes of data have occasionally been gathered, such as when the government collected census data every decade (Kitchin, 2014a). However, since these instances were rare, there was little urgency to analyze the data immediately. This enormous dataset was transferred to a data warehouse to be further examined over time. When the Internet replaced other forms of communication and information flow, the data scenario underwent significant change on several fronts:

The introduction of the Internet hastened the trend of globalization and the expansion of multinational corporations because it has made communication across borders quick, affordable, and simple. Since the Internet's invention, multinational corporations' business volumes have multiplied manyfold. Business organizations have improved their information systems even more to record every detail. Supply chain commercial dealings take place both inside and outside the companies. Sometimes reverse logistics (RL) business operations are mapped to data systems because of their importance for improving customer service or because there are stringent legal requirements in some countries for manufacturers to recover and/or dispose of the products. Retail organizations record millions of customer contacts every hour, resulting in the production of many terabytes of data in just a few hours.

- New semi-structured data formats have appeared, for examples blogs, e-mails, etc. A huge increase in data volume, speed, and type has resulted from the continued addition of social media data from sites like Nyka, First Cry, Ajio, Facebook, Instagram, etc.
- Big data is characterized by a constant influx of data from numerous sources. The data is unstructured and has no fixed source. Every hour, billions of posts, likes, and millions of photos are uploaded to Facebook (Kitchin, 2014).
- The capability of manual analysis has been greatly outpaced by the volume, variety, and velocity of data acquisition. It has occasionally even outperformed the capacity of traditional databases. Technology industry leaders like Microsoft, IBM, and Oracle use the specialized technological framework Hadoop for managing big data in order to analyze such massive volumes of data.

15.8 DIFFERENT BIG DATA SOURCES

In modern information systems, different sources of big data include e-commerce sites, matrimonial sites, social networking websites, cloud applications, software, social influencers, different documents, and corporate applications. The following explains a few sources.

15.8.1 TRANSACTIONAL DATA

In order to develop a model to predict an event, such as a sales projection or the level of success of a new product launch, transactional data must be combined with statistical methods like regression analysis and decision trees. The model can use inputs from historical data to forecast the dependent variable. Statistical software like SPSS or SAS makes it simple to develop these models. All historical data including independent variables is referred to as transactions, and systems used to maintain track of these transactions are commonly characterized as "transactional processing systems." Transaction processing is used to collect information and update data forthe operational decisions in an organization. There are two methods for handling transactions: batch processing, which handles data as a single entity over a period of time, and real-time processing, which handles data instantly. Making operational decisions in any business can be aided by either approach.

15.8.2 SOCIAL MEDIA DATA

Due to social media's growing popularity in recent years, data is being gathered everywhere in the world. As events take place, reports are made. On Facebook, Twitter, or WhatsApp, Internet users are pleased to quickly express their opinions, suggestions for products or services, and movie reviews. For decision-makers, this presents a rare chance to learn about the market. Through the sharing of information on social media, consumers are able to look at reviews, customer complaints, and other services offered with a product to assist in purchasing decisions. Social media is a platform for customer sentiment that aids businesses in decision-making regarding production. Additionally, competitive intelligence regarding the company's products and services provided by rivals in any given market category is gathered through social media analytics. This encourages fresh business concepts to enhance the business life cycle. As a result, social media data are crucial for strategic, operational, and tactical marketing decisions.

With the development of the Internet, countless numbers of users are browsing several websites and conducting numerous web searches for goods and services. Millions of users log in and use a variety of online e-commerce platforms search engines (such as Google, Yahoo, Bing, etc.), or online banking services every day. Their searches and transactions generate numerous click streams and records, some of which may be useful.

15.8.3 DATA FROM ELECTRONIC INSTRUMENTS

There are large number of instruments from where we can collect data like GPS sensors, network-connected equipment, scanners, and cameras are just a few examples of the electronic media that produce large amounts of data. These are known as additional big data collection sources.

15.9 OPPORTUNITIES AND CHALLENGES OF BDA

Massive sample size and high dimensionality are traits of big data (Fan et al., 2014). Dealing with these enormous and continuous data sets presents certain chances for competitive advantage as well as some obstacles when analyzing data of this kind with multiple dimensions, great volume, and heterogeneity. In this section, the authors go into great length about these.

15.9.1 OPPORTUNITIES

A few years ago, a large amount of data was a technological challenge; today, it is an opportunity (Russom, 2011). E-commerce websites and social websites have proven this. Many opportunities and product differentiation are provided by big data. As an early adopter, Amazon.com started collecting information on consumers' tastes, searches, transactions, and book reviews. Based on this data, it provides information about products that nudge clients to acquire similar or comparable goods, boosting the likelihood that they'll make more purchases from the same vendor in the future. To monitor the actions of specific customers and prediction, different models are formed. Walmart uses a system called "social genome" for customer relationship management. Customers who are in-person or online can receive product recommendations through Social Genome. Compared to more traditional data collection techniques like taking samples, big data has several advantages.

15.9.1.1 DATA MINING

Data mining is the analytical technique used to find patterns in datasets, that are used to support the making of decisions and predictions about the future. Finding population patterns and heterogeneities that are not achievable with small-scale data is made possible by this technique. Finding precise information that is not immediately visible is possible with the use of data mining. It can be used, for instance, to track customer satisfaction and loyalty levels or to learn more about the most profitable. This knowledge aids in creating strategies for cross-selling or customer retention.

15.9.1.2 LARGE SAMPLE SIZE FOR ANALYTICS

Massive statistical samples provided by big data improve the outcomes of analytical tools (Russom, 2011). An outlier in the sampling procedure may be a member of a different subgroup. As a result, we may end up with a flawed model and inaccurate outcomes not taking into account all factors that could explain group differences We are examining a comprehensive dataset that contains all subpopulations within big data. As a result, we are better able to comprehend heterogeneity within the dataset and the connections between dependent and independent variables. A model built using the data provides reliable information because it reflects the complete population, which increases the correctness of business decisions. Big data contains information from corporate systems and from different sources like social media, which offers real-time data from the ground such as customer reviews, traffic, and weather updates, and complements information from enterprise systems very effectively. Today's analytical technologies can handle vast amounts of data for affordable prices (Russom, 2011).

15.9.1.3 ADVANCEMENT TECHNOLOGY

It explores massive data sources and information analysis of the same in quest of correlations. The difficulties posed by enormous data sets have inspired the creation of novel computational infrastructure. With improved, less expensive storage and high-speed computing capabilities, technology is prepared with solutions that can keep up with the rate of data generation.

15.9.1.4 REAL TIME

Big data, whether it comes from structured or unstructured sources, gives those who are able to extract value from that specific source of data real-time information. There are many instances where real-time data has been used to address issues. Natural catastrophes have the potential to break key supply chain links impact is greater for nations like India in particular because of its fragmented logistics system, insufficient infrastructure, and a big number of small to large companies. Data from geographic locations, weather, and developing natural disasters (storms, floods, earthquakes, etc.) is used to monitor supply chain risks in real-time, both proactively to avert interruptions and reactively to look into past incidents. Singapore's government uses geo-location information from mobile devices to control traffic during peak hours. In order to direct the taxis to certain regions of the city during rush hour, this information is used to forecast the demand for transportation services in real-time. Social media provides real-time traffic and weather updates, allowing residents to adjust their travel arrangements as necessary. Product suggestions made by e-commerce companies like Amazon, Ajio, Nyka, and Flipkart, which are based on past purchases and search history, increase the sales of new products.

15.9.2 CHALLENGES OF BDA

Big data provides some unique challenges because of its tremendous volume and high dimensionality. Most organizations are overwhelmed by the number of data being collected so quickly. Its size, quality, noise accumulation, false correlation, incidental endogeneity, and measurement mistakes pose the most problems (Fan et al., 2014). One of the crucial things to keep in mind is that big data is fueled by an enormous volume of data that is produced every day and stored more affordably than before.

15.9.2.1 SIZE AND QUALITY OF DATA

The volume of big data presents the biggest difficulty in handling it. Information systems can be used to handle traditional databases with ease, but big data requires a specialized technical framework, such as Hadoop, for data administration. Due to the rapid generation of big data, its storage and transmission necessitate careful planning and infrastructure investment. The second issue relates to data quality, which is measured by the data's completeness, correctness, and prompt availability. In a conventional sampling procedure, a random sample of data is chosen from a sizable population to acquire extensive information, and the sample is then subjected to statistical analysis. Large datasets for big data analysis demand complex statistical and computational techniques.

15.9.2.2 HIGH DIMENSIONALITY

Additionally, it leads to erroneous correlation, which indicates variables may provide false information regarding their association with the model's outcome. Any variable that does not account for the outcome's variability has a probability of being added. It has a high dimension, making it difficult to choose variables and create constructs because there may be erroneous connection. This brings up yet another problem with accidental endogeneity. It results from the model producing erroneous findings due to increased dimensionality.

15.9.2.3 RELIABILITY

The validity of the data poses another challenge. Most unstructured data is frequently untrustworthy and susceptible to outages. Data is gathered in the production environment from a variety of sources, including information systems and various sensors (Le and Pang, 2013). Because of this, the data mining process is highly laborious and requires sorting through a lot of unrelated data to find a tiny amount of useful information. The procedure is like searching for a needle in a haystack.

15.9.2.4 COMPLETENESS

The dataset does not necessarily represent the population, despite its size and the fact that it contains numerous dimensions. A different site, which is a source of a lot of unorganized data, only reflects people who are active there and voice their thoughts or engage in online discussions about the issue. Some websites, such as Twitter, offer access to constrained, filtered datasets that are again a subset of data.

15.9.2.5 FRAUDS

On the one hand, digitalization is making life better, but on the other hand, some people are using it for frauds. Online and offline frauds of all kinds are growing every day. Analysis of the social media fraud data presents a significant problem for researchers.

15.9.2.6 SCALABILITY

This refers to the capacity to modify and expand hardware, software, and storage in order to handle sudden changes in the volume of traffic or the growth of data for quick output generation.

15.9.2.7 COMPLEXITY

Because of the high level of technical complexity, many companies' technocrats are lacking in data science expertise. These are very complex in nature.

15.10 OVERCOMING THE CHALLENGES OF BDS FOR ENHANCED CX

Alharthi et al. (2017) outlined some pertinent issues that organizations must overcome in BDA and provide the desired CX to customers, including infrastructure preparedness, data complexity, a lack of expertise, privacy concerns, and cultural hurdles. Additionally, additional studies have revealed the importance of BDA in increasing CX along with the pertinent issues, namely, the quality of data, availability of data, and systematic challenges. Below are some suggested solutions for overcoming the difficulties.

- Organizations should employ broadly accessible hardware that is less priced and used interchangeable.

- To haul out CX insights from the vast data sets, organizations should employ well-established software technologies (like Hadoop), which are dependable, effective, and cost-friendly. To learn about CX, the employees must get practical training.
- Organizations should carefully handle the security of sensitive customer data; as a result, they must incorporate the required laws as per regulations.
- To ensure a seamless cultural transition, BDA and CX integration into the vision of the business. Because user-generated data is frequently unstructured and qualitative, data quality-related difficulties sometimes render an organization's BDA process. Before doing the analysis, organizations should spend more effort cleaning and organizing the acquired data using the appropriate machine language
- To ensure a seamless cultural transition, BDA and CX integration into a firm's vision is essential.
- Because user-generated data is frequently unstructured and qualitative, data quality-related difficulties sometimes render an organization's BDA process rather inefficient when concluding the required information from that data. Before doing the analysis, organizations should spend more effort cleaning and organizing the acquired data using the appropriate machine language.

15.11 FUTURE RESEARCH DIRECTIONS

Based on the explicit and inferred insights from current literature, some outlines of the scope of further research compiled for future research directions are as follows:

In order to better support the theories of CX and BDA in the literature as well as for practitioners who would employ big data and predictive analytics to benefit the advanced technological community, BDA can reveal novel patterns and previously unrecognized associations; the writers cannot afford to disregard it and the insightful knowledge about complicated phenomena that it offers. We have discovered that CX can be viewed from various perspectives; therefore, the term needs to be redefined. The ideal situation would be to take the customer ecosystem into account, providing organizations more chances to get access to more relevant CX data.

- It remains clear how to get a range of CX insights from the relevant data sets, particularly in the context of BDA. More attention should be paid to describing how CX findings might be helpfully perceived.

- When interacting with a specific organization, it is well recognized that the client experience changes from channel to channel. It would be very beneficial to conduct a comparison study for a range of channels when determining how well BDA can measure CX.
- Based on a range of sociological factors, customers from different nations may differ somewhat from one another. Further research is therefore necessary to examine how individuals define and view CX in various nations in the context of BDA and CX.
- While significant research has been done on the ideas of CX and BDA in the B2C environment, the same has not yet been done in the B2B setting, particularly because an individual client may differ slightly from a business customer.

15.12 CONCLUSION

In this chapter, we concentrated on assembling all the pertinent tactics in the framework of BD, CX, and BDA based on the literature that is available. In this chapter, a detailed conceptual framework of BDA and CX, the evolution of BD, main characteristics and various types of BD, data sources, and opportunities and challenges of BDA is presented. And, the conclusion, followed by future research opportunities, has been presented. This study will help organizations to get beyond the relevant obstacles of putting those tactics into practice. Finally, we discussed some intriguing new CX and BDA research directions. It is anticipated that the information discussed here will significantly benefit practitioners across a wide range of organizations while also adding to the body of knowledge on BD, BDA, and CX.

KEYWORDS

- **customer experience**
- **big data analytics**
- **customers**
- **business**

REFERENCES

Alharthi, A.; Krotov, V.; Bowman, M. Addressing Barriers to Big Data. *Bus. Horizons* **2017,** *60* (3), 285–292.

Artun, O.; Levin, D. *Predictive Marketing: Easy Ways Every Marketer Can Use Customer Analytics and Big Data*; John Wiley & Sons, 2015.

Askari Z. TelecomDrive.com. Smart City Lessons from Singapore—How 'Beeline' Is Redefining Transportation. http://telecomdrive.com/smart-city-lessons-from-singapore-how-beeline-is-redefining-transportation/ (accessed on 23 July 2016).

Berry, L. L.; Carbone, L. P.; Haeckel, S. H. Managing the Total Customer Experience. *MIT Sloan Manag. Rev.* **2002,** *43* (3), 85–89.

Brun, I.; Rajaobelina, L.; Ricard, L.; Berthiaume, B. Impact of Customer Experience on Loyalty: A Multi Channel Examination. *Serv. Ind. J.* **2017,** *37* (5–6), 317–340.

Ballé, M. Transforming Decisions into Action. *Career Dev. Int.* **1998,** *3* (6), 227–232.

Boyd, D.; Crawford, K. Critical Questions for Big Data: Provocations for a Cultural, Technological, and Scholarly Phenomenon. *Inf. Commun. Soc.* **2012,** *15* (5), 662–679.

Chen, H.; Chiang, R. H.; Storey, V. C. Business Intelligence and Analytics: From Big Data to Big Impact. *MIS Quart.* **2012,** *36* (4), 1165–1188.

Coursaris, C. K.; van Osch, W.; Balogh, B. A. Informing Brand Messaging Strategies via Social Media Analytics. *Online Inf. Rev.* **2016,** *40* (1), 6–24.

Davenport, T. H.; Dyché, J. Big Data in Big Companies. *Int. Inst. Anal.* **2013**.

Davenport, T. H. How Strategists Use 'Big Data' to Support Internal Business Decisions, Discovery and Production. *Strategy Leadership* **2014,** *42* (4), 45–50.

De Vries, N. J.; Arefin, A. S.; Mathieson, L.; Lucas, B.; Moscato, P. Relative Neighborhood Graphs Uncover the Dynamics of Social Media Engagement. In: *Advanced Data Mining and Applications: 12th International Conference, ADMA 2016, Gold Coast, QLD, Australia, December 12–15,* **2016,** *Proceedings 12*; Springer International Publishing, 2016; pp. 283–297.

Duan, L.; Xiong, Y. Big Data Analytics and Business Analytics. *J. Manage. Anal.* **2015,** *2* (1), 1–21.

Dubey, R.; Gunasekaran, A.; Childe, S. J.; Wamba, S. F.; Papadopoulos, T. The Impact of Big Data on World- Class Sustainable Manufacturing. *Int. J. Adv. Manuf. Technol.* **2015,** *84* (1–4), 1–15.

Dyche, J. *e-Data: Turning Data into Information with Data Warehousing*; Addison-Wesley. https://www.amazon.com/Data-Turning-Data-Information- Warehousing/dp/0201657805

Dyché, J. Big Data and Discovery, Jills Blog Big Data Digital Innovation, 2014. https://jilldyche.com/2012/12/04/big-data-and-discovery/

Fan, J.; Han, F.;Liu, H. Challenges of Big Data Analysis. *Natl. Sci. Rev.* **2014,** *1* (2), 293–314.

Gareth Bell, I. Interview with Marshall Sponder, Author of Social Media Analytics. *Strat. Direct.* **2012,** *28* (6), 32–35.

Han, J.; Pei, J.; Kamber, M. *Data Mining: Concepts and Techniques*. Elsevier. https://www.elsevier.com/books/data-mining-concepts-and-techniques/han/978-0-12-381479-1

Jeble, S.; Kumari, S.; Patil, Y. Role of Big Data and Predictive Analytics. *Int. J. Autom. Logist.* **2016,** *2* (4), 307–331.

Ji-fan Ren, S.; Fosso Wamba, S.; Akter, S.; Dubey, R.; Childe, S.J. Modelling Quality Dynamics, Business Value and Firm Performance in a Big Data Analytics Environment. *Int. J. Prod. Res.* **2016,** *55* (17), 1–16.

Keeso, A. Big Data and Environmental Sustainability: A Conversation Starter. Smith School Working Paper Series, 2014–04. University of Oxford, 2014. http://www. smithschool. ox.ac. uk/library/workingpapers/workingpaper%2014-04.

Mayer-Schönberger, V.; Cukier, K. *Big Data: A Revolution That Will Transform How We Live, Work, and Think;* Houghton Mifflin Harcourt, 2013. http://www.amazon.in/ Big- Data-Revolution-Transform-Think/dp/0544227751

McAfee, A.; Brynjolfsson, E.; Davenport, T. H.; Patil, D. J.; Barton, D. Big Data: The Management Revolution. *Harv. Bus. Rev.* **2012,** *90* (10), 61–67.

Nair, P. R. Supply Chain Analytics. *CSI Commun.* **2012,** *33* (9), 11.

Provost, F.; Fawcett, T. Data Science and Its Relationship to Big Data and Data-Driven Decision Making. *Big Data* **2013,** *1* (1), 51–59.

Russom, P. Big Data Analytics. *TDWI Best Practices Report, Fourth Quarter* **2011,** 1–35.

Schläfke, M.; Silvi, R.; Möller, K. A Framework for Business Analytics in Performance Management. *Int. Prod. Perform. Manag.* **2012,** *62* (1), 110–122.

Shein, E. Data Analytics Driving Medical Breakthroughs, 2012. http://www.computerworld. com/article/2502520/healthcare-it/data-analytics-driving-medical- breakthroughs. html?page=3

Venkatesh, V. G.; Dubey, R.; Joy, P.; Thomas, M.; Vijeesh, V.; Moosa, A. Supplier Selection in Blood Bags Manufacturing Industry Using TOPSIS Model. *Int. J. Operat. Res.* **2015,** 24 (4), 461–488.

Waller, M. A.; Fawcett, S. E. Click Here for a Data Scientist: Big Data, Predictive Analytics, and Theory Development in the Era of a Maker Movement Supply Chain. *J. Bus. Logist.* **2013,** *34* (4), 249–252.

Waller, M. A.; Fawcett, S. E. Data Science, Predictive Analytics, and Big Data: A Revolution That Will Transform Supply Chain Design and Management. *J. Bus. Logist.* **2013,** *34* (2), 77–84.

Woodie, A. Datanami: How Uber Uses Spark and Hadoop to Optimize Customer Experience, 2015. http://www.datanami.com/2015/10/05/how-uber-uses-spark- and-hadoop-to-optimize-customer-experience/ (accessed on 23 July 2016).

Zhong, R. Y.; Huang, G. Q.; Lan, S.; Dai, Q. Y.; Chen, X.; Zhang, T. A Big Data Approach for Logistics Trajectory Discovery from RFID-Enabled Production Data. *Int. J. Prod. Econ.* **2015,** *165*, 260–272.

CHAPTER 16

Role of Big Data in Customer Acquisition and Retention

AMANDEEP KAUR and RENU BALA

JCD Institute of Business Management, Haryana, India

ABSTRACT

Big data analytics has recently drawn a lot of interest as academic and industrial researchers work to efficiently extract and apply every piece of knowledge from the voluminous amounts of data being produced and received. To achieve a competitive edge, businesses use big data analytics to make data-driven decisions in various areas of the organization. This study aimed to investigate the value of big data for acquiring and keeping customers. This study uses secondary sources of data collection, including books, papers, and online publications. Thereafter, the data will be subjected to a thematic content analysis. The limitations and issues with using big data are also brought up to remind businesses to use it properly. The study also demonstrates how big data is helping businesses acquire and retain customers while providing them with insights that allow them to deliver personalized services. On the other hand, the chapter also discusses the security and privacy risks associated with using big data analytics. Users must therefore take precautions to lessen the possibility of growing privacy and security vulnerabilities in their big data environment.

16.1 INTRODUCTION

Consider a scenario without data storage—a world where all information about individuals or organizations, all transactions, and all observable

Augmenting Customer Retention Through Big Data Analytics.
Reena Malik, Ambuj Sharma, and Prashant Chaudhary (Eds.)

aspects are immediately erased after usage. As a result, organizations would be unable to gather useful data and knowledge, carry out in-depth studies, or offer fresh prospects and advantages. Everyday continuity now depends on information such as client names and addresses, product availability, purchases made, personnel hired, etc. Any organization's success depends on its ability to use data effectively. Now consider the breadth of specifics and the explosion of information and data made available now thanks to technological advances and the internet. Huge volumes of data are now readily accessible, thanks to improvements in storage capacity and data collection techniques. More data are being produced every second, and in order to extract value, it must be stored and evaluated. Organizations must maximize the value of the enormous amounts of stored data because it is now less costly to store data. Such data must be stored and analyzed using new types of big data analytics because of their magnitude, variety, and quick change. Big data of this kind must be correctly evaluated in order to retrieve pertinent information.

Similarly, today's internet world also includes big data. Big data is constantly an important component in the background of everything from search to online commerce to video on demand to editing. The Internet of Things (IoT), according to some, will overtake big data as the most publicized technology. But IOT cannot function without large amounts of data. In this chapter, we examine the problems, tools, and restrictions associated with large datasets. But first, we must comprehend big data. Big data is more diversified, has a higher volume, and comes from a wider variety of sources than standard databases. The secret to using big data is to extract useful information from a sea of data.

Because it enables businesses to adapt their service and offerings to consumers and gain deeper insights into customer behaviors from the vast amount of data, big data is increasingly becoming a critical component of company success in customer relationship management. According to research, businesses using big data analytics outperformed their competitors by 5% in productivity and 6% in profitability. 92% of company executives from 19 different countries were happy with the outcomes of big data analytics, and they anticipated that big data would have a greater overall impact on their organizations, particularly on customer relationship management. Nevertheless, research shows that just 30% of firms use customer experience to their advantage, and 70% of customer data is never leveraged to make improvements. Big data analytics raises worries that customer behavior is changing so quickly that past data and models cannot be trusted and that it is difficult to identify patterns. This can be fixed by using high-quality data, such as the company's internal data or external data, and applying and improving a better model in an agile environment. Many companies and customers moved their operations online during the pandemic, and some marketers are now focusing even more on precision marketing since they are aware that customers will continue to shop online even after the outbreak. It is essential for a business to gain a leading position in the market during and after the digital transformation by gathering online consumer data to do big data analytics to inform its decision-making and business strategy.

16.2 CHARACTERISTICS OF BIG DATA

The following are the characteristics of big data, which are also known as the five Vs.

Volume: The first V, or volume, specifies the rate at which data are produced. It symbolizes the aspect of data that demonstrates the enormous volume of data that is produced. With its 312 terabyte-sized phone records database and about 2 trillion rows, AT&T is thought to have the biggest volume of data in the world (Saluja et al., 2018).

Velocity: It refers to the speed at which data are collected and reacted upon. Data that are sent into memory at the greatest speed is typical. The health and safety implications of some IOT applications necessitate immediate assessment and response. Operationally, users of mobile phones have high user density, increasing network traffic, and expectations for quick responses (Siddardha and Suresh, 2016).

Variety: It relates to the types of data that form big data and includes both structured and unstructured data. This data can include text, sensor data, audio, video, click streams, log files, and so on. Utilizing the most types of data in images, video clips, and documents to enhance customer satisfaction and monitoring different video feeds from security cameras to target interest are just a few examples of the new issues, circumstances, etc. that can arise from the analysis of combined data types (Hadi, Shnain, Hadishaheed, and Ahmad, 2015).

Value: Different types of investigative techniques and quantitative methods can be used to take out value from data. Big data involves the extraction of constructive information from massive amounts of data in order to forecast future trends and make decisions (Siddardha, Suresh 2016).

Veracity: It refers to the level of information trust a leader has when making a decision. It is very important for businesses to find appropriate correlations in big data. Yet, building faith in big data presents a significant difficulty as the number and variety of sources increase, as one in three company leaders does not trust the information utilized to reach judgments (Hadi et al., 2015).

16.3 CHALLENGES AND ISSUES WITH BIG DATA

Large data resources but poor quality: Big data is mainly from diverse types of data sources. Big data cannot be adequately described in a conventional manner. Data in big data may be unreliable, and noise might alter it. For this reason, effective data processing and storing are necessary.

Problems in storing the data and processing it: Big data storage practices have an impact on costs as well as analysis and processing. More availability, improved performance, and minimum storage expenses need to be developed to meet service and logical requirements in big data. Redundancy may result from the fact that data come from various sources. Redundancy detection and elimination may increase storage space.

Difficulty in processing different types of data: Databases and storage facilities fall short when it comes to processing unstructured and semistructured data. For a large number of users, read/write operations with big data are highly concurrent. The algorithm may not be adequate as the database size grows. According to the CAP theorem, a distributed system cannot have all three; we can only select two of the three.

Mass data mining: Studies have demonstrated that the accuracy of machine algorithms increases with the size of the datasets. Large datasets invalidate the majority of conventional data mining algorithms. When data size exceeds petabytes, serial algorithms may not be able to calculate quickly enough.

16.4 CUSTOMER ACQUISITION AND RETENTION

Big data analytics are additionally employed to entice and maintain customers. According to Klein, big data analytics assist firms in acquiring and retaining customers. Innovation makes this possible by ensuring that companies have the necessary data and can provide specific products. Big data, in other words, helps firms focus on what best represents and excites their potential customers. Big data, for instance, enables businesses to comprehend their target markets and provide expertise. By doing this, the company enhances the experience and satisfaction of customers, two elements that are crucial for customer maintenance. Also, by understanding what clients want, firms may make changes that are likely specific toward each customer's preferences. Such rewards encourage more people to stick with a brand.

Together with personalized and customized services, predictive analysis is a prominent application of big data. The automaker Santana is the example that extracts aspects from its historical data using data analysis and computer training, and then it applies those attributes to estimate how buyers would view its goods. It has better customer relationship management because problems can be identified before a client even gets in touch.

The amount of data is very large to store and process in traditional databases; therefore, we use data analytics. It is very convenient if most of the data are to be analyzed, as it is possible to understand the shopping behavior of each customer, and small data is less effective than a larger dataset.

16.4.1 CUSTOMER ACQUISITION

Customer data analytics provide a broad overview of how a company's consumers behave and look, which can be useful for efforts to acquire new customers that are more specifically focused. Companies can strategically plan cross-channel marketing to target potential clients and increase return on campaigns by utilizing data science models. In addition, data analytics can assist you in expanding your consumer base by identifying preferences and purchasing trends like demographics, affinity, in-market, remarketing, etc. With data analytics for client acquisition, you can also automate and optimize data feed updates, build groups to target particular items, manage campaigns like thematic search, retargeting strategy, and implementation, and manage ad extensions more successfully. Other ways that data analytics can assist you with customer acquisition include aligning bidding strategies with KPIs, enhancing Google quality scores, increasing online visibility by enhancing local search results and optimizing the user experience, optimizing marketing strategies, and enhancing the effectiveness of advertising by choosing the right attribution model.

16.4.2 CUSTOMER RETENTION

Profits can rise from 25% to 95% by increasing client retention rates by 5%. By using the RFM (recency, frequency, and monetary) framework to account for acquisition and retention costs, customer retention analytics can assist businesses in calculating the lifetime value of customers. It can also develop churn prediction models by using static and customer engagement variables, selecting the optimal attribution model to optimize marketing strategies, and improving the effectiveness of advertising (Cao, 2021).

16.5 ADVANTAGES OF BIG DATA TO ACQUIRE CUSTOMERS AND THEIR RETENTION

Following are the advantages of data analytics for different parties:

To know more about the customer and be more focused on them: This is the main use of big data in the present scenario. Big data is employed in this case to learn more about customers' preferences and activities. To gain more clarity about their customers, businesses are using more social media data, text analytics, and browser logs to their existing traditional datasets. In many circumstances, developing predictive models is the main goal.

Recognizing and enhancing business processes: Data analytics are also being used more and more to streamline company procedures. Based on forecasts derived from social media platforms, web search portals, and meteorological information, retailers can maximize their inventory. The optimization of the supply chain or delivery routes is one particular business function that makes extensive use of data analytics. These can also be used to enhance HR business processes.

Enhancing research and science: Consider CERN, the Swiss laboratory for nuclear physics, which is home to the largest and most potent particle accelerator in the world, the Large Hadron Collider. Huge volumes of data are produced by experiments to discover the mysteries of our cosmos, including how it began and operates. The 30 petabytes of data in the CERN data center are being analyzed by 65,000 CPUs.

Enhancing public health and healthcare: We can quickly decode complete DNA strings thanks to big data analytics, which will help us better understand and forecast illness trends, discover novel treatments, and decode entire DNA strings. Imagine what would happen if millions of people and their varied ailments could be treated using all the individual data from smart wearable devices. Future clinical trials won't be constrained by small sample sizes and will be able to include everyone.

Increasing the output of devices and machines: The capability of machines and devices can grow autonomous and smarter with the aid of data analytics. Big data techniques can be used to run a self-driving car. The Toyota Prius is equipped with cameras, GPS, and powerful processors, which permit it to safely navigate roads without the need for human assistance. Using information from smart meters, big data techniques are being utilized for energy grids.

Strengthening law enforcement and security: Big data is used extensively to enhance safety measures and support law order. Others employ big data methodologies to recognize and stop cyberattacks. Credit card firms also utilize this data to detect fraudulent transactions; on the other hand, police forces use it to detain different criminals and can also predict illegal activities.

16.6 BIG DATA CHALLENGES IN CUSTOMER ACQUISITION AND RETENTION

Customer acquisition and retention are crucial aspects of any business, and big data can be incredibly helpful in achieving these goals (Kitchens et al., 2018). However, there are also several challenges associated with using big data for the acquisition and retention of customers. Here are some of the most significant challenges:

Data quality: Big data is only valuable if it is accurate, relevant, and up-to-date. Poor data quality can lead to incorrect insights, ineffective decision-making, and wasted resources (Power, 2014).

Data privacy: The use of big data for customer acquisition and retention can raise privacy concerns among customers. Companies must ensure that they are transparent about the data they collect, how it is used, and how it is protected (Phillips and Hoskisson 2015).

Data integration: Big data often comes from multiple sources, and integrating this data can be challenging. Businesses need to ensure that data are properly integrated to avoid inconsistencies and inaccuracies (Benoit et al., 2020).

Data analysis: Big data requires specialized tools and skills for effective analysis. Companies need to ensure that they have the right personnel and technology to analyze data effectively (Grover et al., 2018).

Resource allocation: Big data can generate massive amounts of information, and not all of it is relevant to the acquisition and retention of customers. Businesses need to allocate resources effectively to ensure that they focus on the most valuable insights (Zhao, 2013).

Implementation: Even with accurate insights, implementing changes to customer acquisition and retention strategies can be difficult. Companies must ensure that they have the resources and capabilities to make changes effectively (Raguseo and Vitari 2018).

Overall, using big data for the acquisition and retention of customers can provide valuable insights and improve business outcomes. However, companies must be prepared to address these challenges to ensure that they get the most out of their data (Duan and Xiong, 2015).

16.7 MEASURES TO OVERCOME THE CHALLENGES OF BIG DATA IN THE ACQUISITION AND RETENTION OF CUSTOMERS

Big data has revolutionized the way businesses acquire and retain customers. Howeverw, the abundance of data can pose significant challenges, including data storage, data processing, and data analysis (Banu, 2022). Here are some measures businesses can take to overcome these challenges and improve the acquisition and retention of customers:

Identify relevant data: To avoid getting lost in a sea of data, it is essential to identify the most relevant data points for customer acquisition and retention. Businesses should focus on data that provides insights into customer behavior, preferences, and feedback. This will help them make informed decisions and tailor their marketing strategies to better target customers (Yoseph et al., 2020).

Invest in data management systems: An effective data management system is essential to handle large data volumes. Companies should invest in data storage and processing systems that can handle the scale and complexity of big data. This can include cloud-based data storage solutions or data warehouses (Ascarza et al., 2018).

Use advanced analytics: Big data analytics can provide valuable insights into customer behavior and preferences. Companies should use advanced analytics tools like machine learning algorithms, predictive analytics, and data visualization to uncover patterns and trends in customer data. This will enable them to personalize their marketing strategies and offer more relevant products and services (Fernando et al., 2018).

Maintain data quality: Big data is useless if it is inaccurate, incomplete, or outdated. To ensure data quality, businesses should establish data governance policies and procedures that promote data accuracy, consistency, and completeness. They should also use data cleansing and validation tools to maintain data quality (Meire et al., 2017).

Ensure data security: With the rise of big data, the security of customer data has become more critical than ever. Companies should use data encryption, access controls, and firewalls to protect customer data from unauthorized access or cyberattacks (Kaisler et al., 2013).

Focus on customer experience: While big data provides insights into customer behavior, it's important not to lose sight of the customer experience. Companies should use big data to understand customer needs and preferences, and then tailor their marketing strategies to create a better customer experience. This includes offering personalized recommendations, providing exceptional customer service, and responding quickly to customer feedback (Garcia et al., 2021).

By adopting these measures, businesses can overcome the challenges of big data and improve their customer acquisition and retention efforts (Vassakis et al., 2018).

16.8 FUTURE OF BIG DATA IN CUSTOMER ACQUISITION AND RETENTION

The future of big data in customer acquisition and retention is bright. As the volume of customer data continues to grow, businesses that can effectively analyze this data will gain a competitive advantage (Isson, 2018). Here are some of the key trends that are likely to shape the future of big data in customer acquisition and retention:

Real-time analytics: Real-time analytics will become increasingly important in customer acquisition and retention. With the rise of the IoT, businesses will be able to collect more data on customer behavior and preferences in real time. Real-time analytics will enable companies to make quick decisions and offer personalized experiences that meet customer needs (Fang and Zhang, 2016).

Artificial intelligence: Artificial intelligence (AI) will play a crucial role in customer acquisition and retention. Machine learning algorithms can analyze large datasets and make predictions about customer behavior. AI will enable companies to provide personalized recommendations and improve the customer experience (Oblander et al., 2020).

Data privacy and security: Data privacy and security will continue to be a top concern for customers. Businesses that can demonstrate that they are protecting customer data will have a competitive advantage. Companies will need to implement data privacy and security measures to ensure that customer data are safe from cyberattacks (Chae, 2015).

Personalization: Personalization will become more sophisticated in the future. By leveraging big data, companies will be able to offer personalized experiences that are tailored to individual customers. Personalization will be based on customer preferences, behavior, and purchase history (Degli, 2014).

Multichannel engagement: Multichannel engagement will become more important as customers increasingly use multiple channels to interact with businesses. By analyzing data from different channels, businesses can gain a more comprehensive view of the customer and provide personalized experiences that are consistent across all channels (Batistic et al., 2019).

In summary, big data will play an increasingly important role in customer acquisition and retention. Businesses that can effectively analyze customer data and provide personalized experiences will gain a competitive advantage. Real-time analytics, artificial intelligence, data privacy and security, personalization, and multichannel engagement will be key trends that shape the future of big data in customer acquisition and retention (Chiang and Yang 2018).

16.9 LIMITATIONS OF USING BIG DATA IN CUSTOMER ACQUISITION AND RETENTION

Insufficient team coordination: In an organization, there is sometimes a miscommunication between the many groups from various areas. A small minority of team members' data analysis may be made available to a tiny proportion of managers. Yet, the insights generated by such teams are not particularly useful or have a minimal impact on organizational metrics. Teams may be working in "silos," with each using its own procedures and being separated from other areas, which could be the cause of this.

Insufficient commitment and determination: Information systems are inexpensive, but they are also costly and take patience to pay for themselves. For example, if there is no prior data, setting up methods and procedures to start collecting the data may take some time. Analytics models, by their very nature, improve in accuracy with time and necessitate dedication to be used. Business clients can lose patience when results aren't immediately apparent, which damages their faith in the models. A virtuous cycle and process must be in place when a firm chooses to employ data analytics techniques so that it is evident what is performing and what doesn't, as well as what must be done about it.

Poor data quality: One of the major limitations of data analytics is the inaccessibility of good-quality data. There may already be a ton of data available to businesses, but the true issue is whether they have the specific data they need. A leading approach is required, in which the commercial issues that must be addressed should then be defined, and the data required to address these issues can then be found. Sometimes the data obtained for previous objectives might not even be pertinent to tackle the issues we are facing right now. Even when we are using the right measures to conduct research, the value of the data collection may not always be up to grade.

Privacy issues: Customers' privacy may occasionally be violated by data collection since organizations whose services they use have access to information about their purchases, online transactions, and subscriptions. For mutual benefit, certain businesses might trade their datasets with other businesses. A person, a nation, or a community could potentially be attacked using certain obtained data. Businesses must be careful about the type of customer data they gather and protect the privacy and security of that data. Only the information necessary for the analysis must be collected, and any sensitive information must be anonymized to ensure its security.

Disabled user data: Data cannot be accessed by anyone and must be correctly moved from one device to another because protection is the main factor. Because of this, technical skills are crucial for handling large amounts of data in a successful manner. So, using big data involves a lot of labor.

We must realize that although working with huge data has many restrictions, it may be possible to work with smaller datasets more productively due to the ease of evaluation. Big data, therefore, has a bright future in the IT industry in the years to come. Thus, consider developing your skills in big data again for the foreseeable.

16.10 SIGNIFICANCE OF THE STUDY

This study of big data in customer acquisition and retention is significant in research because it can advance knowledge, develop new tools and techniques, improve business practices, inform public policy, and provide a competitive advantage (Artun and Levin, 2015). By leveraging big data, researchers can generate new insights into customer behavior and preferences and use that information to help businesses create more effective marketing campaigns and retention programs (Wu, 2022).

16.11 IMPLICATIONS OF THE STUDY

The implications of the present study in customer acquisition and retention are that by leveraging the power of big data, businesses can improve their marketing strategies, increase efficiency, and gain a competitive advantage in their respective industries (Galletta et al., 2017). It also provides a strong base for the researchers to conduct their research in the respective field (Sangaralingam et al. 2019).

KEYWORDS

- **big data analytics**
- **customer acquisition**
- **customer retention**
- **customized service**
- **data privacy**

REFERENCES

Artun, O.; Levin, D. *Predictive Marketing: Easy Ways Every Marketer Can Use Customer Analytics and Big Data*; John Wiley & Sons, 2015.

Ascarza, E.; Neslin, S. A.; Netzer, O.; Anderson, Z.; Fader, P. S.; Gupta, S.; Schrift, R. In Pursuit of Enhanced Customer Retention Management: Review, Key Issues, and Future Directions. *Custom. Needs Solut.* **2018,** *5*, 65–81.

Banu, A. Big Data Analytics–Tools and Techniques–Application in the Insurance Sector. In: *Big Data: A Game Changer for Insurance Industry*; Emerald Publishing Limited, 2022; pp 191–212.

Batistic, S.; van der Laken, P. History, Evolution and Future of Big Data and Analytics: A Bibliometric Analysis of Its Relationship to Performance in Organizations. *Br. J. Manag.* **2019,** *30* (2), 229–251.

Benoit, D. F.; Lessmann, S.; Verbeke, W. On Realising the Utopian Potential of Big Data Analytics for Maximising Return on Marketing Investments. *J. Market. Manag.* **2020,** *36* (3–4), 233–247.

Chae, B. K. Big Data and IT-Enabled Services: Ecosystem and Coevolution. *IT Professional* **2015,** *17* (2), 20–25.

Chiang, L. L. L.; Yang, C. S. Does Country-of-Origin Brand Personality Generate Retail Customer Lifetime Value? A Big Data Analytics Approach. *Technol. Forecast. Soc. Change* **2018,** *130*, 177–187.

Degli Esposti, S. When Big Data Meets Dataveillance: The Hidden Side of Analytics. *Surveillance Soc.* **2014,** *12* (2), 209–225.

Duan, L.; Xiong, Y. Big Data Analytics and Business Analytics. *J. Manag. Anal.* **2015,** *2* (1), 1–21.

Fang, B.; Zhang, P. Big Data in Finance. *Big Data Concepts, Theories, and Applications* **2016,** 391–412.

Fernando, Y.; Chidambaram, R. R.; Wahyuni-TD, I. S. The Impact of Big Data Analytics and Data Security Practices on Service Supply Chain Performance. *Benchmarking: Int. J.* **2018,** *25* (9), 4009–4034.

Galletta, A.; Carnevale, L.; Celesti, A.; Fazio, M.; Villari, M. A Cloud-Based System for Improving Retention Marketing Loyalty Programs in Industry 4.0: A Study on Big Data Storage Implications. *IEEE Access* **2017,** *6*, 5485–5492.

Garcia-Arroyo, J.; Osca, A. Big Data Contributions to Human Resource Management: A Systematic Review. *Int. J. Hum. Resour. Manag.* **2021,** *32* (20), 4337–4362.

Grover, V.; Chiang, R. H.; Liang, T. P.; Zhang, D. Creating Strategic Business Value from Big Data Analytics: A Research Framework. *J. Manag. Inf. Syst.* **2018,** *35* (2), 388–423.

Isson, J. P. *Unstructured Data Analytics: How to Improve Customer Acquisition, Customer Retention, and Fraud Detection and Prevention*; John Wiley & Sons, 2018.

Kaisler, S.; Armour, F.; Espinosa, J. A.; Money, W. Big Data: Issues and Challenges Moving Forward. In *2013 46th Hawaii International Conference on System Sciences*; IEEE, 2013; pp 995–1004.

Kitchens, B.; Dobolyi, D.; Li, J.; Abbasi, A. Advanced Customer Analytics: Strategic Value Through Integration of Relationship-Oriented Big Data. *J. Manag. Inf. Syst.* **2018,** *35* (2), 540–574.

Meire, M.; Ballings, M.; Van den Poel, D. The Added Value of Social Media Data in B2B Customer Acquisition Systems: A Real-Life Experiment. *Dec. Support Syst.* **2017,** *104,* 26–37.

Oblander, E. S.; Gupta, S.; Mela, C. F.; Winer, R. S.; Lehmann, D. R. The Past, Present, and Future of Customer Management. *Market. Lett.* **2020,** *31*, 125–136.

Phillips-Wren, G.; Hoskisson, A. An Analytical Journey Towards Big Data. *J. Dec.Syst.* **2015,** *24* (1), 87–102.

Power, D. J. Using 'Big Data' for Analytics and Decision Support. *J. Dec. Syst.* **2014,** *23* (2), 222–228.

Raguseo, E.; Vitari, C. Investments in Big Data Analytics and Firm Performance: An Empirical Investigation of Direct and Mediating Effects. *Int. J. Prod. Res.* **2018,** *56* (15), 5206–5221.

Sangaralingam, K.; Verma, N.; Ravi, A.; Bae, S. W.; Datta, A. High Value Customer Acquisition & Retention Modelling–A Scalable Data Mashup Approach. In: *2019 IEEE International Conference on Big Data (Big Data)*; IEEE, 2019; pp 1907–1916.

Siddardha, K. Suresh Big Data Analytics: Challenges, Tools and Limitations. *Int. J. Eng. Tech. Res. (IJETR)* **2016,** *6* (3), 40–43.

Vassakis, K.; Petrakis, E.; Kopanakis, I. Big Data Analytics: Applications, Prospects and Challenges. In: *Mobile Big Data: A Roadmap from Models to Technologies*; 2018; pp 3–20.

Wu, X. The Use of Big Data in Customer Acquisition and Retention. In: *2022 7th International Conference on Financial Innovation and Economic Development (ICFIED 2022)*; Atlantis Press, 2022; pp 2258–2265.

Yoseph, F.; Ahamed HassainMalim, N. H.; Heikkila, M.; Brezulianu, A.; Geman, O.; Paskhal Rostam, N. A. The Impact of Big Data Market Segmentation Using Data Mining and Clustering Techniques. *J. Intell. Fuzzy Syst.* **2020,** *38* (5), 6159–6173.

Zhao, D. Frontiers of Big Data Business Analytics: Patterns and Cases in Online Marketing. *Big Data Bus. Anal* **2013,** *43*.

CHAPTER 17

Personalization and Customization of Governance Products and Services for Citizens Using Big Data Analytics and Artificial Intelligence

AMNA MIRZA[1] and SACHIN KUMAR SHARMA[2]

[1]*Department of Political Science, Shyama Prasad Mukherji College for Women, University of Delhi, Delhi, India*

[2]*Cluster Innovation Centre, University of Delhi, Delhi, India*

ABSTRACT

Digital technologies have transformed each and every aspect of our life by providing us with personalized products and services. Today, technological advancements, their renewal, and decentralization are important yardsticks of the development of nations. Similarly, on governance aspects, digital e-technologies have transformed governance by transforming it into e-governance which has led to the huge collection of data on citizen behaviors and engagement patterns with governance interface. Data and its management are the new currency type in the digital realm, the fourth industrial revolution, and discussions of globalization 4.0. Big data and artificial intelligence can make more of a contribution to better ensuring the efficiency and effectiveness of governance goods, such as the execution of programs and policies to target segments of citizens. This chapter intends to propose a conceptual model to improve the personalization of e-governance products and services to each citizen of India to his or her socioeconomic, educational, and environmental background. The proposed conceptual theoretical models incorporate the

Augmenting Customer Retention Through Big Data Analytics.
Reena Malik, Ambuj Sharma, and Prashant Chaudhary (Eds.)

political system of the country and its technological interfaces and estimate to improve the governance experiences of citizens.

17.1 INTRODUCTION

Personalization and customization of governance products and services is a relatively new concept that is gaining popularity across the world (Krishnaraju et al., 2016). With the advent of big data analytics and artificial intelligence (AI), governments can now provide services that are tailored to the individual needs of citizens (Mehr et al., 2017). In today's fast-paced and technologically advanced world, new technologies are constantly being developed and they have the potential to revolutionize the way we live and interact with one another (Floridi, 2014).

These advancements have not only impacted our personal lives but also the way governance is conducted. Customization of government services and goods for citizens is a fast-developing concept that makes use of AI and big data analytics to provide citizens with personalized solutions and experiences that are unique to them (Chen et al., 2021). As more data is being gathered from numerous sources, it is now possible to evaluate this data and utilize it to create government services and products tailored to each person's individual needs. Governments can make better decisions and offer better services to citizens by using AI, big data analytics, and other technological advancements to process massive volumes of data, find trends, and make predictions (Pencheva et al., 2020). This approach produces a more effective, receptive, and efficient government, which can enhance the lives of citizens and the overall governing experience. E-governance has been and continues to be essential on a global scale because more and more nations utilize digital technologies to offer their citizens better and more-efficient government services. (Manoharan et al., 2021). It can improve transparency and accountability, reduce corruption and bureaucracy, and increase citizen engagement and participation in the decision-making process (Akpan-Obong et al., 2022).

Additionally, e-governance initiatives can facilitate cross-border collaboration and cooperation among countries, making it a critical component of international relations (Krimmer et al., 2021). Governments everywhere strive to provide their inhabitants with better services. Big data analytics and AI have made it feasible to tailor and customize government services and goods to cater to the unique demands of each citizen. Personalization and customization of governance products and services based on e-governance foundation can have several benefits. One of the most significant benefits is improved citizen satisfaction with government services. Citizens will be more likely to use and recommend government services that are tailored to their needs. Additionally, personalized services can also boost citizens engagement and participation in their governments decision-making process. Personalized services can also increase efficiency and reduce costs by enabling governments to focus their resources on areas of need rather than providing services that are not needed (Al-Mushayt et al., 2019). Personalized services can also improve the quality of life for citizens. For example, personalized healthcare services can help citizens manage chronic conditions or prevent illnesses by identifying and addressing health risks (Bardhan et al., 2020). Similarly, personalized transportation services can help citizens get to where they need to go more efficiently and safely (Duggal et al., 2021). The potential of personalization and customization of governance products and services is vast. Personalized education services can help students learn at their own pace and with methods that suit their learning style (Bhati et al., 2019). This can lead to improved academic outcomes and increased engagement in learning. Personalized financial services can help citizens manage their finances more effectively by identifying areas where they can save money or reduce debt (Mhlanga, 2022). This can lead to increased financial stability and improved quality of life. Personalized transportation services can also help reduce traffic congestion and improve the environment by encouraging citizens to use public transportation or other forms of shared transportation. Despite the benefits, several challenges must be addressed in the implementation of personalized services. One of the biggest challenges is the issue of data privacy. Personalized services require the collection and use of personal data, which can be sensitive and potentially harmful if mishandled (Alexopoulos et al., 2019). Governments must ensure that they have proper data security protocols in place to protect citizen data. Another challenge is the potential for bias in the algorithms used to provide personalized services. The data that algorithms are educated on determines how impartial they are. The algorithm will also be biased if the data is skewed. Governments are required to make sure that the data used to provide personalized services is impartial and representative. An additional issue that needs to be resolved is accessibility. Due to unequal access to technology and the Internet, some people may not be able to take advantage of personalized services.

Although there are undoubtedly some issues that must be resolved, such as data protection and accessibility, tailored services provide many advantages.

It is essential that governments work to develop and implement personalized services that are representative, unbiased, and accessible to all citizens. By doing so, governments can provide services that are tailored to the specific needs of citizens, leading to improved satisfaction, increased engagement, and more efficient use of resources. Under this context, the chapter discusses the work done in this regard and also proposes a conceptual model for the personalization work in the Indian context and discusses the same with critical aspects from all stakeholder's points of view.

Here is how the chapter is structured—the literature review is included in Section 7.2. In Section 7.3, the research mythology is described. A conceptual framework is suggested in Section 7.4. Section 7.5 discusses the findings and analyses together with moral dilemmas. The chapter comes to a close with Section 7.6.

17.2 REVIEW OF LITERATURE

E-governance has emerged as an innovative way to provide more efficient, effective, and accountable governance to citizens. The advent of technology, in particular, big data analytics, AI, and other technological advancements has enabled the development of personalized governance products and services for citizens. Madhu Bala and Deepal Verma, in their published research paper "Governance to Good Governance through e-Governance: A critical review of Concept, Model, Initiatives & Challenges in India" in the *International Journal of Management, IT & Engineering*, provide an extensive analysis of the concept of e-governance. They highlight it as a strategic mechanism used by governance experts to leverage Information and Communication Technology (ICT) to enhance the efficiency, transparency, and cost-effectiveness of governance for the benefit of citizens. In simpler terms, the authors suggest that e-governance involves the use of advanced technological solutions by government officials to streamline processes, improve transparency, and reduce costs in the administration of government services. It emphasizes the significance of knowing the distinction between e-government and e-governance because these terms are frequently used synonymously, but the former refers to procedures and frameworks for the electronic delivery of public services. Former Indian President Dr. APJ Abdul Kalam envisioned e-governance in India as a system characterized by transparency, ease of access, security, and authenticity in the flow of information across departments. This would result in fair and impartial service delivery to citizens.

The following are the four forms of interactions recognized in e-government:

- G2C (government-to-citizen)
- G2B (government-to-business)
- G2G (Government-to-government)
- G2E (government-to-employee)

By providing citizens with greater and more effective access to public services, government-to-citizen engagement seeks to make the government more approachable and user-friendly. G2B contact makes it easier for businesses and the government to communicate, cutting down on bureaucracy and streamlining processes to make commercial operations more transparent. G2G interaction aims to improve productivity, performance, and efficiency by enabling seamless communication between various governmental bodies. Finally, G2E interaction aims to raise employee satisfaction levels by enabling quick and effective ICT-based contact between them and the government. The evolution of e-government in India has gone through numerous stages of development. The introduction of personal computers and their integration into government offices constituted the first phase.

This period was largely concerned with computerization, with word processing and data processing coming later in the use of computers. The development of networking during the second stage allowed the sharing of information and data flow between various government agencies by connecting select units of those organizations through a hub. As Internet connectivity increased in the third stage, there was an increasing demand for government organizations to maintain an online presence. Governmental entities and other organizations created websites in an effort to meet the growing demand for information and services. These websites were created to offer the general public pertinent information, such as specifics of the organizations structure, contact details, reports, periodicals, aspirations, etc. The fourth stage saw the emergence of online engagement, which attempted to limit the amount of face-to-face contact with public officials by making forms, guidelines, laws, regulations, and other pertinent material available for download. The state governments have taken measures to integrate information and communication technologies (ICTs) into connection, networking, and service delivery systems. It has been observed that the focus on e-government has been mostly on automation and computerization. In order to improve residents' quality of life, efforts have been concentrated on improving the citizen–state interaction for a variety of government services, as well as encouraging entrepreneurial models and market knowledge. Each state government has created an IT task group for this reason, and they have started posting citizen charters online and developing an IT policy statement for their state. India has given e-governance a lot of attention, and the government has implemented many initiatives to computerize land records, allow online distribution of land records, and improve the provision of government services to citizens.

Several projects have been launched in the last few years to enhance the e-governance system. India has launched many projects to advance e-governance to enhance the provision of public services to residents. The computerization of land records is one such program that intends to give landowners updated records of their rights, as well as digital copies of their ownership, crop, and tenancy information. This project was completed with the assistance from the National Informatics Center (NIC). The Bhoomi project, which aims to transmit 20 million rural land records to 6.7 million farmers through 177 government-owned kiosks in the state of Karnataka, is another significant effort in the area of e-governance. This self-sustaining e-governance initiative has the potential to help a lot of individuals and improve the effectiveness of land-related procedures.

Another important endeavor in the area of e-governance is the Gyandoot project. The Dhar district of Madhya Pradesh started this Intranet-based government-to-citizen (G2C) service delivery program to give pertinent information to the rural populace and serve as an interface between the people and the district administration.

The Lokvani project in Uttar Pradesh is a public–private collaboration designed to offer a single-window, self-sustaining e-governance system for resolving complaints, keeping land records up-to-date, and offering necessary services. Undoubtedly the project has the potential to increase the effectiveness and accessibility of government services for the general public.

Throughout India, several further e-governance initiatives have been put into practice. In Kerala, for instance, the project FRIENDS is a centralized platform designed to give citizens the means to pay taxes and other financial obligations to the state government. The e-Mitra project in Rajasthan is a comprehensive initiative aiming to provide urban and rural populations with the greatest number of services related to various state government offices through the Lokmitra Janmitra Centers/Kiosks. Government-to-citizen and e-business-to-citizen services are the goals of the Andhra Pradesh e-Seva program. These programs demonstrate the efforts being made to advance e-governance in India and enhance the delivery of governmental services to citizens.

17.3 RESEARCH METHODOLOGY

To conduct this chapter, a methodical and extensive review of the literature on the customization and personalization of governance products and services was carried out. In addition to this, qualitative data and expert opinions were evaluated through semi-structured interviews in the relevant field. The aim was to provide a comprehensive and systematic analysis of the subject matter. This work started with a vision to provide efficient and accurate best possible government services to the citizens. Under this context, several works were identified and worked upon. The work exploration gave the dimensions of the government challenges in India and highlighted the gaps. The work of literature review also helped in indicating of the e-governance products and services implemented by the Indian government. This helped in developing of comprehensive contextual models taking all the challenges and opportunities together and providing the best governance and policy for the citizens. The findings contribute to the advancement of knowledge in this area and inform the design and implementation of personalization and customization of governance products and services in the future.

17.4 CONCEPTUAL FRAMEWORK

To provide personalization and customization of Indian governance products and services for citizens using big data analytics and AI, a conceptual model can be developed that incorporates the following components:

Data Collection and Analysis: The first step in developing personalized services is collecting and analyzing citizen data. This includes demographic information, such as age, gender, and location, as well as information about their preferences, behavior, and needs. This data can be collected through various sources, such as government databases, population census, AADHAAR, PAN card details and text details, social media, and other online platforms.

AI and Machine Learning: Once the data has been collected, it can be processed using AI and machine learning algorithms to identify patterns and insights. These algorithms can be used to create citizen profiles and predict their future behavior and preferences.

Service Customization: Based on the insights gathered from the data analysis, customized services can be developed that cater to the specific needs and preferences of individual citizens. For example, personalized health services can be developed based on a citizen's medical history and current health conditions.

Service Delivery: Personalized services can be delivered to citizens through various channels, such as mobile applications, online portals, or through government service centers. The delivery channels should be designed to be accessible and user-friendly, ensuring that citizens can easily access the services they need.

Monitoring and Evaluation: The final step in the conceptual model is monitoring and evaluating the effectiveness of the personalized services. This includes gathering feedback from citizens on their experience with the services and analyzing the data to determine if the services are achieving the desired outcomes.

The conceptual model also considers the ethical issues that arise in the development and implementation of personalized services. This includes ensuring that citizen data is collected and used in a transparent and secure manner, ensuring that the algorithms used are unbiased and free from discrimination, and ensuring that the personalized services do not create or exacerbate existing social and economic inequalities. Furthermore, the model should consider the unique needs and characteristics of the Indian population, such as language diversity, socio-economic disparities, and differences in technological proficiency. Regardless of their background, including their religion, caste, area, eating habits, environmental conditions, or degree of education, the model should be made inclusive and accessible to all citizens. By incorporating ethical considerations and addressing the unique needs of the Indian population, the model can provide services that are tailored to the specific needs of citizens, while also ensuring that they are fair, unbiased, and respectful of citizens' rights and dignity.

17.5 RESULTS AND ANALYSIS

The terms e-governance, intelligent systems, advanced analytics, big data, and industry 4.0 have become universal concepts that are gaining popularity and significance in today's fast-paced and technologically advanced society.

Governments across the world have come to realize the significance of incorporating the latest technological advancements into their governance structures to keep pace with the rapidly changing world. With the increasing use of technology in all aspects of life, e-governance has become a crucial tool for governments to improve their services and engage with citizens more effectively and efficiently. By embracing the latest technology, governments can enhance their transparency, security, and efficiency, leading to better and more inclusive governance.

Moreover, the advent of AI/ML/industry 4.0 has brought about a transformation in the way work is being done, leading to a more interconnected, automated, and data-driven world. This has the ability to greatly increase the effectiveness and efficiency of government services. Governments can use technology to more closely adapt their services and offerings to the unique requirements and preferences of each citizen, giving them a more personalized experience. Furthermore, with the vast amounts of data generated by these technologies, governments can gain insights into the needs and wants of citizens, allowing them to make more informed decisions and improve their governance processes. The computerization of land records, the Gyandoot initiative, the Lokvani project, Project FRIENDS, the e-Mitra project, the e-Seva project, the admission to professional colleges, the e-Procurement project, MCA 21, the Khajane project, SmartGov, and the National E-governance Plan are just a few of the recent e-governance initiatives that India has put into action (Mufeed, 2015).

These programs seek to make government service delivery to citizens more effective, transparent, and cost-efficient by utilizing technology. Despite these efforts, the existing e-governance structure in India still has several limitations and challenges. One of the major limitations is the lack of personalization of governance products and services to each citizen, taking into account his or her socioeconomic, educational, and environmental background. This has led to a disproportionate distribution of benefits and services to citizens, which is a significant obstacle to India’s successful adoption of e-governance. The absence of information about individual citizens is another major issue. This problem can be solved by utilizing big data analytics and AI to provide a more in-depth understanding of each citizen's socioeconomic, educational, and environmental background. Government organizations can obtain important insights into citizens' preferences and needs by utilizing big data and AI, which can then be used to build and offer services that are specifically suited to their requirements.

To address these limitations, it is necessary to develop a model for the personalization of e-governance products and services to each citizen. Big data analytics and AI should be the foundation of the model, which should also take into consideration each citizens' socioeconomic, educational, and environmental background as well as current e-governance efforts and technology. The goal of achieving e-governance in India is a challenging task that extends beyond just computerizing individual government operations. The successful implementation of e-governance requires a fundamental shift in work culture and objectives, as well as a transformation of current processes. A culture of maintaining, processing, and accessing information electronically must be established for informed decision-making. A smooth transition from traditional processes to automated services must be ensured, without interrupting existing services. This can be accomplished by taking small, well-informed steps promptly and avoiding large, costly moves without fully understanding their social impact. We can say the literature on e-governance in India suggests that there is a need for greater personalization and customization of e-governance products and services and big data analytics, AI, etc. can play a key role in improving the personalization of e-governance services by providing a more nuanced understanding of citizens needs and preferences. Although it is crucial to make sure that the use of big data and AI is constrained by rules of data security and privacy, the models suggested for enhancing personalization are aware of their context and centered on the requirements of users.

The personalization and customization of governance products and services using big data analytics and AI also raises several ethical issues that must be addressed to ensure that the benefits of personalized services do not come at the expense of citizens' privacy and security. One of the most significant ethical issues related to the personalization and customization of governance products and services is the issue of data privacy. Personalized services require the collection and use of personal data, which can be sensitive and potentially harmful if mishandled. Governments must ensure that they have proper data security protocols in place to protect citizen data. They must also ensure that citizens are informed about the collection and use of their data and that they have the right to access, correct, or delete their data at any time. Another ethical issue related to personalized services is the potential for bias in the algorithms used to provide personalized services. Only the data used to train an algorithm can guarantee its objectivity. The algorithm will be biased if the data is skewed. Governments are required to ensure that the data used to provide personalized services is impartial and representative.

They must also regularly monitor and evaluate the algorithms used in personalized services to ensure that they are not unfairly targeting or excluding certain groups of citizens. Transparency is another ethical issue that must be addressed in the development and implementation of personalized services. Citizens have the right to know how personalized services work and how their data is being used. Governments must be transparent about the collection and use of citizen data, as well as the algorithms and decision-making processes used in personalized services. Accessibility is also an ethical issue related to personalized services. Not all citizens have equal access to modern technology or the online world, which can restrict their capacity to use customized services. Governments must ensure that personalized services are accessible to all citizens, regardless of their technological expertise or access to technology. They must also ensure that personalized services do not create or exacerbate existing digital divides between different groups of citizens. In addition, the use of AI in personalized services raises several ethical issues related to accountability and responsibility. As AI becomes more advanced, it becomes more difficult to understand how decisions are being made and who is responsible for those decisions. Governments must ensure that they have clear mechanisms in place to hold those responsible for the development and use of personalized services accountable for any unintended consequences or harm that may result.

Finally, there is an ethical issue related to the potential for personalized services to reinforce existing social and economic inequalities. If personalized services are not designed and implemented with equity and fairness in mind, they may end up perpetuating existing social and economic inequalities. Governments must ensure that personalized services are designed to benefit all citizens, regardless of their socioeconomic status or other demographic characteristics.

In conclusion, while big data analytics and AI have the potential to greatly improve citizen satisfaction, engagement, and quality of life, they also raise many ethical concerns that need to be addressed to make sure that the advantages of personalized services do not jeopardize citizens privacy, security, and other fundamental rights. Governments must work to develop and implement personalized services that are designed with transparency, accessibility, equity, and accountability in mind. By doing so, they can provide services that are tailored to the specific needs of citizens, while also ensuring that they are fair, unbiased, and respectful of citizens' rights and dignity.

17.6 CONCLUSION

The importance of e-governance and AI/ML, big data, and industry 4.0 in today's world cannot be overstated. As the world becomes increasingly technology-driven, it is crucial for governments to embrace and incorporate these advancements into their governance structures. By doing so, they can improve their services, enhance their transparency and security, and create a more inclusive governance experience for all citizens. In conclusion, the way that citizens interact with their government may be completely transformed by the integration of big data analytics and AI into governance products and services. By personalizing and customizing services and products to each citizen based on their socioeconomic, educational, and environmental background, the government can provide a more efficient and effective service. However, the implementation of such a system requires careful consideration of privacy and security concerns, as well as a focus on creating user-friendly interfaces. As technology advances, it is imperative that e-governance evolves alongside it to provide citizens with the best possible service. With proper planning and execution, the personalization and customization of governance products and services through the use of big data analytics and AI can bring about a new era of efficiency, transparency, and responsiveness in government services.

KEYWORDS

- **personalization**
- **governance products**
- **big data**
- **artificial intelligence**
- **services**
- **citizens**

REFERENCES

Akpan-Obong, P. I.; Trinh, M. P.; Ayo, C. K.; Oni, A. E-Governance as Good Governance? Evidence from 15 West African countries. *Inf. Technol. Dev.* **2022,** 1–20.

Alexopoulos, C.; Lachana, Z.; Androutsopoulou, A.; Diamantopoulou, V.; Charalabidis, Y.; Loutsaris, M. A. How Machine Learning Is Changing E-Government. In: *Proceedings of the 12th International Conference on Theory and Practice of Electronic Governance*; April 2019; pp 354–363.

Al-Mushayt, O. S. Automating E-Government Services with Artificial Intelligence. *IEEE Access* **2019,** *7*, 146821–146829.

Bardhan, I.; Chen, H.; Karahanna, E. Connecting Systems, Data, and People: A Multidisciplinary Research Roadmap for Chronic Disease Management. *MIS Quart.* **2020,** *44* (1), 185–200.

Bhati, A.; Song, I. New Methods for Collaborative Experiential Learning to Provide Personalized Formative Assessment. *Int. J. Emerg. Technol. Learn.* **2019,** *14*, 179–195.

Chen, T.; Guo, W.; Gao, X.; Liang, Z. AI-Based Self-Service Technology in Public Service Delivery: User Experience and Influencing Factors. *Gov. Inf. Quart.* **2021,** *38* (4), 101520.

Duggal, A. S.; Singh, R.; Gehlot, A.; Gupta, L. R.; Akram, S. V.; Prakash, C. et al. Infrastructure, Mobility and Safety 4.0: Modernization in Road Transportation. *Technol. Soc.* **2021,** *67*, 101791.

Floridi, L. *The Fourth Revolution: How the Infosphere Is Reshaping Human Reality*; OUP: Oxford, 2014.

Krishnaraju, V.; Mathew, S. K.; Sugumaran, V. Web Personalization for User Acceptance of Technology: An Empirical Investigation of E-Government Services. *Inf. Syst. Front.* **2016,** *18*, 579–595.

Krimmer, R.; Dedovic, S.; Schmidt, C.; Corici, A. A. Developing Cross-Border e-Governance: Exploring Interoperability and Cross-Border Integration. In *Electronic Participation: 13th IFIP WG 8.5 International Conference, ePart* **2021,** *Granada, Spain, September 7–9,* **2021,** *Proceedings 13*; Springer International Publishing, 2021; pp 107–124.

Mhlanga, D. Industry 4.0 in Finance: The Impact of Artificial Intelligence (AI) on Digital Financial Inclusion. *Int. J. Fin. Stud.* **2020,** *8* (3), 45.

Mufeed, S. A.; Charag, O.; Ahmad, I. E-Governance in India: A Review of Developmental Projects, 2015.

Mehr, H.; Ash, H.; Fellow, D. Artificial Intelligence for Citizen Services and Government. *Ash Cent. Democr. Gov. Innov. Harvard Kennedy Sch.* August, 1–12, 2017.

Manoharan, A. P.; Ingrams, A.; Kang, D.; Zhao, H. Globalization and Worldwide Best Practices in E-Government. *Int. J. Pub. Admin.* **2021,** *44* (6), 465–476.

Pencheva, I.; Esteve, M.; Mikhaylov, S. J. Big Data and AI–A Transformational Shift for Government: So, What Next for Research? *Pub. Policy Admin.* **2020,** *35* (1), 24–44.

CHAPTER 18

Retention in the Metaverse: Customer Engagement Using Big Data

SUMEET SINGH LAMBA and REENA MALIK

Chitkara Business School, Chitkara University, Punjab, India

ABSTRACT

In a world where technology constantly evolves, keeping up with the latest trends can be challenging. But one trend that businesses cannot afford to ignore is the metaverse. The metaverse is a digital universe where people can interact with each other and create their own reality. It is a place where avatars (digital representations of people) can meet, socialize, and do business. The term was first coined by science fiction writer Neal Stephenson in his 1992 novel Snow Crash. Today, the metaverse concept is realized through virtual reality (VR) and augmented reality (AR) technology. VR allows users to immerse themselves in a completely artificial environment, while AR overlays digital information on top of the real world. These technologies are giving rise to new ways of interacting with the world and each other.

The potential applications of the metaverse are nearly limitless. For businesses, it provides a new way to engage with customers and build brand awareness. Customer engagement in the metaverse can be used to increase retention rates and customer loyalty. By collecting data on customer activity and preferences, businesses can personalize the user experience for each individual. This allows for a more immersive and engaging experience that keeps customers coming back. In order to keep customers engaged, businesses need to harness the power of big data. Big data can provide insights into customer behavior, preferences, and needs that can be used to create tailored customer experiences. By using big data to better understand their

Augmenting Customer Retention Through Big Data Analytics.
Reena Malik, Ambuj Sharma, and Prashant Chaudhary (Eds.)

customers, businesses can create more engaging experiences that will help retain existing customers and attract new ones.

18.1 INTRODUCTION TO METAVERSE

The term "metaverse" refers to a hypothetical future state of the internet, where virtual and physical worlds merge to create a shared, immersive space. In this world, people can interact with each other and digital objects in real-time using avatars to represent themselves (Stokel-Walker, 2022). The metaverse concept has been popularized in science fiction and video games but has gained momentum in recent years as a potential next step for the internet.

The term "metaverse" was coined by science fiction author Neal Stephenson in his 1992 novel "Snow Crash." In the book, the metaverse is a fully immersive virtual world where people can interact with each other and digital objects in real-time. While Stephenson's vision of the metaverse was fictional, it inspired real-world efforts to create similar virtual worlds. The book that gave the term "metaverse" is Snow Crash, as shown below (Fig. 18.1).

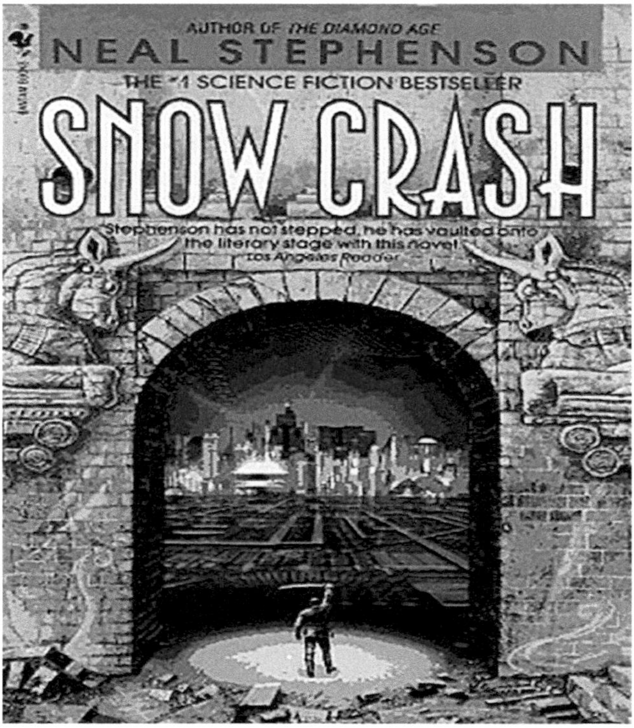

FIGURE 18.1 Cover of Neal Stephenson's novel "Snow Crash" where the term metaverse was first used.

In the years since "Snow Crash," the metaverse concept has been popularized in video games, such as World of Warcraft, Second Life, and Minecraft. These games allow players to create avatars and interact with other players in a shared digital space. While these games are not a true metaverse, they represent early examples of the technology that could enable a metaverse in the future.

The idea of a true metaverse has gained momentum in recent years, driven by advances in virtual reality (VR), augmented reality (AR), and blockchain technology. VR and AR enable immersive, three-dimensional experiences that could make the metaverse feel more realistic and immersive than ever before. Blockchain technology, the underlying technology of cryptocurrencies like Bitcoin, could enable decentralized ownership and governance of digital assets in a metaverse (Murray et al., 2022).

In a true metaverse, people could use avatars to represent themselves and interact with each other and digital objects in real-time (Mozumder et al., 2022). They could explore virtual worlds, participate in events, and even conduct business. For example, a musician could perform a virtual concert in the metaverse, and fans worldwide could attend using their avatars. A businessperson could attend a virtual conference and meet with other attendees to discuss business opportunities. The possibilities for a metaverse are limited only by our imaginations.

While the metaverse is still a hypothetical future state of the internet, many companies are working to make it a reality. Facebook has announced plans to create a metaverse and is investing heavily in VR and AR technology to make it happen. Epic Games, the company behind the popular video game Fortnite, is also exploring the potential of a metaverse and has created a virtual concert venue that can host events with millions of attendees. The potential benefits of a metaverse are significant. A metaverse could create new opportunities for social interaction, entertainment, and commerce. It could enable people to connect with each other in new and meaningful ways and create new business opportunities that were previously impossible. It could also enable new forms of art and expression, allowing people to explore new worlds and experiences currently beyond our reach.

18.2 INTRODUCTION TO BIG DATA

Big data refers to large and complex data sets that are difficult to process using traditional data processing techniques (Elgendy and Elragal, 2014). Various sources, such as social media, e-commerce transactions, and customer interactions, typically generate these data sets. Big data has become an increasingly important tool for businesses as it can provide valuable insights into customer behavior and preferences. Big data can be further explained as shown below (Fig. 18.2).

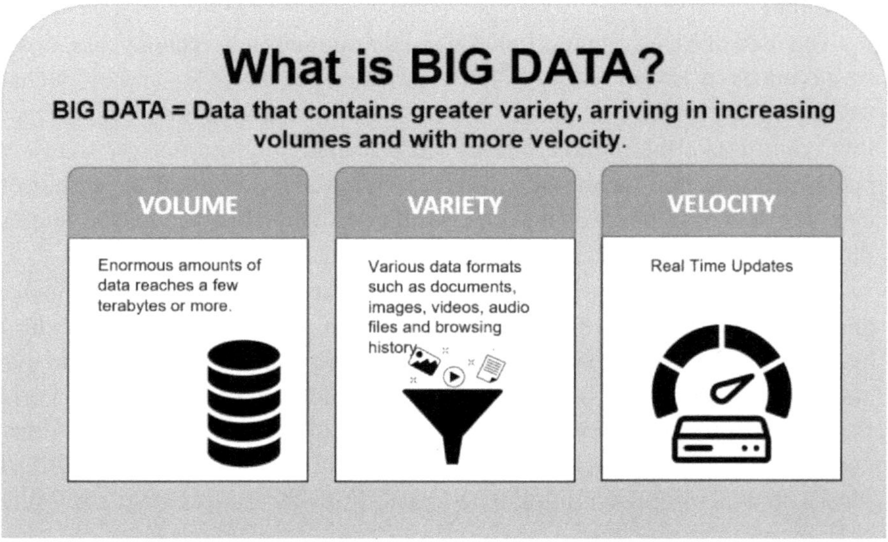

FIGURE 18.2 Big data explained.

Brands can use big data for customer personalization in a number of ways. By analyzing large data sets, brands can better understand their customers' needs and preferences and use this information to create personalized experiences that better meet their customers' expectations. One of the key ways that brands use big data for customer personalization is by analyzing customer behavior. By tracking customer interactions and purchase history, brands can identify patterns and trends in their customers' behavior (Campbell et al., 2020). This information can be used to create personalized recommendations and offers tailored to each customer's interests and preferences.

For example, Amazon is known for its personalized product recommendations. By analyzing customer behavior and purchase history, Amazon is able to suggest products that customers are likely to be interested in. This helps customers find what they are looking for more quickly and increases the likelihood of purchasing.

Another way brands use big data for customer personalization is by analyzing customer feedback. By gathering customer feedback through surveys, social media, and other channels, brands can gain valuable insights into what customers like and dislike about their products and services (Elena, 2016). This information can be used to improve products and services and create personalized experiences that better meet customers' needs.

For example, Starbucks uses customer feedback to create personalized offers for its loyalty program members. By analyzing customer feedback and purchase history, Starbucks can offer personalized promotions tailored to each customer's preferences. This not only increases customer loyalty but also helps to improve the overall customer experience. In addition to analyzing customer behavior and feedback, brands can also use big data for customer segmentation. By segmenting customers into different groups based on factors such as age, gender, and location, brands can create personalized experiences that are tailored to each group's needs and preferences (Cook et al., 2003).

For example, Netflix uses customer segmentation to personalize its content recommendations. By analyzing viewing history and customer feedback, Netflix can recommend content tailored to each customer's preferences. This not only helps to improve the overall customer experience but also helps to retain customers and increase customer loyalty. Another way that brands use big data for customer personalization is by leveraging real-time data. By collecting and analyzing data in real-time, brands can respond quickly to changes in customer behavior and preferences and create personalized experiences that are tailored to each customer's needs (Buhalis and Sinarta, 2019).

For example, Uber uses real-time data to create personalized experiences for its customers. By tracking customer location and ride history, Uber can offer personalized promotions and discounts tailored to each customer's needs. This not only helps to improve the overall customer experience but also helps to retain customers and increase customer loyalty. There are many benefits to using big data for customer personalization. By creating personalized experiences that are tailored to each customer's needs and preferences, brands can improve the overall customer experience, increase customer loyalty, and drive revenue.

While the use of big data for customer personalization offers many benefits for brands, it also presents some challenges. As brands collect and use more data about their customers, there are growing concerns about data privacy. Customers may be uncomfortable with how much data brands collect about them and may be wary of sharing their personal information. Another challenge brands face when using big data for customer personalization is ensuring that the data they use is accurate and of high-quality. Inaccurate or incomplete data can lead to incorrect insights and ineffective personalization strategies. Further, brands may also struggle to integrate data from multiple sources, such as social media, CRM systems, and website analytics tools. This can make it difficult to create a complete picture of the customer journey and personalize experiences effectively. Big data offers brands an opportunity to collect, analyze, and use data to better understand their customers and personalize their experiences. By analyzing customer data, creating targeted marketing campaigns, recommending products, improving customer service, and enhancing the overall customer experience, brands can build stronger relationships with customers, increase loyalty, and ultimately drive more sales and revenue.

However, brands must also be mindful of the challenges of using big data for customer personalization, including data privacy concerns, data quality, and integration issues. By addressing these challenges and developing a comprehensive data strategy, brands can harness the power of big data to create more personalized and engaging experiences for their customers.

18.3 CUSTOMER ENGAGEMENT IN METAVERSE

Customer engagement and customer retention are closely linked, and the metaverse offers a unique opportunity for brands to build lasting relationships with their customers. Metaverse allows brands to create a virtual representation of their stores and to interact with customers in that space (Fig 18.3).

FIGURE 18.3 Illustration showing how brands can create a virtual display for their products and allow customers to interact with it.

Here are some ways in which customer engagement in the metaverse can lead to customer retention:

18.3.1 PERSONALIZED EXPERIENCES

By offering personalized experiences in the metaverse, brands can connect with their customers more deeply. This could include personalized virtual try-ons, customized avatars, or virtual events tailored to a specific audience. By providing a personalized experience, customers are more likely to feel a sense of belonging and loyalty to the brand, which can increase the likelihood of repeat purchases.

18.3.2 COMMUNITY BUILDING

The metaverse offers a platform for community building, where brands can create a sense of belonging and connection among their customers (Pradhan et al., 2021). Brands can create virtual events, social spaces, or games that bring their customers together and foster a sense of community. By building a community around their brand, customers are more likely to feel connected to the brand and to each other, which can increase the likelihood of repeat purchases and brand advocacy (Turri et al., 2013).

18.3.3 GAMIFICATION

Gamification is the process of incorporating game elements into nongame contexts, such as shopping experiences. By using gamification in the metaverse, brands can create an engaging and interactive experience for their customers. This could include virtual scavenger hunts, challenges, or rewards for completing specific tasks. By making the shopping experience more fun and engaging, customers are more likely to return and make additional purchases.

18.3.4 BRAND STORYTELLING

The metaverse provides an opportunity for brands to tell their story in a more immersive and interactive way. Brands can create virtual experiences that showcase their brand history, values, and mission. By creating a compelling narrative around their brand, customers are more likely to feel a sense of connection and loyalty to the brand, which can increase the likelihood of repeat purchases.

18.3.5 CUSTOMER FEEDBACK

Engaging with customers in the metaverse also provides an opportunity for brands to receive direct feedback on their products and services. By creating virtual surveys, feedback forms, or interactive experiences that encourage customer feedback, brands can better understand their customers' needs and preferences. By listening to customer feedback, brands can improve their products and services, increasing customer satisfaction and loyalty.

By using personalized experiences, community building, gamification, brand storytelling, and customer feedback, brands can create a deeper connection with their customers, leading to increased customer retention and loyalty. As the metaverse continues to evolve, it is likely that more brands will experiment with these engagement strategies, leading to even more innovative and creative ways of building lasting relationships with customers.

18.4 BRANDS IN METAVERSE

With the rise of virtual reality and augmented reality, more and more brands are exploring the potential of the metaverse as a new platform for customer engagement. We will now look at some of the brands that use customer engagement in the metaverse and the strategies they use to connect with customers in this new medium.

18.4.1 ADIDAS

Adidas is a sportswear brand that has been exploring the potential of the metaverse for several years. In 2019, the company launched a virtual store in the game "Second Life," where players could purchase real-world Adidas products for their avatars.

Adidas has been experimenting with virtual try-on technology in the metaverse. The company has created virtual sneakers that players can try on and customize in games like "Roblox" and "Animal Crossing." By using virtual try-on technology, Adidas is able to offer a more engaging and interactive shopping experience for customers in the metaverse.

18.4.2 GUCCI

Gucci is a luxury fashion brand that has been at the forefront of the metaverse trend. In 2020, the company launched its own virtual world, "Gucci Garden," which features a series of virtual rooms that customers can explore.

In Gucci Garden, customers can view and purchase the latest Gucci collections and participate in a range of virtual activities, including art exhibitions, games, and interactive experiences. The virtual world is designed to provide customers with a more immersive and engaging experience and to bring the brand to life in a new way.

18.4.3 COCA-COLA

Coca-Cola is a brand that has been experimenting with the metaverse for several years. In 2018, the company launched a virtual reality experience called "Coca-Cola Magic," which allowed customers to explore a virtual world and interact with Coke-themed objects and characters.

More recently, Coca-Cola has been exploring the potential of augmented reality in the metaverse. The company has created a series of AR filters and experiences that customers can use on social media platforms like Snapchat and Instagram. By using AR technology, Coca-Cola is able to offer a more interactive and engaging experience for customers and create a deeper connection between the brand and its audience.

18.4.4 FORTNITE

Fortnite is a popular online game that has become a hub for virtual events and experiences. In 2020, the game hosted a virtual concert by rapper Travis Scott, which over 12 million players attended.

Since then, Fortnite has continued to host virtual events and collaborate with brands, including a partnership with Marvel that featured a series of virtual superhero outfits and items. By partnering with Fortnite, brands are able to reach a massive audience of engaged and enthusiastic players and connect with them in a more interactive and immersive way.

18.4.5 NIKE

Nike is a sportswear brand that has been exploring the potential of the metaverse for several years. In 2019, the company launched a virtual store in the game "Roblox," where players could purchase virtual versions of real-world Nike products for their avatars.

Recently, Nike has been experimenting with virtual try-on technology in the metaverse. The company has created virtual sneakers that players can try on and customize in games like "Roblox" and "Fortnite." By using virtual try-on technology, Nike is able to offer a more engaging and interactive shopping experience for customers in the metaverse. Nike announced a partnership with Roblox to create Nikeland, a free immersive sports space, as shown below (Fig. 18.4).

FIGURE 18.4 Nikeland, a free immersive sports space in Roblox.

Source: Nike. https://www.nike.com/kids/nikeland-roblox

18.4.6 BURBERRY

Burberry is a luxury fashion brand that has been experimenting with the metaverse since 2019. That year, the company launched an AR-powered pop-up store in Tokyo, featuring a range of interactive and immersive experiences for customers. More recently, Burberry has been exploring the potential of virtual try-on technology in the metaverse. The company has created a virtual showroom in the game "Bazaar," where customers can try on virtual versions of Burberry products and purchase them for their avatars. The virtual showroom is designed to provide customers with a more immersive and interactive shopping experience and to showcase the latest Burberry collections in a new and engaging way. Burberry has also created an exclusive virtual handbag collection on Roblox, with a Roblox avatar carrying one of Burberry's exclusive bags (Refer Fig. 18.5).

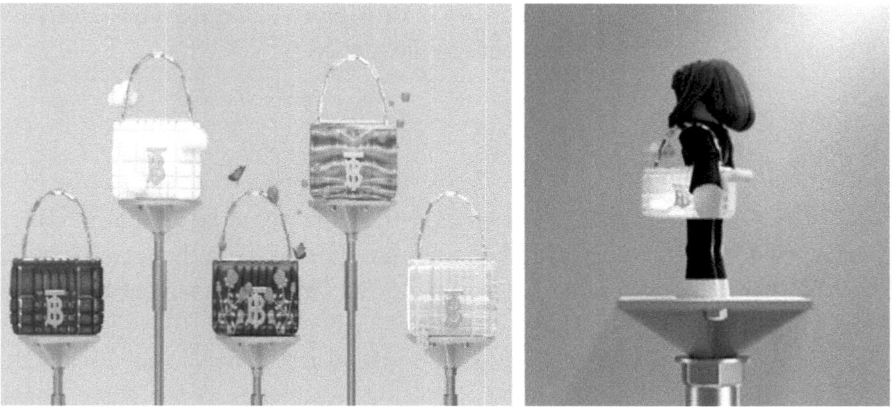

FIGURE 18.5 (a) A virtual handbag collection on display by Burberry on Roblox and (b) a Roblox avatar carrying one of Burberry's exclusive bags.

Image courtesy: Burberry. https://www.burberryplc.com/news/brand/2022/burberry-introduces-virtual-handbag-collection-on-roblox

18.4.7 AMERICAN EAGLE

American Eagle is a fashion brand that has been experimenting with the metaverse since 2020. The company launched a virtual store in the game "Animal Crossing," where players could purchase virtual versions of real-world American Eagle products for their avatars. The American Eagle has been exploring the potential of virtual events in the metaverse. The company hosted a virtual "Pride Prom" in the game "Roblox," which featured a range of interactive experiences and activities for players. By hosting virtual events, American Eagle is able to connect with its audience more engagingly and interactively and create a deeper connection with the brand.

18.4.8 LOUIS VUITTON

Louis Vuitton is a luxury fashion brand that has been exploring the potential of the metaverse since 2019. The company launched an AR-powered pop-up store in Los Angeles, which featured a range of interactive and immersive experiences for customers.

More recently, Louis Vuitton has been experimenting with virtual try-on technology in the metaverse. The company has created virtual versions of its latest collections, which customers can try on and purchase in games like "League of Legends" and "Honour of Kings." By using virtual try-on technology, Louis Vuitton is able to offer a more engaging and interactive shopping experience for customers in the metaverse.

18.4.9 BMW

BMW is a car brand that has been exploring the potential of the metaverse since 2019. The company launched a virtual showroom in the game "Second Life," where players could view and purchase virtual versions of BMW cars for their avatars.

BMW has been experimenting with virtual test drives in the metaverse. The company has created a virtual driving experience in the game "Forza Horizon 4," which allows players to test drive virtual versions of BMW cars. By using virtual test drives, BMW is able to offer a more engaging and interactive experience for customers in the metaverse and showcase the latest BMW models in a new and innovative way.

18.4.10 SEPHORA

Sephora is a beauty brand that has been exploring the potential of the metaverse since 2019. The company launched a virtual store in the game "Second Life," where players could purchase virtual versions of real-world Sephora products for their avatars.

Sephora has been experimenting with virtual try-on technology in the metaverse. The company has created virtual versions of its latest makeup collections, which customers can try on and purchase in games like "Roblox" and "Animal Crossing." By using virtual try-on technology, Sephora is able to offer a more engaging and interactive shopping experience for customers in the metaverse.

The metaverse is a new platform for customer engagement that is being explored by a growing number of brands. By using virtual reality, augmented reality, and other technologies, these brands are able to offer a more immersive and engaging experience for customers in the metaverse and create a deeper connection with their audience. As the metaverse continues to evolve, it is likely that more brands will experiment with this new medium and that we will see even more innovative and creative uses of customer engagement in the virtual world.

18.5 USING BIG DATA IN METAVERSE FOR CUSTOMER ENGAGEMENT

In the metaverse, brands have access to vast customer data, which they can use to understand their customers better and create more personalized and engaging experiences. Big data plays a critical role in this process as it allows brands to analyze and interpret customer data at scale, providing insights into customer behavior, preferences, and trends.

Big data allows brands to collect and analyze data from customer interactions in the metaverse, such as the items they purchase, the virtual spaces they visit, and the activities they participate in. By analyzing this data, brands can identify patterns and preferences that allow them to create more personalized experiences for their customers (Huang and Rust, 2021). For example, if a brand notices that a customer frequently visits a specific virtual space, they can offer promotions or experiences tailored to that space.

Personalization is a critical factor in creating engaging experiences for customers in the metaverse. By analyzing customer data, brands can gain insights into customer behavior and preferences, allowing them to create personalized experiences that better resonate with their customers (Huang and Rust, 2021). For example, a virtual store could use data on a customer's previous purchases to make personalized product recommendations. This can lead to increased customer loyalty and retention as customers are more likely to return to a brand that offers personalized experiences that cater to their individual preferences.

By analyzing customer data, brands can use predictive analytics to anticipate customer needs and behavior, allowing them to create more targeted and effective engagement strategies (Novak et al., 2000). For example, suppose a brand notices that a customer consistently purchases a certain type of product or service. In that case, it can anticipate the customer's needs and make recommendations or offers accordingly.

Predictive analytics is another important application of big data in the metaverse. By analyzing customer data, brands can use machine learning algorithms to identify patterns and trends in customer behavior, allowing them to make predictions about future behavior. This can help brands anticipate customer needs and offer personalized recommendations or promotions. For example, a virtual fashion brand could analyze a customer's past purchases and use predictive analytics to recommend new products that the customer will likely be interested in. This can help to improve customer retention and loyalty as customers are more likely to return to a brand that offers personalized recommendations that cater to their individual preferences.

How predictive analytics models work and how the same can be deployed through big data in the metaverse are shown below (Fig. 18.6).

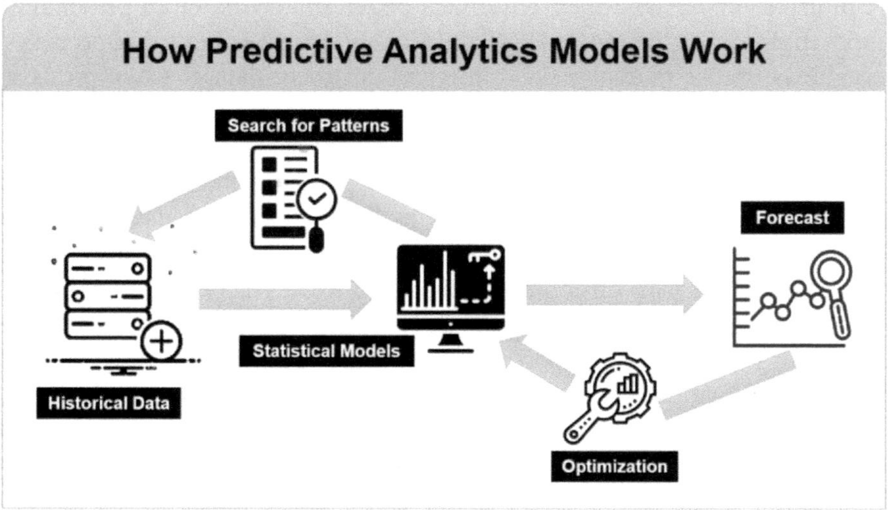

FIGURE 18.6 A chart showing how predictive analytics models work.

Big data allows brands to segment their customers based on their preferences and behaviors, allowing them to create more targeted and effective engagement strategies. By segmenting customers based on data such as their location, age, and interests, brands can create tailored experiences that better resonate with their customers (Cook et al., 2003).

Customer segmentation is the process of dividing customers into groups based on shared characteristics or behaviors. By segmenting customers based on data such as their location, age, and interests, brands can create tailored experiences that better resonate with their customers. For example, a virtual music festival could use data on a customer's location and music preferences to offer personalized recommendations for acts to see at the festival. By tailoring the experience to the customer's individual preferences, brands can create more engaging experiences that are more likely to lead to customer retention and loyalty.

Big data also allows brands to track and measure the effectiveness of their engagement strategies, allowing them to make data-driven decisions for continuous improvement. By analyzing customer data, brands can understand which engagement strategies are working well and which are not, allowing them to make changes and improvements to their strategy. For example, a virtual retailer could track the effectiveness of different promotions and offers and use this data to optimize their engagement strategy for maximum effectiveness. By continuously improving their engagement strategies, brands can create more engaging customer experiences that lead to higher retention and loyalty.

Advanced artificial intelligence and machine learning algorithms can also help brands better understand and engage with their customers (Kumar et al., 2019). These technologies can analyze vast amounts of data and identify patterns and trends that may be difficult or impossible to identify with traditional data analysis methods.

Finally, using advanced AI and machine learning algorithms can help brands better understand and engage with their customers. These technologies can analyze vast amounts of data and identify patterns and trends that may be difficult or impossible to identify with traditional data analysis methods. For example, a virtual retailer could use AI to analyze customer behavior and preferences and use this data to create personalized product recommendations or promotions. By leveraging the power of AI, brands can create more engaging experiences for customers that lead to higher levels of retention and loyalty.

Big data plays a crucial role in helping brands achieve higher customer retention and engagement levels in the metaverse. By using data to personalize experiences, anticipate customer needs, segment customers, continuously improve engagement strategies, and leverage advanced AI, brands can create more effective and engaging experiences for their customers, ultimately leading to increased customer loyalty and retention.

18.6 CHALLENGES

As businesses try to leverage big data for customer retention in the metaverse, they may face several challenges. Here are some of the common challenges:

- Integration of Big Data Tools: Integrating big data tools into existing metaverse platforms can be complex and time-consuming. This can pose a challenge for businesses that lack the technical expertise to manage and integrate these tools effectively.
- Privacy and Security Concerns: Using big data in the metaverse raises concerns about privacy and security (Sun et al., 2022; Malik et al., 2021). Collecting and analyzing customer data raises questions about who has access to it, how it is being used, and how it is protected.

- Limited Customer Data: While big data has the potential to provide valuable insights into customer behavior, some businesses may not have access to enough customer data to make informed decisions. In the metaverse, customer behavior can differ from traditional e-commerce behavior, and businesses may need to gather new data types to make accurate predictions.
- Fragmented Metaverse Landscape: The metaverse is a fragmented landscape with many different platforms, protocols, and technologies. This can make it difficult for businesses to develop a cohesive strategy that works across all platforms.
- Technical Limitations: Some metaverse platforms may have technical limitations that make it difficult to collect and analyze customer data. For example, some platforms may not support data tracking or may not provide access to data in a standardized format.
- High Investment Costs: Adopting big data tools for the metaverse can require significant time and resources. Businesses may need to hire specialized staff, invest in new technology, and undergo extensive training to leverage big data for customer retention effectively.
- Lack of Understanding of the Metaverse: The concept of the metaverse is still new and relatively unknown to many businesses. As a result, there may be a lack of understanding of how big data can be used in the metaverse and what kind of data is most helpful in driving customer retention.
- The challenges of leveraging big data for customer retention in the metaverse require businesses to carefully consider the technical, organizational, and ethical implications of integrating these tools into their operations. The process may require a significant investment of time and resources, and businesses must remain vigilant in their efforts to protect customer privacy and security.

18.7 SHAPE OF THE THINGS TO COME

The future for brands using big data in the metaverse for customer retention and engagement is promising. As the metaverse continues to grow and expand, so will the opportunities for businesses to leverage big data to drive customer loyalty and engagement. With access to more customer behavior data, brands can provide even more personalized experiences for their customers in the metaverse. By using predictive analytics and machine learning algorithms, brands can anticipate customer needs and provide tailored recommendations.

As the metaverse continues to grow, there will be more standardization and integration of data and platforms (Rawal et al., 2022). This will make it easier for businesses to use big data to drive customer retention and engagement across multiple platforms. Real-time data analytics will become more common in the metaverse, allowing brands to track and respond to customer behavior in real-time. This will enable brands to identify trends and adjust their strategies accordingly.

As privacy and data usage concerns continue to grow, brands will need to be more transparent in their use of customer data. Brands that are transparent and ethical in their data usage are likely to be more successful in building customer trust and loyalty (Rani et al., 2023).

Artificial intelligence (AI) and virtual reality (VR) technologies, which are continuously advancing, will become more integrated into the metaverse. This will provide even more opportunities for brands to leverage big data to drive customer engagement and retention.

With technological advancements and increased standardization of data and platforms, businesses can use big data to provide even more personalized customer experiences in the metaverse. As long as brands are transparent and ethical in their data usage, they are likely to successfully build customer trust and loyalty.

KEYWORDS

- **customer retention**
- **customer engagement**
- **customer loyalty**
- **metaverse**
- **web 3.0**
- **virtual reality**

REFERENCES

Buhalis, D.; Sinarta, Y. Real-Time Co-Creation and Nowness Service: Lessons from Tourism and Hospitality. *J. Travel Tour. Market.* **2019,** *36* (5), 563–582. https://doi.org/10.1080/10548408.2019.1592059

Campbell, C.; Sands, S.; Ferraro, C.; Tsao, H.; Mavrommatis, A. From Data to Action: How Marketers Can Leverage AI. *Bus. Horizons* **2020,** *63* (2), 227–243. https://doi.org/10.1016/j.bushor.2019.12.002

Cook, B. I.; Wayne, G. F.; Keithly, L.; Connolly, G. N. One Size Does Not Fit All: How the Tobacco Industry Has Altered Cigarette Design to Target Consumer Groups with Specific Psychological and Psychosocial Needs. *Addiction* **2003,** *98* (11), 1547–1561. https://doi.org/10.1046/j.1360-0443.2003.00563.x

Elena, C. A. Social Media—A Strategy in Developing Customer Relationship Management. Procedia. *Econ. Fin.* **2016,** *39,* 785–790. https://doi.org/10.1016/s2212-5671 (16)30266-0

Elgendy, N.; Elragal, A. Big Data Analytics: A Literature Review Paper. *Lect. Notes Comput. Sci.* **2014,** 214–227. https://doi.org/10.1007/978-3-319-08976-8_16

Huang, M.; Rust, R. T. A Strategic Framework for Artificial Intelligence in Marketing. *J. Acad. Market. Sci.* **2021,** *49* (1), 30–50. https://doi.org/10.1007/s11747-020-00749-9

Kumar, V.; Rajan, B.; Venkatesan, R.; Lecinski, J. Understanding the Role of Artificial Intelligence in Personalized Engagement Marketing. *Calif. Manag. Rev.* **2019,** *61* (4), 135–155. https://doi.org/10.1177/0008125619859317

Mozumder, M. a. I.; Sheeraz, M.; Athar, A.; Aich, S.; Kim, H. Overview: Technology Roadmap of the Future Trend of Metaverse Based on IoT, Blockchain, AI Technique, and Medical Domain Metaverse Activity. In: *2022 24th International Conference on Advanced Communication Technology (ICACT)*; 2022. https://doi.org/10.23919/icact53585.2022.9728808

Malik, R.; Trivedi, S.; Sharma, A.; Mishra, R. Adoption of Chatbots for Learning Among University Students': Role of Perceived Convenience and Enhanced Performance. *iJET* **2021,** *16* (18), 200–212.

Malik, R.; Trivedi, S. Blockchain Technology and Healthcare: Towards Combating COVID-19. In: *Blockchain Technology in Corporate Governance*; Sood, K., Dhanaraj, R., Balusamy, B., Kadry, S., Eds.; Wiley Publications, 2022; pp 57–74.

Murray, A.; Kim, D.; Combs, J. The Promise of a Decentralised Internet: What Is Web 3.0 and HOW Can Firms Prepare? *Bus. Horizons* **2022.** https://doi.org/10.1016/j.bushor.2022.06.002

Novak, T. P.; Hoffman, D. L.; Yung, Y. Measuring the Customer Experience in Online Environments: A Structural Modeling Approach. *Market. Sci.* **2000,** *19* (1), 22–42. https://doi.org/10.1287/mksc.19.1.22.15184

Rawal, B. S.; Mentges, A.; Ahmad, S. The Rise of Metaverse and Interoperability with Split-Protocol. In: *2022 IEEE 23rd International Conference on Information Reuse and Integration for Data Science (IRI)*; 2022. https://doi.org/10.1109/iri54793.2022.00051

Rani, S.; Gupta, D.; Herencsar, N.; Srivastava, G. Blockchain-Enabled Cooperative Computing Strategy for Resource Sharing in Fog Networks. *Internet of Things (Netherlands)* **2023,** *21.*

Pradhan K.; John P.; Sandhu N. Use of Artificial Intelligence in Healthcare Delivery in India. *J. Hosp. Manag. Health Policy* **2021,** *28* (5).

Stokel-Walker, C. Welcome to the Metaverse. *New Scientist* **2022,** *253* (3368), 39–43. https://doi.org/10.1016/s0262-4079 (22)00018-5

Sun, J.; Gan, W.; Chao, H.; Yu, P. S. Metaverse: Survey, Applications, Security, and Opportunities. ArXiv (Cornell University), 2022. https://doi.org/10.48550/arxiv.2210.07990

Turri, A. M.; Smith, K.; Kemp, E. Developing Affective Brand Commitment Through Social Media. *J. Electron. Commerce Res.* **2013,** *14* (3), 201. http://web.csulb.edu/journals/jecr/issues/20133/Paper1.pdf

CHAPTER 19

What Lies in Big Data for Customer Retention? Analyzing the Past, Present, and Future

MANPREET ARORA

HPKVBS, School of Commerce and Management Studies, Central University of Himachal Pradesh, Dharamshala, India

ABSTRACT

The big data is transforming marketing and sales decisions in various aspects. Customer involvement, customer retention, and loyalty are some of the important factors or dimensions contributing toward the success of every business, and big data is proving to be an important tool for achieving all these objectives. The most emerging themes which came out of the data set appear to be the usage of machine learning sentiment analysis in retailing. Another aspect which highlights the use of big data and artificial intelligence is increasing sales and understanding customer intentions in various business scenarios. In the year 2018, the most significant topics of research for "big data and artificial intelligence" were related to tourism, data mining, and social media. After that, the thrust of the researchers shifted toward tourism destinations, big data, and the use/application of big data and related technology in the field of commerce. In 2020, big data was extensively applied in sales forecasting, commerce, and marketing to a great extent. In the later half of the same year, the focus shifted to social networking, artificial intelligence, and retailing. Presently, the research studies that are coming up in the year 2022 are mostly related to machine learning, sentiment analysis, and retailing.

Augmenting Customer Retention Through Big Data Analytics.
Reena Malik, Ambuj Sharma, and Prashant Chaudhary (Eds.)

19.1 INTRODUCTION

Optimizing market performance by saving time and money is the key to the success of businesses in the digital world. "Customer engagement", "customer retention and loyalty", and "market optimization and performance" have become the buzzwords in today's scenario, where the future of every company depends upon how well you are able to retain your customers and satisfy their needs. The use of "big data analysis" and "artificially intelligent systems" in every sphere of life has proven its importance in the digital world, where marketing is no excuse (Arora and Sharma, 2022). The benefits of "big data analytics" are many in the field of marketing, and they have proven to be universally accepted almost in every critical circumstance. If we talk about the direct benefit of big data in the arena/discipline of marketing, it not only comprises gathering, analyzing, or using voluminous data to convert it into information in order to improve the business operations but it also helps us to get a "360-degree view of the audiences" in order to sustain it in the future.

Big data is transforming marketing and sales decisions in various aspects. Customer involvement, customer retention, and loyalty are some of the important factors or dimensions contributing toward the success of every business, and big data is proving to be an important tool for achieving all these objectives. As the amount of data generated by the business houses and the customers is increasing manifold every second, it becomes important for the marketing departments to leverage this heavily increasing data in a way that can help them to make good business decisions which help in gaining strategic advancements for the company. In this world of digitalization, where the voluminous data is not an easy task to handle (Arora, 2020), without big data analytics, it is simply impossible to make accurate business decisions for the future in the absence of technology. Thereby, it becomes pertinent for the businesses to adapt accordingly to the changing technologies in order to face the uncertain business environment. Moreover, the Covid-19 pandemic has brought a serious shift in the whole economy, where digital modes are playing a crucial role (Arora and Sharma, 2022). Social media platforms are becoming a mode of generating databases, and the role of digitalization in every sector is increasing day by day (Arora and Sharma, 2022).

19.2 SCHEMA OF THE PAPER

In order to see and highlight the significance of "big data and emerging technologies" in relation to marketing and customer relations, it becomes pertinent to analyze the existing literature in this field. Therefore, the researcher has attempted to analyze the present literature available in the SCOPUS database. In the first section of the paper, the data collection strategy has been explained; in the second, a review of the literature is presented. And in the third section, performance analysis and thematic analysis have been performed on the existing literature to find out the applicability of big data in diverse areas and different dimensions.

The chapter highlights the emerging importance/role of big data and AI in various segments or fields, especially in the field of marketing. Further, it also highlights how big data can be successfully used to apply and augment customer retention strategies.

19.3 DATA COLLECTION STRATEGY

In the initial search process, the term ("("big data" OR "ÄI" AND "Customer retention" OR "Marketing")") has been used in the "source title" of the SCOPUS database as on February 1, 2023, and then again revisited on February 15, 2023, to confirm any additions in the publications on the search area in the Scopus database.

In the refinement process, before filtration, the results came out from the database between 1980 and 2023 for a total of 3,635 documents. After the filtration, the author considered articles, reviews, books, and book chapters at both the publication stages, that is, final and in-press, and 1350 documents were received. The source type taken is "Journal", published in the English Language, particularly in the discipline of "Business, Management, and Accounting" at the last stage, which gave data from 2002 to 2022 of 653 documents (refer to Fig. 19.1).

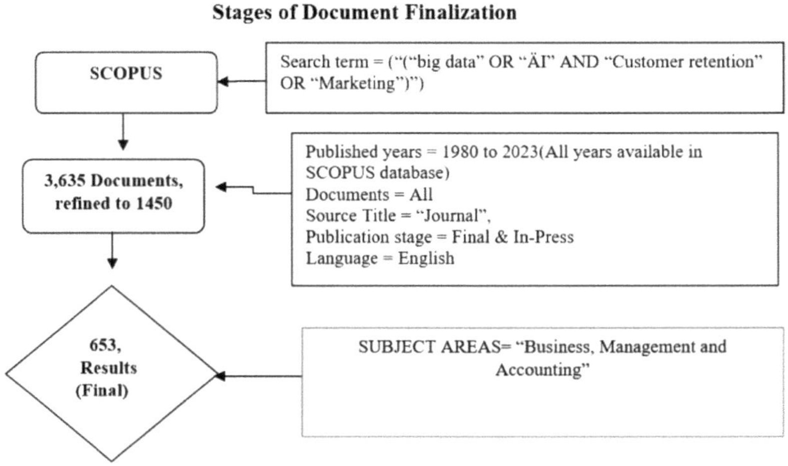

FIGURE 19.1 Stages of document finalization.

Source: Author.

19.4 THE SEARCH STRING

"TITLE-ABS-KEY ("big data" OR "ÄI" AND "Customer retention" OR "Marketing") AND (LIMIT-TO (DOCTYPE, "ar")) AND (LIMIT-TO (SUBJAREA, "BUSI")) AND (LIMIT-TO (LANGUAGE, "English")) AND (LIMIT-TO (SRCTYPE, "j")) 653"

19.5 DATA ANALYSIS METHODS AND TOOLS

In this article, the author has performed a major literature review to gain insights into themes developed and evolving in relation to big data and AI with respect to the fields of marketing and customer retention. Along with reviewing the literature, the thematic evolution, most trending topics, three plot charts, and content analysis have been performed. The author has also performed a partial performance analysis to see the most contributing articles in this field. Performance analysis is a technique which highlights the overall contribution of the article or author in research in a particular area. That is, in general, the evolution of literature over a period of time is highlighted, along with the most prominent countries, authors, and institutions contributing to an area of study. But in this article, the top fifteen most-cited articles are reviewed and highlighted. The author has used RStudio to analyze the Scopus data set.

19.6 THE LITERATURE REVIEW

Erevelles et al. (2016) regard consumer analytics as the epicenter for big data. As for authors, the source of "big data" is individual consumers. The technological advancements help us find out "data on consumer phenomena" on various dimensions in real life. Big data analytics has brought about substantial changes in marketing in addition to consumer behavior activities (Davenport et al., 2020). The organizations which are investing in big data analytics implementation need to address three areas, that is, "Using big data analytics for optimizing the marketing mix, taking advantage of big data analytics for personalization, and utilizing the benefits of big data analytics in securing customer privacy as well as data security" (Wedel and Kannan, 2016). In this digital world, the sources of information for the marketers can be plentiful, especially the online chatter on social media. There can be various dimensions of this online chatter, like quality, customer satisfaction, or dissatisfaction, which can prove useful for marketers in decision-making.

The data on product reviews on the online platforms of a company is a rich source of data for decision-making. Big data analysis is quite helpful in extracting online chatter, which in turn facilitates strategic decision-making (Tirunillai and Tellis, 2014). The applications of "big data, AI, and the emerging technologies" are evident in the hotel marketing and management areas. Jiang and Wen (2020) suggest the use of AI in the areas of health crises and hotel management to increase customer satisfaction in terms of health and hygiene factors. The Covid-19 pandemic hit the tourism sector badly; therefore, in order to deal with the issues of health and hygiene and increase the level of customers' trust and satisfaction in this area, the use of digital technologies, digital platforms, and the application of AI-oriented technologies can help to recover this sector. Without being digital, no business can survive, especially in this internet-dependence-oriented environment. Intelligent solutions are available in the field of marketing in this digital era, but on the same hand, the challenges are also many. It is not very easy for companies to adapt to changing technologies, and there is a strong need to find out about these challenges. Leeflang et al. (2014), in their study, found that companies still have to find the "talent gaps", and there is a need to readjust their "organizational designs", taking care of the digital scenarios. Further, in order to improve their performance, the companies will have to focus on "actionable metrics" as well. Choi et al. (2018) are of the view that the use/applications of big data analytics are indeed critical in the area/field of operations management. The authors strongly advocate the use of big data analytic techniques in "forecasting, inventory management, revenue management, marketing, transportation management, supply chain management, and risk analysis".

19.7 THE MOST CITED PUBLICATIONS WITH THEIR THEMES AND SOURCE TITLES

If we look at the publications which are highly cited out of the data set shown in Table 19.1, then the top ten highly cited publications highlight the role/applications of big data or uses/ benefits of big data in various business scenarios, especially in marketing. Table 19.1 highlights the top fifteen highly cited papers on the theme of "big data, AI, and Marketing and Customer Retention".

TABLE 19.1 Most Cited Publications.

	Document title	Authors	Year	Source	Cited by
1	Big data, consumer analytics, and the transformation of marketing	Erevelles, S., Fukawa, N., Swayne, L.	2016	Journal of Business Research 69(2), pp. 897–904	642
	Theme and keywords of the document	Big data; Consumer analytics; Consumer insights; Ignorance; Induction; and Resource-based theory			
2	How artificial intelligence will change the future of marketing	Davenport, T., Guha, A., Grewal, D., Bressgott, T.	2020	Journal of the Academy of Marketing Science 48(1), pp. 24–42	441
	Theme and keywords of the document	Artificial intelligence; Bias; Ethics; Marketing strategy; Privacy; and Robots			
3	Marketing analytics for data-rich environments	Wedel, M., Kannan, P. K.	2016	Journal of Marketing 80(6), pp. 97–121	415
	Theme and keywords of the document	Big data; Marketing analytics; Marketing mix; Personalization; and Privacy			
4	Mining marketing meaning from online chatter: strategic brand analysis of big data using latent dirichlet allocation	Tirunillai, S., Tellis, G. J.	2014	Journal of Marketing Research 51(4), pp. 463–479	413
	Theme and keywords of the document	Big data; Brand mapping; Consumer satisfaction; Dimensions; Latent dirichlet allocation; Quality; and User-generated content			
5	Effects of COVID-19 on hotel marketing and management: a perspective article	Jiang, Y., Wen, J.	2020	International Journal of Contemporary Hospitality Management 32(8), pp. 2563–2573	378
	Theme and keywords of the document	Artificial intelligence and robotics; COVID-19 pandemic; Health and health care; Hotel management; and Hygiene and cleanliness			
6	Challenges and solutions for marketing in a digital era	Leeflang, P. S. H., Verhoef, P. C., Dahlström, P., Freundt, T.	2014	European Management Journal 32(1), pp. 1–12	334
	Theme and keywords of the document	Analytics; Big data; Customers; Firm strategies; Online marketing; and Social media			
7	Big data analytics in operations management	Choi, T. M., Wallace, S. W., Wang, Y.	2018	Production and Operations Management 27(10), pp. 1868–1883	322
	Theme and keywords of the document	applications and case studies; big data analytics; big data methods; data-driven optimization; and operations management			

TABLE 19.1 *(Continued)*

	Document title	Authors	Year	Source	Cited by
8	SoCoMo marketing for travel and tourism: Empowering cocreation of value	Buhalis, D., Foerste, M.	2015	Journal of Destination Marketing and Management 4(3), pp. 151–161	283
	Theme and keywords of the document	Cocreation; Mobile context awareness; Mobile technologies; Personalization; and Social media marketing			
9	The role of data privacy in marketing	Martin, K. D., Murphy, P. E.	2017	Journal of the Academy of Marketing Science 45(2), pp. 135–155	269
	Theme and keywords of the document	Big data; Ethics; Privacy; and Review article			
10	The service revolution and the transformation of marketing science	Rust, R. T., Huang, M. H.	2014	Marketing Science 33(2), pp. 206–221	252
	Theme and keywords of the document	Big data; Customer equity; Customer lifetime value; Customer loyalty; Customer relationship management; Customization; Information technology; Service; and Service productivity			
11	Exploring the relationship between big data analytics capability and competitive performance: The mediating roles of dynamic and operational capabilities	Mikalef, P., Krogstie, J., Pappas, I. O., Pavlou, P.	2020	Information and Management 57(2),103–169	240
	Theme and keywords of the document	Big data analytics; Business value; Dynamic capabilities; Operational capabilities; and Resource-based view			
12	Toward Industry 4.0: Mapping digital technologies for supply chain management–marketing integration	Ardito, L., Petruzzelli, A. M., Panniello, U., Garavelli, A. C.	2019	Business Process Management Journal 25(2), pp. 323–346	238
	Theme and keywords of the document	Big data analytics; Cloud computing; Customer profiling; Cyber security; Industry 4.0; Innovation; Internet of Things; Marketing; Patent analysis; Supply chain management; and Supply chain management–marketing integration			
13	Real-time cocreation and nowness service: lessons from tourism and hospitality	Buhalis, D., Sinarta, Y.	2019	Journal of Travel and Tourism Marketing 36(5), pp. 563–582	226
	Theme and keywords of the document	hospitality; instant gratification; interactive; marketing; nowness; real time; smart; social media; strategy; and tourism			
14	Effects of big data analytics and traditional marketing analytics on new product success: A knowledge fusion perspective	Xu, Z., Frankwick, G. L., Ramirez, E.	2016	Journal of Business Research 69(5), pp. 1562–1566	226

TABLE 19.1 *(Continued)*

	Document title	Authors	Year	Source	Cited by
	Theme and keywords of the document	Big data analytics; Complexity; Knowledge fusion; NPD; NPS; and Traditional marketing analytics			
15	Tourism analytics with massive user-generated content: A case study of Barcelona	Marine-Roig, E., Anton Clavé, S.	2015	Journal of Destination Marketing and Management 4(3), pp. 162–172	217
	Theme and keyword of the document	Big data; Business intelligence; Catalonia; Smart city; Smart tourism destination; and User-generated content			

Source: Author.

The top 15 most cited articles in the field of "big data and artificial intelligence", especially in relation with customer retention, show that in 2016, the article published by Erevelles et al. on "big data and Consumer Analytics and the Transformation of Marketing" has been cited the most, that is, 642 times. Another article published in 2020 on "how artificial intelligence will change the future of marketing" has been acknowledged by the researchers to a great extent and is being cited 41 times. The major thrust of this article is how the use/application or intervention of artificial intelligence can transform the area of marketing. The article highlights the role of "Bias; Ethics; Marketing strategy; Privacy; and Robots" to build their argument. It is extensively used by the marketers to understand the peculiarities of consumers and consumer behavior, which helps in the prediction of the market, and ultimately, it can be beneficial for the researchers to a great extent. At the third place is the article written by Wedel and Kannan (2016). The article was published in the "Journal of Marketing" and has been cited 415 times. It analyzes the dimensions of consumer behavior and big data. The major thrust of the article is again on big data and its usage: "Marketing analytics; Marketing mix; Personalization; and Privacy".

At number four is the article written by Tirunillai and Tellis, in 2014, published in the "Journal of Marketing Research", which has been cited 413 times again on the theme of using big data to understand the online chatter in order to make strategic business decisions. An extensive use of artificial intelligence has been propagated by the researchers in the field of tourism these days. At number five is the article written by Jiang and Wen in 2020, published in the "International Journal of Contemporary Hospitality Management", which has been cited 378 times and highlights the use of emerging technologies in the field of hotel marketing and management including the use of AI and robotics in the health and hygiene sector.

Emerging technologies and big data analysis not only provide solutions to organizations but on the same hand, they also pose challenges to them. The article at number six, written by Leeflang et al. (2013), highlights the challenges and solutions for marketing in the digital area. It was published in "European Management Journal" and has been cited 334 times. At seventh place is the article written by Choi et al. (2018), which has been cited 322 times and highlights the applications/use of big data analysis in the field/area of operation management. This article is followed by an article by Buhalis and Foerste highlighting "SoCoMo marketing for travel and tourism", which focuses on "mobile context-awareness", "advantages of personalization", excessive use, dependence, and the benefits of "social media marketing". Where big data offers solutions to various customer-oriented issues and challenges, it also offers major threats for companies and stakeholders in the form of data breaches, privacy issues, cybercrimes, etc. Martin and Murphy have thoroughly discussed this sensitive issue in 2017 in the article titled "The role of data privacy in marketing" which is at ninth rank in the list of top-cited articles on big data and AI. Big data has brought various revolutions in the field of service and, undoubtedly, is a mode of transformation in the field of marketing. Rust and Huang (2014) highlighted the use of big data in creating "customer lifetime value". Further, they also talk about how customization is becoming very relevant in today's market, and it becomes very necessary for the marketers to create better customer relationships, in which big data analytics can play an important role. It therefore highlights the very pertinent term, which is customer retention through big data usage by the marketers. This piece of research published in "Marketing Science" in the year 2014 stands at number ten with 252 citations.

Value creation is an emerging concept, and in the last decade, we have seen that businesses are investing a lot of time and money on creating value. The competitive performance of an organization not only depends upon its operational capabilities but in the data-driven world, the use of data in terms of converting it into information and further utilizing it for the creation of knowledge is equally important. Mikalef et al. (2020) have discussed the concepts of business value and the utilization of big data analytics in creating the operational capacities of a business in their article, "Exploring the relationship between big data analytics capability and competitive performance: The mediating roles of dynamic and operational capabilities", published in 2020 and cited by 240. This article was published in one of the leading journals "Information and management" and stands at number eleven.

The research on Industry 4.0 is revolutionizing the world of business, with a greater focus on creativity and innovation. Since the disruptions caused by COVID-19, a lot of research studies have been focusing on providing resilience strategies for the economy, especially in the field of "supply chain management" and various "marketing integration techniques". Ardito et al. (2019) have focused on various emerging concepts related to achieving the goals of Industry 4.0, with a thrust on big data analytics.

Social media is playing a decisive role in excessive big data collection. It has provided a platform for real-time services to a great extent. Buhalis and Sinarta (2019) have discussed the role of interactive marketing and the concept of "nowness" in their article, "Real-time cocreation and nowness service: lessons from tourism and hospitality", published in 2019 in the "Journal of Travel and Tourism Marketing" which received 226 citations. The transformation of traditional marketing concepts with big data analytics has been gaining prominence, and its effects can have larger perspectives, providing directions to the researchers. Xu et al. (2016) have attempted to provide deeper insights through certain fusion techniques in this area. Their article titled "Effects of big data analytics and traditional marketing analytics on new product success: A knowledge fusion perspective" stands at fourteenth position with 226 citations. At number fifteen is the case of Barcelona, which highlights the use of "massive user-generated content" in the field of tourism, as published by Marine-Roig and Anton (2015). This case study has been published in the "Journal of Destination Marketing and Management" and is cited 217 times (refer to Fig. 19.2).

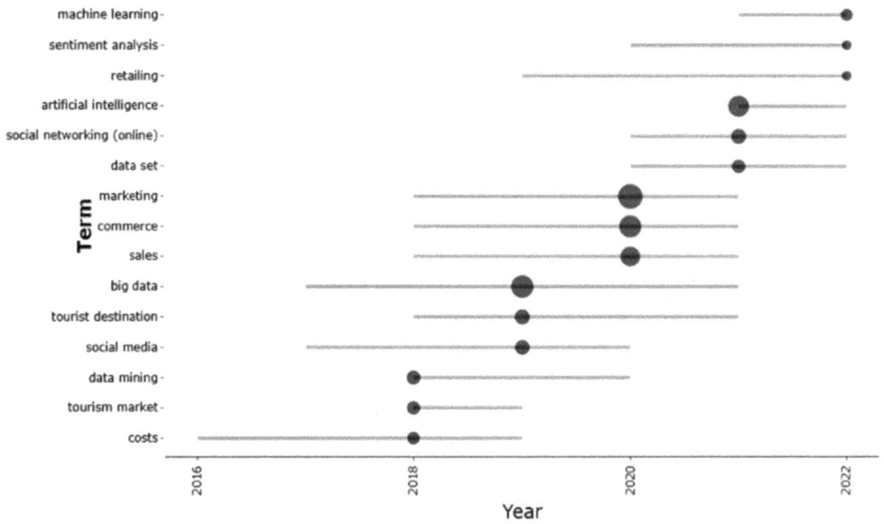

FIGURE 19.2 Most trending topics.

Source: Author.

The most emerging theme that came out of the data set appears to be the usage of machine learning sentiment analysis in retailing. Another aspect that highlights the use of big data and artificial intelligence is increasing sales in various business scenarios. In the year 2018, the most significant topics of research for "big data and artificial intelligence" were related to tourism, data mining, and social media. After that, the thrust of the researchers shifted toward tourism destinations, big data, and the use/application of big data and related technology in the field of commerce. In 2020, big data was extensively applied in sales forecasting, commerce, and marketing to a great extent. In the later half of the same year, the focus shifted to social networking, artificial intelligence, and retailing. Presently, the research studies that are coming up in the year 2022 are mostly related to machine learning, sentiment analysis, and retailing (refer to Fig. 19.3).

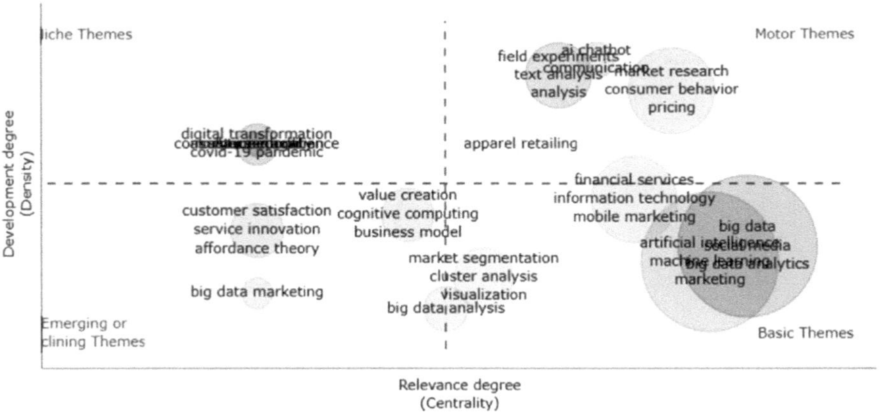

FIGURE 19.3 Highlighting emerging, niche, and basic themes.

Source: Author.

With the help of R software, the researcher has tried to determine the emerging themes, niche teams, and motor themes of the areas related to artificial intelligence and big data analysis. The data set extracted from the Scopus database highlights that the basic themes related to the search that were researched by the researchers are primarily related to big data, artificial intelligence, business analytics, marketing, mobile marketing, IT market segmentation, cluster analysis, visualization, and financial services.

However, the most important themes, which are the motor teams, are related to consumer behavior, pricing, field experiments relating to AI, and other emerging aspects of "Chatbot" and can also be seen in the motor themes that are being researched by the researchers in this area. Text analysis is quite apparent in market research in this area. However, people have also focused on interventions using big data analytics in the area of apparel retailing. It shows that the use of big data and artificial intelligence is being researched in diverse dimensions of marketing, in addition to the most important coming up themes like "chatbot", digital transformation, and various aspects of research relating to the COVID-19 pandemic. However, the most emerging themes are customer satisfaction, service, innovation, big data, and the use of big data in marketing. The data set highlights that there is a great scope of use of big data and marketing, and this area is continuously evolving and growing. A great thrust of research studies using big data and AI in the research of consumer behavior, pricing decisions, and market research decisions can be seen under motor themes (refer to Fig. 19.4).

FIGURE 19.4 Evolution of big data themes.

Source: Author.

The thematic evolution of the data set has divided the data into two slices, that is, from 2002 to 2020 and then 2021 to 2023. In the first decade, the major thrust of the research was artificial intelligence and the use of cost-effective techniques in this area, where big data, economics, and social media were the other thrust areas. Now we can see the connections between the use of big data and creating data sets. It is also being used in sciences like biology. Further, machine learning and big data have shown a greater connection, and a lot of work is being done in the consumer behavior area with the help of "big data". The benefits of big data in solving problems related to economics or economic predictions, as well as social media, can also be seen in understanding the marketing precision areas along with tourist behaviors. The use of "big data and artificial intelligence" is closely related to marketing, showing and highlighting the relevance of big data and artificial intelligence in the field of marketing and prediction.

At last, the word chart has been created by doing content analysis, which highlights the most frequently occurring keywords like "big data", "data analytics", "decision making", "social networking", "tourist destinations", "strategic planning", "data mining", "tourist behaviour," etc., focusing on the uses, benefits, interventions, and applications of big data analytics in these areas and fields (refer to Fig. 19.5).

FIGURE 19.5 Cloud chart.

Source: Author.

19.8 WHAT CAN BIG DATA DO FOR MARKETING?

The above discussion clearly highlights that there can be a series of positive implications and uses of big data for marketing. The uses and applications of big data in the following areas can highlight the benefits of this revolutionary technology, especially in the fields of management and marketing:

- One of the prime objectives of every business is to understand who their customers are, where they are located, what their needs are, and how they like to be engaged. That is, customer involvement is an important task for the marketing team for every business. Big data analytics has the capability to reveal the customers of the business, their needs and wants, and it can also help us provide solutions for customer engagement.
- Retaining the customer in the digital world and maintaining their loyalty are two important and influential factors for every business that determine its success in the long run. big data analytics solutions can help businesses figure out what the drivers of consumer commitment are and why the customers are not loyal to a particular business by evaluating the voluminous data of their choices and preferences available digitally.
- There is always a scope of increasing the market efficiency. By focusing on the production and marketing dimensions of any business or product, big data solutions can help the marketers and producers identify the best possible ways of expenditure in different dimensions in order to take any decision in real-time.
- Dialog with the stakeholders that is too strategic is becoming a key to the success of every corporation. Therefore, it is very important for every organization to deal with the issues of corporate communication in accordance with emerging technologies that are associated with big data and artificial intelligence. The future of communication in every aspect is data-driven and automated.
- Credible and long-term positioning of the companies lies much on effective, fair, and transparent communication with the stakeholders, and the future of communication lies in data orientation and an automated set of communication technologies which are AI-driven.
- Dealing with high and voluminous data is possible only through big data solutions, which will affect the way the organizations communicate, behave, respond, and grow.
- To convert a high volume of data into effective information usable for decision-making is possible only through big data solutions.
- The challenge for organizations is to contribute toward knowledge management in order to sustain themselves in the future. Just processing or handling the data is not sufficient; communication solutions are the inherent essence of knowledge management.

19.9 CONCLUSIONS

The implications for marketing in the field of big data are manifold. It provides a series of benefits in the areas of customer retention, sales, brand reputation, brand management, and sales forecasting. The niche themes of research in relation to big data and marketing are digital transformation and creating companies' competence in the field of sales. The themes which are gaining attention from researchers these days are AI chatbots, understanding customer behavior through big data and AI, undertaking pricing decisions with the help of big data analytics, and carrying out research and developmental activities with the help of big data and AI. The basic themes of research majorly explored by the researcher in the past years were the use of big data analytics in the fields of financial services, information technology, and mobile marketing.

KEYWORDS

- **big data**
- **artificial intelligence**
- **customer retention**
- **customer loyalty**
- **literature review**
- **bibliometrics**
- **big data**
- **evolution of literature**

REFERENCES

Ardito, L.; Petruzzelli, A. M.; Panniello, U.; Garavelli, A. C. Towards Industry 4.0: Mapping Digital Technologies for Supply Chain Management-Marketing Integration. *Bus. Process Manag. J.* **2018,** *25* (2), 323–346.

Arora, M. Post-Truth and Marketing Communication in Technological Age. In: *Handbook of Research on Innovations in Technology and Marketing for the Connected Consumer*; IGI Global, 2020; pp 94–108.

Arora, M.; Sharma, R. L. Artificial Intelligence and Big Data: Ontological and Communicative Perspectives in Multi-Sectoral Scenarios of Modern Businesses. *Foresight* **2022,** (ahead-of-print).

Arora, M.; Sharma, R. L. Coalescing Skills of Gig Players and Fervor of Entrepreneurial Leaders to Provide Resilience Strategies During Global Economic Crises. In: *COVID-19's Impact on the Cryptocurrency Market and the Digital Economy*; IGI Global, 2022; pp 118–140.

Arora, M.; Sharma, R. L. Integrating Gig Economy and Social Media Platforms as a Business Strategy in the Era of Digitalization. In: *Integrated Business Models in the Digital Age: Principles and Practices of Technology Empowered Strategies*; Springer International Publishing: Cham, 2022; pp 67–86.

Buhalis, D.; Foerste, M. SoCoMo Marketing for Travel and Tourism: Empowering Co-Creation of Value. *J. Destin. Market. Manag.* **2015,** *4* (3), 151–161.

Buhalis, D.; Sinarta, Y. Real-Time Co-Creation and Nowness Service: Lessons from Tourism and Hospitality. *J. Travel Tour. Market.* **2019,** *36* (5), 563–582.

Choi, T. M.; Wallace, S. W.; Wang, Y. Big Data Analytics in Operations Management. *Prod. Operat. Manag.* **2018,** *27* (10), 1868–1883.

Davenport, T.; Guha, A.; Grewal, D.; Bressgott, T. How Artificial Intelligence Will Change the Future of Marketing. *J. Acad. Market. Sci.* **2020,** *48*, 24–42.

Erevelles, S.; Fukawa, N.; Swayne, L. Big Data Consumer Analytics and the Transformation of Marketing. *J. Bus. Res.* **2016,** *69* (2), 897–904.

Jiang, Y.; Wen, J. Effects of COVID-19 on Hotel Marketing and Management: A Perspective Article. *Int. J. Contemp. Hosp. Manag.* **2020,** *32* (8), 2563–2573.

Leeflang, P. S.; Verhoef, P. C.; Dahlström, P.; Freundt, T. Challenges and Solutions for Marketing in a Digital Era. *Eur. Manag. J.* **2014,** *32* (1), 1–12.

Marine-Roig, E.; Clavé, S. A. Tourism Analytics with Massive User-Generated Content: A Case Study of Barcelona. *J. Destin. Market. Manag.* **2015,** *4* (3), 162–172.

Martin, K. D.; Murphy, P. E. The role of data privacy in marketing. *J. Acad. Market. Sci.* **2017,** *45*, 135–155.

Mikalef, P.; Krogstie, J.; Pappas, I. O.; Pavlou, P. Exploring the Relationship Between Big Data Analytics Capability and Competitive Performance: The Mediating Roles of Dynamic and Operational Capabilities. *Inf. Manag.* **2020,** *57* (2), 103169.

Rust, R. T.; Huang, M. H. The Service Revolution and the Transformation of Marketing Science. *Market. Sci.* **2014,** *33* (2), 206–221.

Tirunillai, S.; Tellis, G. J. Mining Marketing Meaning from Online Chatter: Strategic Brand Analysis of Big Data Using Latent Dirichlet Allocation. *J. Market. Res.* **2014,** *51* (4), 463–479.

Wedel, M.; Kannan, P. K. Marketing Analytics for Data-Rich Environments. *J. Market.* **2016,** *80* (6), 97–121.

Xu, Z.; Frankwick, G. L.; Ramirez, E. Effects of Big Data Analytics and Traditional Marketing Analytics on New Product Success: A Knowledge Fusion Perspective. *J. Bus. Res.* **2016,** *69* (5), 1562–1566.

Index

D

I

K

L

M